Affordable Housing and the Homeless

Editor: Jürgen Friedrichs

Affordable Housing and the Homeless

Editor
Jürgen Friedrichs

Walter de Gruyter · Berlin · New York   1988

Prof. Dr. Jürgen Friedrichs
Lehrstuhl für Allgemeine Soziologie und Stadtforschung,
Institut für Soziologie der Universität Hamburg,
Leiter der Forschungsstelle Vergleichende Stadtforschung Hamburg

Library of Congress Cataloging in Publication Data

Affordable housing and the homeless / editor, Jürgen Friedrichs.
  p. cm.
  A selection of papers initially presented at a symposium on affordable housing,
organized by the Ad Hoc Group of Housing and the Built Environment of the
International Sociological Association, held Sept. 16-20, 1987 at the University
of Hamburg.
  Bibliography: p.
  ISBN 0-899925-451-9 (U.S.)
  1.Housing--Congresses. 2.Housing policy--Congresses. 3.Homelessness--
Congresses. 4. Self-help housing--Congresses.
I. Friedrichs, Jürgen.
HD7286.A34 1988   88-18919
363.5'8--dc 19   CIP

CIP-Titelaufnahme der Deutschen Bibliothek

Affordable housing and the homeless / Ed. Jürgen Friedrichs. – Berlin ; New York :
de Gruyter, 1988
  ISBN 3-11-011-611-1
NE: Friedrichs, Jürgen [Hrsg.]

CONTENTS

PART THREE: THE NEW HOMELESSNESS

PREFACE

Elizabeth Huttman and Willem van Vliet--

In recent years, a relative decline in national revenue growth rates has prompted many countries worldwide to re-arrange their economic and social priorities. Typically, expenditure cutbacks have affected the provision and maintenance of housing, particularly low-income housing.

Among the results have been homelessness and housing deprivation such as squatter settlements. The ways and the extent in which this situation has been developing vary a great deal from one country to another, depending in part on whether the prevailing ideology views housing primarily as a basic human entitlement or as a consumer good and potentially (private) profit-generating commodity, and whether economic factors such as high interest rates and low return on investment dampen new housing starts. Considering the range of approaches to the existing problems, it is of interest to inquire about their effectiveness, to evaluate the reasons behind their success or failure, and to explore the possibilities for adapting a policy or program that has worked in one country to the conditions specific to other countries.

These and other questions drive the research of a growing international network of housing experts organized under the *Ad Hoc Group of Housing and the Built Environment* of the International Sociological Association. During the past decade this group has held meetings and conferences in Uppsala (Sweden), Mexico City, New Delhi, Amsterdam, and most recently in 1987 in Hamburg, Federal Republic of Germany. At these meetings, researchers (primarily sociologists, but also planners, political scientists, economists, geographers, policy analysts, anthropologists, psychologists and others) as well as practitioners have presented and discussed papers, exchanged information, and laid the groundwork for collaborative work.

At the next conference, to be held in June 1988 in Amsterdam, more than 400 participants from around the world are expected. Future meetings are planned for 1989 (possibly in North America; and a site in Eastern Europe) and 1990 (Barcelona). A periodic Newsletter keeps members abreast of each other's activities, relevant events, current developments, and the like.

This book is a selection of papers initially presented at the group's most recent meeting, the symposium on "Affordable Housing: from participation to self-help and shelter for the homeless", held September 16-20, 1987 at the University of Hamburg, Federal Republic of Germany, under the sponsorship of the Volkswagen Foundation. The preparations for this symposium took place on very short notice after a decision in August 1986 at the World Congress of Sociology in New Delhi to submit a proposal to the Volkswagen Foundation.

Affordable Housing and the Homeless
© 1988 Walter de Gruyter & Co., Berlin · New York – Printed in Germany

An Organization Committee consisting of Dan Ferrand Bechmann (France), Jane Darke (Britain), Jürgen Friedrichs (Federal Republic of Germany), and Jaspal S. Marwaha (India) wrote the proposal. Following its positive reception by the Volkswagen Foundation, Jürgen Friedrichs, who headed the committee, did an exemplary job in making the needed local arrangements in a very short time span and in securing publication of this volume soon thereafter. We hope that this timely dissemination of the papers that were presented, discussed and subsequently revised will enhance their usefulness as contributions to the ongoing discussions of ways in which decent housing can be provided so that it is within everyone's reach.

Elizabeth Huttman, Willem van Vliet--
January 1988

AFFORDABLE HOUSING AND HOMELESSNESS:

A COMPARATIVE VIEW

Jürgen Friedrichs

The contributions in this book indicate a housing shortage and for some countries a dramatic increase in the number of homeless in advanced industrialized societies. Both problems, affordable housing and homelessness, are related. If a society cannot provide affordable housing, for instance by subsidizing rents, the number of homelessness will increase.

It is the market segment of lower-income households which has posed the problem of adequate provision in all capitalist societies. Over the last two decades, in most cities of these countries, it has been argued that a market equilibrium exists despite some deficits in the low-income segment of the housing markets and in some regions. Now we face, in this segment, a much larger deficit than initially assumed, furthermore, a growing number of homeless people. How can these changes be accounted for?

First of all, they are neither based on manipulations of statistics nor do they seem to be a temporary problem of the next five years. This is evident, if we link the problem of affordability to economic changes in advanced industrialized societies.

These societies transform from goods production to information processing and services. This process has been documented in detail for many countries, for instance the United States (e.g., Bluestone and Harrison, 1982; Stanback and Noyelle, 1982). Production and profit declines in those industries where the product cycle has reached its final stage, such as in shipbuilding, mining, steel production, and - if no process innovations have occurred - in textiles (see, Markusen, 1985). New jobs require either a high qualification or are restricted to lower service entry-level jobs. The decrease in the number of jobs in old industries has not been compensated by new jobs, and even if this were possible, the changes in the qualifications required ("mismatch") still lead to mass-unemployment and a rising number of households on public assistance (see, Kasarda and Friedrichs, 1985). Cities such as Liverpool, Lille, Duisburg, Barcelona, and Detroit may serve as examples for the resulting social problems.

The consequences for the homeless are vividly described in the contribution by Culhane and Fried. To cite one homeless, Manny, and his perception of the situation: "These things, when I began to smell myself, these things told me something about society. These things told me that society says 'You are now unprotected. You are now no good to us'".

The exact number of homeless in a country is difficult to estimate. The figuress supplied for France by Bechmann-Ferrand, and for the U.S. by Huttman, indicate the magnitude of the problem and their alarming increase. The term "new" homelessness as used in West Germany to denote the situation - at least for West Germany - appropriately. In the early 1960s there was a large number of homeless as a result of the post-war housing shortage, their figure dropped considerably in the following decades, and rose again in the mid-1980s, this time due to economic problems.

Relating the problems of affordable housing and homelessness to structural economic changes, we may further assume that both problems will aggravate. The number of dwellings available for rent at affordable prices is continuously decreasing. First, the stock is reduced by demolishing old buildings and by modernization of buildings resulting in higher rents. Second, apartments are converted into condominiums, supporting the trend from rent toward ownership. This is documented in the contributions by Thorns and van Vliet--.

In addition, as the U.S. experience shows, hotels often used to house homeless are transformed into appartments, a process described by Huttman. Second, new construction is done in Europe on a very small scale if compared with construction figures in the 1960s and even the 1970s. New construction no longer compensates for the losses in the stock.

Thus, we may forecast a declining supply. On the demand side, there is little hope for an economic recovery in general, and hence an increase in renters able to pay their rent or an even higher rent. Taking West Germany as an example, the Research Institute of the Federal Agency of Labour has calculated that the unemployment rate will increase beyond the year 2000 if the economic growth rate remains below 2.5 percent, and the female participation rate does not increase. Over the last three years, the GNP in West Germany has grown by 2.0 percent (1985), 2.5 percent (1986), and 1.7 percent (1987). In the same period, the unemployment rate was around 9 percent, up to 9.9 in 1987 with a high variation among regions. In addition to these 2.5 million unemployed more two million persons were on public assistance (2,058,000 already in 1985).

Even in those large cities exhibiting economic growth and low unemployment rates such as Munich and Stuttgart in West Germany, London in the United Kingdom, Boston or New York in the United States, growth did not affect all social strata. The number of persons unemployed or on public assistance and the number of homeless did not decrease. Instead, we observe a growing social polarization (e.g., by income). As Murie and Forrest phrase it in their contribution: "Homelessness is one symptom of multi-dimensional exclusion from the social consumption norms of the majority". Processes of gentrification in inner-city neighborhoods are one of the spatial outcomes of these social changes (Berry, 1985; Smith and Williams, 1986).

There is little doubt that the problems of affordability and homelessness will continue to accompany the structural economic changes. As a further consequence, "affordable housing", supplied to a large extent in new housing estates is no longer affordable for many households living there.

Affordability of housing is--like poverty--a relative term, depending upon the level and quality of provision a country wants to supply and can supply. At present, the problem seems to be aggravated by the rising social disparities which were outlined above. It is poverty amongst the plenty. If such processes occur, the "relative deprivation", as conceived by Merton (1957), increases and will result in growing social antagonism.

Socialist Countries

Having discussed the problems of affordable housing in cities in capitalist countries, we may now turn to cities in socialist countries and ask how their local (or federal) administrations try to solve the problem. The contribution about Prague by Kerner gives some clues; to put them into a broader perspective, some data for other cities in Eastern Europe shall be added. (For a more detailed analysis, see Friedrichs, 1988.) The article by Kerner demonstrates the tremendous efforts made in Czechoslovakia, and in Prague in particular, housing is heavily subsidized, rents and repair costs are extremely low compared with prices in capitalist countries. However, neither Prague nor other major cities in socialist countries have managed to cope with the excess demand for housing.

In these countries, the basic problem is to provide housing for all social groups. The estimated housing shortage in capital cities as by 1979/1980 were (Friedrichs, 1988): Budapest: 96,000 dwellings, (stock: 726,691 dwellings), Moscow: 844,148 dwellings, (stock: 2,542,000 dwellings), Prague: 65,728 dwellings (stock: 448,034 dwellings), Warsaw: 80,658 dwellings (stock: 513,501 dwellings).

The considerable housing shortage, in turn, has led to several problems related to the question of affordable housing. First, to cope with the shortage, both in Budapest and Warsaw, communal dwellings are sold to households. Certainly, this is not socialist in a strict sense. The reasoning behind this strategy is twofold: to acquire funds for further communal construction and to benefit from private savings. One of the consequences is that housing is made accessible only to those with a high amount of savings, a further consequence is a reduction in state/communal control over the housing "market".

Second, in Budapest, Prague and Warsaw we find a trend to reduce communal housing construction in favor of cooperative housing. This may be interpreted - irrespective of the extent of this measure in each of these cities - as a trend towards withdrawal from state intervention into the housing market or housing supply.

Third, we can observe the advent of a crisis in affordability of housing. Some of the problems of large new housing estates, as described in the contribution of Friedrichs for West Germany, also refer to such new housing estates in socialist countries. Rents are extremely low, in contrast, prices for consumer goods are very high, but the costs for new construction and repair are increasing. Discussions with representatives from planning departments and universities in Budapest, Prague and Warsaw in two conferences on "Housing Problems in Socialist Countries" (Andrzejewski et al.; 1986, Borovicka and Kerner, 1986; Brenner et al., 1986) revealed that prefabricated elements and the concrete itself show dramatic symptoms of decay in both Western and Eastern European new housing estates. To cope with the rising costs for repair, tenants in Prague, for example, will have to pay a larger share of repair costs. In addition, it is planned to raise the rents.

Policies

The crisis of affordable housing and shelter for the homeless is a result of economic changes, therefore, it is impossible to solve these problems by urban planning by just providing homes or by transfer payments. This brings us to the question of policies to ameliorate these "new" social disparities.

The articles in this volume do refer to highly industrialized societies, which are as well rich societies. However, none of them has solved the problem of affordable housing. Excluding socialist countries, we may argue that all mechanisms of state or local intervention into a capitalist housing market have not achieved - or not secured - equal justice in housing provision for all social groups.

We are facing a situation of rich industrial societies not capable or not willing to supply a sufficient number of affordable dwellings for both the lowest income groups and the homeless. The policies described for Great Britain (Darke and Darke, Murie and Forrest), Australia and New Zealand (Thorns), and the United States (Huttman, van Vliet--) seem to have some elements in common: governments rely upon home-ownership to a growing extent and seem to have little propensity to subsidize social housing on the necessary larger scale.

A different position is proposed by Karyd. He argues that "dwellings are only to a very limited extent substitutes for each other". If this were a correct empirical proposition, we may conclude that only a broad range of dwellings offered would meet the more differentiated demand - which in turn is the result of greater differentiation of lifestyles in advanced societies. However, the situation is more complex: As noted above, we observe differentiation *and* in a larger segment of these societies and a growing social underclass (Wilson, 1985) at the same time. It is this underclass of low-income or transfer-payment depending households which are in need of affordable dwellings; for them substitution is more feasible.

A more provocative point is Karyd's assertion, that housing policies ignoring market laws - like Sweden - are using an "oystrich approach". His assumption, that subsidies to households will rise rent levels and have only a marginal effect on the quantity of housing supplied will be shared by many economists. This is one of the reasons why in West Germany a double subsidy-system was introduced after the Second World War: to subsidize households below a defined net household income and to subsidize the construction of dwellings in social housing projects, and to rent such dwellings by a local administration only to households below that income limit.

As the articles by Darke and Darke and by Thorns show, neither socialist nor conservative governments have succeeded in solving the housing problem, even the socialist governments in Australia have dismissed their initial policies in favor of a free-market, anti-Welfarist, policy. In more general terms: In most countries we can observe a trend toward less state intervention and from collective to individual provision. This holds true even for socialist countries, such as Czechoslovakia, Hungary, and Poland, albeit on a different level and magnitude.

With respect to policy conclusions the contributions in this volume offer mixed suggestions. Most authors agree that it is the responsibility of the government or the society at large to help the lower income groups. Many European countries had the tradition of governmental subsidies for rental dwellings, which were then managed or owned by non-profit housing organizations - sometimes owned by the local government.

An additional strategy may be self-help as suggested in the article by Turpijn. He reports that already half of the Dutch population are self- builders. To increase self-help, the major target group, low-income households, have to be stimulated by local authorities to build and to conform to building standards or regulations. To be effective, one of the main problems of self-help has to be solved by local governments: to define building standards meeting the essential requirements but as well compatible with the financial means and qualifications of the potential self-helpers.

A historic example of self-help strategies is supplied by Andernacht in his review of the Goldstein project from the 1920s. Initially aimed at supplying dwellings for low-income households, the project failed to pass legislation and was suspended. When it was finally realized it served more to supply labour and jobs then to result in a large number of homes, as the author concludes. Could this, nonetheless, be a useful strategy? Can it be transferred to our time and to other countries? These questions remain to be answered.

The final conclusion to be drawn from these trends is pessimistic. Housing departments or private investors cannot solve national economic problems. They can at best alleviate them. The problem of affordable housing thus remains a problem of economic growth of a society.

References

Andrzejewski, A., Dangschat, J. and Gorynski, J., 1986: Wohnungswirtschaft in Polen. *Archiv für Kommunalwissenschaften* 25, 219- 239.
Berry, B.J.L., 1985: Islands of Renewal in Seas of Decay. In: P. E. Peterson (ed.): *The New Urban Reality*. Washington, D.C.: The Brookings Institution.
Bluestone, B. and Harrison, B., 1985: *The Deindustrialization of America*. New York: Basic Books.

Borovicka, B. and Kerner, A., 1986: Wohnungspolitik in der CSSR und in Prag. *Archiv für Kommunalwissenschaften* 25, 240-251.

Brenner, J., Szücs, I. and Kiehl, K., 1986: Die gegenwärtige und zukünftige Wohnungsversorgung in Budapest. *Archiv für Kommunalwissenschaften* 25, 252-266.

Friedrichs, J., 1988: Large Cities in Eastern Europe. In: M. Dogan and J.D. Kasarda (eds.): *The Metropolis Era.* Vol. 1. Beverly Hills-London: Sage, pp..128-154.

Kasarda, J.D. and Friedrichs, J., 1985: Comparative Demographic- Employment Mismatches in U.S. and West German Cities. In: E.L. Simpson and I.D. Simpson (eds.): *Research in the Sociology of Work. Vol. 3: Unemployment.* Greenwich-London: JAI-Press.

Markusen, A.R., 1985: *Profit Cycle, Oligopoly, and Regional Development.* Cambridge, Mass.: MIT-Press.

Merton, R.K., 1957: *Social Theory and Social Structure.* Glencoe, Ill.: Free Press.

Smith, N. and Williams, P. (eds.), 1986: *Gentrification of the City.* Boston: Allen and Unwin.

Stanback, T.M., Jr. and Noyelle, T.J., 1982: *Cities in Transition.* Totowa, N.J.: Allanheld, Osmun.

Wilson, W.J., 1985: The Urban Underclass in Advanced Industrial Society. In: P.E. Peterson (ed.): *The New Urban Reality.* Washington, D.C.: The Brookings Institution.

PART ONE:
GENERAL ISSUES

GROWTH RESTRICTIONS AND AFFORDABLE HOUSING: DWELLINGS VERSUS PEOPLE

Willem van Vliet

Introduction

In the United States, differential patterns of investment and concomitant population shifts have contributed to various regional inequities. Some regions are characterized by disinvestment, unemployment and loss of population, whereas others benefit from new opportunities for economic expansion and experience rapid population increases (Bluestone and Harrison, 1982; Sawers and Tabb, 1984).

In these widely divergent regional contexts, communities have developed quite different, indeed often contrasting, responses to economic and demographic growth. On the one hand, there are communities in depressed areas that go out of their way to offer enticements for private enterprises considering potential business sites. Generous tax abatements and the gratis provision of infrastructure are among the incentives commonly offered (see, e.g., Feagin 1983, ch. 2). A literature that has developed in this connection contains political, demographic and theoretical analyses of the forces favoring growth (e.g., Humphrey and Krannich, 1980; Humphrey and Buttel, 1980; Logan, 1978; Lyon, Felice and Perryman, 1981; Molotch, 1976). The timeliness of the concern with growth is illustrated by a meeting of the U.S. real estate and development industries held this fall, where it was a central agenda topic (Lowenstein, 1987).

On the other hand, there are communities that attempt to restrict growth for fear of adverse effects on the quality of community life. There are concerns, for example, that uncontrolled growth may cause excessive demands upon the community's existing transportation system, medical services, and schools. Other problems may exist with respect to the natural environment, including negative impacts on recreational resources, air quality, and water supplies. In light of these potentially serious threats to the quality of community life, a number of communities have adopted growth management schemes. The stated purpose of these controls is typically to restrict new residential construction. Among the techniques employed in this connection with varying degrees of success are impact fees on new development, building codes, construction moratoria, zoning ordinances, and sub-division regulations (see, e.g. Burrows, 1978; Dowall, 1984; Scott, 1975). There is a growing body of research on the characteristics of people who favor growth controls versus those who oppose it and on the degree to which public officials represent the views of the population at large or those of special interest groups (e.g.,

Baldassare, 1981, 1982; Baldassare and Protash, 1982; Connerly, 1986; Gottdiener and Neiman, 1981; Neiman and Loveridge, 1981; Protash and Baldassare, 1983).

This paper is concerned with a central controversy surrounding the use of growth restrictions. It has been claimed that one of the results of these practices, whether unintended or not, is the exclusion of moderately priced housing (e.g., Frieden, 1982). The scarcity of land, the limited number of building permits issued, and so forth, are viewed as driving up the price of existing stock and newly constructed dwellings. The adoption of such growth limitation ordinances is seen as posing a threat to the provision of moderate-cost housing at a time when home ownership problems are already viewed by many to have reached crisis proportions (Schwartz, Hansen and Green, 1984; Lillydahl and Singell, 1986).

In a recent study, Miller (1986) compared house prices in Boulder, Colorado, (and those in several surrounding communities lacking such controls), before and after the introduction of a growth-control plan in 1977, with those reported by Schwartz, Hansen and Green (1981, 1984) in their comparison of Petaluma and Santa Rosa in California. On the basis of his research results, Miller challenged the conclusion that growth limitations necessarily eliminate low-price housing, suggesting that in the case of Boulder various policy and market factors mitigated the anticipated price increases. Boulder's experience should be of interest to communities elsewhere in the country which face similar circumstances and which might want to consider adapting elements of Boulder's approach to their particular situation. In this light, careful examination of the developments in Boulder is of broader significance.

Without disputing the ostensible validity of Miller's observations, this paper proposes a broader perspective on the issue. Specifically, it argues that it is inappropriate to focus exclusively on (part of) the supply-side of the housing market (i.e., the dwellings and then only the ones sold) and that it is necessary to consider also the demand side (i.e., the people). Additionally collected data on the Boulder population lead to conclusions clearly at variance with the more optimistic assessment arrived at by Miller.

The rest of this paper is structured as follows. First, the methods, findings and conclusions of Miller's study are summarized. Several main points are highlighted. Against this background, the approach based on dwellings is contrasted with a people-oriented approach and corroborative data are presented. The paper concludes with comments that emphasize caution in conclusions regarding effects of growth management and underlines the importance of integral consideration of supply *and* demand in policy-related housing research.

The Dwellings

The purpose of Miller's (1986: 319) study was "to contrast the effects on moderate-priced housing of a growth control ordinance in Petaluma, California, with the effects in Boulder,

Colorado, whose growth control ordinance was modeled after Petaluma's." To this end, Miller examined availability of moderate-priced units, changes in the characteristics of houses sold, and sale prices of new single family homes both before and after enactment of Boulder's growth limitation ordinance, principally re-analyzing data previously collected from the County Assessor's record of transactions.

Results of the comparison point up two chief observations. First, in Petaluma, Ca., the proportions of moderate-price new detached homes (sold at or below $25,000 in 1970 dollars) dropped from 87% in 1973, the year its growth limitation ordinance was enacted, to 15% in 1974 and 3% in 1976. In Santa Rosa, 16 miles north of Petaluma and without a growth limitation, the proportion of new detached dwellings fluctuated around 38% throughout that same period.

In contrast, Boulder was already a relatively expensive housing market even before growth controls were enacted. In the preceding years, the proportions of houses that were sold at moderate prices ranged from 29% (1974) to 34% (1976). In 1977, the onset of the growth limitations, that percentage dropped to 18%, declining further to 12% in 1981, before rising back to 26% in 1984 (Miller, 1986: 322).

Second, Miller explains the continued existence of a relatively high proportion of moderate-priced homes in Boulder (in comparison with Petaluma) by a significant shift to owner-occupied attached housing. Indeed, the number of attached homes as a proportion of all homes sold in Boulder jumped from 3% in 1976, to 9% in 1977, to 32% in 1978, to 49% in 1984 (p. 323). This shift resulted from four factors: (1) the conversion of about 1,000 apartment units into condominiums; (2) incentives in the growth limitation ordinance and Boulder Valley Comprehensive Plan to construct attached units in the center of town; (3) a 1973 ordinance requiring that 10% of all new units be affordable to people of modest means; and (4) the natural market for small attached units associated with universities (ibid.). Miller concludes that the above policy and market factors combined to mitigate the effects of the price increase of detached homes on the housing market overall and, in addition, that Boulder was able to avoid homogenizing consequences to community demography and economy as seen in Petaluma after the adoption of growth restrictions (p. 325).

As phrased, the first part of this conclusion is correct, and we do not wish to take issue with. However, it only partially covers what has, in fact, happened and several additional observations are in order to get a fuller picture of the developments that took place in Boulder.

To begin with, as Miller himself points out (p. 322) the maintenance of a (comparatively) sizeable proportion of housing in the low- to moderate-cost sector in Boulder has been due to very significant changes in characteristics of the housing stock. These changes included in particular the already noted increase in the number of attached homes and a precipitous decline of 22% in the square footage of homes sold (from 1,620 sq. feet in 1973 to 1,260 sq. feet in 1984; p. 325). Significantly, Miller writes that "while Boulder homebuyers paid less, they also received less" (p. 325).

Indeed, when one examines strictly comparable data only, Miller's (1986) findings on the effects on house prices of the growth limitations in Boulder appear to be completely in line with those obtained by Schwartz et al. (1986) for Petaluma. In 1976, the year before the growth ordinance was initiated, a new house in Boulder was only $15,000 more expensive (in 1984 dollars) than like houses in the rest of the county and 16% of all Boulder sales in 1976 were of new detached houses. By 1984, new single-family detached houses were almost $37,000 more expensive than in the rest of Boulder County, and they represented only 3% of the sold stock in the city (Miller 1986: 323).

Figure 1: Assessed Median House Values in Boulder, Census Tracts, 1970-1980

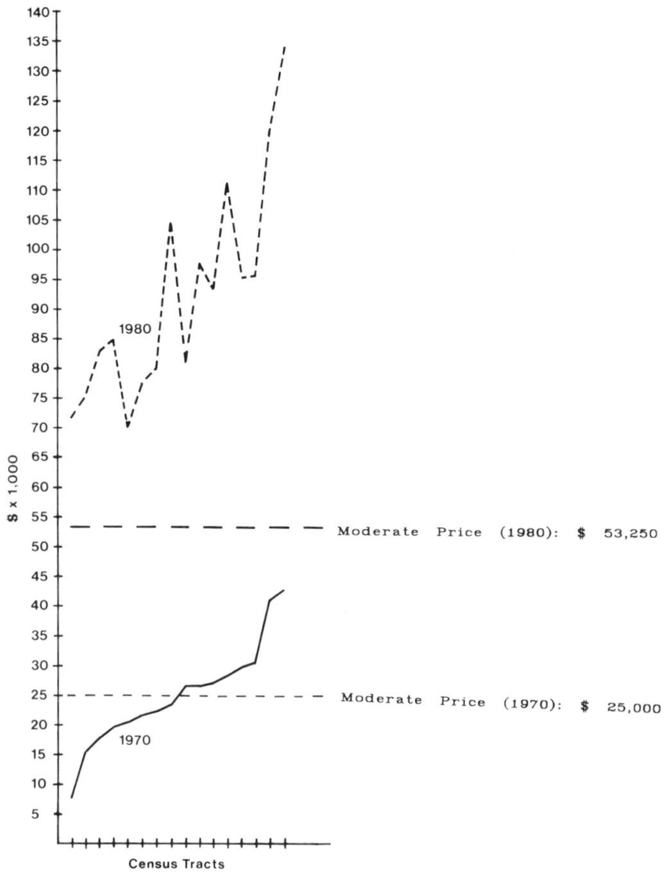

Source: U. S. Bureau of the Census, 1972: Table H-1, pp. H10-11; 1983: Table H-1, pp. 26-28.

To sum up, Miller's study leads to two conclusions. First, after a decline that coincided with the adoption of growth controls, the proportion of moderate-price housing in Boulder was maintained, thanks to various policy and market factors, at a clearly higher level than had been the case in Petaluma. Second, the maintenance of a low-cost housing stock could only occur because the stock underwent a metamorphosis, one which involved a very significant increase in the proportion of attached units and a steep decrease in the average square footage of houses sold.

A Broader View

The second of the above-mentioned conclusions is very important because it begins to give more meaning to the notion of moderate-price housing than a narrow focus on sale price alone. Indeed, labeling moderate-price housing so merely because of its price is misleading, as it says nothing about other important qualities of the house such as its size, type, structural condition and location vis-a-vis jobs, schools, shops, and the like.

It is also important to remember that Miller's analysis included only houses that had actually been sold. A fuller examination of the effects of growth limitations on housing should examine the entire housing market (i.e., owner-occupied and rental units) and not only part thereof (i.e., owner-occupied units that were sold). Such a broader analysis in the case of Boulder reveals several points (see Table 1). Among them, between 1970 and 1980:

1. The renter population *grew* by 19% from 39.7% to 47.2%, when the national figure *fell* by 8.2% to 30.7%.

2. The low-rent index declined by more than 22% to 12.4%.

3. The rental vacancy rate rose by 34%.

4. Median house values jumped up by almost 300% to $86,500 in 1980 (against a 1980 median value of $47,200 for the U.S. as a whole, representing a much lower gain: 178%).

5. Owner-occupied housing as a proportion of all housing units *decreased* by 7.8% when the national rate *increased* by 2.4%.

6. The homeowner vacancy rate jumped by more than 400% (against 50% for the entire U.S.).

The preceding statistics appear to show that, in Boulder during the 1970's, escalating house values put ownership beyond the reach of a growing number of households, resulting, among other things, in higher vacancy rates. Concomitant to this trend has been an increase in renters who were faced with a declining number of low-rent units.

Willem van Vliet

Table 1: Selected Housing Characteristics for Boulder and the U.S,
1970 and 1980

Housing Characteristics	1970	1980	1970-1980 % Change
Detached Houses (%)			
Boulder	54.3	45.3	-16.6
USA	66.2	66.2	- 6.1
Low-Rent Index (%)			
Boulder	15.9	12.4	-22.2
USA	39.8	37.0	7.0
Median House Value			
Boulder	$23,000	$86,500	+296.7
USA	$17,000	$47,200	+177.7
Owner-occupied Housing Units (%)			
Boulder	51.0	47.0	- 7.8
USA	2.9	64.4	+ 2.4
Renter Population (%)			
Boulder	39.7	47.2	+19.0
USA	33.4	30.7	- 8.2
Renter Vacancy Rate			
Boulder	3.5	4.7	+34.0
USA	6.6	7.1	+ 7.6
Homeowner Vacancy Rate			
Boulder	.7	3.6	+414.3
USA	1.2	1.8	+50.0

Source: Pay et al., 1985: 36, 38, 40, 47, 49, 50, 51.

Very clearly, the picture of moderater cost housing that now emerges is quite different from that found by Miller in his more restricted analysis of sold dwellings only. The salience of the shift in the proportion of moderate-price housing is perhaps most clearly illustrated in Figure 1. It shows that in 1970 in eight of the 16 census tracts on which data were available the median house value was below moderate cost ($25,000; the criterion used by Miller (1986: 322), while in 1980 none out of 19 census tracts fell in that category ($53,250 or less).

In view of the shift to attached housing, the decline in square footage, and the sharply increased cost of housing overall, one wonders how the growth restrictions affected people. Did incomes, in fact, increase in pace with housing costs or did cost-income ratios change? Do we find changes in population composition? It is to these questions that we turn next.

Table 2: Income Characteristics of the Boulder and U.S. Population, 1970 and 1980

Income Characteristics	1970	1980	1970-1980 % Change
Low-income Families			
Boulder	32.3%	34.9%	+ 8.1
USA	33.5	35.0	+ 4.5
Middle-income Families			
Boulder	43.0%	37.3%	-16.6
USA	43.1	40.5	- 6.1
High-income Families			
Boulder	24.7%	27.8	+21.0
USA	23.4	24.6	+ 4.9
Families Below Poverty Level			
Boulder	5.2%	6.9%	+32.7
USA	10.7	9.6	-10.3

Source: Pay et al., 1985: 23, 30-32.

The People

Let us first look at income. Table 2 shows a polarization trend, as the proportions of high- as well as low-income families increased, while that of middle-income families declined. These trends are in line with, but very much more pronounced, that those seen for the U.S.

Willem van Vliet

as a whole during the 1970-1980 period. Moreover, while nationally the proportion of families below the poverty line dropped by more than 10%, in Boulder it rose by almost 33%. In and of themselves, these figures are relatively meaningless because they must be seen in relation to changes in housing cost.Information in this connection is found in Figures 2 and 3.

Figure 2: Ratios of Mean Family over Median Assessed House Values in Boulder, Census Tracts, 1970-1980

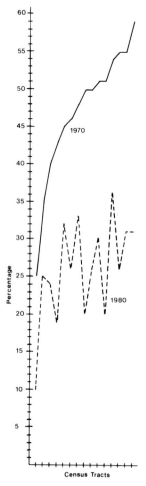

Source: U.S. Bureau of the Census, 1972: Table P-4, pp. P100-101; 1983: Table P-11, pp. P305-307.

Figure 2 shows the ratio of median family income over median assessed house value for Boulder census tracts in 1970 and 1980. During this ten-year period, this ratio declined very significantly without exception. This development provided existing owners with tremendous equity gains, but made home purchase greatly more costly for those wanting to trade up and much more so still for new and first-time buyers.

Figure 3: Median Rent as a Proportion of Median Family Income in Boulder, Census Tracts, 1970-1980

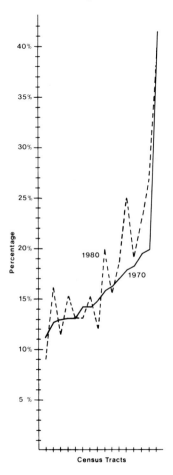

Source: Bureau of the Census, 1972: Table H-1, pp. H10-11; 1983: Table H-1, pp. H26-28.

Table 3: A Comparison of Selected Demographic Characteristics of the Boulder and U.S. Population, 1970 and 1980

Demographic Aspect	1970	1980	1970-1980 % Change
Family Households (%)			
Boulder	68.5	50.2	-26.8
USA	81.2	73.9	- 9.0
Population Under 5 (%)			
Boulder	7.5	3.9	-47.5
USA	8.4	7.2	-14.5
Population Between 5-18 (%)			
Boulder	24.2	13.4	-29.7
USA	25.8	20.9	-18.8
Single Parent Families (%)			
Boulder	10.3	24.2	+136.3
USA	12.3	19.5	+ 59.1
Married Persons (%)			
Boulder	55.5	38.1	-31.3
USA	68.8	61.7	-10.3
Ratio of Married to Unmarried Persons			
Boulder	1.04	.57	-45.2
USA	1.60	1.45	- 9.4
Divorced and Separated Persons (%)			
Boulder	4.5	9.9	+120.9
USA	5.9	9.3	+ 57.3
Total Number of Households			
Boulder			+ 21.8
USA			+ 24.6

Sources: Pay et al., 1985: 6, 7, 10, 12, 14, 15, 16, 18.

In a detailed study, the National Association of Home Builders (1981: 16) concluded that the artificial growth limitations imposed on. Boulder had accelerated house price increases to an extent that the majority of new and first-time buyers bought less expensive homes built in increasing numbers in surrounding towns. Similarly, Figure 3 shows how median rent in Boulder census tracts as a proportion of median family income rose steeply virtually without exception.

Furthermore, while median family income in Boulder increased by 100.7% between 1970 and 1980, this rise was less than for the U.S. in general (107.6%). More importantly, the gains in family income fell far short of the increase in housing costs. In fact, the house value to family income ratio rose by 84% from 1970 to 1980. In contrast, the income of unrelated individuals during the corresponding period rose by 243% and for them the house value to income ratio increased by only 1.1%.

Considering that between 1970 and 1980 the Boulder housing stock became less congent with family living (attached and much smaller units which had become also more expansive per square foot), one logically asks: did the Boulder population change, too?

The Boulder population did indeed change. Table 3 shows that family households decreased by 27% between 1970 and 1980 (U.S.A.: - 9%). The decline was most evident among families with children under five years (-48%). At the same time, the total number of households grew by 22%. Single-parent families and divorced or separated parents increased by, respectively, 136% and 121%, more than twice the national rate.

Only a more complete analysis than is possible here can clarify why fewer families stayed in or came to Boulder. However, it seems safe to conclude that a lack of affordable housing of the appropriate type and size ranks high among the reasons, notwithstanding Boulder's long-standing commitment to the provision of low-income housing. A 1985 survey of low-income households in Boulder (less than $15,000 per year) found that 27% mentioned affordable housing as a problem and 41% of those sampled complained about affordable rent (Kathlene, 1985b: 3).

Conclusion

The data presented in this paper indicate that following the enactment of growth restrictions in Boulder, the housing stock and the composition of the population have changed significantly. However, research on the effects of growth control on housing is fraught with many difficulties (Schwartz, Zorn, and Hansen, 1986). Obviously, there are other factors that should be considered as well. In the case of Boulder, the open space (Green Belt) program, the comprehensive plan, employment opportunities and a growing student population, no doubt, affected developments during the 1970's. The changes observed here are not exclusively attributable to growth controls.

The data presented in the preceeding discussions have several limitations. For example, it would be good to trace developments year-by-year, not constrained by the decennial interval of census data collection. It would also be good to compare the Boulder data not only with national figures, but with those for nearby communities as well (a task currently underway). Such a strategy would hold constant any effects that are specific to the region.

Of course, one would also want to know how many of the moderate-*price* houses sold were bought by moderate-*income* households, a question that requires information not available from accessible records. It would also be desirable to include a more encompassing analysis ramifications of growth control on the quality of public services and community infrastructure (cf. Huttman, 1979). A similarly broad approach is also argued in a pilot study by Anselin and Arias (1983) in which a multi-criteria framework is proposed as a decision support system for urban growth management.

Notwithstanding these and other limitations, the data that were presented suffice to make the argument that an examination of the implications of growth restrictions for housing must go beyond an analysis of the effects on the prices of houses sold. Also part of the housing market are the houses that are not sold (owner-occupied as well as rental) and the people living in and seeking these houses. The literature contains numerous examples of ill-fated housing polices, programs and projects that failed to recognize the needs of the very people they were intended to serve. In attempts to effectuate congruence between people and their housing environment, integral consideration of problems in the dynamics of supply *and* demand is essential (Studer and Van Vliet--, 1987).

References

Anselin, L. and Arias, E. G., 1983.: A Multi-Criteria Framework as a Decision Support System for Urban Growth Management Applications: Central City Redevelopment.. *European Journal of Operational Research* 13, 300-309.

Baldassare, M., 1981: *The Growth Dilemma: Residents' Views and Local Population Change in the United States*. Berkeley, CA: University of California Press.

----, 1982a: Predicting Local Concern about Growth: the Roots of Citizen Discontent.. *Journal of Urban Affairs* 4, 9-49.

---- **and Protash, W.**, 1982b: Growth Controls, Population Growth, and Community Satisfaction. *American Sociological Review* 47, 339-346.

Bluestone, B. and Harrison, B., 1982: *The Deindustrialization of America*. New York: Basic Books.

Burrows, L.B., 1978: *Growth Management: Issues, Techniques, and Policy Implications*. New Brunswick, NJ: Center for Urban Policy Research.

Connerly, C.E., 1986: Growth Management Concern. The Impact of its Definition on Support for Local Growth Controls. *Environment and Behavior* 18, 707-732.

Dowall, D.E., 1980: The Effects of Land Use and Environmental Regulations on Housing Cost. *Policy Studies* 8, 277-288.

Feagan, J.R., 1983: *The Urban Real Estate Game: Playing Monopoly with Real Money.* Englewood Cliffs, NJ: Prentice Hall.

Finkler, E., Toner, W. and Popper, F., 1976: *Urban Nongrowth: City Planning for People.* New York: Praeger.

Frieden, B., 1982: The Exclusionary Effect of Growth Controls. In: M.B. Johnson (ed.): *Resolving the Housing Crisis.* Cambridge, MA: Ballinger.

Gleeson, M.E., 1979: The Effects of an Urban Growth Management System on Land Values. *Land Economics* 55, 350-365.

Gottdiener, M. and Neiman, M., 1981: Characteristics of Support for Local Growth Control. *Urban Affairs Quarterly* 17, 55-73.

Humphrey, C. and R. Krannich, R., 1980: The Promotion of Growth in Small Urban Places and its Impact on Population Change, 1975-78. *Social Science Quarterly* 61, 581-594.

---- **and Buttel, F.** 1980: "The Sociology of the Growth/No Growth Debate. *Policy Studies Journal* 9, 336-345.

Huttman, E.D., 1979: Social Inequality and the "No Growth" Movement: a Further Barrier to Low Income Families' Entry into Desirable Residential Areas. In: A.J. Mayer and L. Gordon (eds.): *Urban Life and the Struggle to be Human*, pp. 191-197. Dubuque, IA: Kendall-Hunt.

Kamara, S.G. 1987: Effect of Local Variations in Public Service on Housing Production at the Fringe of a Growth-Controlled Multi-County Metropolitan Area. *Urban Studies* 24, 109-117.

Kathlene, L., 1985a: *Female Single Parents in Boulder County.* Boulder, CO: University of Colorado, Center for Public Policy Research.

----, 1985b: Low-income Households in Boulder County. Boulder, CO: University of Colorado, Center for Public Policy Research.

Lillydahl, J.H. and Singell, L.D., 1987: The Effects of Growth Management on the Housing Market: a Review of the Theoretical and Empirical Evidence. *Journal of Urban Affairs* 9, 63-77.

Logan, J., 1978: Growth, Politics and the Stratification of Places.. *American Journal of Sociology* 84, 404-416.

Lowenstein, R., 1987: When Developers Meet, Talk Turns to 'No-Growth' Trends. *The Wall Street Journal.* October 14, 1987, p. 35.

Lyon, L., Felice, L. and Perryman, M.R., 1981: Community Power and Population Increase: an Empirical Test of the Growth Machine Model. *American Journal of Sociology* 86, 1387-1400.

Miller, T. and Fitch, S., m.d.: *Impacts of the Danish Plan on Housing Prices in Boulder.* Boulder, CO: City Department of Human Resources/University of Colorado, Center for Public Policy Research.

Miller, T.I., 1986: Must Growth Restrictions Eliminate Moderate-Priced Housing? *Journal of the American Planning Association* 52, 319-325.

Molotch, H., 1976: The City as a Growth Machine: Toward a Political Economy of Place. American Journal of Sociology 82:309-32.

National Association of Home Builders, 1981: *The Danish Plan in Retrospect.* Washington, D.C.: NAHB, State, Local and Environmental Affairs Division.

Neiman, M. and Loveridge, R.D., 1981: Environmentalism and Local Growth Control: a Probe into the Class Bias Thesis. *Environment and Behavior* 13, 759-772.

Pay, W.S., Dane, S., Davis, J.N. and T. Miller, T., 1985: *The Handbook of Comparative Municipal Statistics.* Boulder: Division of Research and Evaluation, Dept. of Community Planning and Development.

Protash, W. and Baldassare, M., 1983: Growth Policies and Community Status: A Test and Modification of Logan's Theory. *Urban Affairs Quarterly* 18, 397-412.

Sawers, L. and Tabb, W.K., 1984: *Sunbelt/Snowbelt: Urban Development and Regional Restructuring.* New York: Oxford University Press.

Schwartz, S. I., 1984: The Effect of Growth Control on the Production of Moderate Priced Housing. *Land Economics* 60, 110-14.

----, **Zorn, P.M. and Hansen, D.E.**, 1986: Research Design Issues and Pitfalls in Growth Control Studies. *Land Economics* 62, 223-233.

Studer, R.G. and Van Vliet--, W., 1987: Sociophysical Congruence as Problem of Supply and Demand. *Architecture and Behavior* 3, 159-173.

Wolch, J.R. and Gabriel., S.A., 1981: Local Land Development Policies and Urban Housing Values. *Environment and Planning* 13, 1253-76.

WHO GETS HOUSED: THE CHANGING NATURE OF HOUSING AFFORDABILITY AND ACCESS IN ADVANCED CAPITALIST SOCIETIES

David C. Thorns

Housing Policy Context

Housing policy was a key ingredient of the post-war development of social-democratic style Labour administrations in a number of Western capitalist economies. These economies were shaped by the policies drawn from the economic theories of Keynes and as such emphasized an approach centered on the control of "demand" for commodities rather than upon the "supply" of money. The first two decades of the post 1945 period were generally ones of economic growth, interrupted by the short-term fluctuations associated with trade cycles. Over these years levels of inflation were modest, unemployment rates were low and economic growth was obtained. However, as the 1960s progressed the economies of western nations began to develop more acute problems. Inflation and unemployment became more pronounced leading to the growing realization that the capitalist state was moving into a new "crisis".

The crisis it was suggested resulted from the inability of the state to manage capital during a period when profitability was falling and restructuring was required to revitalize capitalist production and so increase the level of profits (Gamble 1979). State intervention into this process was re-fashioned during the 1960s with much rhetoric about the use of scientific and technological skills and improved economic management (Massey, 1984; Massey and Meegan, 1982). However, the limited ability of a particular nation state, during a general period of crisis within capitalist societies, to develop a viable strategy to reshape their economy increasingly became evident (Mandel, 1978).

The 1970s provided the decade in which the break with post war social democratic welfare state policy occurred. Nearly all western capitalist nations during this decade moved towards policies of fiscal austerity shifting attention from the "demand" side of the economic equation to the supply, especially of money.

The new emphasis on monetarism was accompanied by a revival of a new era of market individualism. The revival of economic well-being and consequently social progress was to be based on a new wave of entrepreneurial activity creating not a welfare culture but an entrepreneurial culture. This shift brought with it attacks upon the structure of the welfare state and an argument that this structure should be dismantled as it had grown into a large and inefficient bureaucracy no longer able to deliver efficiently, health, housing, educational and social services to the population. This move was seen by many writers as one of "recommodification" (Forrest and Williams, 1980; Harloe, 1981), of "recapitalization" of capital (Miller, 1978). The more popularist presentation was of the "privatization" of services with the return to the individual of a greater capacity to choose the services or provisions required. The consequence of this has been growth in such areas as private medical insurance and in some western capitalist societies the expansion of owner-occupation.

One example of how these macro-changes have led to a re-direction of housing policy is the case of the United Kingdom. The policies followed by the Thatcher Government in the 1980s have led to the role of the State in housing being redefined. The state has become a residual provider only entering the housing arena when no other possibility existed with the normal expectations being that housing demand would be satisfied by the activities of the private market. Policy therefore has changed from one of support for public housing to one emphasizing the further expansion of home ownership, an attempt to revive the private rental sector and an attack on the level of existing public housing through vigorous sale policy (Murie and Forrest, in this volume). The shift in policy was based upon ideology as much as economics and cost cutting. This can be demonstrated by the increasing cost to the state of home ownership through the taxation system and through the policies adopted with respect to the homeless.

The taxation system provides assistance to owner-occupiers in the form of tax relief on mortgage interest payments, exemption from capital gains tax and inheritance tax, and discount on the sale of council houses. These varied forms of assistance collectively provide over 9 billion pounds annually (Darke and Drake, in this volume). The second area where the ideological thrust of the Conservative Government policy is clear is in the area of provisions for the homeless. In order to carry out these statutory obligations to house the homeless local authorities have increasingly had to spend large amounts of money on temporary accommodation in both hotels and bed and breakfast boarding houses. The costs of such provisions is now in many cases, especially in the London area, well in excess of the costs of providing a more permanent solution in the form of additional public housing stock. The permanent solution is, however, prevented by the Conservative Central Government's opposition to the expansion or maintenance of the public stock and its control over local authorities' capital expenditure (Murie and Forrest, in this volume).

The increased levels of home ownership that have resulted from the changes of the 1960s and 1970s has led to debate within the sociological literature regarding whether this movement from rental, both private and public, to home ownership has major social and political consequences. One position to emerge argues that housing changes lead to a restratification of the urban population around consumption sectors rather than production producing political changes in terms of voting behaviour, the formation of local social movements committed to the support of local property interests and a general resistance to change (Edel, 1982; Pratt, 1982; Saunders, 1979, 1984, 1986; Thorns, 1981).

The particularities of the British case need, however, to be seen in the light of comparative data. Not all western capitalist societies had this particular pattern of housing change, and it may well be that the tenure shift itself is not the most important consequence of the major structural changes that occurred during the 1960s and 1970s (Harloe and Paris, 1984; Kemeny, 1983, 1987). The shift to monetarist policies, the removal of housing's protected circuit of finance and the consequence of a much more mobile and global finance capital have all had impacts upon housing structure effecting the key aspects of housing policy, i.e., access, costs, construction and availability. In order to explore some of these impacts more closely it is necessary to examine some case study material. The next section of this paper will, therefore, focus upon Australian and New Zealand data.

Changing Housing Contexts: Australia and New Zealand

Australia

Owner-occupation for the whole of the post-war period has been the dominant form of tenure. However, it has increased over the period from 52% in 1947 to 69% by 1986 (see Watson, 1986, and Table 1). This broadening of the base of owner-occupation occurred during the 1950s and 1960s and was brought about through a combination of low rates of inflation of house and land prices, full employment, rising real wages and government policies designed to assist owner-occupiers. The mechanism of assistance chosen was through such devices as tax relief and incentive savings schemes and Commonwealth (i.e., Federal Government) State housing agreements which assisted in the provision of loans through building societies (Neutze, 1977).

The 1970s and 1980s, however, were in contrast to the 1950s and 1960s a period of rapid inflation in house and land prices with the result that considerable strain was placed upon the ability of households to gain access to housing, particularly in Sydney and to a lesser extent Melbourne (Burke et al., 1984; Kilmartin et al., 1985): During the 1970s, for example, the cost of an average (110 sq.m.) house in Sydney rose 238%, 220% in Melbourne and 141% in Adelaide. Within the total costs of house and land, the cost of land relative to the house changed markedly. For example, in Sydney in the 1950s land on average contributed to 14% of the total cost whereas in the 1980s this had risen to 50% (Daly and Paris, 1985). Over this period, the cost of houses and land, especially for those entering the market for the first time and not having the advantage of capital gains on their existing property, clearly escalated.

The impact of these changes upon the capacity of households to afford housing can be seen from the rising levels of deposit now required to purchase and in the increasing proportion of income that housing consumes (Burke et al. 1984, Australian Bureau of Statistics 1986). Research in the 1970s has shown evidence of a growing housing problem,

David C. Thorns

more especially in Sydney and Melbourne, with the numbers of those living in caravans, boarding houses, emergency houses and homeless increasing (Daly and Paris, 1985; Fopp, 1986; Kilmartin et al., 1985; Paris and Stimson, 1986).

Table 1: Tenure Status of Occupied Private Dwellings/Households, Australia, 1911-1981

	1911		1947		1954	
	No.	%	No.	%	No.	%
Owner	402637	45.0	338025	44.7	1121814	47.9
Purchased by Instalments	39318	4.4	147677	7.9	353093	15.1
Owner/Purchaser undefined	na	na	na	na	na	na
Owner/Purchaser	441955	49.4	985702	52.6	14704907	62.9
Goverment Tenant	0	0.0	0	0.0	99376	4.2
Other Tenant	404371	45.2	812750	43.4	699854	29.9
Other Meth. of Occup.	48063	5.4	48867	2.6	56257	2.4
Not Stated	na	na	26304	1.4	13027	0.6
Total	894389	100.0	1873623	100.0	2343241	100.0

Table 1: Continued

	1966		1976		1981	
	No.	%	No.	%	No.	%
Owner	na	na	1306293	31.5	1548873	33.2
Purchased by Instalments	na	na	437770	34.7	1542282	33.0
Owner/Purchaser Undef.	na	na	17434	0.4	87110	1.9
Owner/Purchaser	2231913	70.8	2761497	66.7	3178265	68.1
Goverment Tenant	161722	5.1	204627	4.9	228938	4.9
Other Tenant	673357	21.4	839873	20.3	935543	20.3
Other Meth. of Occup.	59552	1.9	232477	5.6	190647	4.1
Not Stated	25382	0.8	102047	2.5	135516	2.9
Total	3151926	100.0	4140521	100.0	4668909	100.0

Source: Burke et al., 1984: 3

The collective impact of internal housing market changes and those of the external economic environment have created a housing situation in most of the Australian states in which waiting lists for public housing have grown, low vacancy rates exist in the private rental sector pushing up rental levels and high cost to income ratios from low and modest income earners are becoming common (Burke et al., 1984; Paris, 1984). The result is an increasingly differentiated housing market within which some substantial gains are sustained at the upper speculative end of the market, and money is available for loans but at a price many modest and low income earners cannot afford.

New Zealand

The tenure structure in New Zealand, like that of Australia, has been one dominated by owner-occupation rising from 55% in 1945 to 72% in 1986 (Thorns, 1983, and Figure 1). The 1950s and 1960s were decades of relatively stable prices, full employment and rising real incomes (Rosenberg 1986). The state provided considerable assistance to home owners through the operation of the State Advances Corporation which provided low interest loans to first home buyers purchasing a home. The loans were subject to income restrictions, thus ensuring they were available to households of low to modest income. The linkage of the loans to the purchase of a new house (until the late 1970s when the policy was changed) assisted in the growth of new housing subdivisions in the 1950s and 1960s and provided a ready market for the products of the larger group builders who became important suppliers of housing in the main urban centres, especially in New Zealand's largest city, Auckland.

Figure 1: Tenure, 1951-1986

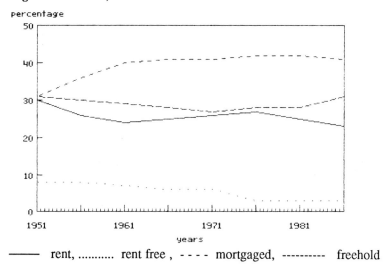

——— rent, ……… rent free , - - - - mortgaged, ---------- freehold

The 1970s and 1980s, however, were in marked contrast, decades of high inflation, rising unemployment and falling real wages. These conditions have created a growing affordability problem especially for those attempting to enter the housing market for the first time. House and land prices have grown rapidly in a number of boom periods, from

1972-75, 1980-83 and 1984-85 (Figure 2). These booms are linked to construction cycles and also changes to monetary policy which encouraged the growth of credit in the early 1970s and the early 1980s (Thorns, 1986). The most recent boom, however, is different from the two earlier periods as it has resulted from a more radical restructuring of finance policies as part of a move towards a more general deregulation of the New Zealand economy after mid-1984 (Deane, 1985).

Figure 2: Graph of Percentage Increases per Year in House Prices, Weekly Wages and C.P.I.

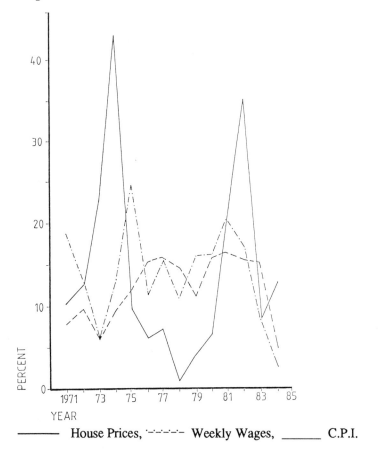

House Prices, ‒‒‒‒‒ Weekly Wages, _____ C.P.I.

The changes to affordability of housing can be shown by examining the relationship of the average house and land price to the average weekly income. In 1974 it took 42% of the average weekly income to purchase an existing property and 49% to purchase a new property. By the mid 1980s this had changed to requiring 63% and 73% respectively

(National Housing Commission, 1986). Clearly such averages provide only a crude measure of change, nonetheless they indicate the direction of change and the erosion of many households' capacity to afford housing unless they have access either to capital or multiple incomes within the household.

Housing Policy Debate: The Retreat from Welfarism?

The growing problem of affordability of housing has now been demonstrated for Australia and New Zealand and growing housing pressures within the early and mid 1980s identified. In both countries the mid 1980s brought into office Labour Governments (1983 Australia, 1984 New Zealand) with housing as an area of priority in their election manifestos.

The Australian Labour Party's housing programme set out at the end of 1982, prior to the 1983 election campaign provided a traditional social democrat style solution to the perceived housing crisis within Australia. The policy aimed at increasing the supply of housing improving the planning and management of housing development and a firm commitment to public rental housing. The policy included specific commitments within this broad framework to increase the number of units built per year from 135,000 to 160,000 during the first three years of office of a Labour Government, to set up a Department of Housing and Urban and Regional Affairs and to expand public housing. Further the policy includes the rejection of the idea of deregulating the finance industry and so ending housing's protected position (Paris and Stimson, 1986).

The New Zealand Labour Party going into the 1984 election also campaigned with housing as a central area of concern. The housing policy that was advocated was based around increased assistance to home owners through the provision of "deposit gap" financial assistance to first home buyers. One scheme viewed as a possibility was the Australian Labour party's first home owner grant scheme. In addition the policy sought to encourage the construction of more housing with the restoration of the state within the public rental sector through an increased stock of public housing for rental and the reforms of landlord tenant relations to improve tenant security. Again an Australian model was chosen as a guide to reform. In this case the South Australian Tenancy reform legislation was chosen as a guide to developing New Zealand Law.

In office both the Australian and New Zealand Labour Governments have modified their housing policies from ones based upon equity and general Governmental assistance and involvement to policies which increasingly emphasize targeting of assistance to the "most needy" and the introduction of more "market" rents and interest rates for the users of public housing and mortgage loan assistance. Their moves have led to public housing occupying a much less prominent place within the respective Governments' housing policies. In the Australian case this has led to the abandonment of a commitment to double the size of the state rental sector and the adoption of a more general and non-specific commitment to increased funding. In New Zealand the Government initially stopped the sale of public housing, which had been strongly encouraged by the previous Government, and increased the rate of public house acquisitions. However, at the same time they have introduced a policy of adjustment to rents bringing them closer to the rates prevailing in the private market. The policy is designed in part to encourage the better-off tenants to vacate public housing and move into private home ownership. The adoption of this move to more modest rents provided a rent strike by state tenants in one area of Wellington in 1987.

The other major departure from their pre-election housing policies has been in the moves both Governments have made towards the deregulation of the financial sector and the resulting ending of a protected circuit for housing finance. This deregulation in both cases has made competition for money more intense driving up interest rates. Although it has not reduced the amount of funds available for housing within the economy it has increased substantially the cost of borrowing rather than decreased it as the advocates of deregulation forecasted. A consequence, therefore, of the deregulatory policies has been the necessity to produce new mechanisms to preserve access to housing for the low and modest income earning households who have been excluded from traditional financial arrangements by the increases in costs (Thorns, 1987).

The first question of interest is why did Labour administrations adopt macro-economic policies which were essentially anti-Welfarist? The answer here lies in the general trends of capitalist development as much as in the particularities of the two societies.

The end of the long boom of the 1950s and 1960s was a product of changes in the relative position of both countries with respect to their export commodities and world markets. The re-organization of Europe into the E.E.C. posed problems for the continuation of the export of primary products, important based for both societies. The 1970s recessions within the world economy further depressed raw material prices such as minerals which constituted another element of Australia's export income. Further the competition of cheaper products from especially South East Asia and Japan had important impacts upon domestic manufacturing with rationalizations and closures becoming a dominant feature of the 1970s and 1980s. The period, therefore, became one of extensive restructuring of both capital and State activity in an attempt to create conditions for continued economic growth (Martin, 1981; Rosenberg, 1986). Part of this process was to reduce the level of State expenditure on consumption and support for welfare provisions in order to re-direct subsidies and State assistance to the development of export industries. One victim of this change was the housing sector. Finance was removed from housing in part to finance other areas of Government expenditure. For example, in New Zealand the Government moved from subsidizing consumption in the form of welfare services to subsidizing production in the form of a "think big" energy related sector to develop among other things synthetic petrol and steel production (Pearce, 1987). The limited success of this strategy became clear by the middle of the 1980s when the level of unemployment was rising and the extent of control over the economy in New Zealand by the State was seen as the "most extensive of any western democratic nation" (Deane, 1985).

The new governments in the mid 1980s came to power at a time when market liberalism was re-emerging as a dominant economic theory. The experience of America and Britain notwithstanding, it was argued that the revitalization of the domestic economies of Australia and New Zealand required the re-emergence of entrepreneurial skills and these would only be facilitated through creating a climate of greater competition and new patterns of investment. The requirements for this were seen to be a less regulated and protected economy and society where risk-taking was encouraged. This produced the current paradox in which Labour administrations have become the champions of a free-market capitalism based upon a return to individualistic competition and action.

The shift with respect to housing policy in particular has been quite radical. In mid 1984 the New Zealand economy had been subjected to an extended freeze on wages, dividends, rents, prices interest rates and exchange rates. Further this freeze was imposed on an economy already subject to extensive import protection, export subsidies, compulsory ratio requirements for all financial institutions to invest in government stock, qualitative and quantitative credit guidelines and an array of other regulatory devices (Deane, 1985). The main elements of the new approach were the abandonment of wage and price controls, the abolition of interest rate and rent controls, a 20% devaluation followed by a floating exchange rate, the abolition of exchange controls over foreign currency transactions and a commitment to reducing the government deficit through a combination of cuts in Government spending, increases in charges for services and corporatization of Government departments. The Australian Government has also moved to de-regulate the finance industry removing the asset and interest rate controls that previously protected the housing sector.

The impacts of this welter of changes upon the housing sector have been extensive. They have pushed up interest rates, e.g. in Australia the deregulation of savings banks mortgages in April 1986 resulted in an immediate increase from a rate of 13.5% to one of 15.5%. In New Zealand the rate rose from 12% in July 1984 to 15% by December 1984. It has, however, continued to climb rather than to fall in the new more competitive environment with average first mortgage rates approaching 20% by March 1987 (Figure 3). Rent levels have also risen as has availability but at a much increased cost. In February 1987 the average weekly rental for a three-bedroomed house in Auckland was $235 which represented 67% of the average weekly wage (National Housing Commission, 1988). The increases in rents that have been charged for private rental accommodation have not led to an increase in the size of this sector as with the deregulation of the financial markets a higher rate of return became available in other sectors of the economy leading to a property and share boom during 1986 and into the first half of 1987. With the stock market crash of late 1987 money appears to be flowing into the banking system and again failing to stimulate the growth of accommodation. The removal of rent controls and financial deregulation therefore do not seem to have produced any direct benefits for the housing sector. Housing construction after an initial burst also does not seem to have been sustained by the new deregulated finance sector. For example, in New Zealand, housing permits grew through the latter part of 1984 and through 1985. However, towards the end of 1986 and into 1987 there has been a substantial fall in building activity especially outside of the Auckland area (Table 2).

Figure 3: Mortgage Interest Rates 1970-1987

Interest rates

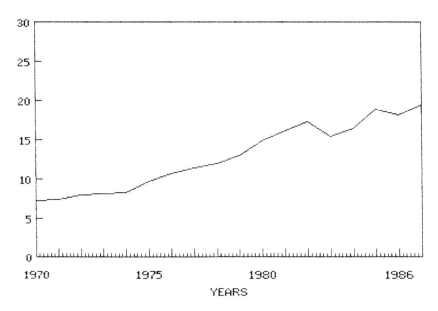

The Australian figures present a similar picture. The level of house building in 1982 was at a historically low point with 105,000 new units constructed which was the lowest since the 1950s. During the initial years of the Labour administration the numbers grew quite rapidly so that by the end of 1984 the annual rate had increased to 153,000. However, as the rising interest rate and prices of the mid 1980s caused growing affordability problems the rate of construction has declined. The final consequence of note is the extent to which the move towards market liberalism and a more deregulated economy has rapidly increased regional variations in house prices.

Absolute housing costs, for example, are highest in New South Wales, especially in Sydney (Henderson and Hough 1984), with the highest prices and rate of increase in values of land and houses and therefore the highest cost of home ownership. In 1983, the median house price in Sydney was $83,000, by 1985 this had risen to $91,000, this compares with $81,000 in 1985 for Melbourne. In New Zealand, the Auckland area stands out as the one with the highest prices and greatest housing pressures. In December 1986, for example, the average sale price of a house in Auckland at $153,653 was nearly twice the national average of $87,591. (Sydney Metropolitan area in 1986 contained 3,204,696 making it the largest urban centre in Australia. - Auckland Metropolitan area in 1986 contained 809,142 making it by far the largest urban centre in New Zealand. Wellington is next in size but has less than half the Auckland population.)

Table 2: Building Permits 1970-1987

Years	Houses	Flats	Total
1970	16990	6094	23084
1971	16230	7449	23679
1972	15577	8756	24333
1973	19916	12857	32773
1974	23582	16152	39734
1975	21436	11665	33101
1976	20932	11257	32189
1977	19160	10994	30154
1978	14358	6847	21205
1979	13669	5380	19049
1980	11687	3510	15197
1981	11108	3334	14442
1982	13996	5010	19006
1983	11854	4145	15999
1984	15488	4738	20226
1985	15664	6118	21782
1986	15907	7128	23035

Source: N.Z. Statistics Department

The Australian figures present a similar picture. The level of house building in 1982 was at a historically low point with 105,000 new units constructed which was the lowest since the 1950s. During the initial years of the Labour administration the numbers grew quite rapidly so that by the end of 1984 the annual rate had increased to 153,000. However, as the rising interest rate and prices of the mid 1980s caused growing affordability problems the rate of construction has declined. The final consequence of note is the extent to which the move towards market liberalism and a more deregulated economy has rapidly increased regional variations in house prices. Absolute housing costs, for example, are highest in New South Wales, especially in Sydney (Henderson and Hough, 1984), with the highest prices and rate of increase in values of land and houses and therefore the highest cost of home ownership. In 1983 the median house price in

Sydney was $83,000, by 1985 this had risen to $91,000, this compares with $81,000 in 1985 for Melbourne. In New Zealand, the Auckland area stands out as the one with the highest prices and greatest housing pressures. In December 1986, for example, the average sale price of a house in Auckland at $153,653 was nearly twice the national average of $87,591. (Sydney Metropolitan area in 1986 contained 3,204,696 making it the largest urban centre in Australia. - Auckland Metropolitan area in 1986 contained 809,142 making it by far the largest urban centre in New Zealand. Wellington is next in size but has less than half the Auckland population.)

Policy Initiatives

The high costs of housing access and the deterioration in affordability experienced in the 1980s have led to new policy initiatives in both countries based around new designs for mortgages. They do not, therefore, challenge the assumption that the continuance of owner-occupation is the most suitable form of housing tenure, they simply accept this as taken for granted and devote attention to trying to continue to facilitate it in the face of a deteriorating capacity of modest and low income earners to afford home ownership (Kemeny, 1983; Thorns, 1987).

oth the schemes devised have two main features. A cash grant to assist with the deposit for home purchase and a repayment plan which is designed around a constant real rate of interest and a fixed proportion of household income. In both cases the chosen levels have been a real interest rate of 3% and a repayment level of 25% of total household income. The nominal rate of interest in the scheme would be based on movements in the consumer price index and the capital sum outstanding would be adjusted by movements in the consumer price index over the previous twelve months. The repayments and the sum loaned are, therefore, indexed to inflation and so ensure a smoother repayments path and a more equitable return to the lender than a conventional mortgage.

The Australian scheme was launched in Victoria in 1984 with a pilot programme of 520 loans, subsequently in 1985 the state government changed all its housing loans to operate on this basis (Carter, 1986). Other state governments have also initiated schemes to try and reduce the costs of house purchase (see Bethune, 1986; Rose, 1986). In New Zealand the Government-controlled Housing Corporation has developed a scheme similar to the Victorian one and, since its inception in December 1985, 500 houses have been made available under its provisions. Evaluative data, available at present, suggests that these new schemes have assisted two groups of people, those with substantial deposits but with low income (e.g., those on benefits as a result of marriage splits, unemployment etc.) and modest income earners. The appeal of the scheme beyond these groups to middle and upper income earners is likely to be limited as they are unlikely to find it difficult to raise money from private sector financial institutions or be willing to forego the capital gains through sharing these with the lenders.

Future Directions

The restructuring process within most Western capitalist societies of the 1970s and 1980s brought in a new set of policies based around market monetarism and individual provision and away from the policies of collective provisions of welfare characteristics of the immediate post-war decades. Consequently, it is targeting rather than universalism, housing allowances and negative income tax rather than the building of state housing which become the dominant issues debated.

The failures during the 1950s and 1960s to promote continued economic growth are blamed on the inadequacies of state management and the growth of unwieldy bureaucracies. These in turn become cited as the cause of the fiscal and other crises of the 1970s and 1980s. Such critiques suffer from a limited analysis of the historical development of Western capitalist societies and a failure to carry out comparative analysis. Capitalist societies are characterized by sequential crises of varying severity and in this respect the 1970s and 1980s are yet one more such crisis (Mandel, 1983). However, each crisis comes with its own particular set of characteristics and its impact is not uniform across all societies.

The examination of the responses of two particular nation states to the prevailing economic conditions of the 1970s and 1980s has identified both common and unique features in their responses. They have both followed the path of economic liberalism, but at varying speeds. New Zealand has moved the most rapidly and extensively to deregulate and transform its economy through a restructuring of its finance system, corporatization of its public services and a progressive removal of support mechanisms to farmers and manufacturers, exposing both groups much more to the vagaries of international markets and flows of capital. The Australians while adopting a broadly monetarist strategy have been less wholesale in their adoption of such policies and have maintained a more corporatist style of economic management.

The consequences of these changes for housing provision have been similar and in both countries costs have risen and access to housing for low and modest income earners has got appreciably more difficult resulting in waiting lists for public housing growing, overcrowding increasing, pressure upon the cheaper end of the private rental market pushing up rents, and homelessness appearing.

The policy responses have been ones attempting to cheapen the costs of home ownership through new forms of mortgage arrangement rather than those which would confront the often outmoded building and subdivision practices, planning regulations, or attempt to tax or limit land speculation and the capital gains made through property sales. Further no real challenge has yet appeared to the continuation of home ownership as the main objective of public housing policy.

References

Australian Bureau of Statistics, 1986: *Household Expenditure Survey, Australia: Summary of Results. 1984.* ABS Cat No. 65300.

Bethune, G., 1986: *Lowering the Threshold: Recent Innovations in Housing Finance.* Paper presented at World Planning and Housing Congress. Adelaide.

Burke, T., Hancock, L. and Newton, R., 1984: *A Roof Over Their Heads.* Institute of Family Studies, Monograph No. 4.

Carter, R.A., 1986: *Innovations in Financial Mechanisms for Housing Markets.* Paper presented to World Planning and Housing Congress.

Daly, M. and Paris, C., 1985: *From the General to the Particular. Global Economic Re-structuring and the Local Housing Crisis in New South Wales.* Paper presented to a conference on Urban and Regional Impacts of the New International Division of Labour, Hong Kong.

Deane, R., 1985: *Financial Sector Reform: The Case of New Zealand.* Paper presented to a Conference on Financial Reform in the Pacific Basin Countries. San Francisco.

Edel, M., 1982: Home Ownership and Working Class Unity. *International Journal of Urban and Regional Research* 6, 205-222.

Fopp, R., 1986: *Youth Housing: Pre-requisites for Planning.* Paper presented to the World Planning and Housing Congress.

Forrest, R. and Williams, P., 1980: *The Commodification of Housing: Emerging Issues and Contradictions.* Centre for Urban and Regional Studies. University of Birmingham, WP.73.

Gamble, A., 1979: *Decline of Britain.* London.

Harloe, M., 1981: The Recommodification of Housing. In: M. Harloe, and E. Lebas. (eds.): *City Class and Capital.* London.

---- and Paris, C., 1984: The Decollectivization of Consumption. In: I. Szelenyi (ed.): *Cities in Recession.* Beverly Hills, 70-98.

Henderson, R. and Hough, D., 1984: Sydney's Poor Get Squeezed. *Australian Society,* 3, 6-8.

Kemeny, J., 1983: *The Great Australian Nightmare.* Melbourne.

---, 1987: Toward a Theorised Housing Studies. A Counter Critique of the Provision Thesis. *Housing Studies* 2, 249-260.

Kilmartin, L., Thorns, D.C. and Burke, T., 1985: Social Theory and The Australian City. Sydney.

Martin, J., 1981: *State Papers.* Department of Sociology, Massey University. Palmerston North.

Massey, D., 1984: *Social Divisions of Labour.* London.

----, and Meegan, R., 1982: *The Anatomy of Job Loss.* .London.

Mandel, E., 1978: *The Second Slump.* London.

----, 1983: World Crisis and the Monetarist Answer. In: K. Jansen (ed.): *Monetarism, Economic Crisis and the 3rd World. London.*

Miller, S.M., 1978: The Recapitalization of Capitalism. *International Journal of Urban and Regional Research* 2, 202-212.

Murie, A. and Forrest, R., 1980: Wealth, Inheritance and Housing Policy. *Policy and Politics* 8, 1-19.

National Housing Commission, 1986: *Report for Year Ended 31st March..* Government Printer. Wellington.

----, 1988: *Five Yearly Report. 1983-1988.* Forthcoming. Government Printer. Wellington.

Neutze, M., 1977: *Urban Development in Australia.* Sydney.

Paris, C., 1984: *Affordable and Available Housing: The Role of the Private Rental Sector.* Australian Institute of Urban Studies. Canberra.

---- **and Stimson, R.,** 1986: *Housing Tenure, Costs and Policies in Australia.* Paper presented to World Planning and Housing Congress. Op. cit.

Pearce, G., 1987: *Where is New Zealand Going?* PhD. University of Canterbury.

Pratt, G., 1982: Class Analysis and Urban Domestic Property: a Critical Re-examination. *International Journal of Urban and Regional Research* 6, 481-502.

Rose, R.A., 1986: *Affordable Housing Finance..* Paper presented at the World Planning and Housing Congress, op. cit.

Rosenberg, W., 1986: *The Magic Square.* Monthly Review Society. Christchurch.

Saunders, P., 1979: Urban Politics. London.

----, 1984: Beyond Housing Classes. *International Journal of Urban and Regional Research* 8, 202-225.

----, 1986: Social Theory and the Urban Question. London.

Thorns, D.C., 1981: The Implications of Differential Rates of Capital Gains from Owner-occupation for the Formation and Development of Housing Classes. International *Journal of Urban and Regional Research* 5, 205-227.

----, 1983: Owner-occupation, The State and Class Relations in New Zealand. In: C. **Wilkes and I. Shirley** (eds.): *In the Public Interest.* Auckland.

----, 1986: New Zealand Housing Policy: Continuities and Changes. *Housing Studies* 1, 180-191.

----, 1987: New Solutions to Old Problems: Housing Affordability and Access within Australia and New Zealand. *Environment and Planning A,* forthcoming.

Watson, S., 1986: *Whose Great Australian Dream. Home Ownership and the Exclusion of Women.* Paper presented to World Planning and Housing Congress. Op. cit.

AFFORDABLE HOUSING: ROLES FOR THE STATE AND THE COMMUNITY

Jane Darke and Roy Darke

Introduction

At first sight affordability appears to be a useful objective with respect to housing, and one on which there would be substantial agreement: a dwelling should be affordable just as it should be structurally sound. Actually, the term conceals certain implications about the form of housing provision. An implication is that it is for the individual household to procure housing, according to its means, with the state intervening at the margins to render housing affordable. It recognises that poorer households in any society find it very difficult to afford adequate housing, but it still places responsibility for providing shelter with those households rather than the state which could provide "to each according to his needs". We suggest that the concept of affordability could be broadened to apply to expenditure by the state as well as by individuals, and that we need to examine what a state can afford to provide, or in some cases, whether a state can afford *not* to make certain provisions.

It might be thought that the idea of affordability has greater applicability in less developed countries. State provision in less developed countries, unlike the West, tends to be directed to the needs of middle income groups rather than the poorest, and often at lower paid government officials, where it is in the interests of the state as employer to have a contented workforce in good quality affordable housing. However, affordability applied to provision for the poorer sections has limited usefulness because these groups may literally be able to afford nothing, and obtain their shelter at present through occupying structures they find: ruins, concrete pipes etc. or through building makeshift shelters made of scrap materials. It is difficult to use affordability criteria as the basis for policy where the intention is to help households with very low and unpredictable incomes.

We return later to the idea of affordability but just note here that affordability is only one of several possible objectives of the state in intervening in the housing system.. The main part of this paper seeks to analyse different forms and degrees of state intervention. There is a tendency for state intervention to be seen as a single continuum, where a command economy would have a high score and a free market economy a low one. We wish to argue that state intervention has a number of different dimensions in relation to the changes in housing policy brought about in eight years of Conservative government in Britain.

Reasons for State Intervention in Housing

Before we look at various forms of state involvement, we should identify why, in principle, the state should have an interest in becoming involved at all in housing provision. There are various possible reasons.

Firstly, inadequate housing may be an actual or perceived threat to social order. It has been argued (Swenarton, 1981) that this was the main motivation behind the housing drive in Britain at the end of the First World War, with the threat of Bolshevism, as a potentially appealing option for the British working class, diffused by promises of excellent housing (in the event only partly delivered). More recently, inner city riots have often called forth increased investment in housing for the area concerned for the local authority, although it is also paradoxically the case that many neighbourhoods which have seen riots have also seen considerable housing investment *before* the disturbances (for example, neighbourhood offices and environmental improvements at Broadwater Farm, Tottenham, London; enveloping at Handsworth in Birmingham).

Secondly, there is a desire on the part of the state to produce a better quality population. In some cases, poor standard housing for the poor carried threats to the bourgeoisie: diseases resulting from poor sanitation that might then spread to all groups, or imperfectly inculcated sexual modesty due to overcrowding potentially leading to corruption of young men in other classes. Such risks in late 19th century Britain influenced the climate of opinion in favour of increased state intervention. There was also alarm at the poor physical health and condition of conscripts for military service. In analogous cases, employers have provided good quality housing in order to attract, retain and reproduce a high quality workforce (for example, Titus Salt who built Saltaire). In all these cases, apparently altruistic motives on the part of middle class legislators and opinion-formers may contain a strong admixture of self interest.

Thirdly, there is an idea linked with various forms of partnership between the state and households (individually or in small groups) to do with "housing as a verb" (Turner, 1972), namely, that the process of producing, acquiring or managing housing can empower the individual and engender new capacities and skills. This may be an important by-product of collective self-build projects in countries such as Nicaragua (Darke, 1987). Some such idea is a significant part of the newer housing objectives of the Thatcher government, including the breaking up of local authorities' large holdings of low cost rented housing. The first speech of the newly appointed Housing Minister, William Waldegrave, given at the Institute of Housing conference on 19th June 1987, promised to "wean people off the deadly drug of dependency" and to increase private sector involvement in public sector housing. .(Reported in the *Guardian,* June 20, 1987, p.3, and *Inside Housing,* June 26, 1987, p.3.).

Fourthly, the state may sometimes use housing production as a tool of macro-economic policy. In Britain this has more often taken the form of cutting production at times of economic difficulties, than being a positive element in employment planning. The "stop-go" policies of post- war governments have been one of the obstacles to developing an efficient construction industry. However, the policies on which the Labour party unsuccessfully fought the 1987 general election included a large increase in housing investment as a cost effective way of reducing unemployment. As an indication of the continued interest in the employment potential of housebuilding a national pressure group emerged in the mid 1980s under the campaigning slogan of "Homes and Jobs".

A final possible motive for state intervention, more characteristic of governments representing the interests of the working class or the economically weaker groups, is an objective to reduce inequalities in housing standards and to apply the resources of the state to collective benefit. The resources thus applied may include expertise in organisation, overheads such as research and development costs, interventions to achieve economies of scale and so on. In some instances, including Britain, there is a pooling of costs and cross subsidisation. Unlike owner occupiers, council tenants' costs are based on historic costs. Rent levels are pooled across all the properties in a particular authority's ownership and this pooling could be extended to a national sharing of costs. In countries where collective financing of housing and social equalisation through housing provisions are part of the state's objectives, housing intervention will probably be accompanied by extensive intervention in health care and education.

These five motives for state intervention can be summarised as: maintenance of social order, promotion of quality of the population, encouragement of self development, economic planning and collective equalisation. We return to them later.

Forms of State Intervention: Housing in Britain

We now turn to the various forms that state intervention may take. It has been suggested (Le Grand and Robinson, 1984) that state intervention in welfare goods is through *provision, subsidy or regulations*. These take place in the context of particular goals which relate to the five objectives described above. Obviously provision, subsidy and regulations are not *alternative* options: typically there is a mixture of all types of measure in government actions.

In discussing state intervention in housing in Britain, the situation is complicated by the existence of a local government system where the local authorities are responsible for housing provision in their own districts. In areas of greatest housing need, that is, the larger cities and in London (apart from the outer suburbs), most of these areas are controlled by the Labour party while since 1979 the national government has been Conservative: thus the two levels of government have been following different objectives, and each level carries different powers and obligations with respect to housing.

To expand on the question of housing goals, it has been suggested that, until the election of the Thatcher government in 1979, there was broad consensus on the need for state intervention to deliver welfare goods (Hall and Jaques, 1983). In the case of housing policy this is an oversimplification. Thatcherism *has* taken housing policy sharply into new directions but there were changes of emphasis before then.

To understand the goals of postwar governments we must look first at earlier phases of state housing. During the half century of state housing provision before the Second World War, the Conservative party never fully accepted that either state provision or a system of subsidies would be a permanent part of housing supply. In this sense Thatcher's housing policy *is* an extension of Conservative "victorian values". State intervention was seen as occasionally necessary to meet an exceptional situation: the high cost of removal and replacement of insanitary housing, the shortage of homes after World War One, the continuing high level of building costs, the threat to public health and social order posed by slums and overcrowding. The assumption was that the market could and would be the normal channel of provision for most households, including the working class. This provision was expected to take the form of private housing for rent rather than owner occupation.

Labour, by contrast, envisaged the provision of good quality housing by local authorities as a normal component of housing supply, potentially catering for most working class households. The housing policies of the first Labour government, a short lived minority administration in 1924, were based on this objective. In the Labour administration of 1945-51, this was extended to encompass households of all social classes (Merrett, 979). In this their housing policies paralleled their education and health care policies. It was thought potentially beneficial for professionals such as doctors and teachers to live among the communities they served. We see high levels of provision, subsidy and regulation from this government: controls over the building industry and building materials supply to ensure that these met social needs (although stopping well short of nationalisation of the industry), high space standards for new housing, a powerful system of town planning and so on. There was however a certain vagueness with respect to goal setting in terms of output targets (Merrett, 1979). This was exploited by the Conservative party during the 1951 election campaign in their promise to build 300 000 homes a year, and this was a significant factor in their victory.

The goal was still to achieve high housing output, but the emphasis gradually shifted to owner occupation as the mainstream housing provision, to which it was assumed all families aspired, with council housing as a second-best tenure for sections of the working class. Output of council housing halved between 1953 and 1959, while private sector output rose steadily until the 1960s. When Labour finally returned to power in 1964, it accepted this shift of ideology, as seen from the following statement of their objectives:

> "once the country has overcome its huge social problem of slumdom and obsolescence, and met the needs of the great cities for more houses let at moderate rents, the programme of subsidisied council housing should decrease. The expansion of the public programme now proposed is to meet exceptional needs...The expansion of building for owner occupation on the other hand is normal; it reflects a long term social advance" (Ministry of Housing and Local Government, 1964).

These broad assumptions continued under the Conservative government of the early 1970s and the Labour government of 1974-1979, although there were considerable fluctuations in output and subsidy levels. Thus, only between 1951 and 1979 was there some degree of consensus on national housing objectives.

British Housing Policy since 1979

The steady postwar improvement in housing conditions for the mass of the population was checked by the policies introduced in 1979. The goals of the Thatcher government have been to *reduce* the size of the state sector, expand home ownership and latterly to *revive* the private rented sector. The aim is to encourage and reward enterprise, and it is believed that dependence on a local authority landlord is peculiarly destructive of such enterprise. State investment has been cut, and for the first time since the war there has been a *decrease* in the numbers and the quality of the local authority stock. Numbers are shown in Figure 1, and the increasingly poor quality is evident from statistics on disrepair in successive House Condition surveys (Department of the Environment, 1973, 1978, 1982) and from a major "Inquiry into the Condition of the Local Authority Housing Stock" undertaken by the Department of the Environment in 1985, showing that 3.8 million of the 4.6 million council houses in England needed renovation and repair at an average cost of almost £5 000 each: a total bill of some £19 000 million at 1985 prices (Association of Metropolitan Authorities, 1984; Department of the Environment, 1985).:). In other words, the scale of *provision* is being reduced. The level of investment which the government permits local authorities to make has been reduced by 75% since 1978/79, although spending has been slightly greater than 25% of the 1978/79 level due to the forced sale of council houses and local authority land.

As well as reductions in stock through sales at a discount to tenants there are now to be opportunities for council tenants to vote for their existing home to be transferred from local authority ownership to a housing trust. he terms of the transfer, and what happens to the outstanding debt, have not been made clear. There are also pressures on local authorities to enter into various partnership arrangements with the private sector in order to increase housing provision, in particular through renovation and sometimes resale of run-down estates.

Home ownership has been supposedly made easier for people at the margins by a variety of initiatives, in addition to the right to buy their home (Whitehead, 1986). he aggregate effect of these measures has been slight compared to over a million dwellings sold under the Right to Buy legislation in Britain up to the end of 1987, representing one in six of council dwellings.

Figure 1: Post War Trends in Housing in Britain

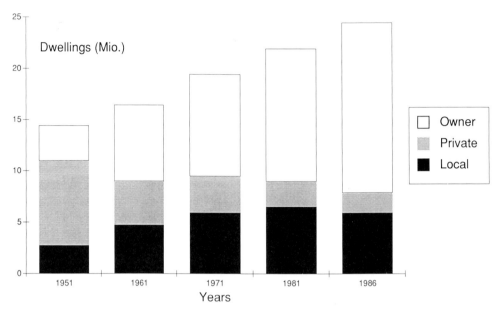

Source: Social Trends, No.17, 1987.

Initially the goal of privatising the public sector was obscured by an apparent objective to cut public expenditure. In adopting the LeGrand and Robinson framework, the category of subsidies must be expanded to include *capital* investment controlled by government, as well as current subsidies, although investment will appear under "provision". In the early years of the Thatcher government, with Michael Heseltine as Secretary of State for the Environment, the cuts in housing expenditure resulted in steep reductions in current subsidies to local authorities. Tenants faced large rent increases to compensate for this: between 1980 and 1982 rents rose by 75% while the retail price index rose by only 23%. Housing expenditure was cut very much more severely than other areas of welfare spending such as health and education. There were also severe reductions in *capital* expenditure which meant a drastic cut in housebuilding as we have already seen, and insufficient money to spend on repairs, maintenance and remedial work.

Yet it has become apparent in subsequent years that the housing goals of Thatcherism consist in an *ideological* attack on the public sector, rather than an objective of saving money. This is seen in various ways.

Table 1: Housing Statistics, Britain: Selected Comparisons.

	1978 or 1978/79	1980 or 1980/81	1985 or 1985/86	1987 or 1987/88
A.	114 000	94 000	33 000	12 700*
B.	£4 849m	£3 097m	£1 672m	£1 225m
C.	£1 258m	£1 393m	£ 457m	na
D.	£#2 100m	£2 720m	£4 750m	-
E.	£12 023	£17 533	£23 742	£27 444**
F.	£5.20	£7.71	£15.59	-
G.	53 000	63 000	93 000	53 450*
H.	100	134.1	189.6	200.4

* Figures for first six months; ** Figure for 1986.

A. Public Sector Housebuilding: Completions (England).

B. Housing Investment Programme Allocations (England), 1986/87 prices.

C. Exchequer Subsidy to Local Authorities (England).

D. Tax Relief on Mortgage Interest (Great Britain), 1985/86 prices.

E. Average House Price for First Time Buyers (UK).

F. Average Weekly Local Authority Rent (England and Wales).

G. Homeless Households accepted by Local Authorities (England).

H. Retail Price Index (Great Britain).

Sources: Dept. of the Environment., various dates, *Housing and Construction Statistics*; DOE., various dates, *Local Housing Statistics;* Association of Metropolitan Authorities; Parliamentary Written Answers, various dates; Public Expenditure White Papers; *Accountancy,* June 1987.

Firstly, the accounting conventions used in public expenditure do not include the cost of tax foregone through support to owner occupation, but in fact this represents a loss to the public purse far greater than the savings in housing subsidies. In the five years from 1980/81 to 1985/86, tax relief on mortgage interest increased from £ 720 million to £4 750 million: its abolition would have meant a 13.4% increase in revenue from income tax and surtax. Over the same period, Exchequer housing subsidies to local authorities decreased from £1 393 million to £457 million. Thus the increased subsidies to home owners were more than double the reduction in subsidies to council tenants with, of course, richer owners getting the greatest support.

Subsidies to housing costs of individual householders through housing benefit (including rate rebates) reach about 3.6 million householders each in the public and private sectors and cost about £2 300 million in each sector, so this does not increase the imbalance. However, support for owner occupation does not end with mortgage tax relief: if we add exemption from Capital Gains tax, Inheritance tax and discount on the sales of council housing, the total cost to public funds exceeds £9 000 million and even this leaves out supplementary benefit payments of mortgage interest, development grants and relief from Value Added tax.

Secondly, public expenditure is taken to include both *capital* expenditure by local authorities, where there is a real asset as a result of the expenditure, *and* current subsidies on costs. Capital expenditure is financed by borrowing through the money market, and we have the illogical position where such expenditure through an individual loan is seen as useful expenditure to be encouraged through tax incentives, but a similar house built by a local authority with a similar loan is seen as an intolerable drain on public resources.

A further instance where the anti-public sector project triumphs over saving in public expenditure is in provision for the homeless. This is an issue which Forrest and Murie address in their chapter. Suffice it to say here that there are some 100 000 households annually accepted as homeless and in priority need, a figure which has doubled since 1978, and a proportionof these will spend several months in temporary accomodation in bed and breakfast hotels at a cost of some £11 000 a year per household in hotel bills, where the actual costs of providing permanent rehousing would be half of this. (Figures given in the House of Commons in January 1987 by John Patten, then Minister of Housing.)

Another instance of state intervention over subsidies has been promised by the recently re-elected government which again affects the Treasury's costs adversely and will increase costs to some council tenants. There is to be a ban on transfers from local authorities' General Rate Fund (that is, their general income from property tax) to the Housing Revenue Account. Local authorities will not be allowed to subsidise their tenants, and in some areas (mainly London boroughs) this will mean doubling of rents. Where this impacts on the Treasury is that about two thirds of these tenants will be having some or all their rent paid by the Department of Health and Social Security as Housing Benefit. (Transfers in the other direction will not be banned, so the situation will continue where some ratepayers in rural areas are being subsidised by rents of council tenants which more than cover the outgoings from the Housing Revenue Account.)

In summary, the goal of reducing provision has taken precedence over that of reducing expenditure: provision *will* be cut even if this means *higher* costs, to say nothing of the social costs.

The Government's alterations in *regulations* significantly affected housing activity have shown greater consistency. Early in their term they abandoned regulations on minimum space standards to which local authorities had to adhere. The other main area where regulations have been relaxed is in rent controls and security of tenure in the private rented sector. There has already been a partial abandonment of fair rents, and fixed term "shorthold" letting is now permitted instead of the greater security previously enjoyed. It has been announced that this relaxation of controls will go further; that landlords should be allowed to make "a reasonable rate of return" and that they will not be subjected to a process of approval.. "Assured tenancies" introduced on a limited scale will be extended more widely.

One area of regulation introduced by the last Labour government may well be relaxed, although this prediction is the authors' supposition rather than any "promise" or advance warning by the government.. The Housing (Homeless Persons) Act of 1977 placed on local authorities a duty to rehouse homeless families, provided they had dependent children, or were vulnerable (includiing being pregnant, elderly or ill), *and* had a "local connection", *and* had not brought about their homelessness intentionally.

These conditions are fairly restrictive and exclude most homeless households, but for many authorities, particularly in London, the incidence of homelessness is greater than the incidence of available vacancies, given other obligations such as transferring tenants subject to violence or harassment. Unless the flow of homeless households can be reduced, the government will not be able to achieve its aim of reducing the size of the council stock in these areas. We would therefore expect an enforced change in the regulations on who qualifies for rehousing by the local authority when homeless, to make them even more restrictive.

The aggregate effect of all these changes, some merely outline proposals, is virtually impossible to calculate. Expenditure on housing takes many forms and there is little sensible correspondence between those having an impact on the national economy, those regarded as public expenditure, and those which the government seeks to control. However, if the cost of all forms of support for owner occupation is taken into account, the total cost of the government's housing policy has certainly increased massively, despite the continued emphasis on pressing the nation to live within its means. Government assistance has been heavily redistributed from poor to rich. The aim is not to render housing affordable but to de-collectivise housing provision.

Summary

To summarise the case of Britain under the Conservatives, the evidence shows that state intervention cannot be seen as a single dimension. The ousing objectives of previous governments were, first to meet the overall *shortage* of housing then to tackle *unfit* housing. The Thatcher government has aimed firstly to reduce public expenditure, then reduce individual households' dependence on a local authority. We have seen that public sector newbuild has been severely cut, and that together with disposal of existing public sector stock this has resulted in a shrinking public sector, for the first time this century. Regulations have been relaxed to supposedly provide the conditions where private landlords can meet the needs that local authorities are prevented from meeting. Taking all forms of expenditure on housing, these have massively increased, mainly in order to achieve the objective of extending owner occupation. Yet there has been *no* action with respect to the main problem facing prospective housebuyers in the prosperous South East, that of rapidly inflating house prices.

Affordability is not a useful concept for understanding the objectives of the Thatcher government. The word may be used by government ministers as in the promise of "affordable rents": a piece of Orwellian 'newspeak' referring to rent levels very much higher than present fair rents or council rents; that is, *unaffordable* rents.

In terms of the original five objectives for state housing policy, the maintenance of social order has been achieved by increasing police powers and more sophisticated weaponry rather than by housing provision. Quality of population is scarcely an issue when those in steady jobs are increasingly in owner occupation: the state shows little interest in maintaining health, morale or dignity in a population without an economic role, and dependent on state benefits.

The social costs and damage to quality of life arising from occupation of an area where not only are *you* poor and trying to cope with the associated problems, but this is also true of all your neighbours, have not been recognised by the government, still less addressed. The government has deliberately rejected the idea of planning to reduce unemployment, believing that market forces will in time bring this about provided that workers do not price themselves out of the market through excessive wage demands. The encouragement of self sufficiency, in a highly individualised form, is clearly paramount. any merits in a collective approach, from support for research through overall direction of resources to meet the particular targets, to allowing individuals' housing costs to be based on historic costs, have effectively been ignored.

State Intervention in Housing Policy: The Developing World

Turning to Third World countries, the pattern of state intervention is very different. Concern with the objective of maintaining social order is often significant for governments in the developing world although social unrest is rarely precipitated by poor housing conditions alone. The fight for survival against the tyranny of hunger and poverty is so dominant in the life of many families in the less developed countries (LDCs) that political organisation and collective mobilisation is less widespread than might be expected. Where poverty is widespread and social change relatively slow, expectations of improvement may be limited. On the other hand the state in the developing world is also much more likely to exert coercion and direct force in quelling unrest. Open use of power may be used on a scale and in a manner that would not be considered legitimate in the West. Indeed, state power has frequently been used in LDCs to *reduce* housing provision directly, for example, by the bulldozing of barrios and squatter settlements built without state approval.

The second principal objective for the state is a concern to improve the health and physical well-being of the population. However, in the LDCs the burgeoning population with large numbers of young people capable of carrying out unskilled tasks means that labour supply outstrips demand. Many workers or prospective workers turn to the service sector in order to earn some money. The conventional wisdom about strategies for development in LDCs stresses the need for investment in human capital but priority normally goes to educating professional and highly skilled workers leaving the majority without adequate education and training. In the advanced nations a similar position may be emerging with mechanisation in production and advanced communications in other sectors resulting in smaller workforces for similar levels of wealth creation. A consequence is that governments show less interest than before in sustaining social and welfare programmes for all.

Enhancing self sufficiency and creating opportunities for development of skills as a third aim of government with respect to housing policy has come to prominence over the past decade. Self build housing programmes as a principal policy in the poorer nations has been given prominence by the World Bank's emphasis on "sites and services" schemes (Williams, 1984; World Bank, 1972, 1975). How far governments go in terms of treating self build as a means to develop the abilities and skills of the population depends on the circumstances within particular nations.

The goal of employment planning takes on a different form in the less developed countries. In most such countries there is plentiful cheap labour, although technical, organisational and building craft skills may be scarce. Economic planning related to housebuilding may centre on other objectives such as reducing dependence on expensive imported materials and construction plant.

The final objective of reducing inequalities and achieving redistribution through some form of pooled costs or central sharing of resources is on the agenda for many governments in the developing world. Progress towards this aim is limited given the relatively low levels of GNP, high levels of international debt and small size of the surplus in most LDCs. The experience of housing programmes has often shown that beneficiaries are from the middle economic strata rather than those households in greatest need (Dwyer, 1975; Harms, 1972). An explicit commitment to equalisation of housing conditions has been associated with socialist and collectivist governments.

Conclusions

Many people have seen the self actualising potential of participation in decision-making from Plato to Habermas whilst it is also said that the broader the participation the more democratic the process becomes (Pateman, 1970). When the organisation of housing provision is undertaken at the broader level, cross subsidisation and redistribution can be more easily effected. We believe this ability to pool resources in order to achieve equalisation was a principal benefit from state intervention in the housing system in the UK during the mid 20th century and that this remains a principal justification for maintaining a major governmental presence in the housing systems of the developed world today. Whilst not wishing to underplay the problems that have beset programmes of state housing in Britain particularly since 1956 when the subsidy system was altered to encourage the building of high rise housing, the record is not all bad. Against the catalogue of unpopular high flats, technical mistakes, bad construction, "sink" estates, poor repairs services and indifferent management, there are recent efforts to improve that reputation.

Principal among these are decentralisation of housing management in order to provide a more accesible and approachable service. Often decentralisation has been accompanied by some degree of greater tenant consultation and participation in the decision-making process. rogress is slow and some of the changes appear limited but they are pointing in the right direction in order to overcome the unpopularity of past management practices. Compared with other agents of housing provision (housing associations and private landlords), local authorities can be more effective and more responsive to tenant demands. In the realm of housing management, modernisation of dwellings and newbuild, the more adventurous efforts to obtain tenant participation in decision-making have been in the public sector. On the other hand those households on the margins of owner occcupation who have sought to buy their homes when on low incomes are faced with escalating difficulties of debt, as the scale of disrepair for which they have responsibility increases and the lack of experience to tackle these problems threaten to overwhelm them (Karn, Kemeny and Williams, 1986).

The rising scale of disrepair and lack of maintenance shows the limits to a vision of a property owning democracy in Britain. This growing problem will only be resolved by some form of collective state-led intervention such as direct provision and management (for example, enveloping) or subsidy (for example, grant aid). With a widening disparity in the developed nations between the well- and poorly-housed the case for greater equalisation of housing conditions and collectivisation of housing policy grows more pressing. Affordability as a concept might be turned on its head from its conceptual basis in the notion of individual responsiblity to offer a revised definition which indicates that the developing and developed worlds cannot neglect housing distress or decline in the quality of the housing stock. The corollary is that nations cannot afford *not* to develop collective programmes for improvement of housing conditions. Affordability would then become a matter of national accounting which presents housing costs as an input to national well-being and not a drain on resources.

Thus we do not decry the present British government's aim of promoting participation and reducing passive dependence on a local authority, but feel that this can be achieved through increased tenant participation in decisions about their housing. Where we disagree with the present government's approach is that these measures are not offered within a broader context of collective improvement or equalisation of housing conditions nor within a framework which offers wider democratic opportunities. Local authorities, being elected bodies, are accountable to local people; as stated above, the system of financing state housing through local authorities has many advantages and despite their failings, local authorities have a much better record of involving their clients than other agencies providing housing.

References

Association of Metropolitan Authorities, 1984: *Submission to the Inquiry into British Housing*. London: The Association.

Darke, R., 19xx: Housing in Nicaragua. International Journal of Urban and Regional *Research* 11, 100-114.

Department of the Environment, 1973: House Condition Survey 1971: England and Wales London: Her Majesty's Stationery Office.

----, 1978: *English House Condition Survey 1976*. London: Her Majesty's Stationery Office.

----, 1982: *English House Condition Survey 1981*. London: Her Majesty's Stationery Office.

----, 1985: *Inquiry into the Condition of the Local Authority Housing Stock*. London: The Department.

Dwyer, D., 1975: *People and Housing in Third World Cities*. London: Longman.

Hall, S. and Jaques, M., eds., 1983: *The Politics of Thatcherism*. London: Lawrence & Wishart.

Harms, H., 1972: The Housing Problem for Low Income People. In: J.F.C. Turner and R. Fichter (eds.): *Freedom to Build: Dweller Control of the Housing Process*. London: Collier-Macmillan, pp. 73-94.

Karn, V., Kemeny, J. and Williams, P., 1986: Low Cost Home Ownership in the Inner City. In: P.A. Booth and A.D.H. Crook (eds.): *Low Cost Home Ownership: An Evaluation of Housing Policy under the Conservatives*. London: Gower, pp. 149-169.

Le Grand, J. and Robinson, R., 1984: *Privatisation and the Welfare State*. London: Allen and Unwin.

Merrett, S., 1979: *State Housing in Britain London*. Routledge and Kegan Paul.

Ministry of Housing and Local Government, 1964: *The Housing Programme 1965 to 1970*. Cmnd. 2838. London: Her Majesty's Stationery Office.

Pateman, C., 1970: *Participation and Democratic Theory*. Cambridge: Cambridge University Press.

Swenarton, M., 1981: *Homes Fit for Heroes: The Politics and Architecture of Early State Housing in Britain.* London: Heinemann Educational.

Turner, J.F.C., 1972: Housing as a Verb. In: J.F.C. Turner and R. Fichter (eds.): *Freedom To Build: Dweller Control of the Housing Process.* London: Collier-Macmillan, pp. 148-175.

Whitehead, C.M.E., 1986: Low Cost Home Ownership in the Context of Current Government Policy. In: P.A. Booth and A.H.D. Crook (eds.): *Low Cost Home Ownership: An Evaluation of Housing Policy under the Conservatives.* London: Gower, pp. 59-79.

World Bank, 1972: *Urbanisation: Sector Policy Paper.* New York: World Bank.

----, 1975: *Housing: Sector Policy Paper.* New York: World Bank.

Williams, D.G., 1984: The Role of International Agencies: The World Bank. In: G.K. Kayne (ed.): *Low Income Housing in the Developing World.* Chichester: Wiley, pp. 173C. Exchequer Subsidy to Local Authorities (England).

PART TWO:
THE PROBLEM OF AFFORDABLE HOUSING

AFFORDABLE HOUSING AND THE MARKET

Arne Karyd

Introduction

In his lifetime, a physician will probably perform many deep sighs over what he perceives as mere supersticion and misconceptions among the people surrounding him. Staying outside in chilly weather without proper clothing neither makes you catch a cold nor brings pneumonia around; it just lowers your resistance against contageon. Probably the same kind of problems face most professionals whatever the art of their profession. The situation for the economist revealing his occupation at the cocktail party is most accurately described as the dealing with myths, some of which displaying extreme survival capability.[1] For example, it is commonly believed that the optimal state of any activity is maximum, sufficient or at least profit. Any deficit-producing activity should preferably be abandonned. Among all myths of economics, this is probably the worst and its origin is often to be found in completely erroneous parallells between the economy of the nation and the economy of the household. The economy of the nation cannot be derived or described as a mere sum of every household. The assumed eternal life of the nation is but one crucial difference.

A closely situated illustration is the traffic policy of Western Europe and the Federal Republic of Germany (FRG). In the FRG, the state railways - impressivly effective to a foreign utilizer - display an annual deficit of some four billion DM. Many people are alarmed by this fact and advocate the reallocation of traffic from railways to roads. However, if the financial result of the roads was measured in the same way as the result of the railways, the deficit would render most business accountants unconscious. Consider for instance the annual interest and depletion on the capital invested in the 9000 km FRG highway net.[2]

---

1. It should be kept in mind that economists deal with questions of economy facing a nation, region, branch, socio-economic layer, group of people etc, normally disregarding organizational boundaries. The science dealing with economy within an organizational framework, e.g. costs and revenues of a business firm, is labeled business administration..

2. Note, that although - contrary to a widespread misconception - German highway construction began as early as 1913 less than one third of the present net was completed by the end of World War II. Hence even the nominal cost of production is immense.

Affordable Housing and the Homeless
© 1988 Walter de Gruyter & Co., Berlin · New York – Printed in Germany

In addition, it can be shown that there is an optimal price level for railway transport as well as any other service or merchandise. To the economist, "optimal" means optimal to the society rather than to the railway administration. It can also be shown that in the railway case this price level is very low and will bring about a substantial deficit. The conclusion is that railways should be run with a certain deficit. If a profit is displayed, this normally indicates too high a price level, insufficient volume of production or both. This conclusion is probably backed up by the relatives of some 10,000 men, women and displayed, this normally indicates too high a price level, insufficient volume of production or both. This conclusion is probably backed up by the relatives of some 10,000 men, women and children annually killed by road traffic in the FRG. To them, to the transportation economist and to those distressed by dying woods, the railway deficit removed from its economic context means less than nothing.

Now the connection between this line of reasoning and affordable housing may seem more than obscure. My point is the following: If basic economics is disregarded, the effects on society might be more profound and widespread than most policymaker realize.

Although there may be no lives to be saved by altered housing olicy, vast sums now spent in vain may be saved and used better. The aim of this paper is to discuss o the nature of the "market" in the housing framework o some frequently disregarded market-related facts of economics within the housing policy sector o some effects of this neglect.

Swedish Housing Conditions

Housing policy and housing conditions in Sweden differ significantly from those of continental Europe. 178 years of peace, rapid urbanization, a high rate of economic growth, powerful unions and a powerful construction industry, a high level of ambition in social policy etc. all put their marks on development. It is also obvious that housing policy makers in a country slightly larger than the FRG, Austria, Switzerland and the Benelux together inhabited by a population comparable to that of greater Paris (8,4 million) face different problems than those facing their continental colleagues. However, these differences apply to the size of the problems rather than to their kind. In other words, probably all questions troubling Occident housing policy makers can be found in Sweden but their extent and severity are less pronounced. A possible exception is the problem of homelessness. Facing winter, social authorities in Gothenburg, our second largest city, scanned the city for outdoor sleepers. Their total findings were one man sleeping in his car as a victim of a raging wife rather than housing policy (Göteborgs-Posten, Nov 22, 1987). In Stockholm, comparable to Hamburg in size, conditions are somewhat harsher and in a recent TV-programme social authorities estimated the number of outdoor lodgers to less than 100.

The Present Swedish Housing Situation

In order to save paper space for discussion rather than description, the present situation and its background will be summarized into a few points. Details are found in the Benton and Karyd (1986) paper.

- As far back as in 1970, Sweden probably outstripped most if not all comparable countries in housing standard measured as the number of occupied dwellings per 1.000 inhabitants (Luijanen, 1981). The same conclusion is valid for the average size of *completed* dwellings by that time but not for the average size in the existing stock.

- Basic housing objectives (discussed at length in e.g., Lundquist, 1981; Malmsten, 1969) were fulfilled in the mid-1970s, at least on the macro level (see Jussil, 1981).

- By this time, construction activity dropped to one third of its 1970 peak level which was some 110.000 completed dwellings. Simultaneously, construction price index *increased* its rate of growth (Wickman, 1987) and housing subsidy volume started skyrocketing.

- Construction of new dwellings has from time to time turned into "houseomania". From 1949 to the present day, some 2.6 million dwellings have been completed. The whole population could be very well housed without utilizing any part of the housing heritage from centuries past. The ratio of post-war dwellings to all dwellings is roughly the same as in the FRG, a country which - to put it mildly - had a slightly different starting point (see the contribution by Friedrichs).

- Direct governmental financial support - housing allowances, interest allowances and miscellaneous supports - amount to some SEK 20 billion at present. In comparison, the defence budget is some 25% larger.

- The financial burden of interest allowances to already existing dwellings will continue to grow for about 18 years at the present inflation level (Wickman, 1987).

- Strong evidence suggest that income distributive effects of housing subsidies conflict with fundamental housing policy objectives in Sweden as well as in the other Nordic countries (Åhren, 1986, and to some extent also Turner, 1986).

- In spite of alleged severe conditions on urban housing markets, hardly any attempts have been made to use the second hand market for housing policy purposes although this sector comprises vast policy opportunities (Brzesky, 1986).

Affordable Housing Policy

Most developed countries recognize the responsibility of government to provide housing to its citizens. How, and to which extent, government should intervene in the housing sector is an issue of considerable debate. The disagreement is extremely profound when the attitude of government towards "housing markets" is under debate. In order to provide a point of departure for the subsequent discussion, I will characterize two different types of opinion in this field and trace their economic implications.

Market believers: "Almost every kind of services and goods are available on a market which means that there are sellers as well as buyers. There are markets for single-dwelling houses, condominiums and multi-dwelling houses. Although illegal in Sweden, there is also a market for rent agreements in the big cities. The need for housing will be satisfied by the forces of the market - demand and supply. Compared to these real forces, the power of government is small. Because of its limited power and because the market is the best way to distribute housing, the role of government should be confined to lubricate and facilitate activities on the markets. If extremely high rents or sales profits are observed, this is not an indication of unsufficient government control but a sign of improper market function. The reasons are often to be found in vainful attempts from the government to offset the market, e.g. by constraints on construction and supply".

Market opposers: "Adequate housing is a basic human right, not a merchandise. The influence of markets over such an essential sector of human life should be removed or at least rendered harmless. Government should excise control over physical planning, construction of new housing, rent levels and price levels. Although private-owned single- and multi-family dwellings may be tolerated, realized capital gains occuring at sale should be heavily taxed. For multi-family dwellings, prospective buyers should be subject to approval by the local tenant organization. The forming of condominiums should not be encouraged. In general, housing should be subsidized to prevent people from choosing inferior housing conditions in order to use the money for other kinds of consumption".

For reasons of discussion, the opinions characterized above are somewhat exaggerated. Although there may be straightforward advocates of each version, most opinions encountered in every-day life are compromises between the two. This should be kept in mind but has no impact on the following discussion.

The Nature of the Market

Part of this antagonism is explained by the fact that "market" is a word with very different meaning to different groups. To the believer, it is a nice sunny place where neatly behaving sellers and buyers agree upon fair deals to the benefit of all and the omnipotent, wellinformed consumer is free to choose. To the opposer, it is a ghastly location where top-hat- dressed, tax-evading sharks already well off make incredible profits by exploiting basic needs and ignorance among powerless people.

No more than anyone else could the economist supply a description of the market that both parties would agree upon. Another approach is to find the necessary conditions for the existence of a market. In other words, which factors must be present before we can say that the situation is best described as a "market"? Economics shows that only three factors are necessary:

- There must be buyers, i.e. someone willing to increase his possession of the merchandise and pay a price for it;

- There must be sellers, i.e. someone in possession of the merchandise but willing to dispose of it at a price;

- Finally there must be some way for sellers and buyers to find each other: A market place, advertisements, brokers etc.

In particular, it should be noted that the approval of government or of society in general are not necessary conditions. This is proven by the perpetual existence of semi-legal and illegal markets like those for prostitution, narcotics, and even housing (see the contribution by Kerner). If the market offers profits high enough, it will resist almost any kind of extermination attempts.

From this scenario it should be clear that the market exists whether you like it or not. Housing policy can make it shrink or expand and improve or obstruct its activities but housing policy can never make the market disappear. Facing this harsh reality, the best way to act for the housing policy maker is to travesty the proverb If you can't beat them - join them and say: I can't beat the market, so I will accept its existence and use it for my housing policy purposes. Unfortunately this confession is slightly too much for many a housing politician. The result is an at least in Sweden frequent attitude, namely the ostrich approach to housing policy. This is characterized by the denieing, neglecting or disregarding of the market in the futile hope that if you pretend it is not there, it will cause you no harm. 1) I will provide some examples in section 4.

Market-Believer Policy Implications

Even the most superficial glance at 20th-century housing history clearly reveals the inability of a market left to its own to provide adequate housing for the poor. Market believers are seldom crude enogh to deny this conclusion. More often, the market believer escapes this lacking feature of the market: If the poor are poor, then general social policy and general subsidies like allowances, not housing subsidies, should relieve the poor from their poverty and make them fit for fight in the market. In the market, existing whether we like it or not, income redistribution by means of subsidizing specific goods like housing causes price- and behaviour adjustments and in the end, the redistributional effect may be offset or inverted. In short, poverty should be fought by social policy, not housing policy, and the latter is fairly useless even as a tool in social policy. A possible exception is the housing voucher system used in the U.S. contribution to This is not a general subsidy - it is directed towards housing - but its use can be confined to those who really need it.

Normally the inability to combine housing policy tools with such a restriction is put forward as a major disadvantage by the market believer. This line of reasoning is quite powerful and necessitates a brief discussion of the housing policy advocated by the market believer. For goods and services in general, the quantity can be sufficiently described by using units as number, weight, volume or number of man-hours. Measuring the volume of housing is immensely more complicated. Popular units as sq.m. or number of dwellings do not incorporate the quality and equipment standard of housing. Consequently these measurements provide only a very rough estimate of housing volume.[1]

For the discussion we will disregard this complication and assume that square meters, is an adequate measurement of housing volume. Then the main argument of market believers can be sketced as follows.

Figure 1: Market Believer Housing Market

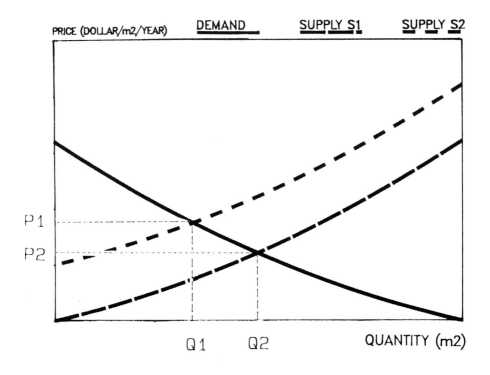

1. See Eriksson (1981) for a discussion of the relation between "useful floorspace" and "floorspace for housing purposes". Comparing 1970 and 1978, Eriksson concluded that in spite of a 50% drop in the number of dwellings annually produced, the produced useful floorspace.

In Figure 1, the vertical axis measures the price of housing in SEK per square meter and year. (The precise nature of this price - rent, costs for a condominium or cost for a single-family dwelling - has no bearing on the discussion.) The "quantity of housing" is measured along the horizontal axis in square meter. The demand for housing is downward sloping, i.e. the lower the cost for housing, the higher the quantity of housing demanded. The supply for housing is upward-sloping, i.e. the higher the price for housing, the higher the volume of housing offered on the market.

While the *exact* properties of the demand and supply curves are very hard to establish, there is no doubt whatsoever regarding the general relationships between price and volume. The market, if left to its own, will find a point of equilibrium at the quantity q_1 and the price level p_1. (It can be shown that some combinations of slopes will make the price and quantity fluctuate around the equilibrium point rather than reaching it. This possibility is disregarded in the following.)

The prevailing price level p_1 may be unattainable to large groups of citizens. According to the market believer, the first commandment is that this situation never should be attacked by interfering with the market. Instead, general subsidies to the low income earners should make them able to face the price level p_1. Hence no "housing policy" is necessary. If, however, a housing policy really must be implemented it should be directed towards the supply of housing.

The demand curve is a reflection of consumer preferences and these should not be tampered with. Instead, action should be taken in order to shift the supply curve to the right. Possible steps are the introduction of construction-encouraging policy instrument such as (more) favourable tax rules for the owners of multi- family dwellings, conversion of abandoned industrial sites into housing sites, changers in the building code, etc. (The existence of a building code - a book of technical construction requirements - is justified inter alia by the fact that the lifespan of a building normally exceeds the lifespan of its constructor. Hence society, as heir to the building, has the right to impose rules otherwise neglected by the constructor. This point is normally accepted also by market believers.) The supply of housing will increase to the S' curve and the market will reach a new equilibrium at the lower price level p_2 and the higher volume level q_2. Everyone but landlords are better off than before.

This sketchy example is of course a very rough description of the market believer line of reasoning. Nevertheless it serves fairly well as a basic tool for evaluating a market-centered policy. The rough sketch also contains the main objection to this kind of policy.

Macro- and micromarkets

The Swedish word for real estate, "fastighet", has the same inherent meaning as the German "Immobilien" and the French "immeubles", i.e. the basic property of sites and buildings of not being movable. This means that "housing" at the macro level discussed above is a fairly useless concept. Dwellings are only to a very limited extent substitutes for each other. Normally the housing consumer is faced with a micro housing market within reasonable range from his work..

 Most people, especially in the lower income groups, cannot choose their housing first and their work later. Their choice of housing must be confined to available opportunities within a few hundred square kilometers. In addition, this limited market can be further divided into markets for tenancy agreements (where the price is the rent), condominiums and single-family dwellings. In the latter cases, the "price" is the paid or lost rent for the necessary capital plus, in the condominium case, the yearly fee.

     In urban areas, all these markets are characterized by next to vertical supply curves, i.e. the quantity of housing offered at the market will remain practically constant regardless of the housing price level. The offered quantity is not totally insensitive to the price level because very high price levels would make the conversion of present non-housing premises into dwellings profitable and even tempt some owners of single-family dwellings to offer a room or two for rent. In general, though, the supply of housing is quite stiff because there are very few sites suitable for housing construction and very few dwellings not already occupied. Under these circumstances it is impossible to implement a housing policy aiming at increased supply and furthermore, the real cost of housing (the cost expressed in e.g constant 1987 dollars) may rise all by itself. According to a disputed but interesting theory of economist Södersten (1976), three factors contribute to a long-run upward push of market-determined housing costs: The growth of cities, making remote areas less and less remote; inflation, raising the general price level more than the costs of owning multi-family dwellings; and finally the fact that productivity (production per unit of input, e.g. man-hours) tends to grow slower in the construction industry than in general, thus raising the cost of new construction and pushing the price of existing buildings upward.

The Vicious Circle

However, even if the market works like the ideal case depicted in figure 1, the general subsidies preferred by market believers will affect the market. If the subsidy works as intended, it will rise the income level of the recipients. Consequently, their demand for all goods and services *including housing* will rise. The demand curve in Figure 2 is shifted to the right.

     As a result, the price level will rise to p_2 and the quantity of housing to q_2. Landlords and property owners will also receive part of the subsidy, materialized in a higher price level. The rising price level will create a need for additional subsidies which in turn will rise the price level still further and so on. This vicious circle will not continue for ever but the final subsidy level might be much higher than originally calculated.

Applied to the small urban markets discussed above, the conclusion will will be that the subsidy will have but marginal effects on the quantity of housing offered to the market. Instead, the housing price level will rise and the bulk of the subsidy will be received by landlords. Summing up, a policy tool such as general household subsidies requires more than the existence of a market in order to work as intended by market believers. It requires a market with a *price-sensitive supply* of housing. This complication is frequently overlooked by market believers.

Figure 2: Subsidy Effect in the Market

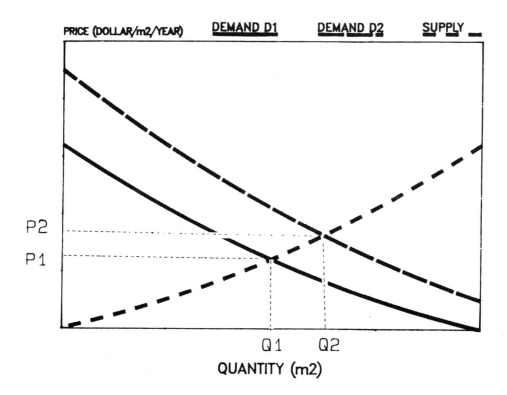

Market-Opposer Policy Implications

For the market opposer, the correct ways to act differ somewhat between the different kind of dwellings. For reasons of space I will confine the discussion to one specific issue. The example concerns rent levels for rented dwellings. If market rents are too high, the market opposer will advocate the replacement of market rents by some other standard, e.g. dictated or negotiated rents. To the lawyer and the policy-maker contaminated by the ostrich approach, this is done by adding an additional paragraph to the law. The economist would say that the task is slightly more complicated.

Negotiated Rent Levels

In Sweden, rent levels are set in negotiations between the tenant organizations and their landlord counterpart. Semi-public bodies are assumed to be rent leaders. (A detailed discussion of negotiated rents versus market rents is found in Nyman and Torne, 1985). Differences in location have a profound effect on the demand but are only to a minor extent reflected in the negotiated rent levels. Compared to the rent levels emerging in a free market, the central city rents will be lower and the remote suburban rents higher. This means empty dwellings in the suburbs and excess demand in the center (Figure 3).

To the economist, as separated from the business administrator, both empty suburban dewellings and excess demand in the center indicates ineffectiver housing policy. In the first case, we could all agree upon the fact that if the house already exists, it will normally stand there for fifty or a hundred years and in fact it will deteriorate more rapidly if it is not occupied. Nothing is to gain by keeping the rent level so high that none finds it worthwhile to live in the house. Instead, the rent level should be lowered, the house filled with tenants and we will all benefit from the fact that still another part of our common capital is utilized. (Provided, of course, that the deterrent factor really is the rent level. As indicated in the contribution by Friedrichs in this book, also the physical and social environment and the constructive quality of the house may serve as intimidating factors. These factors may be too powerful to be offset by rent decreases and in that case demolition or drastic reconstruction may be the only remedies.)

Under negotiated rents, the counterpart of empty suburban dwellings is normally excess demand in the central parts of the city. "Excess demand" means that at the prevailing rent level, there will be a queue of prospective tenants for each available dwelling because the benefits associated with these dwellings are perceived as having a value greater than the rent.

. Suppose a centrally located, attractive dwelling has a negotiated rent of x dollars per month. If the rent was determined at a free market instead, it would be x plus an additional z dollars, i.e. someone is willing to pay not only x but x+z dollars for the benefit of occupying this dwelling. Anyone moving into the dwelling would, though, only have to pay x dollars monthly because this is the negotiated rent. Realizing that if I could get hold of the dwelling and will have to pay only x dollars per month, I may conclude that it would be profitable to offer the present inhabitant a sum of money for the lease contract. In fact, it would be profitable to offer a sum up to the present value of the z dollars per month I would be willing to pay but do not have to pay if I get hold of the dwelling. Further realizing that if I pay this sum of money the money is not lost but constitutes an investment, the value of which I will be able to recover if I sell the lease contract, my willingness to pay the present inhabitant for his contract increases additionally.

Figure 3: Negotiated and Market Rents

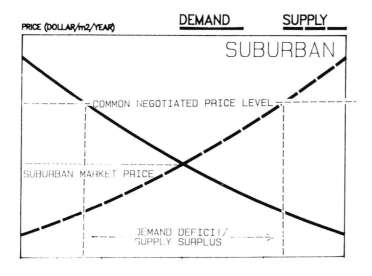

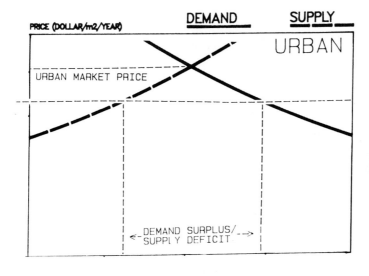

The prospect that a small group of happy central dwellers should be able to make vast profits just because they happen to inhabit an attractive dwelling is unacceptable not only to the market opposer. Consequently this kind of business arrangement is prohibited in Sweden. Unfortunately - as we have already seen - the approval of government is not a necessary condition for the existence of a market. In other words, the market cannot be banned away.

For the present Swedish government, active regional policy is hardly a hallmark and the urbanization pressure is back to its 1960s level. This means increased demand for centrally located dwellings and a rising difference between negotiated and market rents. As mentioned above, one is not allowed to sell ones tenancy agreement but to switch it for another or hand it over to the seller of a single-family dwelling one is buying. These possibilities set the stage for profitable circumvening. If someone switches his tenure against another of less market value, he can always capitalize the difference in market value by simultaneously selling some furniture or your 1972 Volkswagen wreck for 10,000 dollars. This may be illegal but no one can do anything about it because the car price is never made public. Accompanying rising demand, these transactions are performed less and less tacitly and at present may find notes in the most popular areas offering thousands of dollars to anyone who will hand over a lease contract. While the offer is not illegal, accepting it is doubtlessly illegal.

In the case where a tenant moves to a single-family dwelling and the former owner will take over the tenancy agreement, the situation is even more advantageous. The seller will pay the tenant the whole market value of his tenure by simply reducing the price of the single-family dwelling. For reasonable proportions between selling price and tenure value, this transaction is invisible, unattackable and probably not even illegal.

Capitalizing market value by circumvening the law is a phenomenon rapidly aggravating the problem of implementing a rent level policy. Law enforcement when the criminal action is totally confined to two *consenting* parties is next to impossible. Even the market opposer must give the market believer some credit for the statement that government power is small compared to the real forces of demand and supply.

To this problem no easy remedies are visible. My impression is that negotiated rents perform their redistributional task reasonably well as long as the difference between negotiated and market rent is not too big. When this difference reaches a certain magnitude though, negotiated rents have to take at least part of the market pressure into consideration. This will give rise to new problems, for instance rapid increases in the price of centrally located buildings, but the alternative is inevitably black- market adjustments described above. These adjustment can be assumed to be even less desirable than increased rents and property values from a social point of view.

The Problem of Subsidized Single-Family Dwellings

Practically all single-family dwellings constructed in later years are financed by means of heavily subsidized government loans. One salient problem with such an arrangement is how to confine the subsidy to those who really need it. Until mid-1986, the construction of a government-financed house was surrounded by tight regulations on maximum floorspace and equipment standards. For instance, a sauna occasionally disqualified the house for government loans. The same effect was brought about if the maximum permissable floorspace was exceeded. Such regulations are sitting ducks for the ingenuity of the construction industry: Attics with no staircase (to be delivered later) and the windows hidden behind the wooden panel, spaces remarkably similar to saunas but labeled closet, supply room or something else. In 1986, these rules and the production cost control, equally circumvenable, were simply lifted. This was the right thing to do because these restrictions did not work. However, one could raise the question whether the social profile of the housing policy still remains when a castle-building millionaire receives a heavy subsidy for the first 5-6 rooms.

While the subsidizing of single-family houses regardless of size and standard in itself is enough to cause hesitation, the trouble really starts when the house is being sold at the second-hand market. Real estate broker advertisements clearly reveal an evident feature of a subsidized loan connected to the house and not to the inhabitant: The loan has a market value corresponding to the size of its remaining subsidy content. The second-hand buyer will buy not only the house but also the subsidized loan at its present value. Consequently the subsidy, intended to last for some 15-20 years, may be cashed at present value by the first owner if the market is functioning reasonably well. This is probably the most obvious and most omitted property of a subsidized loan. A detailed example is given by Benton and Karyd (1986: 311); a remedy - attaching the loan to persons instead of houses - is also suggested. If at all recognized, the problem has been attacked only by vague and easily circumvenable means like transfer price control.

Conclusions

In a research report as well as in a discussion paper the author should be granted the right to use the last lines at his own discretion, e.g. to present the deductions he wants to present regardless of the degree of background support in the preceding text. Straining this freedom to the limit, I would suggest that the "Swedish model" housing policy is mainly influenced by the ostrich approach to housing markets. It is tacitly assumed that if you refuse to see or discuss the market, it will cease to exist. Unfortunately, the market does not require the approval of anyone to be fully operational and it will tend to offset the most ambitious policy programs insofar as these programs are designed without due consideration to basic laws of the market. Housing policy could make use of the market (see, Brzeski, 1986) but this possibility is rarely utilized. Out of the immense volume of housing subsidies, the bulk will serve to boost the housing standard of people who do not really need it. Only to a marginal extent will the provision of affordable housing to those who cannot afford it be promoted by this system.

Furthermore there does not seem to be much hope of rapid recovery from the ostrich syndrom. On the contrary, even recent actions reveal ignorance of basic market laws. According to the municipalities of Gothenburg, the best way to stop black market transactions with tenancy contracts would be to force the landlord to sign an affidavit that no money was involved when a tenancy agreement was taken over. Sancta simplicitas would be the comment from the market believer and also from those who do not believe in but understand the market (Göteborgs-Posten, Sept. 22, 1987: 7).

Another policy instrument recently introduced confirms the prevailing ostrich approach. In order to enable low income earners with children to buy used single-family dwellings, acquisition loans were introduced during 1987. Someone having at least two children and a low household income is entitled to a very favorable loan. This fact is of course known to the seller. Hence the price will be pushed upward and this effect cannot be offset by transfer price control for reasons stated above. Furthermore, the fact that one may be entitled to a vast subsidy if his household income is low enough makes income tax evasion even more profitable than before. Note that the income requirement is assesed for one year only while the subsidized loan will yield revenue for many years (Göteborgs-Posten, Sept. 9, 1987: 4, "Sydost" enclosure). Finally, this kind of arrangement divides the buyers on the market into one non-subsidized and one extremely subsidized group on the very dubious basis of taxable income. The members of the latter group will be much more competible in the housing market than even high-income earners of the former group. It is a riddle how the housing policy can go on and on creating such profound cleavages.

References

Åhren, P, 1986.: *Housing Subsidies in the Nordic Countries*. Discussion paper to the 1986 International Research Conference on Housing Policy at the National Institute for Building Research

Benton, L. and Karyd, A., 1986: *How to Spend Billions. Waste Aspects of the Swedish Housing Loans System*. Discussion paper to the 1986 International Research Conference on Housing Policy at the National Institute for Building Research.

Brzeski, W.J., 1986: *Resale Home Finance and Market Reallocation of Households - a Viable Option for Swedish Housing Policy Research?* Discussion paper to the 1986

International Research Conference on Housing Policy at the National Institute for Building Research.

Eriksson, J., 1981: Har vi byggt bort trångboddheten? Contribution to the anthology *Bostadsfrågan inför 80-talet*. Stockholm.

Jussil, S., 1981: Kredit- och skattepolitikens samband med bostadspolitiken. Contribution to the anthology *Bostadsfrågan inför 80-talet*. Stockholm.

Luijanen, M., 1981: Svensk bostadspolitik vid internationell jmfrelse. Contribution to the anthology *Bostadsfrågan inför 80-talet*. Stockholm.

Lundqvist, L.J., 1981: Bostadskostnaderna. Statens Institut för Byggnadsforskning t:19.

Malmsten, B.: Bostadsbyggandet i plan och verklighet. *Byggforskningsrådet* R69:84

Nyman, B. and Tornée, P., 1985: *Marknadsmässiga hyror för en rättvisare bostadsmarknad.* Discussion paper to the 1985 housing seminar at the National Institute for Building Research.

Södersten, B., 1976: Bostadsförsörjning och bostadspolitik under efterkrigstiden. In: B. Södersten (ed.): *Svensk Ekonomi*. Stockholm.

Turner, B., 1986: *Housing Finance in the Nordic Countries*. Discussion paper to the 1986 International Research Conference on Housing Policy at the National Institute for Building Research.

AFFORDABLE HOUSING IN A SOCIALIST COUNTRY
THE CASE OF PRAGUE

Antonín Kerner

This chapter focusses on experiences in a socialist country, the CSSR, and in particular its capital, Prague, with no housing "market" but a housing policy with a strong impact on social interventions. The non-existence of a housing market, however, does not imply that there are no economic problems with regard to housing policy and other services connected with dwellings.

The Socialist Economy

The Czechoslovak national economy is being developed on the basis of social ownership of the means of production. It is the state-owned socialist enterprises together with co-operative enterprises that play a decisive role, even though there is a relatively wide range of various organizational forms differing in their ways of management and financing, in the scope of economic activity etc. Private ownership of small-scale producers in agriculture or in services (craftsmen) is of little importance.

The practice of building up socialism in Czechoslovakia is based on Marx's thesis that it is not the realization of private ownership of the means of production but only human labor that can be the source of individual income.

The socialist economy is a planned economy. The system of overall economic balance-accounting is a precondition for economic growth and balance. The system of balance-accounting of income, investments, manpower and external economic relations is a prerequisite for future-related decision-making. The quality of balance-accounting also influences the quality of decision-making processes which are outlined in the general scheme in the objectives of the plan. Further working out of the balance-accounting method and all other information systems makes possible approaching the drafting of middle-term and long-term structure plans. Middle-term plans (for five years) can perform their target and programme function. The five-year plan integrates main targets such as the number of flats, subsidies, capital investment in the form of technical and social infrastructure.

First of all the planning scheme programme is orientated towards locating capital investments and the labor force as the main conditions for economic equilibrium. The real economic growth rate and the proportion of all kinds of goods and services depend on many other circumstances. The responsibility of enterprises to fulfill the main targets laid

Affordable Housing and the Homeless
© 1988 Walter de Gruyter & Co., Berlin · New York – Printed in Germany

down in the state plan on the one hand and to introduce marketing on the other hand are the important points of today's socialist economy. The decentralization of decision-making processes is very important for the material and moral initiative.

The system of economic planning is a very important background for the social policy. Economic and social policy are very closely integrated. Positive results in economy policy influence social policy.

Social policy safeguards important social rights and certainties for all people. Czechoslovakia is a country with full employment, a country in which everyone can work corresponding to his education, training and abilities. In Czechoslovakia today social security covers the entire working population - mothers, children, old and sick people.

Young families with children receive help, free education and free health care is provided for the whole population. The socialist state is also increasingly caring for retired people (men over the age of sixty and women aged between 53 and 57 depending on their number of children).

Housing Policy

The housing problem seen as an imbalance between the number, size, and location of flats on the one hand and the real demand for them on the other hand was the historical problem. Socio-economic and technological progress which is the basis for the development of productive forces has led man to engage in constant improvements in his way of living and has improved his real possibilities to satisfy his demand for housing. However, in the past the use of these possibilities depended not only on the socio-economic level of society as a whole but mainly on the status of a given social stratum or group in the process of the production and distribution of the national product.

The basic housing paradox of the past was the massive deterioration of the housing conditions of the industrial proletariat and the impoverished lower middle classes, despite the general economic growth which could easily have fully satisfied the housing requirements of those days.

Industrialization also spurred great social changes, in particular a rapid growth of cities which became industrial and economic centres. City populations continued to grow much faster than national populations - a fact attributed to the influx of people from rural areas.

The developing industries drew new blood not only from the villages, but their labor force was also reinforced by smallholders and minor craftsmen pouring in from smaller towns.

This process inevitably led to the worsening of their housing situation compared with their earlier smallholder existence as craftsmen or farmers. The transition to hired labor meant the separation of work and home - earlier a harmonic unity. No sooner had a smallholder been denied the possibility to use his own means of production and forced to seek employment in the city than he lost the benefit of keeping his own house or apartment. His options narrowed to renting a flat either from his employer or a landlord.

Many things have changed after the Second World War in the period of the construction of the socialist system. Radical changes that occurred in this period led to a broad democratization and to the humanization of housing with standards rapidly improving. The main objective was to satisfy the housing needs of workers, providing each and every family with their own flat. A new housing policy was formulated as part of the social policy characterized by a strong government influence.

Housing policy can be defined as an inventory of means and methods applied by any society to achieve certain goals in the sphere of housing. These goals differ depending on which class rules society or, better still, whose interests are pursued by those who formulate and implement such a policy. The socialist housing policy strives to eliminate the housing shortages which in the past affected most strongly the low-income, poorly qualified and socially underprivileged classes.

The socialist society with its political and management bodies provides all citizens equal access to housing. In this process it gives priority to the improvement of the conditions under which those on a lower social level must live. To ensure that housing needs are met is primarily the job of social institutions. These include first of all the national committees, i.e. local bodies of state power and administration, social organizations and co-operatives.

An inevitable part of housing policy is the consistent satisfaction of housing requirements in harmony with the requirements of production and society, and with the social needs of the different groups of the population. Czechoslovakia's socialist housing policy emphasizes a comprehensive approach to housing, comprising both housing construction and the provision of all basic amenities for residents. Its goal is to create a hygienic and first-rate housing environment consistent in all aspects with the modern demands of housing culture.

The architectural solution and physical planning of housing complexes stem from the tenet that newly built and existing housing projects must ensure equal access to the basic components of social consumption of finance from public funds, such as education, health care and culture.

In the post-war years Czechoslovakia experienced positive demographic trends resulting in an upswing in new families and new households. This, conversely, dramatically increased the demand for housing, especially in newly industrialized regions. The new organization of the national economy naturally changed the national demographic pattern. The housing problem became a hot issue, largely because of the ever fuller satisfaction of the other vital needs of the population. Thus, housing emerged as a crucial condition for keeping the rapidly growing living standards in good proportions. With regard to the number of finished flats per 1,000 inhabitants, Czechoslovakia in the mid-seventies ranked among the leading European countries.

The following Table 1 shows the gross total of housing construction in ten-year periods since the end of the Second World War (all types of dwellings):

Table 1: Housing Construction in Czechoslovakia, 1946-1985

Period	Number of finished homes
1946-1955	307,000
1956-1965	722,000
1966-1975	1,055,000
1976-1985	1,133,000

Current estimates stand at 336 housing units per 1,000 inhabitants on a national scale. More than two-thirds of all Czechoslovak citizens live in houses and flats built after the year 1945. The rapid growth of houses during the sixties and seventies brought with it the need to use pre-fabricated elements and to apply industrial elements in constructing new districts. Concerning quantity this was a big advantage. On the other hand there are many problems with technical and architectural standards, with maintenance, and with regard to social aspects.

It goes without saying that the satisfaction of housing needs, just like other spheres of consumption, is limited in socialist societies by the means and resources accrued. Thus, economic progress and consequently even housing construction are determined by the level of social production reached so far. They do not depend exclusively on individual wishes or the co-operativeness of state organs, but also on the objective availability of resources that can be realized for housing projects in the spheres of financial investment, material or capacity. Demands are rising as far as the quality of housing and related services is concerned. The situation is better in villages and small towns; demand is higher in cities, especially in Prague, the capital city.

Forms of Housing

The following forms of housing construction co-exist in Czechoslovakia: state (communal), based on state ownership, co-operative based on the principle of group socialist ownership and construction of family houses which are the personal property of citizens. It is possible for private citizens to buy state-owned apartments.

Housing policy as part of social policy is not only realized through state-owned housing. This form dominates in big cities but not in the country as a whole. The majority of all houses are in personal property (family houses). Czechoslovak Constitution Law distinguishes between private property (means of production) and personal property (means of consumption, originating in labor income). It is also possible to buy apartments from state ownership in personal property (newly built or older ones). This is not common, however, mainly because of the price compared with the low rents in state housing.

The forms of housing in Czechoslovakia in 1986 were: state ownership: 24%, co-operative based: 16%, and personal ownership: 60%. In total, there are 5.4 million flats of all forms of ownership in Czechoslovakia. Their average age was 35.6 years in total Czechoslovakia, 39.4 years in the Czech Republik, and 26.1 years in the Slovak Republic.

Determining the proportion of each form of housing construction and to make decisions regarding overall scope, location and standard are component parts of the housing policy of the central government (technical standard, financing) and also of local governments (location, distribution etc.). The influencing and limiting factors include in the first place the building, material and financial considerations but also the need to save and protect such priceless resources as farm land, water and other components of the living environment. Another important factor influencing decisions about the location and form of construction in different parts of the country is the actual state of development and the distribution of the labor force.

Social subsidies concern all forms of housing construction and are granted predominantly from state funds. The investment process of housing and related construction starts with physical planning in regions and districts. The national committees decide about the use and functions of different areas and allocations for housing, economic and other public ventures. Among other things they mark off areas designed for housing projects, zones of rest and recreation, protected areas, reserves etc.

The national committees are also responsible for the protection of farm land and therefore offer non-farm land for housing construction without any fee or with a very small fee for family houses (permanent personal land use). In fact the cost of land for housing construction has no important role. Some administrative rules are more complicated.

The national committees therefore function as direct sponsors of housing and related projects. This arrangement is called "communal housing construction" and also includes, apart from state-financed housing construction, the construction of technical amenities of housing estates - roads, parking lots, parks and public green, playgrounds, water supply, sewerage networks, gas, electricity and heat distribution etc. Moreover, communal housing projects also include the social infrastructure, i.e. creches, kindergartens, basic schools, health care centers, communal services, retail networks, restaurants, cultural centers, sports centers. All these projects are financed by the state irrespective of whether they serve the occupants of state-owned, co-operative or private houses.

The national committees and their organs do not have to fulfill all functions prescribed by the law. They are free to appoint special agencies to work in their stead in certain areas, e.g. building project investments. Completed projects are handed over to organizations which manage them. Housing complexes pass over to the so-called housing economy enterprises (non-profit organizations) which also report to the national committees. Their task is to provide services relating to the use of flats. They oversee the maintenance and servicing of flats and keep in touch with their occupants.

The national committees also function as construction authorities issuing building permits for all projects, be they executed by socialist organizations or private builders. The construction authority also checks building projects for their societal aspects, such as safety, aesthetic value, environmental considerations etc. In the final stage it decides whether the project meets all functional requirements and authorizes its use. The construction authority also sees to it that buildings are properly maintained.

Social housing (communal dwellings) are financed completely from the budget of national committees (in fact there are subsidies from the state budget according to the number of flats, because local revenues are insufficient). The subsidies also include the technical and social infrastructure. Furthermore, the state bears the bigger part of the maintenance costs. Rents per sq.m. have been constant for a long period, at present since 1964. They equal about 8% of the household income.

The legal regulations for the distribution of housing proceed from the following main principles:

- Homes managed by the national committees are primarily for bigger families with lower incomes.

- The distribution of homes is subject to public control.

- State control and supervision prevents speculation and ensures proper use of flats.

- The right of tenancy can be suspended only in cases specified by the law.

- Nobody may be evicted from his home without being assigned an alternative apartment or another form of accommodation.

Homes rented from the state are distributed by the local national committees. This distribution is a direct instrument of the state housing policy. Applicants are put on the housing list. Here, the national committee will give priority to applicants without a home of their own in the constituency, married couples living in separate households and persons who have flats of their own in other communities than their place of work. Priority is further given to applicants whose flats are considered in unsanitary condition or unsuitable in any other way, and to applicants who have been ordered to move out through a decision of a court or a national committee.

The "unsanitary" status applies to premises marked by the health officer or the construction authority as unsuited for habitation because of technical flaws adversely affecting human health. The Czechoslovak legal system thus defines circumstances under which applicants are put on the housing list so that all legitimate reasons for citizens to apply for a new flat are covered.

Homes are distributed to applicants who are on the waiting list. One criterium is that priority should be given to applicants in urgent need of housing, who should be assigned flats before others on the grounds of their housing situation and other circumstances (e.g., the social importance of their work). Thus waiting lists are drawn up following guidelines similar to those binding for housing lists, i.e. the applicant's housing situation in his community, the sanitary condition of his flat, his state of health etc. The more points an applicant has accrued the sooner he qualifies for a new flat. The importance of the applicant's work is classified according to the significance of his profession and his professional results.

Rents in state-owned homes are dependent on the respective housing quality. According to their amenities flats are divided into four categories that determine their rents:

I. Category - Flats with central heating and complete facilities
II. Category - Flats without central heating with other facilities
III. Category - Without central heating with some facilities
IV. Category - Without any facilities

The basic rents are determined according to floorspace. If a dweller undertakes private efforts to modernize his flat this does not change the category of the flat and thus the rent. Of course the other communal services are paid for individually depending on the amount consumed (e.g., water, gas, electricity, etc.). The rent (excluding services) is then modified by different social considerations. It is reduced progressively for families with children: one child: 5%, two children: 15%, three children: 30%, four children: 50%, etc. Rents are determined according to fixed legal regulations and do not rise with the tenant's income. Rents for communal flats have not been raised since 1964.

Once a flat is assigned by the national committee nobody (except in cases specified by the law) has the right to prevent the user from moving in. The right of tenancy can be voided either by the user (through death or other circumstances, e.g., renunciation of his right of tenancy, moving to another flat etc.) or by court order or the national committee.

In no case of suspension of user right for whatever reason must the user be left without shelter. In most cases he has the right to be assigned an adequate substitute home or accommodation. The substitute flat must be either of the same quality (not in unsanitary condition, unsuitable or inadequate) or at least adequate to the user's requirements.

Housing Construction Co-operatives

Czechoslovakia has gradually evolved several types of people's co-operatives differing in their economic orientation. In the first place there are agricultural co-operatives engaging in livestock and vegetable production on co-operative farmland which is still the property of its original, now associated smallholders. Then there are producer co-operatives in which former smallholders are associated and consumer co-operatives engaged in trading. Finally, there are the housing construction co-operatives.

Their role is to satisfy the housing requirements of their members and to provide economic, social and cultural services of vital importance in the sphere of housing. They build and secure construction of co-operative flats for their members as well as of non-residential structures (studios, garages etc.). In addition, the housing construction co-operatives

- assign co-operative flats and non-residential facilities to members;

- secure users' unobstructed exercise of rights ensuing from the use of these flats etc. by conducting proper and timely maintenance and servicing of co-operative property;

- ensure the proper provision of services related to the use of flats and organize additional projects and works connected with the building of co-operative flats.

A housing construction co-operative is set up by a founding meeting of members which admits founder-members, approves the statutes of the co-operative and elects co-operative bodies. Membership is open to all citizens who do not join co-operatives for speculative reasons and who, by fulfilling their financial duties (deposition of an acceptance fee and the basic membership deposit) demonstrate their preparedness and ability to meet their obligations towards the co-operative.

Membership rights include the personal use of the flat, the right to participate in all co-operative activities, to enjoy all advantages ensuing from membership, to use the flat for the accommodation of relatives and other persons with whom the user intends to live in one household, the right to have the flat at one's disposal and to decide about the transfer of membership after one's death.

The supreme body of the co-operative is the general meeting which decides on all crucial affairs, endorses the housing statutes, outlines the main directions of the co-operative's work and its activities. It decides over the lists of applicants and the waiting lists that are binding for the distribution of flats. The executive organ of the co-operative is its presiding committee which steers co-operative work and decides on all matters unrelegated by the statutes to other organs. The smallest organizational and economic units of the co-operative are the self-management committees of groups of resident and non-resident members. They operate only in larger co-operatives and their purpose is to active and coordinate the direct participation of members in their co-operative's activities.

The Czechoslovak housing co-operative movement acts on the assumption that *one* flat satisfies the personal requirements of an individual. Therefore, a citizen can be a member of only one housing construction co-operative - except under precisely defined circumstances. This, however, does not prevent a member of a housing construction co-operative from simultaneously being a member in another type of co-operative, e.g., one dealing with the construction of family houses, the building and administration of garages etc. Apart from admission as a member, a citizen can also acquire membership of a housing construction co-operative through the transfer of membership rights from another member under an agreement whereby he replaces the former member, or by inheritance.

Co-operative housing construction enjoys full government support through either direct assistance of state organs and subordinated organizations in the preparation and execution of co-operative housing projects or financial aid. Direct assistance implies primarily free-of-charge allotments of construction sites for co-operative housing schemes. If a co-operative develops a housing estate the local national committee, by means of its investment engineering organization, helps safeguard predesign stage blueprints and handles, on behalf of the co-operative, all matters involving qualified personnel for investment-type projects.

The financing of co-operative housing projects is based on two sources: First, state subsidies, consisting of a fixed sum per flat and of a sum per sq.m. of the actual usable floorspace. Apart from this basic contribution the state also provides special payments to compensate for higher costs which may arise, e.g. due to the size of the building. These subsidies amount to about 30% of total costs. Second, the co-operative itself. Funds needed are drawn from membership shares and special investment credits granted by the Czechoslovak State Bank.

Organizations committed to stabilizing their labor force can grant special aid to co-operatives. This type of housing construction is widely used by virtually all Czechoslovak organizations whose employees are entitled compensation of the full amount of their co-operative membership shares. This compensation presents a kind of loan written off after the employee has worked for the enterprise for a given period.

This sponsored or "stabilization" housing construction is very popular in Czechoslovakia and has by now largely replaced earlier forms of enterprise-sponsored state housing schemes. All other costs such as for maintenance are financed with the co-operative's own funds. Therefore, "rents" are approximately three times higher than in state-owned flats.

The co-operative housing system is an example of participation, of a self-help system in housing policy. It has many favorable consequences for the economic and moral initiatives of citizens. The interest of citizens in the maintenance of buildings and in saving money for running costs etc. is enhanced. On the other hand there is the competition with state-owned flats, which are sometimes of the same quality level but with cheaper and fixed rents.

The Family Houses

The Czechoslovak socialist legal system guarantees the protection of personal property. This concerns property acquired by virtue of work for the benefit of society and which serves the personal needs of the citizen and his family. The remaining amount of certain means of production still owned by individuals, such as a certain small acreage of farmland or a negligible proportion of the housing stock, is not considered personal property but private property which does not fall under the above-mentioned legal protection. A small house in personal ownership enjoys protection just like all other personal property.

To avoid conflicts over the question which houses can serve for renting and which are explicitly designed to suit the needs of their owners and their families, the Czechoslovak Civil Code sets a certain objective limit for houses considered as personal property. Such buildings are called family houses.

First of all, such houses must be designed for non-seasonal residents. Since many village buildings serve both housing purposes and farm production, even a part of a farming estate can be considered a family house. Size is further criterium. A family house must not have more than five habitable rooms, excluding kitchen, bathroom, entrance hall, basement, attic etc. If there are more than five habitable rooms, then the total floorspace must not exceed 120 square meters.

The Czechoslovak housing policy strives for every citizen to build a house of his own, to be able to acquire a plot of land of basically the same quality and size to suit the needs of housing in personal property. However, densely populated Czechoslovakia cannot afford to waste farm land. Therefore the Czechoslovak legal system prescribes certain limitations to ensure that these building sites are adequate to the builder's needs and also to the capacities of our society concerning the distribution of such priceless natural resources as land. The right of personal use is a new type of civic liberty designed to enable citizens to use sites in socialist ownership for their private benefit.

Society even supports individual housing projects with its resources. It mainly helps the individual to acquire the building site for his family house. Apart from the low charges for the right of personal use of the site, the state may under certain conditions grant this right free of charge. In order to minimize the loss of farmland the state gives particular support to the "group building" of family houses which, by its nature, requires less space. In this case the user rights are free.

Family housing construction is an efficient tool for the economic use of labor and a major factor for stabilizing the workforce where it is needed most badly. Employees of socialist organizations can claim family housing construction loans from their employers. Such loans are granted under agreements between the employee and his organization provided that he has worked in the enterprise for a specified period of time. If an employee meets his obligations the organization will refrain from claiming the sum back.

A similar type of loan is granted to citizens who do not fulfill the conditions of this "stabilization" agreement with socialist organizations. These are granted non-returnable loans by national committees. Apart from non-returnable loans, individual builders may also be granted loans returnable in not less than thirty years from the banking system. The interest rate is fixed at 2.7%, in the case of group building at only 2%.

Newly built family houses are exempted from housing taxes for a period of fifteen years. On average, family houses are financed as follows: 25% by social resources, 25% by loans from savings banks, the rest by the builders private financial resources. The family houses project is more popular in the countryside than in cities where total costs are higher. In the cities there are many problems with the land, with the technical infrastructure, with the cost of transporting materials etc.

The previous facts have demonstrated the ways and means used by the Czechoslovak state to regulate new housing construction projects and what is possible in affordable housing. But it should be stressed that in the past emphasis was placed less on a maximum increase in the number of homes than on the replacement of inadequate housing.

Between 1961 and 1970 for example some 455,000 homes in Czechoslovakia were phased out from permanent use, and this number went up to 534,000 in the period 1970-1980. Thus, not less than 47.8% of all newly built homes were used to replace outdated housing. Over the past forty years housing has been subject to major modernization programmes as shown by the steep increase of the share of flats built after 1945 whose quality is incomparably higher than that of the majority of older flats. In 1980, 65.1% of all Czechoslovak citizens (CSR: 57.8%, SSR: up to 80.2%) lived in houses and flats not older than 35 years.

Over the same period the number of occupants per housing unit declined. Thus, in 1961 there were 278 housing units per 1000 inhabitants on a national scale (296 in the Czech Lands and 236 in Slovakia). In 1970, that number increased to 296 (CSR: 315, SSR: 253), and according to the 1980 census, the national figure was 321 (CSR: 340, SSR: 283). Thus the number of occupants per housing unit has dropped since 1961 by about 15.4% (CSR: 14.9, SSR: 19.7). Current national estimates are 336 housing units per 1,000 inhabitants.

Together with the increase in floorspace and the number of homes there were improvements in basic equipment and amenities. The percentage of homes with bathrooms or shower facilities increased from 24.8% in 1961 to 79.7% in 1980 and is now estimated at 85%. Heating arrangements also changed. The percentage of centrally heated flats increased over the same period from 8.6% to 56.8% and is now believed to be in the neighborhood of 65%. Coal-heated flats have all but disappeared from the cities, and where central heating is not available, coal stoves have been replaced by electricity or gas. The percentage of households connected to natural or city gas supply networks rose from 19.7% in 1961 to 40.4% in 1980. At present, about 45% of all flats and the majority of city households use this amenity.

Apart from its quantitative aspects the housing problem also has a qualitative aspect indicated by shortcomings with regard to the size and standard of flats. The general rise of living standards leads to increased demands on housing standards and thus a new housing problem.

Man's needs (at least from a subjective point of view) continue to grow much faster than the possibilities to satisfy them. This concerns not only the quality of flats and other housing amenities but also their quantity. Not even the extensive housing construction drive that has been going on in Czechoslovakia has until now succeeded in satisfying all applicants. One reason is the growing concentration of people in big cities due to the increasing number of urban housing projects. Hence the relative shortage of housing in some big cities despite the fact that the number of buildings completed actually exceeded the quotas previously planned by more than three times. On the other hand housing is more than abundant in other places. This does not mean that some families are left without shelter. We have in fact no homeless people. Rather, some young families simply cannot break free as soon as they would like and have to continue, at least temporarily, living with their parents. Also, divorced younger couples face problems finding new suitable flats within a short period of time.

In evaluating housing quality not only the size and equipment of a flat are taken into account, but also its location within the house, housing complex, architectural unit and neighborhood, e.g. relating to the living environment and lifestyle of a given group of residents, its distance from places of work, shopping amenities, transport routes, sports and recreational facilities.

Solving the housing problem in Czechoslovakia, i.e. the creation of housing whose availability, size, quality and location correspond to existing structures and the needs of both entire households and individuals, is obviously a continuing process which is unlikely to end at a certain future date. For both the individual and group concepts of housing are subject to constant change and development.

Prague

All the above information on housing policy is valid for the capital of Prague, too, although some of the problems are multiplied by the population density. Prague is not a giant city, but with its 1,2 million inhabitants and its size of 498 sq.km it shares many of the problems of big cities everywhere in the world.

The first problem lies in the historical character of the city. Prague has many monuments from medieval times, from the 14th century but also from earlier and later periods. All styles of architecture and various building systems can be found. It is our duty to save historical monuments not only for our generation but also for future ones. This maintenance creates many problems, not only financially, but also materially and technically. The old town square and the King's way (finished in 1987) are good examples.

But the city's history is not based exclusively on public monuments. There are also simple flats (the majority being inhabited by older people) with a generally very low standard. Some of them, dating back to the last century when they were built in suburbs during the industrialization boom, will be demolished and replaced by new houses (for example Prague 3 - Zizkov). Some that were built at the beginning of this century are in relatively good condition but need modernization.

In Prague, like in other cities, we started after World War II with new districts which were built in the new areas using pre-fabricated elements. Of course many people were drawn from the inner city to these districts. The inner city now has less residential dwellings and a large share of older people. Modernization in Prague started ten years ago and we now have the first experiences. The project will continue with the modernization of whole blocks of units and single houses. The necessary funds will come from the city budget, and the majority of flats will remain state property. We also support all initiative steps of individuals intending to modernize their flats (fixed rents).

The types of housing in Prague differ somewhat from the rest of Czechoslovakia. While in Czechoslovakia as a whole more than 70% of all flats are in individual houses (personal property and co-operatives) and the remaining 30% are state flats, the situation in Prague is different (see Table 2). The average size of a flat is 20 sq.m., whreas the average in newly constructed flöats is 48 sq.m.

Table 2: Flats in Prague, by Proprietor (a) and by Category (b), 1986
a) Proprietor

Proprietor	abs.	%
State	296,474	63%
Co-operative	100,030	21%
Personal	65,315	14%
Other	10,000	2%

b) Categories (State and Co-operative Property)

I.: 224,590; II.: 108,889; III.: 27,582; IV.: 49,000

The majority of the flats are in communal ownership, and therefore there is strong pressure from applicants who need a flat. Two groups stand out in this respect: young and divorced couples (with or without children). Very often these applicants need small flats, whereas the majority of new communal flats has three or more rooms.

On the other hand the big share of communal houses is based on the great responsibility for the maintenance of buildings. The Civil Code strictly regulates the duties of house owners, and people are well aware of their rights and strongly criticize any shortcomings regarding maintenance, cleaning etc.

True, it is sometimes impossible to fulfill all these needs. Therefore we also find self-help, do-it-yourself etc. Tenants can receive materials and tools to paint corridors, windows, doors etc., and also for maintaining lawns, parks etc. Such activities take place on a voluntary basis without remuneration. The problem is sometimes to organize such self-help activities on a larger scale. People are more initiative when the maintenance of their flats is concerned than that of whole buildings.

The tendency in city-funded flat modernization is first of all to improve the flats of categories III and IV. A pressing need is to improve some older districts constructed with prefabricated elements. Architectural design, roofs, walls, green spaces etc. have to be improved. Other special problems are presented by important communal services closely connected with housing policy (water supply, sewage systems, gas, electricity, cleaning, urban transport, central heating).

In Czechoslovakia, the prices of major communal services are subsidized and will remain so in the future. The problem is only that the subsidies are higher every year because the technical infrastructure is getting ever more complicated (underground, water supply, sewage systems etc.). Since it also depends on the population density, we do not intend to stimulate the further growth of Prague's population.

Outlook

In 1986 the master plan for the growth of the capital Prague until the year 2000 was completed. It lists the main goals in all aspects of urban development including housing. It is estimated that the population will grow very slowly from 1,192,000 in 1985 to 1,228,000 by the year 2000. The number of households will rise only slightly: from 551,000 in 1985 to 567,000 by the year 2000. The project of housing policy is to increase the number of flats from 487,000 in 1985 to 567,000 by the year 2000. The goal is to have one dwelling for each household. During the period 1986-2000 it is estimated that 110,000 new flats will be constructed in newly developed areas and 7,000 flats in modernization areas. During this period it is planned to modernize 28,000 flats in the city and historical areas.

Czechoslovakia's experiences during the last 40 years clearly demonstrate the necessity of social efforts in housing policy. In the period ahead popular participation in solving housing-related problems will increase. We will support all forms of co-operative and family housing through state subsidies. We wish to continue providing communal housing but not to increase its share of total construction efforts. The construction of new buildings will continue in the large estates located at the periphery but also in the inner city.

The present and future problem is to modernize the existing housing stock with private financing for the smaller units and state financing for the larger ones. Among the more recent elements of the housing policy are a decentralization of the administration especially in the communal dwellings and the promotion of self-help in small-scale maintenance.

LARGE NEW HOUSING ESTATES:
THE CRISIS OF AFFORDABLE HOUSING

Jürgen Friedrichs

The Problem

After the Second World War, in the territorry of West Germany 2,1 million dwellings were destroyed (18% of the pre-war stock), in addition, it is estimated that two to three million dwellings were damaged. In many cities the figures were even higher, such as in Hamburg, where out of 560,00 dwelling more than 270,000 (54%) were destroyed and further 60,000 damaged (Kinder and Pause, 1964). As a consequence, a large percent age of the population lived in poor housing conditions, often barracks at the periphery of the city. The enormous housing shortage was aggravated by the influx of more than eight million refugees, residents of the eastern parts of the former Reich.

Hence, West Germany (as well as East Germany) was confronted with a tremendous housing shortage and new construction became one of the major tasks of the country. The main instrument to cope with this shortage was a program of social housing which started in the late 1940s.

Since during the war period rehabilitation and repair of residential buildings was neglected, and the housing shortage was to be alleviated soon, the construction of new housing estates was given absolute priority over rehabilitation of older residential buildings in inner-city residential areas. Furthermore, a rent control did not allow a sufficient amount of private investment in multi-story residential buildings.

The new housing estates were predominantly built on large sites at the periphery, but inside the central city, where larger lots of vacant or agricultural land was available at low prices. This post-war policy of solving housing problems can be found in most cities in Western and Eastern Europe.

In Table 1, data on the housing production in West Germany are presented. They indicate the high percentage of social housing compared to other forms of construction (cooperative, private). The figures indicate as well the decline of social housing in the late 1970s, mainly due to high construction costs. As the construction became more and more industrialized, the new housing estates became larger, often scheduled for more than 40,000 inhabitants. By 1985, there were more than 233 new housing estates, of 52% are large housing estates (LHEs), defined as estates with more than 1,000 dwelling units. The are distributed over 100 cities of the F.R.G., comprising a total of 500,000-600,000 dwelling units (Schmidt-Bartel and Meuter, 1986: 15).

Table 1: Dwelling Units Completed, F.R.G., 1949-1980

		Social Housing	
Year	Total	abs.	%
1949	221,960	153,340	69.1
1950	371,924	254,990	68.1
1955	568,403	288,988	50.8
1960	574,402	263,205	45.8
1965	591,916	228,606	38.6
1970	478,050	137,095	28.7
1975	436,829	126,660	29.0
1980	388,904	103,700	26.7
1984	387,607	77,808	20.1

Sources: Statistisches Jahrbuch für die Bundesrepublik Deutschland, 1986: 219, 223; Ziercke, 1982: 96.

By 1980, more than 16,5 new dwellings had been completed since 1949, the average rate per 1,000 residents was 8,8 new dwellings. A considerable amount of these dwellings were owned by the non-profit housing organizations, as the data in Table 1 show. In the LHEs, they often own and manage more than 70 percent of all dwellings. From the total stock of 26,8 million dwellings in 1984, the non-profit organizations held 12.9%.

The basic aim of these LHEs was to make housing affordable for families with lower incomes (below a defined limit) and to those living in bad housing conditions, either due to the war or due to substandard dwellings in inner-city neighborhoods. Note, that the programs of modernization for inner city areas came much later (in the mid-1970s) than new construction. This priority for new construction over modernization of the existing stock can be observed in many cities in Western and Eastern Europe (Friedrichs, 1985, 1988).

Despite the impressive amount of new construction especially social housing in the LHEs experienced several problems since the early 1980s (e.g. BfLR, 1987; Herlyn, 1986; Köhler, 1981; SAGA, 1980; Schmidt-Bartel and Meuter, 1986; SRL, 1986; Strubelt and Kauwetter, 1982). The major problems these estates exhibited were:

- A growing non-occupancy rate (defined as a dwelling unit continuously not occupied for three month, later revised as empty for six month). For 1984 the rate for the entire stock of social housing is estimated to be one percent (Thoss, 1986: 2), but up to 3.2 percent in new estates (Schmidt-Bartel and Meuter, 1986: 25). Mainly apartments of 70-80 sq. m. are vacant (Schmidt-Bartel and Meuter, 1986: 26; Pohl, 1986: 34).

Table 2: Demolition, Fluctuation, and Non-Occupancy, Selected Cities
a) Demolition

	Construction Period	Dwellings	Demolition
St. Louis (USA), Pruitt-Igoe	1950-54	2780	1972/76
Newcastle (UK), Noble Street Flats	1956-58	434	1975
Leeuwarden (NL), Linneasstraat	1947-55	414	1977

b) Non-Occupancy

City, LHE	Rate	Year	Dwelling Units
Kiel (D), Mettenhof	11	1984/85	7300
Bremen (D), Osterholz-Tenever	15	1985	2600
Malmö (S), Rosengaard	17/9	1977/85	7000
Lyon (F), Les Minguettes	16	1980	9200
Briey-la-Foret (F), Unit	59/100	1983/85	339
Amsterdam (NL), Bijlmermeer	25	1982	12500
St. Louis (USA), Pruitt-Igoe	66	1969	2780
Boston (USA), Columbia Point	75	1984	na
Boston (USA), Mission Main	60	1984	na

c) Fluctuation

City, LHE	Rate	Year
Hamburg (FRG), Kirchdorf-Süd	16	1985
Bremen (FRG), Osterholz-Tenever	21	1985
Essen (FRG), Hörsterfeld	25	1984
Leeds (UK), Hunslet Grange	40	1976+
Amsterdam (NL), Bijlmermeer	30	1984

Source: Autzen and Becker, 1985: 138.

The major problems these estates exhibit are:

- an increasing fluctuation of renters, resulting in high costs for renovation of the apartment and administrative costs;

- a negative image of the LHEs, in particular, the negative evaluation of the low accessibility and insufficient infrastructure (shops, crafts, cultural facilities, jobs);

- a negative evaluation of the dominant (especially concentrated) high-rise apartment buildings, hence, perceived high density;

- increasing incidences of crime and vandalism;

- a growing concentration of "problem families", such as families living on transfer payments (public assistance, unemployment aid), foreign-born;

- a growing number of households in delay with their rent payments;

- increasing deterioration of the buildings, especially defects in the pre-fabricated concrete segments, resulting in high costs of repair not calculated in the rent, for instance of DM 500 million for the 95,000 dwelling units by the nonprofit organization SAGA in Hamburg.

The crisis of the affordability of affordable housing was indicated and officially recognized be a program "The Amelioration of Large New Housing Estates from the 1960s and 1970s", launched by the Federal Department of Housing in 1982.

Most of these problems are not specific to LHEs in West Germany, but can be found in many other countries. In Table 2, some data pertinent to these almost intricate and universal problems of LHEs are presented. The main reasons for this crisis of LHEs were: an overall equilibrium in the housing market (yet deficits in the submarket of low-cost housing), the financing system of social housing resulting in a higher increase in rents in social housing than in private, construction costs and rents rising faster than incomes (see Table 3), a growing tendency to rent social housing apartments to "problem families", a declining population but increasing number of households, amongst them many young unmarried seeking inner-city locations.

Table 3: Construction Costs for Residential Buildings With Three or More Dwelling Units, F.R.G., 1970, 1975, and 1980

Indicator	1970	1975	1980
Construction costs			
(DM per square meter)	914	1,523	2,227
Index	100	166	244
Net income (DM/month)*	1256	2200	2993
Index	100	175	238
Index Living costs	100	134	162
Expenditures for rent (DM/month)	168	280	401

* Four person blue collar household, medium income

Source: Ziercke, 1982: 123, 1258.

To analyze the problems of LHEs greater detail, in the following section one of the largest new housing estates in Hamburg will serve as an example. In the final section, the findings will be discussed in the context of LHEs in general.

Figure 1: Mümmelmannsberg and its Neigborhoods

The Example: The New Housing Estate "Mümmelmannsberg"

The estate of Mümmelmannsberg (in the following abbreviated as "MMB") is located at the eastern fringe of Hamburg; the layout of the residential area and its component nine neighborhoods are shown in Figure 1. MBB was built between 1972 and 1984 and has 7,200 dwelling units. In 1985, it had 18,228 inhabitants with a percentage of foreign-born of 19.1 (Hamburg: 9.7%) and with 29% of all households living on public assistance.

To analyze the existing problems and to implement an amelioration program a study was conducted in 1986; field research was done in September/October, and the report was completed in December of 1986 (Friedrichs and Dangschat, 1986). A random sample of residents, drawn from the Central Directory of Residents, were interviewed either by telephone or - if the household had no telephone - face-to-face. From a total of 1,217 addresses 727 interviews were completed, 82% by telephone. The non-response rate of 40% was mainly accounted for by incorrect addresses, households that had moved and - to a smaller extent - refusals to be interviewed. Due to the fact that the 1981 census had been postponed in West Germany, there are very few data on the population structure; judged by these, the sample is not biased; however, the percentage of foreign-born is only 11.5% compared with 17.5% according to official statistics.

Some important characteristics of the population composition and housing conditions are shown in Table 4. Compared with Hamburg, the residents of MMB are younger, households are larger, and figures for income (as far as data are available) and years of schooling are lower. Net monthly household incomes are considerably lower in social housing apartments than in cooperative or private apartments; a similar difference can be found for years of schooling. Many households pay relatively high rents per square meter.

Population Change. The population in MMB changed considerably between 1980 and 1985. The total number of residents dropped by 11%, in the section constructed first (neighborhoods 1-5, 9) even by 17.6%, and in neighborhood 2 by almost one-third (886 residents). Since more German than foreign-born residents moved out, the latter percentage rose, increasing by 80% between 1980 and 1985. A particular increase was shown by the number of foreign-born residents from non-European Community countries such as Polish citizens or Asians seeking political asylum - their figure tripled. By 1985, they accounted for half of the foreign-born population. The highest concentration of foreign-born residents with 55% was in block 222 in neighborhood 1, followed by two blocks with over 27% in neighborhood 4.

Fluctuation and Non-Occupancy. As indicated by the data on population change, the fluctuation rate rose in MMB. Data were available only for the dwellings owned by two non-profit organizations, Neue Heimat and SAGA. The fluctuation rate for the apartments of the former was 20% in 1985 (Handwerkskammer, 1986: 20), for the latter, the state-owned SAGA, fluctuation rose from 6.7% 1981 to 9.9% in 1985.

The non-occupancy rate in non-profit social housing was 14% for the Neue Heimat apartments in July 1986, but 30% for one particular block in neighborhood 2 (Ziercke,

1986: 5). The highest rates were in neighborhoods 2, 3, 4 and 7. In summer 1986, the total number of vacant apartments was 581.

Table 4: Socio-Demographic Composition of Mümmelmannsberg Residents, in Percent

Age		Household Size	
14-18 years	9.4	1 person	7.7
19-34 years	29.8	2 persons	27.5
35-59 years	52.2	3 persons	23.1
60+ years	8.7	4 persons	23.1
		5+ persons	11.6

Years of Schooling		Household Net Income	
9 years	61.8	DM -1499	14.0
10 years	24.9	DM 1500-2999	22.4
13 years	13.2	DM 3000-3999	22.4
		DM 4000+	8.0

Owner of Dwelling		Size of Dwelling in sq.m.	
Non-Profit	57.9	-69	25.8
Cooperative	32.0	70-79	32.0
Respondent	10.1	80-99	35.4
		100+	6.9

Monthly Rent (incl. Heating)		Monthly Rent per sq.m.	
DM -699	33.6	DM -7.99	6.0
DM 700-799	32.4	DM 8.00-9.99	59.4
DM 800+	34.0	DM10.00-10.99	23.5
		DM 11.00+	9.5

Source: Friedrichs and Dangschat, 1986

Problems Perceived by Residents. The residents were asked (in open-ended questions) to state their content and discontent with the estate. The responses given revealed a broad range of problems - the number of responses to the question what was disliked was 20 percent higher than to the question what was liked. Responses to both questions can be grouped in three major areas: the dwelling, the environment (area around the dwelling), and the estate. In Table 5 the distribution of responses for both questions is given.

The responses exhibit a plausible pattern: People moved into the area for low-cost housing in a green environment, hence we find more positive responses for both the dwelling and the environment, and "the green" is the most often cited reason in the category "estate".

In contrast, dislike concentrates on features of the estate in general. The four most often mentioned topics were: "high-rises, architecture, concrete" (20.0%), "vandalism, crime, antisocial people, unsafe" (12.4%), "dirt" (11.6%), and "social environment" (11.3%). Respondents living in cooperative or private houses showed less criticism of the dwelling but more of the environment and the estate.

Table 5: Major Areas of Content and Discontent with Mümmelmannsberg, Multiple Responses

Resposes Pertaining to	Content	Discontent
Dwelling	15.6	8.6
Dwelling Environment	16.3	6.2
Estate	58.9	84.5
"Nothing"	8.3	0.1
Other	0.8	0.6
Total %	100.0	100.0
Total Responses	1397	1847
Total Respondents	678	696

Source: Friedrichs and Dangschat, 1986: 69, 71.

Analyses of responses by socio-demographic characteristics revealed some surprising results. Among respondents critical of the architecture ("high-rises", "concrete") a higher percentage had a higher education (more than 13 years of schooling) and income. However, respondents criticizing dirt, crime and vandalism were overproportionately those with a low education and a low income. In seeking to explain this finding, we assumed a social segregation correlated with unpleasant living conditions in the neighborhood. Indices of segregation (Duncan's IS) resulted in low values for both education and income (9.8 resp. 23.9).

Segregation alone cannot explain the attitudes met. Hence, to account for the higher rate of low-status residents complaining about "crime" and "dirt" we may refer to social norms: Persons with low status are oriented toward middle-class values and react more strongly when the respective norms are violated. Furthermore, we may assume that for the majority of this group moving into the new estate represented a social achievement which they do not want to be spoiled by a negative image resulting from crime. In this context, two further findings are important.

1. As noted above, many negative responses pertained to the "social environment". To explore this dimension the respondents were asked a) whether they agreed or disagreed with the statements "Some people say there are too many antisocial people in MMB" and "Some people say there are too many foreign-born people in MMB". Two-thirds of the respondents agreed with both statements; for the second statement there was *no* statistically significant difference between German and foreign-born residents. Clearly, the residents perceive the social problems of the estate and the unfavourable social mix as detrimental to their conceptions of a good neighborhood and the image of the estate.

This conclusion is supported by two additional findings: When asked for their opinion about MMB today compared with the time when they moved in, 41% did not state any change, 13% said it had changed to the better, and 46% responded that MMB had changed to the worse, predominantly due to changes in its resident structure. The second finding refers to the image of the estate. Respondents had to rate it on a six-point scale ("1" being the best grade), for themselves, the presumed note friends and relatives would give the estate and the presumed note Hamburg residents would give. The average notes given were 3.5 for respondents, 3.9 for friends, and 4.5 for Hamburg residents indicating the negative image MMB residents think the estate has in Hamburg.

How to Improve Living Conditions in MMB. Besides exploring the deficits of the estate as perceived by its residents the major aim of the study was to explore the type and feasibility of measures to improve living conditions. This was done in two ways: by asking the respondents what sort of improvements they thought of or wished, and by presenting a catalogue of possible improvements, asking respondents to grade each of these improvement by importance. The main suggestions emerging from both types of questions were: 1. improvement of infrastructure, e.g. shopping facilities, improvement of shopping center, give tenants individual gardens, more small craftmen's businesses; 2. demolition of high-rise buildings, in particular of one block in neighborhood 2; 3. other building-related changes, e.g., "more color", "painting of facades", "more green"; 4. to improve the social structure; 5. to lower rents.

The results of the study summarized here require several interlocking measures of amelioration quickly to be implemented; many of them will cause enormous costs if conditions are to be stopped from further deteriorating.

Conclusions

Initially, the LHEs supplied favorable housing for low-income families. When first surveyed, most residents were satisfied with their new apartments and - contrary to preconceptions of many social scientist and architects - with their environment and the estate as well. This is well documented in the numerous studies published in the early 1970s (e.g., Dittrich, 1973, 1974; Dorsch, 1972; Heil, 1971; Kob et al., 1972; Lüdtke, 1973; Sample, 1974; Weeber, 1971; Zapf, Heil and Rudolph, 1969). At that time, the housing shortage resulted in positive responses which can be explained by the transfer of positive judgements on dwellings to the estate in general. However, by this time many deficits had already become apparent, such as the lack of infrastructure and job facilities and the poor accessibility.

Rents at this period were low and took only a relatively small percentage of the disposable household net income (see Table 3). Over the last five years this major advantage - to have a well-equipped apartment at a low rent - has changed dramatically. The major reason that accounts for this change lies in the German system of financing social housing.

Capital subsidies (repayable mortgage loans) are granted for the construction of social housing, implying rent limits to secure rent ceilings. Apartments can be rented legally only to families with lower incomes; the present limit, e.g. for a family with two children, is an average gross monthly income of DM 4,417.

These subsidies were granted for a period of 20 years. As instalments are repaid and interest rates rise, rents rise automatically as well. As a result of this financing system the rents rise higher in older LHEs whereas the more recently constructed LHEs have low rents. For example, a dwelling in one of the first blocks constructed in 1973 had a monthly rent of DM 6.76 per sq.m. In 1985, the subsidized cost rent was DM 14.03, of which the tenants had to pay DM 11.14 and the owner, a non-profit housing organization, DM 2.89 (Ziercke, 1986a: 72). In contrast, in more recently constructed LHEs, which are smaller and better designed, the rent will be DM 7.30. Social housing thus competes with social housing.

The system of degressive loans was based upon the premise of rising incomes, so that income and rent increases would ideally be in equilibrium. This has apparently not been the case, in contrast, since 1982 households in the lower income brackets either had no net gain or even lower net incomes. In addition, the rising number of persons unemployed or on public assistance has aggravated the problem of renting older social housing apartments.

Furthermore, the financing system became a burden for the budget of the city, the city-state of Hamburg in this case. The Hamburg Senate had to raise the initial rent (not including heating) from DM 3.47 in 1970 to DM 7.80 since 1984 (Plesner, 1986: 64). As more and more social housing apartments exceed this limit the city has to finance the difference between DM 7.80 and the actual rent by a "post-subsidy". The dramatic increase in the number of dwellings above this limit is documented by the amount of money spent by the Hamburg Senate for this post-subsidy: it went up from DM 2 million in 1986 to DM 40 million in 1985 (Plessner, 1986: 65). Finally, subsidies became higher due to rising construction cost; at present the cost per square meter (without heating) is DM 19-22, the maximum rent in new social housing is DM 7.80 - the difference has to be subsidized.

The second major reason for the problems faced by LHEs is the change in their social structure. Social housing apartments, constituting the majority of the entire dwelling stock in LHEs, are let by governmental agencies - as outlined above - to persons or households under specific conditions. This already limits the social range of households living in these apartments, and due to their large share - as compared with dwellings owned by cooperatives or privately - also determines the overall mix in LHEs.

Over the last five years more vacant apartments were let to "problem families" (low income, homeless, single-parent) and to households from inner-city modernization areas. Furthermore, to supply housing for foreign-born residents, their households were often directed toward LHEs, in recent years especially foreigners seeking political asylum in West Germany. As the findings of our study of MMB indicate, residents do not approve of the present social composition.

Judged by the sparse empirical evidence available, the imbalanced social composition of the LHEs has led to a selective outmigration of households with a (meanwhile) higher social status (Kob et al., 1972; Wiemann, 1978; cf. Herlyn, 1986: 46). A recent survey of 194 new estates showed that these changes take place particularly in LHEs with more than 5,000 dwelling units (Schmidt-Bartel and Meuter, 1986: 30). This tendency was also apparent in the study on MMB: Two-thirds of the residents interviewed intended to move out of the estate, 22 percent of all respondents had already actively searched for a new apartment, of these the majority had above-average social status judged by income and education.

The combination of the three factors: increasing rents, an imbalanced social structure and the perception of competing new and better social housing has led to a *spiral of decline* and impaired the market position of the apartments within LHEs.

As a consequence, urban governments are faced with an almost paradoxical situation: Either they regard social housing as a means of social policy and hence rent apartments in LHEs mainly to low-income German or foreign-born households, thus facing a continuation of the spiral of decline (higher fluctuation and non-occupancy rates causing financial losses), or leave the apartments to the market, diminish losses and eventually break the spiral, but at the price of being blamed for an "unsocial" housing policy.

Hamburg's Social Democrat government has taken the latter position. In March 1987, they decided to abolish the income limit for social apartments in MBB, to reduce the rents by DM 0.50 per sq.m./month, and to let non-profit housing organizations rent their apartments themselves - instead of a governmental agency. This market-oriented decision has drastically reduced the number of non-occupied dwellings from 581 in 1985 to 80 by July 1987, and to almost zero by early 1988.

Additional measures have been implemented to ameliorate the living conditions in MMB and other LHEs in Hamburg. Residents were asked to participate actively in improving the environment ("parliament of tenants"), and some of the above-mentioned deficits perceived by residents may be reduced. *The long-run results and the improvement of market chances are to be awaited.* For instance, the question of whether to demolish part of the high-rise buildings in LHEs has created a considerable controversy in West Germany (e.g., Feldhusen, 1986; SRL, 1986). (Note, that 66% of the respondents in MMB voted for the demolition of one block.) Planning authorities and non-profit organizations have in general reacted negatively to such suggestions, for reasons of costs and the loss of apartments, but also, presumably, for fear such acts would visibly acknowledge prior errors of architects and planners.

A further problem needs attention. The correct decision to break the spiral of decline by attracting middle-income families to LHEs does not resolve the question of where to locate families with an even lower income or living by transfer payments. The price for ameliorating the conditions in one LHE seems to be to shuffle the latter groups to another LHE - thus posing the question of affordable housing even more dramatically.

References

Autzen, R. and Becker, H., 1985: Moderne Zeiten: Aufwertung, Rückbau oder was sonst? *Stadtbauwelt* 86, 134-142.

Dittrich, G., 1973: *Neue Siedlungen und alte Viertel.* Stuttgart: Deutsche Verlags-Anstalt.

----, 1974: *Menschen in neuen Siedlungen.* Stuttgart: Deutsche Verlags-Anstalt.

Dorsch, P., 1972: *Eine neue Heimat in Perlach. München: Piper*

Feldhusen, G., 1986: Rückbau oder Gnadentod? Das komplexe Problem der Großsiedlungen in der BRD. *Bausubstanz*, 3/86, 6-13.

Friedrichs, J. (ed.): *Stadtentwicklungen in West- und Osteuropa.* Berlin-New York: de Gruyter.

-----, 1988: Large Cities in Eastern Europe, In: M. Dogan and J.D. Kasarda (eds.). *The Metropolis Era. Vol.* 1. Berverly Hills-London: Sage (in print).

----- **and Dangschat, J.**, 1986: *Gutachten zur Nachbesserung des Stadtteils Mümmelmannsberg.* Hamburg (Unpublished research report).

Handwerkskammer Hamburg, (ed.), 1986: *Zukunftswerkstatt - Entwicklungschancen* des *Stadtteils Mümmelmannsberg.* Werkstattbericht No. 2. Hamburg: Handelskammer.

Heil, K., 1987: *Kommunikation und Entfremdung.* Stuttgart: Krämer.

Herlyn, U., 1986: Lebensbedingungen und Lebenschancen in den Großsiedlungen der 60er Jahre. In: R. Guldager (ed.): *Wohnquartier im Wandel - in Braunschweig und anderenorts.* Braunschweig: Seminar für Planungswesen (Veröffentlichungen Heft 25).

Kinder, H. and Pause, G., 1949: Soziographische Untersuchungen im Raum Hamburg. In: *Schriften zum Bau-, Wohnungs- und Siedlungswesen,* Ausg. 2. Hamburg: Hammonia.

Kob, J., Kurth, M., Voss, R. and Schulte-Altedorneburg, M., 1972: *Städtebauliche Konzeption in der Bewährung:* Neue Vahr. Bremen-Göttingen: Vandenhoek und Ruprecht.

Köhler, H.-J., 1981: *Neuere Wohngebiete - Wohnlager der 80er Jahre?* Denkschrift der SAGA. Hamburg: SAGA.

Lüdtke, H., 1973: *Bauform und Wohnverhalten*. Hamburg:: Hammonia (Gewos-Schriften-reihe, Neue Folge 8).

Plessner, R, K., 1986: Lösungsansätze aus der Sicht der Mieten- und Belegungspolitik. In: SRL 1986.

Pöhl, H., 1986: Wohnungsleerstände in Westfalen-Lippe - Marketing auch in der Gemeinnützigen Wohnungswirtschaft gefragt. In: R. Thoss et al. (eds.): *Wohnungs-leerstände - Was tun?* Münster: Institut für Wohnungs- und Siedlungswesen.

SAGA (Gemeinnützige Siedlungs-Aktiengesellschaft Hamburg) (ed.), 1980: *Neuere Wohnungsgebiete - Wohnlagen der 80er Jahre?* Hamburg: SAGA (Unpublished paper).

Schmidt-Bartel, J. and Meuter, H., 1986: *Der Wohnungsbestand in Großsiedlungen in der Bundesrepublik Deutschland*. Bonn-Bad Godesberg: Schriftenreihe des BMBau.

SRL (Vereinigung der Stadt-, Regional- und Landesplaner e.V.) (ed.), 1986: Nachbesserung von Großsiedlungen der 60er und 70er Jahre. In: *SRL-Information* 20. Bochum: SRL.

Strubelt, W. and Kauwetter, K., 1982: *Soziale Probleme in ausgewählten Neubaugebieten ausgewählter Städte der Bundesrepublik Deutschland*. Bonn-Bad Godesberg: Schriftenreihe des BMBau.

Thoss, R., 1986: Wohnungsleerstände als volkswirtschaftliches Problem. In: R. Thoss et al. (eds.): *Wohnungsleerstände - Was tun?* Münster: Institut für Wohnungs- und Siedlungswesen.

Weeber, R., 1971: *Eine neue Wohnumwelt*. Stuttgart-Bern: Krämer.

Wiemann, U., 1979: *Wohnungswechsel bei Bewohnern von Neubausiedlungen*. Hamburg: Universität Hamburg (Unpublished Diploma thesis).

Zapf, K., Heil, K. and Rudolph, J., 1969: *Stadt am Stadtrand*. Frankfurt/M.: Europäische Verlagsanstalt.

Ziercke, M., 1982: *Entwicklungen auf den Wohnungsmärkten der Bundesrepublik Deutschland*. Hamburg: Verlag Weltarchiv.

----, 1986: *Vorschläge für ein umfassendes Handlungskonzept zur Verbesserung der wirtschaftlichen, sozialen und technischen Situation in Hamburg-Mümmelmannsberg*. Hamburg (Unpublished research report).

SHADOW-HOUSING

SELF-HELP OF DWELLERS IN THE NETHERLANDS

Wouter Turpijn

All that is of interest occurs
in the shadow, decidedly. One
knows nothing of the true
history of man.
Céline, 1952

Introduction

The central questions posed in this chapter are the following: What is the present relationship in the Netherlands between the self-help of dwellers and the care of the authorities and other professional institutions for housing; which historical developments have led to this relationship, and what perspective does the subject offer for the future?

Self-help by dwellers is defined hereby as all activities concerning the realization and maintenance of the built environment, carried out by the dwellers themselves for the benefit of their own housing, with a minimum of interference from authorities and other professional institutions.

It will be clear that this chapter is mainly concerned with the situation in the Netherlands. At certain points, however, in particular in section two, general comparisons are made with the situation in other countries. Moreover, the ideas and theoretical concepts of writers such as Illich (1971, 1972, 1981), Gorz (1980) and Turner (1976) form an important basis for the analysis of the current phenomenon of self-help of dwellers in the Netherlands.

Historical Developments in the Netherlands and Other Countries

As in many other countries the care for housing in the Netherlands has become increasingly subjected to the rule of government and other professional institutions since about the middle of the nineteenth century. While in times long past the building and maintenance of houses and housing areas were largely a matter for the dwellers

Affordable Housing and the Homeless
© 1988 Walter de Gruyter & Co., Berlin · New York – Printed in Germany

themselves, nowadays in the Netherlands we are confronted with a government policy that emphasizes the role of professional institutions in building and maintenance. In other words, the Netherlands has not only become a welfare state regarding social security and medical, educational and social-cultural services, but also regarding the field of housing.

In this development the activity of the Dutch government has always been concentrated on the financing and subsidizing of the construction of rented dwellings which are managed by housing associations or local authorities. This is an important point of departure in the Housing Act of 1901, for instance. The consequence in the present situation is that of the more than 5 million dwellings in the Netherlands about 45% are let by (semi-governmental) housing associations or local authorities and 15% by private enterprises or individuals, 40% are owned by dwellers. Many dwellings of the latter two categories are also subsidized by the government.

Emphasis on the building of rented dwellings has meant that until now the Dutch government, formally speaking, has hardly made any allowance for the self-help of dwellers. For rented dwellings are not the property of the dwellers. When moving out tenants are obliged to leave the dwelling "in the original condition" as it was when they moved in. If they have permission from the owner/landlord to rebuild the dwelling, the owner is in principle not obliged to give any remuneration. Financially, therefore, it is hardly worthwhile for tenants to go beyond painting and decorating the interior. In practice, however, do-it-yourself tenants do much more, with or without the owner's permission, and regardless of the financial consequences upon discovery or when they move house.

Apart from the emphasis in governmental policy on the building of rented dwellings, and its effects on the self-help of dwellers, the Dutch government has never generally stimulated the self-help of dwellers as defined in my introduction. Although the government and other professionals have allowed for dwellers' participation in the building and management of dwellings since the 1960s (involvement in discussion and decision-making), we are in fact dealing here with a controlled organ of governmental policy. In this respect, dwellers' participation procedures are dominated by the negative aspects of inflexibility and technocracy. The government and other professional institutions continue to pull the strings while the influence of dwellers is usually limited. The activities of squatters and the squatters movement are sometimes even considered as a reaction to the "participation ideology" (Nelissen, 1980; Van der Loo, Snel and Van Steenbergen, 1984). In this context the fact that many do-it-yourself dwellers build without governmental subsidy and/or building permit (Turpijn, 1987) is also worth mentioning. To me these seem to be clear examples of a development from dwellers' participation to self-help of dwellers.

In the 1970s and 1980s in addition, local authorities, especially in Rotterdam, embarked on several projects in which dwellings were actually built for a large part by dwellers themselves. But in this case too strict governmental regulations were of decisive influence, while the Rotterdam projects were not followed up due to strong protest and political lobbying on the part of employers and employees in the building trade who perceived their position as threatened.

It is remarkable that in spite of the current austerity policy in the Netherlands the authorities and other professional institutions in the field of housing still do not show much intereste in the self-help of dwellers. This situation is quite different from the situation in other already mentioned fields of the Dutch welfare state. In the fields of medical services, services for the elderly etc., the government nowadays pleads for a "caring society" with extensive self-help and less services paid for by the state and provided professionally.

The situation in the Dutch field of housing is also quite opposite to the assumption of Harms (1982) that in times of crisis governments like to stimulate the self-help of people. Even in the 1930s the Dutch government did not stimulate the self-help of dwellers. To my knowledge Dutch governmental policy concerning the self-help of dwellers differs considerably from that in other welfare states. In Sweden, Danmark, the United Kingdom, West Germany and Belgium the historical development has certainly been towards increased care of government and other professionals for housing. In comparison with the Netherlands, however, the governmental policy of these countries has been more strongly geared towards encouragement of home-ownership. The owner-status implies that the legal possibilities for self-help of dwellers are considerably greater than those of tenants.

Generally speaking, indeed, self-help housing is more strongly propagated by the governments of these countries than in the Netherlands. In the United Kingdom the government and the national Housing Corporation stimulate self-help housing in several ways (e.g., tax and mortage facilities, housing co-operatives). The German government did the same in the 1920s and 1930s, after World War II ("First German Self-Help Day", for instance, organized by the Standing Committee of Self-Help in September 1950) and in our days. Swedish dwellers in Stockholm and Göteborg have built over 20.000 houses with their own hands, stimulated by the municipal organization Småa. In Belgium do-it-yourself building is even an integrated aspect of the prevailing culture; it is so common that no sociological information on the subject is available (Nitsche, 1981; Neue Ansätze, 1981 and 1982; Harms, 1982; Kroes and IJmkers, 1982; Goossens, 1984).

Great differences can also be seen between the Dutch situation and that of countries which are no welfare states, such as the U.S.A. and Canada. A much more reserved role of the authorities in these countries implies that dwellers have, and utilize, considerable formal freedom in self-help housing. American dwellers buy a lot more building materials than professional builders in the U.S.A. and in Canada; among other things, over a thousand housing co-operatives, established by dwellers themselves, maintain some 50.000 houses (Kern, 1975; Kern, Kogon and Thallon, 1976; Toffler, 1980; Turner and Fichter, 1972; Woonkoöperatieven in Canada, 1985).

Finally, the even greater discrepances between the Dutch situation and that of the so-called "third-world countries" are familiar. In many Latin American, Asian and African countries the only opportunity for most people to get a shelter is self-help housing, using all kinds of material and often building on squatted land. Sometimes dwellers are stimulated to do so by the government in question, the United Nations or other organizations (site and services projects, for instance), in other cases self-help housing occurs in spite of or in the absence of governmental and professional intervention.

With respect to the historical development of the phenomenon of self-help in general, finally, it should be mentioned that this term, as far as I have been able to ascertain, was first used in Western Europe by Huber (1848). Its history goes back to the seventeenth century. Under the influence of puritan ethics of work, poverty was no longer considered a symbol of evangelical simplicity and a subject of Christian charity. From then on poverty was viewed as a moral scandal and an obstacle to progress. The voluntary and charitable care provided by others, the *caritas*, lost at least the central position which it had occupied until then. People were held responsible for all their deeds with the motto: "God helps those who help themselves" (Adriaansens and Zijderveld, 1981). The Enlightenment later served to secularize and radicalize this puritanic vision concerning the personal responsibility of man. Thus the English utilitarianism of the eighteenth and nineteenth centuries saw the development of the idea of a natural harmony between the interest of the individual and the collective interest of society; see, for instance, Samuel Smiles' *Self-Help* of 1860. In the words of Adriaansens and Zijderveld (1981) "the concept of self-help then becomes a corner-stone of the ideology of *laissez-faire*". With the rise of liberalism this ideology found response far beyond England.

Mention must be made, however, of the fact that contemporary self-help theoreticians such as Katz and Bender (1976) do not view liberalism as its historical source, but rather utopian socialism - with Saint-Simon, Fourier and Owen as the most important thinkers - and the later but related social-anarchistic analysis of mutual help by Kropotkin (1914, 1972).

This varying emphasis is not surprising since both liberalism and utopian socialism are mutually influenced products of the Enlightenment, gaining concrete form particularly at the time of the French Revolution. The term self-help indeed has its origin within the orbit of liberalism. But this mainly concerns the more individualistic variant. Collective forms, on the contrary, in the sense of voluntary cooperation and mutual help, arose especially within utopian socialism and, later, social anarchism.

With regard to the current self-help of dwellers, the more individualistic principles of liberalism can be recognized to a certain extent in contemporary do-it-yourself building. In other words, this is a form of self-help of dwellers on an individual level, in which dwellers care for themselves as much as possible, with only occasional help from outside.

The more collectivist principles of utopian socialism and Kropotkin's social anarchism can today be recognized to a certain extent in the many dweller organizations and in the squatters movement, for instance. In these cases we are concerned with self-help of dwellers on a collective level. The distinction between self-help on an individual level and on a collective level will again be referred to later.

A Framework for the Analysis of the Current Self-Help of Dwellers

It will be clear from what has been said that currently the self-help of dwellers in the Netherlands is hardly taken into account by the official governmental housing policy. We have also seen that self-help housing does occur outside this field (self-builders, self-help by tenants, and the squatters movement, for instance). In other words, there is mention of "Shadow-Housing".

In order to analyse the present relationship between the self-help of dwellers and the care of the authorities and other professional institutions for housing, an analytical framework has been developed. Based on the theoretical notions of Illich, Gorz and Turner a continuum has been created, ranging from absolute autonomy to absolute heteronomy, in which heteronomy is defined as "subjection to the rule of another person or power".

These two extremes will never occur as such in reality. They are ideal types, concepts of a certain phenomenon with an overemphasis on the essential characteristics. In this case the phenomenon concerns the presence or absence of the self-help of dwellers; the essential characteristic is formed by the degree of interference of authorities and other professionals in the housing activities of dwellers.

Since both extremes of the continuum can never be reached, the analysis of the phenomenon self-help can "only" serve to establish which extreme it is closest to. Relatively autonomous and relatively heteronomous housing zones can therefore be distinguished on the continuum. The more dwellers' activities can be placed in the autonomous housing zone, the more there is mention of self-help. A clear distinction between the two zones cannot be made. In this respect only relative differences can be perceived in our complicated and interdependent society. That is why I prefer to speak of "zones" rather than "systems", as Turner (1976) does, for instance. In comparison with the latter term the word zone does not imply an exclusive entirely to the same degree. The following diagram illustrates the continuum.

```
absolute autonomy           absolute heteronomy
X                                             X

------------------------- - - - -------------------------

autonomous                  heteronomous
housing zone                housing zone
```

Description and Analysis of the Current Self-Help of Dwellers

In the Netherlands, more or less outside the field of official governmental housing policy, the phenomenon of self-help of dwellers nowadays occurs on a large scale. Considering *self-help on an individual level*, more than half of the Dutch population can be regarded as self-builders. There are even some 600.000 people who are capable of tackling virtually any job and who can be qualified as experts or even "professionals" (Knulst, 1983).

As already mentioned, many self-building dwellers work without governmental subsidy and/or building permit, and therefore with a minimum of interference from the authorities. These persons hardly seem to be known to local authorities, although from my own survey of 1,153 customers of do-it-yourself shops it appeared that one out of three respondents was personally acquainted with this kind of self-builder, and that one out of five operated in this way himself (Turpijn, 1987).

Dwellers also practise self-help in finding a place to live. In 1984, for instance, about 10.000 houses were sold or bought without the assistance of an estate agent (Turpijn, 1987). Around 1980, 21,000 caravans and barracks, 10,000 houseboats and more than 3,500 houses built on allotments were more or less permanently inhabited (NIROV, 1986; Over volkstuinen, 1978). A considerable number of these were illegally occupied, i.e. without permission from the authorities concerned.

In addition, one should take into account some tens of thousands of squatters still estimated to be active in the Netherlands. Because of the collective element in squatting (the squatters movement) this phenomenon is considered as a form of *self-help housing on a collective level*. In the mid-1980s we also counted some 20,000 communes, between one and two-hundred so-called "central-living" groups (i.e. mostly large groups of independent households sharing certain facilities) and some 7,000 dweller organizations of various types (Knoope and Jansen, 1981; Turpijn, 1987).

With respect to the relationship in the Netherlands between self-help dwellers on the one hand and authorities and other professional institutions in the field of housing on the other, the following can be established. Under present (and future) regulations the autonomous zone seems to flourish as far as *self-help of dwellers on an individual level* is concerned. This goes both for self-help in finding somewhere to live and for self-help in building acitivities. As far as the latter is concerned, many do-it-yourself dwellers avoid contact with authorities and other professionals as far as possible because they are afraid that demands will be made which will increase costs, cause bureaucratic fuss and--partly because of this--delay.

The interference of authorities in do-it-yourself activities of dwellers seems to become even less than before. Though largely a question of economic cuts, a policy geared towards reducing government regulations (laws and ordinances) and responsibility (deregulation, decentralization, privatization, liberalization) has this effect in any case.

But with regard to the quality of do-it-yourself activities, for example, the question is whether a continuing reduction in the role of the authorities really is such a good thing. Lower income groups in particular will need stimulation by the government, both financial and other, if they are to be willing and able to conform to minimum safety standards in their do-it-yourself activities.

Structural problems remain in the relationship between do-it-yourself tenants and their owners/landlords. There is a clear desire among tenants to engage in do-it-yourself activities; but the opportunity to do so hardly exists, legally speaking. Formal recognition by the government of the value of do-it-yourself activities in the field of housing would at any rate offer a solution to this problem.

Finally, employers and employees in the building trade have sometimes felt threatened in recent years by do-it-yourself dwelling construction. There is no reason for such fears, however, since research has shown that self-help in building and improving dwellings in fact offers the professionals new opportunities of trade and work. Here we are concerned with activities which would probably never be undertaken without the phenomenon of self-help, while these same activities may now offer all sorts of positive secondary effects for the benefit of professionals. The professional participation which I have in mind would include the building of the basic structures of dwellings (the finishing being left to the dwellers), the supply services of larger building firms as well as consultation and other assistance against payment. The money saved by the government through such self-building efforts could perhaps be put to use in other professional building projects, for not every dweller wants to be a self-builder or has the necessary skills. These also present new opportunities of trade and work for professionals (Boekhorst, 1982; Baartmans, Meijer and Van Schaik, 1987).

The self-help of dwellers on a collective level presents a somewhat different situation. In the case of self-help on an individual level the contact with authorities and other professionals seems to be avoided as far as possible, this self-help occurring largely in the autonomous housing zone. In the case of the differentiated forms of self-help on a collective level there is more contact with these insitutions from the heteronomous housing zone. This is hardly surprising since discrepancy has to do with the specific problems on both levels.

Self-help on a collective level concerns in all cases a problem which a person cannot solve satisfactorily alone (on an individual level). With the help of companions this is usually easier. The best conditions, however, for solving the problem (policy, finances, organizational skill, legal qualifications, influence) can usually be supplied by the authorities. Even if this is not the case, it is at any rate often seen this way by the dwellers concerned. In this context it is more effective to approach the authorities collectively than individually.

For these reasons a certain amount of switching to and fro between the autonomous and heteronomous housing zones can be observed in all the differentiated forms of self-help on a collective level - communes, "central-living" groups, dweller organizations and squatters. Solutions are attempted in all cases through intervention of the authorities. If for some reason this is unsuccessful then a withdrawal from the influence of the authorities may occur for a longer or shorter period, a solution being sought in the autonomous housing zone. Together with other sorts of action this autonomous search for solutions may in itself pressurize the authority concerned to formulate as yet the desired policy.

Such oscillation between the autonomous and heteronomous housing zones may occur more frequently, depending on the period in question and the nature of the problem concerned. It is in fact a continuous interplay of action and reaction. In other words, the autonomous and heteronomous housing zones seem to expand and contract periodically at each other's expense; they can be compared with a pair of communicating vessels.

Analysis of current self-help by dwellers raises the question whether the thesis of Illich, Gorz and Turner concerning the growing dominance of the heteronomous zone should not be toned down. People do indeed experience a dominant heteronomy in many social fields. But in the field of housing at least they continually seem to find answers, seek new ways to live their own lives, or to effectuate an adequate reaction to their problems from the heteronomous zone.

At the moment, however, a certain aversion to authorities and other professionals seems to be evident in all the differentiated forms of self-help on a collective level. The heteronomous zone is apparently adapted insufficiently to the needs of communes, "central-living" groups, dweller organizations and squatters. In the latter case this quite regularly leads to violent escalations which are a cause of anxiety for the future.

Self-Help of Dwellers in the Future

The problem discussed in this last section, when summarized, is that at present in the Netherlands we are concerned on the one hand with considerable self-help of dwellers in various forms and with differing needs in terms of recognition and support from the authorities, while on the other hand these authorities have generally not been able or willing to respond. With a policy of deregulation, decentralization, privatization and liberalization the authorities rather seem to go along with the interest of professional institutions concerned with housing. The possible and already partially evident negative consequences of this antithesis have been described above. The question, therefore, is how this antithesis can be removed. In other words, how can the self-help of dwellers in Dutch society function in harmony with the authorities and other professional institutions in the field of housing?

In my opinion the answer to this question, in contrast to what seems to be happening in the Netherlands at present, is that housing should not primarily become the responsibility of all kinds of professionals if the authorities wish to withdraw from this sector to a certain extent. Even now the professional care for housing is not satisfactory for dwellers as the present function of self-help demonstrates.

It is of utmost importance that dwellers themselves have a reasonable grasp, recognized by all parties, on developments in and around their housing area. But dwellers will not manage on their own. By far not all of them will be able or willing to look after themselves through self-help. In this respect the care of the authorities and other professional institutions should form a complement to the care of dwellers in the form of self-help rather than substitute it.

In other words, what applies to other fields applies to housing as well: The welfare state may not simply be dismantled. It is not just a question of what Schuyt (1986) called the "decline of planning". It should rather be a question of a "planning of decline", the deliberate creation of new and better balanced relationships between authorities, other professional institutions and citizens. According to Schuyt both government and citizens will have to learn "to be content with less, to accept limitations and to work together in a fruitful and efficient manner". It would seem to me that the emphasis here should be on working together fruitfully, from which I would certainly not wish to exclude all (semi-) private professionals.

It is impossible to give a concrete and detailed description here of the form of the proposed complementary relationship between the care of authorities and other professional institutions and the self-help of dwellers. But an "ideal model" in the spirit of Illich, Gorz and Turner may provide some indication. According to this model, authorities and other professionals in the heteronomous housing zone offer a number of basic facilities, such as financial and technical support (money, skills and advice, tools, materials, land), which can be used by dwellers themselves, or under their direct supervision, in the autonomous housing zone. In this way maximum co-ordination between the heteronomous and autonomous housing zones can be achieved. In offering basic facilities, points of attention should be the problem of do-it-yourself tenants and lower income groups.

Generally speaking, in all forms of self-help both on individual and collective levels the rights of dwellers to have land and the buildings on it at their disposal play an all-important role. This has a crucial influence on the problems of do-it-yourself tenants and lower income groups, communes and "central-living" groups, numerous dweller organizations and squatters. As long as users' rights have no priority over owners' rights the opportunities for dwellers to give satisfactory form and content to their home situation remain too limited. For the Netherlands too the International Year of the Homeless in 1987 could have been an opportunity *par excellence* to recognize and effectuate that the right to dwell is of a higher order than the right to own land and the buildings on it. Unfortunately this did not happen.

It is doubtful whether such a maximal or even ideal relationship between autonomy and heteronomy will be a final phase. There is always the danger that, in the course of time, responsibilities given to dwellers will become strongly regulated, canalized and steered by the authorities or other professionals, therefore becoming inflexible. The heteronomous housing zone will then once again expand at the expense of the autonomous zone. Another reaction will undoubtedly emerge in the form of an expansion of the autonomous housing zone. In this respect self-help housing will always continue. For, as Céline said in the quotation with which the chapter began: all things that are of interest to man--the real history of man--take place in the shadow.

References

Adriaansens, H.P.M. and Zijderveld, A.C., 1981: *Vrijwillig Initiatief en de Verzorgingsstaat.* Deventer.

Baartmans, K., Meijer, F. and van Schaik, A., 1987: *Zelfwerk-zaamheid, Woningonderhoud en Bouwwerkgelegenheid.* Delft.

Boekhorst, F.W., 1982: Werkgelegenheid Gediend bij Zelfbouwprojecten. *Bouw* 12, 31-34.

Céline, L.F., 1952: *Voyage au Bout de la Nuit.* Paris.

Goossens, L., 1984: *Het Fenomeen van de Zelfwerkzaamheid in België.* Antwerpen.

Gorz, A., 1980: *Adieux au Prolétariat. Au Delà du Socialisme.* Paris.

Harms, H., 1982: Historical Perspectives on the Practice and Purpose of Self-Help Housing. In: P.M. Ward (ed.): *Self-Help Housing. A Critique.* pp. 17-53.

Huber, V.A., 1848: *Die Selbsthülfe der Arbeitenden Klassen durch Wirtschaftsvereine und Innere Ansiedelung.* Berlin.

Illich, I.I., 1971: *Deschooling Society.* New York.

----, 1972: *Tools for Conviviality.* New York.

----, 1981: *Shadow Work.* London.

Katz, A.H. and Bender, E.I., 1976: Self-Help Groups in Western Society; History and Prospects. *Journal of Applied Behavioral Science* 12, 265-282.

Kern, K., 1975 (1972): *The Owner Built Home.* New York.

---- , **Kogon, T. and Thallon, R.,** 1976: *The Owner Builder and the Code.* Oakhurst.

Knoope, R. and Jansen, H., 1981: *Woongroepen in Nederland. Deel I: Dataverzameling.* Rotterdam.

Knulst, W.P., 1983: Doe het Zelf; Wat Weten Wij Erover?. In: P. Groetelaers and H. Priemus (eds.): *Doe het Zelf; Inleidingen Konfrontatiekollege Volkshuisvesting.* Delft, pp. 5-22..

Kroes, J.H. and Ijmkers, F., 1982: *Buitenlandse Vormen van Woningbeheer.* Delft.

Kropotkin, P., 1972 (1902, 1904, 1914): *Mutual Aid, a Factor of Evolution.* New York.

Loo, H. van der, Snel, E. and van Steenbergen, B., 1984: *Een Wenkend Perspectief? Nieuwe Sociale Bewegingen en Kulturele Veranderingen.* Amersfoort.

Nelissen, N..J.M., 1980: Geïnstitutionaliseerde Beweging; De Verstening van de Participatie op het Terrein van de Ruimtelijke Ordening. In: J.M.G. Thurlings, O. Schreuder, J.A.P. van Hoof, N.J.M. Nelissen and J.A. Janssen, J.A. (eds.): *Institutie en Beweging.* Deventer, pp. 135-181.

Neue Ansätze im Wohnungsbau und Konzepte zur Wohnraumerhaltung: Beispiele - Experimente - Modelle 1981 und 1982. Band I: Lesebuch zum Kongress in Saarbrücken und Band II (J. Brech, ed.). Darmstadt.

NIROV (Nederlands Instituut voor Ruimtelijke Ordening en Volkshuisvesting), 1986: *Andere Woonvormen Goed Geregeld? Een Verkennende Studie.* Den Haag.

Nitsche, R. (ed.), 1981: *Häuserkämpfe 1872, 1920, 1945, 1982.* Berlin.

Over Volkstuinen...Nu, 1978: *Amsterdam: Stichting Recreatie i.s.m.* Algemeen Verbond van Volkstuindersverenigingen.

Schuyt, K., 1986: De Verzorgingsstaat met het Oog op Morgen. In: K. Schuyt and R. van der Veen (eds.): *De Verdeelde Samenleving*. Leiden-Antwerpen, pp. 229-234.

Smiles, S., 1860: *Self-Help; with Illustrations of Character and Conduct*. London.

Toffler, A., 1980: *The Third Wave*. New York.

Turner, J.F.C., 1976: *Housing by People. Towards Autonomy in Building Environments*. London.

---- **and Fichter, R.** (eds.), 1972: *Freedom to Build*. New York.

Turpijn, W., 1987: *In de Schaduw van de Volkshuisvesting. Een Studie over de Zelfwerkzaamheid van Bewoners*. Den Haag.

Woonkoöperatieven in Canada, 1985. Amsterdam

THE GOLDSTEIN PROJECT
TWO WAYS TO AFFORDABLE HOUSING IN THE 1920S

Dieter Andernacht

Introduction

In the period before World War I the migration of people from rural areas towards industrial and urban regions led to very uncomfortable housing conditions in German cities. It is understood that during the wartime itself and soon after, no construction activity took place. This is even true till the end of the inflation period in November 1923. Thus, with the beginning of the reconstruction period the housing problem was considered as a main issue of public activity. The living conditions had to be improved under the aspect of a better reproduction of the working force, including a healthier life. The slogan of these days was "sunlight, fresh air and green environments for everybody".

In urban policy, the main idea was the separation of the working sphere and the living sphere, and the construction of large housing estates. It is the time of the Bauhaus-movement which was not only a movement for a new style, but also a movement where the social aspect of housing was of great importance, too. The modern architects wanted to minimize the rents by standardization and industrialization of construction. The aim was the affordable housing even for the low-income groups. It finally led to the concept of housing for the so-called "minimum of existence" at the CIAM congress in 1929.

By the end of the 1920s, housing construction slowed down due to the world economic crisis. The resulting unemployment led to a change in public policy. Many authors see the end of the Bauhaus period with the beginning of the Nazi regime in 1933 which obliged numerous modern architects to emigrate from Germany. I will argue that housing policy had already changed some years ago, and to demostrate this, an important housing project in Frankfurt, the so-called "Goldstein" project is chosen as an example.

Mass Construction for a "New Frankfurt"

When the Weimar Republic was founded after World War I, the leading political parties had to cope with drastic social changes in the German society since the end of the 19th century. The pacification of social conflicts was of great importance for the consolidation of the republic. The housing shortage had become such an urgent problem that the development of a strategy in housing provision got a fairly symbolic value.

The lack of capital was very important after the inflation period. Any funds could be raised for construction in the free market. The private housing construction came rather to an end and the public sector had to take charge of it. The government created a special tax on the existing stock of houses as a mean to raise funds for new construction. The local authorities were enabled to manage the allocation of mortgage loans to private and public constructors. The interest rate of these mortgages was fixed from 1% to 3 %. By taking over this task "the cities had to assume the main part in the struggle against housing shortage" (Landmann, 1925: 28).

Frankfurt is regarded as the city in Germany which was almost leading in the realization of this idea. From 1925 to 1930 about 15000 dwellings were constructed in Frankfurt by public non-profit societies. Nearly every 11th household moved into a new dwelling during this period.

In Frankfurt, the number of inhabitants had increased rapidly since the beginning of the century. The old city was overcrowded, many families did not have a dwelling of their own and lived in lodgings. The housing office registered about 15000 families in need for housing. So the struggle for better housing became the central point in urban policy. The Mayor, Ludwig Landmann, a far-seeing liberal thought that the industry needs "technically and mentally qualified workers....Under this aspect social politics aiming at the furtherance of the working class have to become preponderant in local economic policy" (Kuhn, 1986b: 21). An important part of the housing program was e.g. realized to favour the localization of the I.G. Farben (the major chemistry company) headquarters in Frankfurt in 1928.

As the City of Frankfurt was the main shareholder in several local non- profit housing companies, the local authorities could push the construction by their own activity. A far-seeing policy in acquisition of land gave them the opportunity to build on a large scale. Inside the local government a special branch, the "Siedlungsamt" (office for settlement) was created to realize the communal housing program. The famous architect Ernst May was engaged in 1925 as head of this department.

Ernst May was a modern architect and a follower of the garden-city movement. His first task was the elaboration of a concept for the construction of large housing areas. Among the settlements he proposed to construct in the following years, there was one outside the city borders. This area of about 500 acres is situated on the riverside of the Main at about 4 miles from the inner city. This area already belonged to a foundation under the control of the City of Frankfurt. So it seemed to be a good choice for the construction of a large housing area with cheap dwellings for the workers in the nearby industrial enterprises.

The Initial Project

The Goldstein area, situated between the city borders and the adjacent village of Schwanheim got its name from the Goldstein farm-house in the middle of the area. The surrounding acres belonged to the farm and were cultivated by a tenant. The first document indicating future activities at Goldstein area dates back to 1926.[1] The department responsible for the farming out of the Goldstein farm wrote a letter to the Mayor and wanted to know, whether it could farm out Goldstein for another year or not. In his answer the Mayor said that a pre-project already existed in the Siedlungsamt but had to be reviewed for different reasons. He announced a new plan for the so-called "Schwanheim Garden Suburb" to come in about four weeks time.

In the following months no sign of any activity can be found in the documents. Presumably, this was due to the complicated negotiation with the federal government concerning the incorporation of Schwanheim and other surrounding villages and small towns into the Frankfurt Urban Community. Only when the incorporation had been accomplished in April 1928 preparatory work for the Goldstein project started again. The settlement office was now very busy to advance its project. The aim was the construction of 6000 dwellings at Goldstein. In August 1928 the office announced the construction of 2000 dwellings each year in 1930, 1931 and 1932. For the realization of the project the settlement office proposed to create an independent construction society and wanted to start the development of the area in spring 1929.[2]

The size of the other great housing areas within the Frankfurt housing program had been or was planned to be between 1200 and 1600 dwellings. Thus, the Goldstein project was by far the most important one. There was also a certain opposition against the Frankfurt housing program. Some people thought that the activity of the local government was too wide- spread and the financial engagement too important. Generally, they deplored the regression of private activity in the construction. We should not be surprised to learn that the opponents of the housing program opposed the Goldstein project above all.

This project had to face stiff opposition inside and outside the city administration. Especially the department for underground engineering tried to hinder the project. So they argued against the dislocation of the sewerage plant advancing by the high costs that would generate from it. Following the plans of the settlement office a tramway to Goldstein should have been constructed. When the opponents got this tramway project cancelled in late 1928 it was their most important success. The construction society had been created in February 1929, but work on the site did not start in spring 1929 as planned

---

1. Letter of 20-11-26 in document T 877 of the Frankfurt municipal archives.
2. Letters of 9-8-28 and 8-9-28 in document T 877.

A New Plan

From 1928 to 1929 construction activity in Germany had declined. But at the same time the need of cheap dwellings increased. In consequence the settlement department had worked out a new plan during spring and summer 1929. In response to the new demand the plan had been reviewed in two aspects:

- the average size of the dwellings had been diminished and a higher density of population in the area was planned,

- due to financing problems, a lower annual rate of construction was projected.

The new plan proposed for the Goldstein area the construction of 8500 dwellings instead of 6000. 5020 of the 8500 appartments were planned as smallest dwellings (41 to 53 sq.m.), another 2380 dwellings of medium size (53 to 60 sq.m.) and only 1130 dwellings of larger size were planned. Most of the houses were suggested to be two-storey serial houses, only 2800 dwellings were provided in four-storey buildings.[1]

The construction of the serial houses was proposed to be done in long rows. Goldstein was to become the most abstract kind of housing area. The simple multiplication of homogenous elements stood at the end of the evolution of the modern architecture in Frankfurt. "The negation of all organic idea comes to its peak" (Uhlig, 1986: 96). But not only the standardization of the appearance should go on. The Goldstein project also played an important role in the industrialization of construction. As it had been done before in the Praunheim housing area, most of the houses were to be built up by fitting of slabs. The City of Frankfurt together with two private constructors had created a factory for the production of slabs. This factory started production in Oktober 1928. The communal housing societies were supposed to give orders continuously to the factory to make it run regularly. But the retardation in the construction program already forced the factory in 1929 to work below its capacity.

Due to financial problems the construction at Goldstein was now conceived to take five years instead of three as in the initial plan. This meant a lower annual rate, 1700 dwellings per year instead of 2000. The costs of the whole project were estimated to 118,4 million Marks. The City of Frankfurt had to invest 10% of this amount into shares of the new construction society to start the operation. The executive council of Frankfurt decided on the payment of the first part (five millions) on September 2, 1929.[2] The decision of the executive council indicates that its majority was still willing to go forward in the realization of the Goldstein garden city. The official map of the Frankfurt urban area edited in spring 1930 also shows the Goldstein garden city and the legend says that this area was "under construction"

---

1. See document 2073 II.

2. See document 1335 in document p. 159.

Retardations and Objections

From September 1929 onwards the city council had to decide on the Goldstein project following the propositions made by the executive council. On one hand the councellors required a multitude of social regards, e.g. they required that the rent for the smallest type of dwellings should not exceed 1.20 Marks (M) per sq.m[1] and that no bonds had to be signed by the future inhabitants.

The social aspect of housing seemed to be of great importance for them. On the other hand they made a lot of objections to the program as a whole and insisted e.g. on a new expert evidence on the ground water table. Obviously some of these objections were advanced to prohibit a positive decision on the project.

The election campaign for city council votes had started in autumn 1929 and the propaganda of the right wing parties against the republican majority and their housing policy had become more and more aggressive. Up to the elections which took place in November 1929 the majority was composed of the social-democratic party, the democratic party and the "Zentrum".[2] The elections gave more influence to the opposition. The social-democratic and the democratic party declined. The so-called "republican coalition" held only the relative majority. Only the "Zentrum" gained some votes, but the Zentrum had been the most critical in the republican coalition concerning the mass-construction of houses. The executive council had to recognize the results of this election as a public vote against his housing program, because it had played an important role in the political campaign. The social-democratic newspaper had commented the propaganda against the housing program as follows: "The defenders of capitalist interests have begun to fight against social housing in a frank way. They officially refused the construction of the garden city at Goldstein."[3]

But not only the pressure of the opposition became stronger. The more important obstacle to the realization of the project was the lack of financial means. From December 1929 onwards the settlement office had no hope that they could realize the Goldstein project. The office did not even deliver the necessary documents the city council had asked for. Several times the Mayor pushed the settlement office to respect the appointed terms.

---

1. In December 1928, the standard wage of a fully employed male worker was M 214.90 for skilled, and M 177.70 for an unskilled worker in the chemical industry; M 232.60 for skilled workmen and M 202.47 for unskilled workmen in printing; M 161.50 for skilled workmen and M 135.53 for unskilled workmen in textile industry.

2. The "Zentrum" ("Centre") was a catholic-republican party.

3. Volkszeitung of 20-9-29 in document of the city council No 439.

Finally in July 1930, Ernst May, the head of the settlement department, himself wrote a letter to the Mayor to tell him that his department had renounced to start construction at Goldstein in 1931 and that any work on the planning should be deferred until further notice. Thus the original Goldstein project which had been the most important project within the Frankfurt housing program was stopped and Ernst May who had been the major inspirer of this program left Frankfurt some weeks later for the Soviet Union where he tried to realize his ideas in the following years (until 1934).

The Government Wants to Create Suburban Settlements

Lacking financial ressources, German cities were not able to continue their own housing policy. This is also true for Frankfurt. Thus the central government could force the cities to follow its orientation by the mean of the financial allocations. At that time more than seven million people were unemployed in Germany. In view of this mass-unemployment the central government proposed a program for rural settlements. Included in this program and as a first step the government projected the creation of suburban settlements with allotments. The general directions for suburban settlements on which the government had decided in autumn 1931 were very strict. They forbid sewerage for these settlements and insisted on building roads in the cheapest manner possible.

For the near future, a decline in the standard of living was expected by the government and these measures were taken to "accustom the homecrofters with more primitive living conditions" (Naleppa and Karger, 1938: 17). Another very important aspect of the suburban settlements was the self-help activity of the future settlers. The self-help activity gave a unemployed persons a task and it was considered to be a preventive measure against social violence. For many distressed families the settlements became the only hope. This psychological effect was intended by the government. The comments of the Third Emergency Decree clearly underlined this point. The Minister of Labour said in 1932, that the most important aspect in provision of work was "to divert the minds" (Köhler, 1969: 290).

Frankfurt's city council doubted that someone could earn his living by gardening in such an allotment. But the majority thought that the only chance for unmployed people to start a new life was to be found in agricultural activities. Following the arguments of the conservative party the majority asked the executive council to elaborate a plan for a rural settlement in Frankfurt.

Towards a New Goldstein Project

Without an approval of the State Commissioner for the Rural Settlement the City of Frankfurt could not raise funds for a suburban settlement. The restrictions he made were so strict that he finally forced the city to choose the Goldstein area for the localization of a settlement. In February 1932, the executive council proposed to construct the first 380 settlements on the Goldstein area.

To prove its intention, the executive council underlined the social and economical importance of the suburban settlements: "The settlement will enable its occupant to get a part of his victuals by gardening. As the short-time work will be very important in the future, the settlement will become an important mean to facilitate the subsistence of its occupant. We will give to the settler the possibility to lease more land nearby; so he can increase his receipts if he wants to. The breeding of small cattle (especially rabbits) will bring casual emoluments and with a good evolution the settler will perhaps completely convert to this activity".[1] These arguments correspond to the commissioner's view.

The costs for the settler's house were 3000 Marks. The government provided 2500 Marks per settlement while the self-help of the future inhabitants had to bring the equivalent of 500 Marks. The allotment around the house was of 700 sq.m. (27 roods); the settler's house had two rooms and a great kitchen, a little stable for chicken, rabbits or goats and a hay-loft. The settlers had to construct the roads by themselves. A labour service, organized and payed by the Labour Office had to help them in this task. The municipality only paid the material for the roads.

If we compare the projected houses with projects already completed in the Frankfurt housing program there is no doubt that there was a regress in living standard. Councellor Rebholz from the social-democratic party was very sceptical: "Everyone who is interested in progress of living style has to characterize the suburban settlements as a regress....There will be no sanitation....The houses are as primitive as in the remotest villages and we should worry about the hygienic conditions".[2]

Rebholz still believed in the idea of progress on which the Frankfurt housing program was based in the years before. Therefore he argued against the emplacement of the suburban settlement at Goldstein refering to the costs which would incur from the clearing of the area once when the "real buildings" would be constructed. And he saw a further contradiction in the concept as a whole. It was neither an urban nor a rural settlement. The defenders of the suburban settlements themselves said in public that the existence of a second job would be the condition to the realization of such a project. The settlers would need a stable income besides their benefits from gardening. Rebholz saw the danger that further wage-cut could be aspired by that. The employers or the government could argue that the second job would help these persons to earn their living. Despite these objections the social-democratic party finally decided to follow the propositions of the executive council. In their view such a project seemed to be the only way to raise funds for housing construction at that time. The Zentrum party agreed as well to the planning. It only required the tightning of the basement and a third room under the roof-top.

1. See document M 258 (31) in document of the city council No 445.
2. See 213 in session of city council on 23-2-32, document of city council No 445.

The communists were the only party remaining opposed to the Goldstein settlement as actually planned. They refused "to build up a village at a place where a modern town should be."[1] They critized the fact that at the same time more than 1000 dwellings in Frankfurt remained inoccupied because of their high rent. A communist councellor said: "You cut the rental allowance, you are not willing to give a reduction on gaz, nor on water and electricity for the unemployed; but you force those people to move to these settlements".[2] But the successor of Ernst May at the head of the settlement office, councellor Niemeyer, did not accept these objections. He referred to the fact that among the aspirants waiting for an allotment at Goldstein were also many adherents of the communist party. Indeed, the intended psychological effect of the Third Emergency Decree was visible. Under this influence the social-democratic newspaper of the Frankfurt region wrote in April 1932 that "by the construction of the Goldstein settlement 380 families have already been delivered from dejection and despair, effects of a long-time unemployment".[3]

The choice of the future settlers was done by the welfare centre in Frankfurt. Since January 1932, even before the official announcement of the project, about 400 applicants to settle at Goldstein were already inscribed on a waiting list. At that time the public assistance had to pay on an average 35 Marks per month as rental allowance. The welfare centre hoped to lower this allowance to 25 Marks per month once when the assisted people could move into the self-help houses at Goldstein. The applicants had to accept a personal contribution of at least 2700 hours of work on the site. The welfare centre gave priority to families with many children and to persons whose profession could be useful in the construction.

Construction at Goldstein started in April 1932. Twelve to twenty men joined to form a working team under the guidance of a foreman. The 380 houses had to be built before one knew which house would be his own one. Only when the construction had been accomplished they would cast lots for the attribution of the houses.

They got 0.20 Marks a day for additional support, but some of them even reinvested this small sum to permit additional works on the houses, e.g. the finishing of a third room under the roof-top. The municipality offered a cup of soup each day to all of them. Relatives often came to help them. A group of 300 volunteers, organized and payed by the Labour Office, came to carry out the construction of the roads in the area.

The future settlers worked from 8 a.m. to 5 p.m. They decided soon to start working earlier in the morning and also extended their working time until sunset. The first houses were finished in September 1932 and the first settlers could move in one month later.

1. Councellor Lang at the session of city council on 23-2-32.

2. Councellor Fischer at the session of city council on 5-4-32.

3. Volkszeitung, edition of 19-4-32.

The welfare centre had registered 900 aspirants at the beginning of the project. Another 500 families asked for a settlement before July 1932. So the city council decided on July 1, 1932 to build a second segment at Goldstein. To found this resolution the council pointed to the fact that illegal breeding of small cattle was spreading everywhere, even in normal dwellings.[1] A third segment of houses was built up at Goldstein from 1933 to 1935. Finally, the settlement became the home for 926 families. It was one of the most important suburban settlements which have been constructed in Germany at that period.

Discussion: Housing Supply or Provision of Work?

The modern architects thought that provision of work would not make sense in housing policy. They thought that only a maximum of efficiency could lead to affordable housing with high living standard. In the view of May, Wagner and their collegues, the provision of work to unqualified workers, the self-help activities and the labor service represented an enormous waste of labor force:

- while unqualified men work on the site, qualified workers go to the Labor Office;

- in spite of the fact that a cheaper construction can only be realized with a higher level of industrialization machines were not used.

Once a councellor of the Zentrum party had asked to start a public employment program by the settlement department. Ernst May said that this program would be much more expensive than applying modern machines and he asked him if he would be ready to pay the difference of the rent in that case. In May's view the planning of the housing program should only be guided by the search for a physiological and economical optimum. Following these ideas the plan for the Goldstein settlement became an original product of welfare state policy.

The Goldstein project always reflected the changing priorities in housing policy. The housing shortage for the low-income groups had led to a concept for a housing area with 8500 dwellings. But in spite of standardization and in spite of construction of smallest dwellings the rents remained too high. In the same time the need to attract labor force to urban regions had declined with the beginning of the economic crisis. So the majority of the city council gave priority to a program under the aspect of employment.

The reason for the creation of suburban settlements was not the housing shortage but the mass-unemployment. The housing shortage was not even mentioned to substantiate the project of a suburban settlement in Frankfurt. In a matter of fact, the new project brought a reduction from 8500 to 926 dwellings in the Goldstein area, and this cannot be regarded as an answer to housing shortage.

---

1. City council, session on 1-7-32.

A study on the economic value of the Goldstein settlement was made in 1938 at Frankfurt University. The study aimed especially at the benefits of gardening and breeding and thus at the indirect raise in income. The authors of the study, W. Karger and W. Naleppa, posit that the government hoped to lower the costs of assistance to the poor by this way. This confirms the objections made by councellor Rebholz in 1932.

The authors reach the following conclusion: "The main force that made the projects of suburban settlements work was only the fear of an instantaneous discharge of political tension. The measures applied aimed primarily at a psychological effect and less at an economic one. The unemployed should feel that there was at least an attempt made to alleviate their misery" (Karger and Naleppa, 1938: 16).

In my view, the final shape of the Goldstein settlement was a symbol for the termination of a policy aiming at housing supply. Hence, we should see the self-help activities primarily as an answer to unemployment and only in second rank as an instrument of housing policy.

The Crisis of Welfare State Policy

Nowadays many economists believe that we have to face a long stagnation period and that the mass-unemployment will last for a long time. More and more people cannot be integrated into the normal economy. That is one of the reasons for the interest in strategies of self-help in housing provision. A lot of experiences are made and much research is done nowadays in the field of informal economy. By introducing concepts of self-reliance we try to join informal economy and housing problems.

A retrospective view could be useful then. Around 1930 the subjacent idea of all the applied measures was the inevitable persistence of mass- unemployment. Housing policy became a mean to provide employment in informal economy. In a critical examination it is not important that at that time informal economy could only be imagined in the agricultural sector. The main ideas were the same and the problems were either the same.

The initial motivation was to turn away from the welfare state policy, the costs of which could no more be afforded by the society. Another element that reoccurs today is the sedentariness as one aspect of social pacification besides the employment. Everyone who is engaged in such projects should clearly point out the priority of the employment aspect on the housing problem - today as well as they did at that period.

References

Andernacht, D., 1985: *L'activité d'Ernst May à Francfort; un enjeu politique*. Grenoble: IUG.

---- **and Kuhn, G.**, 1986: Frankfurter Fordismus. In: R. Höpfner and V. Fischer (eds.): *Ernst May und das Neue Frankfurt 1925-1930*. Berlin.

Stadt Frankfurt, 1926-1932: *Bericht über die Verhandlungen der Stadtverordneten-versammlung der Stadt Frankfurt am Main*. Vols. 58-64. Frankfurt.

Karger, W. and Naleppa, W., 1938: *Die volkswirtschaftliche Leistung einer Kleinsiedlung*. Frankfurt.

Köhler, H., 1969: Arbeitsbeschaffung, Siedlung und Reparationen in der Schluaphase der Regierung Brüning. *Vierteljahreshefte für Zeitgeschichte*, No 3, 276-307.

Kuhn, G., 1986a: *Das Neue Bauen in Frankfurt in der Ära May*. Franfurt: University of Frankfurt, Department of History.

---, 1986b: Landmann, Asch, May. In: R. Höpfner and V. Fischer (eds.): *Ernst May und das Neue Frankfurt 1925-1930*. Berlin.

Landmann, L., 1925: Das Siedlungswesen. *Jahrbuch der Frankfurter Bürgerschaft*. Frankfurt.

Miller-Lane, B., 1968: *Architecture and Politics in Germany 1918-1945*. Cambridge, Mass.: Harvard University Press.

Mohr, C. and Müller, M., 1984: *Funktionalität und Moderne. Das Neue Frankfurt und seine Bauten 1925-1933*. Köln.

Prigge, W., 1986: Regulierung. In: R. Höpfner and V. Fischer (eds.): *Ernst May und das Neue Frankfurt 1925-1930*. Berlin.

Uhlig, G., 1986: Sozialräumliche Konzeption der Frankfurter Siedlung. In: R. Höpfner and V. Fischer (eds.): *Ernst May und das Neue Frankfurt 1925- 1930*. Berlin.

PART THREE:
THE NEW HOMELESSNESS

THE NEW HOMELESS IN BRITAIN

Alan Murie and Ray Forrest

Introduction

Unlike many countries the definition of homelessness in Britain has an official and legislative dimension. This is associated with a long tradition of direct state intervention in the housing market and the existence of a large public rental sector administered by local authorities with a range of statutory responsibilities. In Britain, popular images of the homeless family are far removed from the stereotypical vagrant or drifter and more closely associated with the impact of changes in personal and financial circumstances on working class households in general. Explanation and analysis of homelessness among families (but less so among single persons) is more likely to be in terms of shifts in the social and economic structure and to emphasize housing market processes and constraints rather than pathological factors. There is inevitably considerable debate regarding the extent and nature of homelessness in Britain, the adequacy of official definitions and policies and the avoidance of statutory responsibilities. Nevertheless, the existence of a clear homeless category does enable certain trends and developments to be analyzed.

In this chapter particular attention is given to two related contemporary features of an increasing level of homelessness - a greater awareness of homelessness as a consequence of economic and labor market change and the development of low standard of housing provision compatible with a strengthening of the definition of the homeless as an undeserving or powerless category. In this context discussion of the housing experiences of homeless households in contemporary Britain links to broader discussions of the downgrading and residualization of council housing in general (see, for example, Forrest and Murie, 1983, 1986).

What is new about the homeless and homelessness in Britain in the 1980s? Is it to do with numerical increase, the changing characteristics of homeless households or the transformed pattern of housing tenures and opportunities? All these factors are certainly evident. There has been an explosion of homelessness which has been most apparent in the major urban areas; young people and ethnic minorities are more heavily represented; and the mono-tenurial nature of recent housing policy with its preoccupation with the extension of home ownership has placed less emphasis on the provision of cheaper, easy access rental accommodation. Those in more vulnerable and insecure social and financial circumstances have faced an increasingly hostile housing environment. What is novel, however, is the changed context in which homelessness is increasing and becoming more diverse in nature and origin. There is recognition that homelessness is one symptom of multi-dimensional exclusion from the social consumption norms of the majority and that whatever the housing policy response, those who become homeless (in both official and unofficial categories) are likely to experience much more intractable and long-term problems of social and economic disadvantage. Pessimistic scenarios abound of the widening and deep-seated divisions between the haves and have-nots. In the British context, Halsey (1987: 19) has referred to a new form of polarization in society and the emergence of:

"a more unequal society as between a majority in secure attachment to a still prosperous country and a minority in marginal economic and social conditions, the former moving into the suburban locations of the newer economy of a "green and pleasant land", the latter tending to be trapped into the old provincial industrial cities and their displaced fragments of peripheral council housing estates".

In a similar vein Gamble (1987: 16) has asserted that the pressures:

"to maintain public order in civil society and continuing prosperity has produced policies that have increased the freedom and mobility of private capital while strengthening the powers of the state against those groups excluded and marginalized".

Others have noted (e.g. Pahl, 1986) that the pursuance of majority politics whereby most households experience real economic gain and a minority real economic loss is contributing to a changed income structure. The privileged minority at the top progress on an ever upward wealth and income trajectory, the middle mass of the employed benefit from appreciating domestic property and rising real incomes (often in multiple earning households) and a diverse and expanding group of the socially, economically and electorally marginal represent the bottom part of this onion-shaped structure. Whilst the increase in social polarization is now widely accepted, it is recognised that the diversity and complexity of this process require more subtle and sensitive analysis. It is, for example, inappropriate to conflate the various forms of official and concealed homelessness, young black unemployed, marginal home owners, low paid workers and so forth into a general category thus implying common origins, destinations and consequences. Nevertheless, the common pattern is of divergence and bifurcation, of increasing disparities of wealth, income, lifestyle and life chances among different groups at different stages of the life cycle. In housing terms, in Britain, this polarization has apparently striking dimensions dividing the population into the home owning privatized majority and those dependent on the rental sectors. Transformations in patterns of employment, the impact of recession, the specific history of housing tenures and the recent phase of privatization has strengthened this division. As the majority are drawn into home ownership and public housing becomes the stigmatized tenure for the dispossessed and homeless this division becomes more evident. Over time, however, the penetration of home ownership down the income structure, the impact of government policy aimed at reviving private renting and the further rounds of privatization of public housing is likely to lead to a less clear tenure polarization.

Evidence on the re-emergence of mass poverty and growing social polarization is by no means confined to Britain. Ferge and Miller (1987) have pointed to a commonality of processes in Europe as a whole. And Dahrendorf (1987: 13) has commented on the growth of an underclass (and those balanced precariously on the edge) in all OECD countries:

"For many people in the OECD world, there is today - and has been since the 1970s - a sense of downward movement, or at least of the precariousness of what has been achieved. This is not incompatible with the spectacular success of a few: on the contrary casino capitalism would seem a fitting concomitant of general decline. This negative propensity may well be one of the reasons why the underclass is so important. It represents, so to speak, the ultimate extrapolation of the fate of many. And indeed, it is growing in significance, if not always in size".

It is then this chronic and pervasive deprivation in the context of burgeoning affluence which gives rising homelessness a new and worrying dimension. It is a prospect of entrapment, containment and social and spatial immobility rather than temporary disruption which faces many households. The inner urban areas are gentrified and revalorized and the hi-tech architecture and exclusive waterside residences co-exist with low grade hostels for the homeless and displaced. It is a very different context from the homelessness of the 1960s with elements which parallel many of the characteristics of third world cities and the emergence of what Townsend (1987) has referred to as "market value" poverty with an emphasis on reduced public spending, the minimization of welfare assistance, and the acceptance of much higher levels of "natural" unemployment. It is this sort of perspective which has characterized recent policy responses to rising homelessness.

Background

The post-1945 history of policies towards the homeless is fully described elsewhere (Richards, 1981). War time measures including the provision of hutment camps and billeting were regarded as temporary emergency measures. The continuing responsibility for homelessness was laid down in the National Assistance Act 1948. This abolished the Poor Law and established local authority Welfare Departments. It was these departments which assumed responsibility, as successors to the Poor Law authorities, for care (including residential care) of the old, infirm and handicapped. The emphasis was placed on rehabilitation rather than institutional care and the duty (under Part III of the Act) in respect of homelessness was "to provide ... temporary accommodation for persons who are in urgent need thereof ... in circumstances which could not reasonably have been foreseen". Richards notes that the relevant Ministry of Health Circular (87/48) emphasized that the section was "primarily intended to cover persons temporarily without accommodation as a result of such circumstances as fire, flood or eviction" and *not* for "dealing with the inadequately housed". Temporary accommodation was provided for homeless *families* only and welfare departments had no statutory obligation to accept responsibility for single people who were below retirement age and not infirm. The only statutory provision for the single homeless was in reception centres provided by central government through the National Assistance Board. These reception centres were the successors to workhouse casual wards which had been provided on a deterrent basis under the Poor Law and were to be less punitive than their predecessors and to encourage "resettlement".

The Welfare Departments located at county council level were not also housing departments - and housing departments which in Britain developed an unusually important social housing role were often located in a different tier of local government. Welfare Departments operated under the general guidance of the Minister and as the successors to Poor Law authorities had access to former workhouses which could be used as hostels. Rather than this being a transitional arrangement it remained normal and there was a reluctance to build new units. Local authorities tended to interpret the Act as a hostel and casework service and to draw on the experience of previous administration (Glastonbury, 1971). This involved provision of communal facilities, limited stays (resulting in children being taken into care), sex segregation and restricted contact between husband and wife.

These and other deterrent aspects did not prevent numbers rising but did contribute to the increasing concern about the inadequacy of provision. This limited family based provision was always deficient. However, its shortcomings were made more apparent by the restructuring of the housing market in the subsequent period. The common lodging house, charitable provision and more generally the private rented sector underwent significant decline. Full employment in the post-war period and major investment in housing provision raised general housing standards but the supply of lower priced, easy access accommodation was being steadily eroded. Slum clearance and the decontrol of rents had specific repercussions. Watson (1986) refers to a changing climate in the 1960s in which homelessness reentered the public arena. Households were splitting into small units, marital breakdown was increasing, remarriage decreasing and the population was ageing. New legislation relating to the mentally ill emphasized care in the community - effectively competing for the declining supply of less secure private rented accommodation.

Rent decontrol did not increase the supply of private renting - indeed it speeded its decline - and insecurity of tenure and speculative sale and redevelopment had serious impacts. The decline in lodging houses, hostels and reception centres was dramatic as these forms of accommodation gave way to more profitable land use.

All of these changes led to a considerable growth in homelessness as measured by admittance to accommodation provided under the National Assistance Act 1948 (generally referred to as Part III Accommodation). The Milner Holland Report and more directly the TV play "Cathy Come Home" (1966) focused attention on housing stress and homelessness. Following "Cathy Come Home", five housing-aid organizations combined to launch a new national charitable organization, Shelter: The National Campaign for the Homeless. Shelter's success in attracting funds and public interest was very considerable. This campaign, the continuing growth of homelessness and the result of a series of enquiries into homelessness (Glastonbury, 1971; Greve, 1964; Greve et al., 1971) were of considerable importance. The recurrence of a squatting campaign which had not been apparent since the 1940s was an associated development. Watson (1986) has outlined the revival of interest in homelessness in the voluntary sector in the 1960s and concluded that the emphasis in these agencies and government funding was on the defiance of the homeless rather than on structural changes which generated homelessness. In the 1970s the emphasis clearly shifted towards problems in the housing market. In a full employment economy the problem was increasingly recognised as one of supply and access to housing - although it was sometimes acknowledged that differences in income were key factors - especially for single parents with children.

Evidence about the nature and causes of homelessness grew considerably after the development of public interest in the topic in the mid-1960s. The evictions and harassment that followed the Rent Act 1957 and the continued decline of rental accommodation are generally referred to in explaining the growth of homelessness in the 1960s and its continuation through the 1970s (Burke, 1981). In 1966, there were 2,558 households in temporary accommodation in England and Wales; in 1970, 4,926; in 1976, 10,270. In 1970, 6,544 families were accepted as homeless in England; in 1976, 33,720 and in 1978, 53,000.

The studies by Greve (1964) and Glastonbury (1971) indicated that the characteristics of homeless families in temporary accommodation were similar throughout the late 1950s and 1960s. In addition to low-paid wage earners and unskilled or semi-skilled manual workers, there were high proportions of unemployed men and fatherless families dependent on Supplementary Benefits. Young families and those sharing accommodation were particularly important. Most of those becoming homeless had previously been in privately rented accommodation (87% in London and 62% in South Wales and the West), while only 3% and 10% were owner occupiers. Greve et al. (1981) confirmed this general pattern but identified larger proportions of black households and larger families among the homeless. This study confirmed housing shortage as a major underlying cause of homelessness.

How far family dispute is a response to impossible living conditions arising from enforced sharing and overcrowding while waiting for council or other separate accommodation will vary from case to case. However, Greve et al. (1971: 256) were quite clear that the predominantly young households with larger than average families and lower than average incomes who become homeless were "ordinary decent Londoners". The households concerned were at considerable disadvantage in their housing, the majority living in overcrowded conditions in furnished tenancies where they were at a high risk of becoming homeless through landlord action. Their long-term dependence on the furnished sector derived from local housing shortages and their lack of power in competition for council or owner occupied housing. "Difficult" or "problem" families were a small minority among the homeless, and housing shortage rather than fecklessness was the major factor.

New Legislation

Increasing numbers, increasing concern, increasingly effective pressure group activity and increasing identification of homelessness as a housing problem led to a series of policy adjustments in the 1970s. In an environment in which local authorities were being exhorted to liberalize their housing policies and take a wider view of their responsibilities especially towards those who in the past would have been housed in the private rented sector some local housing departments began to take responsibility for the homeless. They were encouraged to do this in Ministerial Circulars which attempted to overcome the lack of co-operation between welfare and housing authorities. It is worth bearing in mind that some of this lack of co-operation derived from housing departments' concerns to favour the respectable working class and to see the homeless as the disreputable. Rehousing the homeless into the permanent stock was seen as penalizing others who waited their turn or were more responsible.

A Ministry of Health Circular in 1966 had broken new ground in emphasizing that losing ones home was a socially damaging experience in itself and in attempting to lay down minimum standards for hostels. But it had resisted recommending that permanent accommodation should be provided. By 1967 increased pressure and publicity led to joint action by the Ministries of Health and of Housing and Local Government. A joint circular emphasized that homeless families (sic) "have a legitimate claim on local authority housing...". But it was not until 1974 that a more substantial response was made to changing awareness and political pressure (especially through the Joint Charities Group made up of five lobbying organizations). This response in the form of another joint circular was the precursor for legislation which shifted responsibility for homelessness to housing departments. The Circular stated that the provision of accommodation for the homeless should be an integral part of the housing function and therefore that housing authorities should take over the responsibility. It identified priority categories, recommended standards and procedures and identified homelessness as "almost always the extreme form of housing need" rather than as a personal problem of inadequate people. The new circular coincided with local government reorganization in 1974 and did promote changes in local policy. The following period however was marked by evidence of authorities which were not responding positively to new advice and pressure for legislation to bring these authorities into line. The Housing (Homeless Persons) Act 1977 completed this process.

The Housing (Homeless Persons) Act was significantly amended in the process of legislation and never reflected the aspirations of pressure groups, especially in relation to definitions of priority needs and to the inclusion of "tests" of intentionality and a local connection. The Act imposed a duty on local authorities to provide housing for people who were "unintentionally homeless" if they were in "priority need" of accommodation and had a "local connection". The Act was primarily intended for those with dependent children. The notion of vulnerability which was applied to homeless single people served to marginalize their homelessness. The Act also emphasized the role of the voluntary organizations, as opposed to statutory ones, in providing accommodation for the single. Local authorities were empowered to give financial and other assistance to such bodies. Nevertheless, the Act shifted responsibility for housing the homeless from social services departments to housing departments and represented a recognition that homelessness was primarily a housing rather than a social problem.

Reflection on Legislation

Having noted that legislation relating to homelessness was flawed from the outset it is important to reflect upon the experience of it. Britain is unusual in explicitly acknowledging homelessness and treating it as a housing problem involving rights for homeless people which are enforceable in the courts. The numbers of people being accepted in the homelessness category have risen significantly (Table 1) and many local authorities in developing their housing service have redirected resources towards the homeless and others in the greatest housing need.

Table 1a: Homelessness Acceptances

Year	England	London
1979	56,750	16,600
1980	2,920	17,480
1981	70,010	18,470
1982	74,800	21,100
1983	78,240	24,050
1984	83,550	24,820
1985	93,980	27,390
1986	102,980	30,036

Source: Shelter Factsheets and Department of Environment.

However, this is by no means an indication of even qualified success. Four initial observations on the operation of legislation are relevant:

1. Many of those currently housed as homeless would previously have been housed through another route (say the waiting list).

2. Many local authorities use the legislation to minimize the number of households accepted as priority homeless.

3. Many local authorities have continued to use "deterrent" hostel and temporary accommodation for priority homeless households.

4. Homeless households commonly are given fewer offers and "worse" offers for accommodation than others being allocated permanent council housing.

Table 1b: Homeless Households as Percent New Local Authority Lettings, England and Wales

Year	All new tenants (000s)	% as homeless
1976	287	9
1978/79	303	13
1979/80	288	15
1980/81	291	15
1981/82	265	16
1982/83	271	17
1983/84	260	17
1984/85	255	19
1985/86	261	22

Source: CSO, Social Trends.

One view of this is that the development of homelessness legislation has not increased the supply of housing available to those in the most acute housing need and that "homelessness" has been absorbed into council housing management. It provides an "official" category which helps allocators and managers to categorize applicants and ensure that there are households desperate enough to accept and unable to refuse (if they refuse they can be seen as intentionally homeless and undeserving) those properties which other categories of applicants would not accept. This absorption of the homeless category so that it is of mixed benefit to those who are in it is not an inevitable consequence of legislation although the pre-occupation with abuse and intentionality does make this more likely. Nor do the attributes of the post-legislation homeless explain this.

Experience in respect of homeless since the passage of the Housing (Homeless Persons) Act 1977 has reinforced the view that those who become homeless are normal, local households affected by housing shortages. Some local authorities have gone to great lengths to minimize the number of households accepted as homeless and some have in particular interpreted intentions in respect of homelessness in a remarkable way. Nevertheless, over 90% of households accepted as homeless lived in the same borough, district or county as the borough of acceptance one month before acceptance and this applied to over 80% of cases one year before acceptance.

Table 1c: Homeless Households as Percent of New Local Authority Lettings by Region (England), 1983/84 and 1985/86

Region	1983/84 All new tenants (000s)	1983/84 % as homeless	1985/86 All new tenants (000s)	1985/86 % as homeless
North	24	11	24	11
Yorkshire and Humberside	33	14	36	15
East Midlands	22	10	22	15
East Anglia	8	11	8	20
South East	71	27	67	34
Greater London	37	36	34	47
Rest of South East	34	18	33	21
South West	15	20	15	27
West Midlands	30	17	32	27
North West	42	12	43	17

Sources: CSO, Regional Trends, HMSO, 1986; Housing Construction Statistics, 1976-86, HMSO, 1987.

Nor is the practice of local authorities best explained by scapegoating the manager. As Henderson and Karn (1987) argue in relation to racially discriminatory housing allocations "contrary to the prevailing view of racial discrimination ... discriminatory housing allocations are not primarily a consequence of a housing department having in its employ particular racially and socially prejudiced individuals ...". Rather the tasks and interests of officers predispose them to categorize both applicants and properties and to draw on a variety of positive and negative codes, images and stereotypes to make categorizations.

These considerations lead back to a focus on supply and demand. Rather than the legislation, the homeless themselves or the policy implementors being "at fault" it is acknowledged that the time *when* the legislation was introduced was not the most favourable. The housing market restructuring and decline of private renting which are widely recognised as generating the demand for legislation were not terminated by it. The decline has continued. Moreover, other factors have exacerbated the situation. Watson (1986) states:

"The most important point about the Act was the economic context in which it was passed. The Act was brought into force at a time when Britain was suffering severe effects of economic recession. By 1977 in Britain the gross domestic product was below the 1973-74 level in real terms; there had been successive cutbacks, in current spending on public housing since 1976, and capital expenditure (on new and renovated housing) in the public sector (including housing associations) had fallen in real terms every year since 1975. The crucial point, therefore, was that there was a wide gap between the intentions of the Act and the resources provided to meet its requirements. Inevitably the result of the situation was an increased hostility towards the homeless. They were seen to be "jumping the queue" of those people in "real housing need" on the waiting list, they were the new scroungers and rent evaders. The right wing elements of the media had a hey-day".

In the 1980s the decline of public renting has been added to the decline of private renting leading to a general contraction of rental opportunities. This is a new situation in the 1980s. At the same time economic recession and the end of the period of full employment have generated new demands for lower price accommodation. There are a growing number of failed owners and poorer households who are priced out of private renting in inner city areas. The increase in the size of the marginalized population has coincided with a decline in the supply of accommodation available to them. Various evidence is referred to to show a trend for the marginalized poor to funnel towards social rented housing (e.g., Forrest and Murie, 1983). However, in the 1980s the outlet from the funnel has been becoming more restricted.

As suggested earlier, it is this changing environment which involves some *new* elements in homelessness. There are important continuities in the class characteristics of households. However, in contrast to the 1960s, homelessness is less likely to result from landlord action and the households involved are less likely to be in employment.

The early studies of homelessness identified key causes as rent arrears, landlord requiring accommodation, unauthorized occupancy and family disputes. Landlord action and rent arrears have declined in importance and mortgage defaults grow - reflecting changes in the housing market. Violent and non-violent disputes with spouse or inability of parents, relatives or friends to accommodate account for some 60% of the reasons for homelessness in the 1980s compared with between 17% and 25% in London in 1959-61 (Greve, 1964), 34% in South Wales and the South West between 1963 and 1969 (Glastonbury, 1971) and 17% in London in 1970 (Greve et al., 1971). Differences in definitions, some of which emanate from the passing of the Housing (Homeless Persons) Act, 1977, create difficulties in comparing figures. Nevertheless, the growth of marital and family disputes as a cause of homelessness is undeniable. The problems facing women, especially battered wives, have become more apparent in recent years. Court orders to prevent molestation are unlikely to prevent recurrence of violence but many local authorities have been reluctant to accept claims of violence as grounds for rehousing, and the extent of this problem is not likely to be fully indicated by homelessness acceptances.

There is a further perspective on this view of "causes of homelessness". It is to seek to distinguish between immediate and underlying causes and argues that, for example, family disputes result from tensions created by problems of obtaining employment - especially for younger people.

The new homeless are more obviously affected by economic change and restructuring rather than housing market changes alone. The problem of homelessness is exacerbated by a closer fit between economic situation, income, employment and housing situation. In this sense the way the economy has developed and the increasing dominance of home ownership in the housing market have resulted in problems of negotiating access to housing being more dominated by affordability issues rather than questions of rent control, and bureaucratic management. One consequence is that the homeless include those most vulnerable to economic change and those who have not yet negotiated access to council housing or home ownership or whose economic vulnerability threatens their continuing occupation of current housing. This involves younger households and those in vulnerable economic groups, those with recent or substantial mortgages or affected by marital breakdown. The prominence of black households reflects both a historic underrepresentation in council housing and economic position. Recent research has shown that more Asians and West Indian tenants than white tenants are likely to have been housed because they were homeless; and the properties occupied by black people in the public sector are markedly inferior to those occupied by white people (Brown, 1984, P. 81). The decline in rented opportunities and discriminatory practice in relation to homelessness represent aspects of institutional racism. Women headed households form another group more heavily represented among the new homeless. The changing environment in which homelessness has developed includes a significant shift in policy towards housing. Especially since 1979 there has been an increase in the encouragement of home ownership and a shift of subsidy towards owner occupation. But this shift of subsidy has not directly addressed the affordability problem affecting rates of homelessness. Few of the new initiatives and special schemes to increase levels of home ownership have the capacity to draw in households with significantly lower incomes than first time buyers in general and the most significant measure - the sale of council dwellings - benefits those already well housed and results in a change in patterns of access which will over time reduce access for those who look to the rented sector.

Bed and Breakfast Homelessness

There is another dimension to the new homelessness in Britain. The significant growth of homelessness in recent years has been accompanied by an increasing use of temporary accommodation in bed and breakfast hotels. In 1980/81 there were 32,000 homeless households in temporary accommodation in England and Wales. By 1985/86 this figure had risen to 41,100. In 1985/86 some 17% of homeless households were initially housed in bed and breakfast accommodation and 20% in hostels (compared with 12% and 16% respectively in 1979/80). Although the homeless took up a larger proportion of local authority lettings (Table 1) the use of temporary accommodation also rose. The position was most striking in London (Table 1a, 1c and Table 2).

The experience of the new homeless is less likely to be of rapid permanent rehousing or of a short stay in temporary accommodation than was true in the past. Homelessness acceptances and the use of bed and breakfast accommodation in London is highest in some Inner London boroughs where high prices in the owner occupied and privately rented market pose particularly severe problems for lower income households (see Table 1c). In Brent, for example, there are currently 1,000 households in bed and breakfast accommodation. This compares with less than half that number in 1983 (Hansard, 21..10.1987, Vol 120, No 26: col 831).

Table 2: Homeless Households Placed by London Councils in Bed and Breakfast and Other Types of Temporary Aaccommodation

Year	Numbers in B & B	Numbers in other temporary accommodation
June 1981	890	3,760
June 1982	1,300	3,570
June 1983	1,807	3,280
June 1984	2,357	3,730
June 1985	3,251	4,140
June 1986	5,206	5,522
September 1986	6,142	5,901
September 1987	7,970	7,256

Sources: Shelter Fact Sheet and Surveys, 1986, and Association of London Authorities.

Perhaps the most effective way of illustrating the new position of the homeless is to refer to interview data for households in bed and breakfast accommodation (see Murie, 1987). Interviews completed in London do not present identical histories. There is a variation in the nature of accommodation, in previous experience and in encounters with officialdom. However, the variation is within a low standard sector. For families, cramped space, lack of privacy and absence of playspace is severe. While lack of privacy is most likely to be expressed by adults, children's awareness of their housing situation is evident in expressions about their lack of a home. All of these factors contribute to behavioural and psychological problems and to increasing stress in the family. These problems are made worse the longer the time spent in such accommodation. Moreover, they are complicated by the impact of this form of housing on ability to maintain or obtain work, by the lack of social service, health care and other facilities targeted on a "temporary" population and by the distancing from kinship and community networks.

A wider range of health and safety issues are directly linked with conditions in the hotel. The inadequacy of cooking, toilet facilities, problems of sharing and overuse, and inadequate cleaning are directly linked to bouts of sickness, weight loss and faster development of latent health conditions and are also linked to lack of fresh air and play space and dependence on takeaway food often with low nutritional value. The lack of kitchen, cooking and food storage facilities forces families to rely on what is an expensive as well as unhealthy coping strategy. Pressure on budgets also arises from lack of laundry and especially drying facilities for clothes. The facilities in hotels are not suitable for long stay residents in these and other ways. The status of the homeless has turned full circle - from households with individual and personal problems rather than housing problems, to households where the response to their housing needs generates health, work and other personal problems! Heating, electrical and other safety, the provision of hot water and facilities for visiting or telephoning all leave a lot to be desired. In late 1984 a fire in a hotel in Westminster resulted in the death of an Asian mother and two young children placed in the hotel by the London borough of Camden. Other fires and incidents have not led to any response which has reduced the use of bed and breakfast accommodation.

Even though the costs of hotels are higher than almost any alternative form of provision (Greve et al., 1986; Walker, 1987), the pressure for policy change has had almost no impact. The antagonism of central government to increased spending on municipal housing has not been affected by evidence of wasted expenditure or low standards. The lack of political power of the homeless has been evident from evictions by Tower Hamlets and is apparent in the actual histories of individuals. One explanation for the quality of service being delivered lies in the very powerlessness of the homeless, their lack of economic and political bargaining power and the ease with which the category "homeless" can be manipulated and associated with undeserving and undesirable categories. Hotels are expensive and although the accommodation is totally inadequate there is a confusion over how generous provision is. The families involved are aware that if they were able to use the same level of resources to obtain other accommodation they could establish more satisfactory homes for their families. They could also begin to increase their independence because it would be easier to find work. The benefit and "credibility" problems associated with working (usually in low paid jobs) while living in a hotel are generally regarded as insurmountable. And, in some cases, becoming homeless had led to loss of employment.

The response to this situation adds to depression and frustration. Some families retain a belief that they should wait patiently for rehousing - others make more vociferous demands. While a feeling of powerlessness pervades this should not be interpreted as resignation or apathy. The families involved develop active coping strategies to help children attend schools and to develop social contacts. Some adults (usually the men) can spend a lot of time away from the hotel and their family. Women and especially those with younger children and those most at risk of harassment are trapped all day long in hotels.

The disruption experienced by the bed and breakfast homeless has various dimensions. The location of hotels is in established hotelling areas - not the areas where families lived. Schooling and friendships have been disrupted and the neighbourhoods are more threatening. Distance from familiar neighbourhoods and communities involves a break in caring and friendship networks and less familiarity with available services and resources. General problems of poverty and low income are exacerbated by loss of possessions and loss of community support. The very fact of moving requires renegotiation with health and income maintenance services and "temporary" status means that this negotiation is often difficult. The experience of homeless families (which have moved house regularly) in these negotiations is more difficult than that of poor families in general although some have found real support from health visitors, social workers or voluntary organizations. The most directly involved local authority department - the housing department - often maintains sporadic contact and homeless families have no real appreciation of how long they will be in hotels or of how best they can negotiate permanent housing. Some of this reflects the general pressures placed on local authority housing but there is variation in response which reflects policy. The number and reasonableness of offers varies and in one case (Tower Hamlets) large numbers of homeless families have been evicted.

Many of these problems are equally experienced by homeless single people although issues of crowding and privacy are less apparent. Among both families and single homeless people issues of racism and racial harassment are important, given the disproportionate number of families from ethnic minority groups among the homeless. The households involved have a variety of employment and housing histories - including former owner occupiers. However, the largest group have worked in low skill service sector jobs which are essential to London but which are insecure and low paid. In the London housing market such essential workers are not in a strong position to obtain housing. They are generally dependent on the private rented sector and early housing histories are of moves as single people in bed and breakfast and insecure private rented homes. Marriage, family growth and the coming together of families previously living apart changes housing needs but does not change ability to obtain housing. It means eligibility to apply for and wait for the only low price adequate housing (which is in the social rented sector). Waiting involves moving between hotels and between rooms in hotels.

Other Dimensions

Most of this paper has referred to official homelessness and it has been argued that there are new elements in relation to this group. It is important to acknowledge (briefly) that these same new elements also affect other homeless households. The preceding discussion has referred to families in priority need and the groups of "vulnerable" persons accepted in official policies. Clearly these do not represent the full extent of homelessness. Representing the full extent raises questions of definition which have been widely discussed elsewhere. Watson (1986: 6) argues that it is useful to consider this question in terms of a continuum with sleeping rough at one end and absolute security of tenure at the other. She states:

> "There would be little disagreement with the notion of the former state as literally homeless and the latter as not. In between, however, lies an extensive grey area, ranging across hostels, hotels, temporary accommodation, sleeping on friends' floors, licenses, to insecure private rented accommodation, mortgaged accommodation and so on".

It is not intended to pursue this discussion here, but it is important to acknowledge that while in London in 1984/85 some 42,000 homeless households were placed in temporary accommodation and some 75,000 were accepted in official priority need homeless categories there were some 150,000 to 200,000 sharers, 80% of whom would prefer to live separately. On another estimate there were some 300,000 potential households, many of which could be regarded as potentially homeless, given their modest incomes and savings and poor prospects of rehousing in the rented sector. Moreover, it is also important to distinguish between the flow of new homeless households and the number in homeless categories at any time. All of these issues are concerned both with numbers and with the characteristics of the homeless - for example moving away from official definitions increases the importance of the single homeless.

Discussion

Legislative and public acknowledgment of homelessness as the extreme form of housing stress experienced by ordinary decent people has resulted in substantial rehousing of homeless people. In comparison with some countries and with the past this may imply increasing the bargaining power and access of the homeless. However, the change is not as dramatic as might be assumed. Flaws in the legislation, lack of resources to mobilize on behalf of the homeless and a changing economic housing and political environment have been reflected both in the nature and scale of homelessness and in responses to it. The homeless have in important ways been absorbed into housing allocation and management becoming a convenient category which has low esteem and low priority. In this sense official recognition does not alter the reality of being regarded as undeserving or less desirable. The realities of this process have been described in a variety of studies of housing allocations (e.g., Henderson and Karn, 1987; Phillips, 1986).

One important perspective on how this has arisen relates to ideas of bargaining power and to labor market position. The idea of bargaining power has been widely mobilized to explain differential outcomes from housing allocation processes in Britain. It is argued that those households in the most desperate housing circumstances and least able to wait for a better offer will accept the least desirable properties on offer. Those who obtain better quality rehousing are those with more bargaining power. This feature and the allocation practices which enable it to operate provide part of the explanation for the position of homeless households. However, as we outlined at the beginning of this chapter, there is a wider perspective on bargaining power which relates to economic and political marginalization and not solely to the housing process. The new homeless in the 1980s are not just those at the extreme of housing need. They are also those in the most marginalized sections of the labor market and with least political power. It may be argued that the form of service provided is both a demonstration of this and in turn exacerbates it. The most obvious conclusion from this discussion is that the experience of homelessness is critically affected by the economic and political position of the homeless and by the changing economic and housing environment in which homelessness emerges as well as - and to a greater extent than - by the development of formal policies.

References

Brown, C., 1984: *Black and White Britain: The Third PSI Survey.* London: Gower.

Burke, G., 1981: *Housing and Social Justice.* London: Longman.

Dahrendorf, R., 1987: The Erosion of Citizenship and its Consequences for us all. *New Statesman,* June 12, 1987.

Ferge, Z. and Miller, S.M., 1987: *The Dynamics of Deprivation: A Cross-National Study.* London: Gower.

Forrest, R. and Murie, A., 1983: Residualization and Council Housing: Aspects of the Changing Social Relations of Housing Tenure. *Journal of Social Policy* 12, 453-68.

----, 1986: Marginalization and Subsidized Individualism: the Sale of Council Houses in the Restructuring of the British Welfare State. *International Journal of Urban and Regional Research* 10, 46-65.

Gamble, A., 1987: The Great Divide. *Marxism Today,* March, 12-17.

Glastonberry, B., 1971: *Homeless Near a Thousand Homes.* London: Allen and Unwin.

Greve, J., 1964: *London's Homeless.* London: Bell and Sons.

---- et al., 1971: *Homelessness in London.* Glasgow: Scottish Academic Press.

-----, 1976: *Homelessness in London.* Bristol: University of Bristol, School for Advanced Urban Studies.

Halsey, A.H., 1987: Social Trends Since World War Two. *Social Trends,* No. 17, 11-19.

Henderson, J. and Karn, V., 1987: *Race, Class and State Housing.* London: Gower.

Murie, A. (ed.), 1987: *Living in Bed and Breakfast: The Experience of Homelessness in London.* Bristol: University of Bristol, School for Advanced Urban Studies.

Pahl, R., 1986: *Social Polarization and the Economic Crisis.* Paper presented to Seminar organized by the Hungarian Academy of Sciences. Budapest (Mimeo).

Phillips, D., 1986: *What Price Equality.* London: GLC.

Richards, J., 1981: *The Making of the Housing (Homeless Persons) Act 1977.* Bristol: University of Bristol, School for Advanced Urban Studies.

Townsend, P., 1987: *Combatting Poverty.* Paper presented to the 35th Annual Summer School Conference, 1-6 August, Inchigeela, Co. Cork (Mimeo).

Walker, B., 1987: Public Sector Costs of Board and Lodging Accommodation for Homeless Households in London. *Housing Studies* 2, No. 4.

Watson, S., (with Austerberry, H.), 1986: *Housing and Homelessness.* London: Routledge and Kegan Paul.

HOMELESS IN FRANCE:
PUBLIC AND PRIVATE POLICIES

Dan Ferrand-Bechmann

Poverty and Homeless: An Increasing Problem in a Rich Society

It is a strange paradox to write about poverty and homeless in France 1987, since there is a social policy. Yet, the problem exists. The reason is, like in many capitalist countries, that housing is more for profit than for social purposes. One of the symptoms of poverty, to be homeless, is visible and is taken in account by the media. Each of us can see these bag people or imply a caravan still occupied after the period of holidays. These facts that were formerly marginal or seldom are now occuring more frequently. It provokes each of us in our deepest phantasms and imagination and remains quite scandalous in our comfortable society.

If many authors admit there is a problem of poverty, they insist that people can answer of their primary needs (Milano, 1983). Few begin to claim that to be a dramatic new problem and the collectivity wakes up. But new solutions are created to maintain people in social lodging and to help them to pay for electricity, heating and gas, but fewer solutions are offered to help those without lodging. In fact, our social policy is quite sufficient to cover the needs of handicapped people, elderly, recently jobless and families with dependent children. But there are groups not having the qualifications to apply to special locations and thus remain in a deep misery. The media inform more about the public policy than about those who cannot apply especially because they cannot give an address. If they can obtain food they still remain homeless or do not have their own lodging being in collective institutions, such as welfare hotels, in emergency shelters or in the streets under the bridge or in the underground. All these homeless people are first poor and isolated and then homeless.

A recent statuary report indicates that the number of people homeless or in emergency lodging would be 200,000 or 400,000 (Wresinski, 1986). Among them are about 10,000 errants. The places offered in emergency shelters would be officially of 30,000 and 8,000 in hotels, providing a total of 500,000 nights. Statistics indicate officially in the census of 1982: 20,620 emergency dwellings and 120,700 people living in lodgings.

It is difficult to obtain the exact number of homeless, because our statistics are mainly built on the household and also on people that are qualified to ask for a social lodging. They are not done for the people who cannot apply for these lodging because they have not enough revenues, children or because the municipalities have asked that or that criterion to be admitted on a list. But by the admissions to emergency shelters and some census made in the street, relatively precise data can be provided. Same remarks have been made by Marcuse (1987), but in the U.S. there are probably more people sleeping on the street (see, the article by Huttman in this book). There are also less statistics made in social centers and welfare hotels.

Local inquiries are better to know the real situation: among 323 persons asking for social housing, one third were really without lodging. They were with families or friends, in caravans or cars, or squattered. Among the same number of people asking to be admitted in an emergency shelter a quarter were living with families or friends, a quarter should be evicted, others were really homeless (sleeping in huts, cars or cellars or on streets), others were in prisons, hospitals.

Emergency shelters are more numerous because there are more applicants. The vagrants in Paris or elsewhere go to these centersto sleep when the winter is deep cold or are sent into them by the police. The freedom to sleep in the fresh air does not exist really and every citizen is guilty not to have a shelter or a home. Consequently, the local authorities have to provide a bed to anyone that needs one. In fact the possibilities are not every time sufficient and the conditions of living in these shelters quite unbearable for new poor. The famous Maison de Nanterre is not really very comfortable and new shelters built recently in Paris with four storied beds were not a perfect solution.

The municipality could have said in the media, there ere enough beds and despite it, many people were still on the streets. Did they really choose to be out in that cold January or did they could not accept to be lodged in inadequate conditions? Apart from this problem of cold, there is also violence and robbery; if these people could find a proper shelter they would accept it. Why were people to whom I talked, for instance, women begging in the stations, saying there are no more beds in Paris? It is sure that these persons were homeless and that beds in shelters were vacant.

Normally, all our legislations offers various forms of affordable housing, however, not for families with small revenues (Petrequin, 1986). Probably two million households with 75% of the minimum revenu exist in France and have urgent problems to pay their rents and housing expenses. Many efforts are made to resolve the problems of such persons before they could be evicted. Special collective social funds have been set up. Charitable efforts have been made to help people to pay their rents and housing expenses. Public legislations have been voted by the congress to give more rights to people as tenants during the socialist government, since then some of the laws have been abolished. Among the 20% poorest, a third have no comfort at all in their lodging. Private owners wishing to evict their tenants and sell their lands for profit, were able in Paris that winter to let fire empty their property quite easely and rapidly. Even with a strong legislation, informal procedures and pressures are such that the situation of families could be to sleep on the streets the next morning after a fire. Similar is the situation of those without revenues, that can give no guarantee to private owners or public institutions providing social housing. These people even with children are evicted and become homeless.

Lodging is a dominant problem for poor people. Many of the clients of social workers come to the services to ask for a help concerning lodging. The poverty programme's first goals appeared to be lodging.

What are the solutions? Emergency shelters, collective institutions with the aim of social reintegration, families and friends, welfare and normal cheap hotels, cars, caravans, bridges, huts, cellars, old buildings, undergrounds, prisons, hospitals and streets.

Who are the Homeless People?

Part of them are the tramps that tourists have seen and that could be one of the exotic charms of France. Some of them could have really choosen that situation and that freedom (Declerck, 1983). Part of them (10%?) sleep in the underground stations, others find spaces under the bridges and in old houses. It appears they are younger and younger and more and more numerous. Violence becomes more severe, and alcoholism still a huge problem. There is a real society of tramps with norms, solidarity, friendship, sex, violence, crimes and day to day life and pleasure. The police knows them because they are sent to the Maison of Nanterre or go there by themselves when it is too cold or too dangerous.

There are also young mothers with children around 27 years old, and hobos, male or female vagrants. People with drug problems or not, some mentally ill, others not. Probably less than 10% of women and 20% of foreign-born; a study in the north of France indicated that they are more often men. Women have their children and are given social housing or beds in special homes because of their children. Training and qualifications are low.

In many cases they wander from emergency shelters or collectives homes to another in a vagrant system. Those who were living with parents or friends are numerous, indicating the importance of this solidarity. Despite our welfare state, the role of the nuclear and extensive family and of the networks of friends still remains important. 16% of the jobless with no more allocations are living in other's flats or houses. More people are poor, even more ask for help from these networks and give it, as enquiries of A.T.D., a voluntary organization with its own social survey center, have shown. More and more families are obliged to lodge their children still living with a friend or a husband or wife. Surveys show that among homeless people 50% have no revenues at all. The others have a special allocation for single-parents with dependent children, or allocations for handicapped people. Few have jobs. More and more young people come to be homeless. On the contrary, elderly benefit of a good public policy and have no big problem but loneliness.

These people are without money, without job and homeless. They are not in that situation due to mentally illness, but due to the economic crisis and because of the gaps and holes of the public policies. Perhaps the fact that the commissions whose roles are to define who should have a special allocation for handicapped people are less generous. For years these allocations were one solution for people without revenues. They were said not to be able to work and could apply, for this allocation. That generous period is over and there are less and less solutions. Certain categories of people have no minimum revenues and are very poor indeed (Ferrand-Bechmann, 1987).

It appears that the present social programmes are not appropriate to cope with these new situations. The existing structures are neither sufficiently numerous, nor suited to the new jobless situations. The social problems are new in their dimensions and in their caracteristics. The new normal families structure are such that half of the families among poor people are with only one adult. This is one of the reasons, why the government was obliged to set up a new poverty programme in 1985.

The Poverty Programme

To cope with this emergency problem, French social institutions have established a special programme against poverty, of which mainly non-profit organizations are in charge. It runs during the winter, one of its aims is to alleviaftae the needs of the homeless. The organizations that running the programme are:
- Salvation Army,
- A.T.D. Quart Monde (Fourth World),
- Banques alimentaires (Food Bank),
- Emmaus,
- F.N.A.R.S.,
- Entraide Protestante,
- Federation des Equipes Saint-Vincent,
- Fonds Social Juif Unifie,
- OFIVAL,
- Petits Frères des Pauvres (Brothers of the Poor),
- Secours Catholique (Catholic Help),
- Secours Populaire Francais,
- Red Cross,
- Societe Saint-Vincent de Paul
- Union des Foyers de Jeunes Travailleurs.

They have different actions against poverty and homeless. 43,9% of their actions concern problems of lodging; 7,500 emergency beds have been added. Part of the financial aid assistis given to these organizations, part to the départements (90 in France), but the départments give it to these organizations at the local level, being in a way unable to organize that programme without the help of these private charitable organizations.

Part of these actions is just to assist such persons, part is to give them an emergency lodging with the aim of social reintegration or just for giving a shelter: in a normal lodging, in young workers housing, in a hotel. 500,000 nights have been apparently offered during the winter to 40,000 places, an average of ten nights. Where do the people sleep the others nights? Why the beds are empty some nights?

The organizations themselves give the equivalent of the amount given by the state and the département, this money comes from the estates, real estates, gifts, works or benefits etc. These lodging are emergency or more permanent ones. Clients can be helped by a social action or social reinsertion or just with a bed and a soup. These shelters are more or less subsidized by the state. Some places offered in these charitable organizations are funded up to $ 100 a day. A quick calculation shows that the total sum given for a month could pay for a decent rent. But in many cases, these people could not pay regulary rents and could not apply for housing. Very few collective action or self-help groups have been organized neither by the organisations nor by the people themselves. What are the specific actions of these organizations mainly focussed on homeless? (cf. D.A.S., 1986).

Salvation Army

Different types of action are provided by the Salvation Army such as: lodging in hostels and emergency shelters, but also special funds to pay for the rents. This organization pays for more than 2,000 nights in hotels, 58,000 nights in shelters, 361 months of rents. The people who came to ask for help are normally without any money or say they are in such a situation, because it is the key of entrance in this organization. Mainly they are bachelors without family even when they had had one: they cannot support it anymore. Paris is the most important place for these homeless people and would be where the Salvation Army has the largest center. The hotels are the only solutions for families without lodging. Especially in Paris or in the big cities where there is no emergency other solutions for these people. This traditional organization has a very strong programme toward homeless since years but also because of the actual crisis and shortage of other possibilities for those homeless. The Salvation Army has an evangelical organization but welcomes everyone without money and if left without help forced to sleep on the pavement.

A.T.D. Quart Monde

This organization is one of the most radical one in France. It does not run any shelter but helps people to pay their rents and covers their housing expenses. More than half of its budget is devoted to it. It gives a guarantee to the owners even collectives ones or public ones, it has special collective funds managed with others institutions and struggles in the day to day life to help the people not to become homeless despite their lack of money. It has a community action and a political activity. On a larger scale, it gives a minimum revenue to very poor people and works with some local community. It acts with the people and not for them, living with people in need in their poor neighborhood.

Emmaus

This organization is very well known in France because of its famous leader l'Abbé Pierre. This extraordinary charismatic man had been a member of parliament after 1945 and began an anti-poverty campaign, and struggled with a dramatic faith to destroy the slums and to help the homeless families. He was able to collect sufficieent money to have his own social housing and to offer a home to vagrants and homeless people. But he claimed for the right to work and develop an industry of recycling. Many French give to that famous organization old furniture, electric equipment or clothes. The key to join these communities is to accept to work and to contribute to the expenses through work's products. The homeless people ecoming members of Emmaus communities repair and sell these objects, using all the rubbish of our consumption society. They live on the money provided by that industry of recuperation and recycling. With their benefits and the public help, but also the gifts and real estates they run emergency shelters and soup kitchens. The poor help the poorest!

They have two kinds of action toward homelessness, one is emergency shelters, especially in winter, in where homeless people can have a warm night and a soup, the other is the system of community. There are permanent communities, all around France, where people work and live for one or more years. Some are totally isolated from their families and friends and are unable to find a new autonomy, the Emmaus communities are their new families and communities. Facing dangerous situations in underground, vagrants and tramps prefer more and more to exchange their freedom for a home even with a compulsory work. Some have been isolated by illness, by war, by crime or delinquency or just after a family break or the lost of a job.

The Emmaus communities are all around France and well known, they are a safety belt. The poverty programme has helped them to settle more place in their emergency shelters. They also help families to pay for their housing expenses, rents and debts. In some cases they pay for hotels when families with children have no more solutions.

Fédération Nationale des Associations d'Accueil et de Réadaptation Sociale (FNARS)

This is a federation: a network of organizations whose main task is lodging but also social reintegration. By its special poverty programme, the federation has helped to create more than 600 new beds in the organizations, but also has given money to emergency shelters etc.. Part of the voluntary organizations linked to them are subsidized by the state and have a social action goals. The total amount of money they control, directly or indirectly, is quite large, including 150,000 places in permanent centers that are shelters for the homeless, isolated, and jobless, whose situation gives them access to these centers. But the places are fewer than the demand.

Fédération Nationale de l'Entraide Protestante

Their action is mainly toward persons who have just found a job or are in job programme. Like other organizations, they pay for special expenses or hotels or offer shelters. More specific is the way they give money for renewing and repairing collective housing. Their main organizations are near Montpelliers a famous calvinist city in the south of France and in Paris, where the needs are much more acute than in others big cities. It has also tried to organize a meeting place for homeless people in the north of France.

Fonds Social Juif Unifie

This organization does not run special shelters but tries to help financially the people who are homeless. They use more than the third of their funds for that type of problems. Their action is more important in Paris and Marseille where the jewish community is more numerous.

Les Petits Frères des Pauvres

This organization focusses on elderly persons. Though it has special actions to help them to pay for housing expenses and it help others age groups. They run a shelter. The following few statistical data characterize this group: single: 63%, married: 37%; French: 78%. After a period in that home, some obtain a retirement pension, only few a job.

Le Secours Catholique

This powerful organization was also obliged to face the new situation created by the increasing number of homeless people or people that cannot face the expenses of their housing and who would be evicted if they could be helped to pay their debts. It runs a large home near Paris where more than 10,000 nights have been offered to adults and children and also to families. It is a specific situation. But a quarter is women, and three quarter men. Half of the families are single parents families. It gives a good image of the different situations: men ithout families relatively young, women without families more jobless than the men, couples without children very young too, single parents families sometimes recently evicted despite young children. Since there is no other solution, families come to that organization that tries to indicates them social welfare institutions, but it seems that the actual difficult situation for families finds little solutions.

Red Cross

This large traditional organization is also involved in actions to help the homeless especially to run emergency shelters for families and vagrants. It has not more beds in Paris than in others cities.

Société Saint-Vincent de Paul

Like many others, this organization spends a large sum for shelters. It tries to welcome the people during a longer period to help them to find a solution and social help.

Union des Foyers de Jeunes Travailleurs

This organization generally has one aim: to give lodging to young workers. But in fact, because of the economic crisis, it is more and more obliged to have also a social programme and eventually to welcome young people that cannot pay their rents. They run about 500 centers, however, this association has had an important action in the poverty programme and could have welcome more people or give them a better help. Because the beneficiaries are young and mainly jobless, the action was not only toward a shelter but also a training.

Conclusion

The question of poverty and homeless are partly resolved by public policies, partly by private ones through a new collaboration between the voluntary associations organizing flexible actions and programmes, and the state on the national and the local level, providing supplementary additional money through the poverty programme. The state provides social affordable housing and homes for handicapped and elderly people, the voluntary organizations are concerned with the more urgent problems and provide especially emergency shelters during winter and after. The role of families and friends is still crucial and appears to be the one best or the last solution for many people when they are not isolated and could still benefit from this mutual help. The urban question has to include homeless question. Selection made for affordable housing applicants is probably too limited. People remain without qualification to apply and even to be counted by official statistics as people in need for housing. Homeless is no more the question of tramps or new immigrants, it becomes a social question that has to be studied by urban sociologists, political scientists and economists.

References

A.T.D., 1986: *Enquete sur Caen en 1986*. Caen: Ave. du Gal. Leclerc Pierreelaye 78. Coordination des associations du logement, 1985: Etude sur 79 familles en situation d'éxpulsion. Toulouse: 274 rte Seysses 31100.

C.R.E.D.O.C., 1986: *Pauvreté, Precarité, Tentatives de Mésure*. Paris: 142 rue du Chevaleret.

D.A.S., 1986: *Bilan du programme d'action contre la pauvréte et la precarité. July 1986*. Amiens: 123, rue Sadi Carnot Vanves 92.

Declerck, P., 1983: *Ethnographie des marginaux vivant dans le metro Parisien*. Paris: E.H.E.S.S.

Ferrand-Bechmann, D., 1987: Pauvres et tres Pauvres. *Revue Solidarité-Santé*, April (Paris: Edition Masson).

Lae, J.F. and Murard, N., 1986: *L'argent des Pauvres*. Editions Sociales.

Marcuse, P., 1987: *Isolating the Homeless*. New York. Columbia University

Milano, S., 1983: *La Pauvreté en France*. Paris: Syros.

Observatoire Regional de la Sante de Picardie, 1985: D.A.S *L'hébergement social des adultes en Picardie octobre 1985*. Amiens.

Wresinski, J., 1987: Grande Pauvrete et Precarite Economique et Sociale. *Journal Officiel* February 11-12, 1987. Paris: 26, rue Desaix.

HOMELESSNESS AS A HOUSING PROBLEM
IN AN INNER CITY IN THE U.S.

Elizabeth Huttman

Homelessness is essentially a problem of lack of one's own permanent shelter, forcing one instead to resort to such temporary solutions as emergency shelters, use of one's car, tent or such, or sleeping in public places, or doubling up with relatives or friends. Homelessness is due to inability to find a private or public accommodation, usually because of inability to pay for such, but in some cases because of social problem characteristics such as substance abuse or mental illness that make landlords reluctant to rent to the person in a housing scarcity situation.

Focus of this Paper

Much of the literature on the homeless has focused on their characteristics including social problems, rather than the essential shelter problem stemming above all from lack of affordable housing (Baxter and Hopper, 1984; Campbell, 1987; Hensell, 1986; Wright et al., 1987). This paper concentrates on the latter. It gives evidence of the decreasing availability of affordable housing in one major American city, San Francisco, due to loss of stock, vacancy rate, rent level, and housing start situation, as well as availability of subsidized housing. It also mentions effect of rent control on decrease in the rental stock. The paper then discusses demand for low rent housing, and then homelessness and demand, and finally type of homeless and type of demand. It especially covers demand of the "new homeless" such as families, women with children, and singles, including aged without substance abuse problems.

This focus on the underlying housing cause of the homeless situation is partly stressed to point out that long-term permanent shelter accommodations are the end solution to the problem, rather than the present solution of short term emergency accommodations. (As Marcuse [1987] does.) As a San Francisco official has said, today we are using short-term solutions to a long-term problem. In San Francisco where it is estimated there are eight to ten thousand homeless (National Coalition for the Homeless Survey, 1986), over $9.8 million was spent in 1986 by the city for housing the homeless, with half going for use of 32 hotels for 2500, the rest to help the non-profit agency shelters that house another large group. A complaint about this short-term shelter approach has also been made by the New York Times editorial (June 2, 1987), criticizing the lack of focus on preventiveness measures when the city, state, and federal agencies spend $125 million to house 4,800 New York homeless. Experts are saying, that with shelters across the country housing more than 111,000 (1985) each night (Hoch and Huth, forthcoming), there is a need for a more permanent housing solution. San Francisco community shelter workers (Goode, 1986) demanded, there is "a need to get the poorest of the poor off the low rent merry-go-round that keeps them moving from the streets to the dormitory-like shelters operated by non-profit foundations (for limited short stays), to the hotels and then back again." As Hoch and Huth emphasize, a variety of long-term types of housing for this diverse homeless population are needed, for the problem refused to go away. As a San Francisco city leader in 1986 said: we didn't realize in 1983 that the homeless were going to stay around" (Goode, 1986). But they have, partly due to the increased scarcity of affordable housing, as the below shows for San Francisco.

Loss of SROs and Apartments

Homelessness is due to inability to find shelter, whether an apartment, house or room. This is most likely to occur when one moves to a new area; returns from an institutional setting such as hospital; mental health facility; prison; moves out of a relative's home whether parents, spouse, or such; is displaced from the present unit due to property sale or conversion or demolition; or eviction from one's present unit. The hunt for alternative housing is not successful in the case of the homeless.

Lack of affordable apartments can be shown for San Francisco in terms of loss of cheap housing units in the city, especially single resident occupancy (SRO) hotels, number and proportion of units at cheap rents, vacancy rates, and lack of units qualifying as fair market rent units under Section 8, the American housing allowance program.

San Francisco traditionally has had a large stock of SRO units (Koch, 1987). But in the 1970s these were taken out of the stock in large numbers for use as tourist hotels or conversion to quality apartments. For example Hartman, Keating, and LeGates (1982) point out that between 1975 and 1979, 17% (5723 units) were lost of the 32,214 SRO units. Ovrebo et al. (1984) reported that around 1200 SRO units were lost on average each year between 1975 and 1984. The city, due to major protests and demonstrations on loss of these SROs, such as the International Hotel, had a moratorium on conversion from November 1979 to December 1980, but due to loopholes it is reported 2374 more units were lost and even after the city's permanent restrictions on conversion more were lost (Hartman, Keating and LeGates, 1982). Examples were conversion of ten Tenderloin SROs (1,192 units) to tourist hotels; and conversion of others to Section 8 rehabilitated units (Lincoln, 1980; Kasinitz, 1984). In New York City a similar large drop in SRO units occurred, from 50,454 in 1975 to 18,853 in 1981; here the city gave tax abatement incentives to upgrade SROs and this, Kasinitz (1984) reports, caused units to be removed from the cheap rental pool. Ironically, this government action, as with the San Francisco

Section 8 conversion, increased homelessness. And in addition the city of San Francisco program of using SROs (32 hotels housing 2500) for housing the homeless decreased the units available and in addition upped the rental price of the remaining SROs. The city in 1986 paid $7.50 to $14 a night for these contracted SRO units. (Goode, 1986; Weeden and Linehan, 1987).

This loss of SROs is a serious cause of homelessness since SROs are the most likely accommodation for those homeless or at risk of displacement; of Weeden and Linehan's San Francisco sample of those 60 and over, 42% in temporary shelters (or board and care or transitional mental health housing) had formerly been housed in SROs; a third of their "at risk of displacement" from housing (selected from social service agency information) were in SROs. In addition to the loss of SROs the decrease in board and care facilities in San Francisco also caused homelessness; in 1980 there were about 1100 such beds and by 1983 only 800 (Goode and Hsu, 1986). As did the earlier closing of mental hospitals in California.

Loss of Low Rent Housing in General

There are debates on how serious displacement is in U.S. cities (Palen, forthcoming) but in general the Annual Housing Survey (1981) shows 1.7 to 2.4 million persons displaced annually. Studies show this more serious in San Francisco than many other cities (Grier, 1980; U.S. HUD, 1981). The HUD (1981) study found, particularly for San Francisco of the six cities studied, those most affected in displacement were renters, short term residents (three years or less), those working part-time, poorer families, minorities - though not the elderly.

Condominium conversion is another reason for loss of units and this is major in San Francisco. While, as Kain (1983) argues, many such units are sold to the former renter, or returned to the rental market, and are mainly units occupied by the higher income person, some are low rent units. In many cities in the 1970's more than 5% of the rental stock was converted to condomiums (O'Connell, forthcoming); San Francisco was among the leaders. The pace however has now slowed, with less interest in condominium purchase. The HUD 1980 study of conversions show while more than half of the former residents were angry over the situation, the majority (90%) were satisfied with their new housing; yet among those who rented elsewhere (23% turned to ownership), 28% had to pay at least 25% more rent than they did in the pre-conversion building. O'Connell warns this HUD sample did not include what he calls the "invisible evictions" (also see Hartman, 1979) from threats, arson and other forms of harassment. He adds, "but the increasing numbers of homeless must make us look at the 'invisible evictions' that result in the turmoil that often precedes formal conversion".

Loss of rental units can also be attributed to the existence of strict rent control laws. The HUD 1980 condominium conversion study found rental control was not a major reason for conversions. However, Downs (1983) and others see the existence of rent control causing a disincentive for investors to be in the rental business. Certainly a number of apartment house owners moved out of the business in San Francisco, yet for others they benefited by the law that allowed 7% yearly rent increases that they had not before tried to obtain from ongoing good tenants. Second, the law allowed greater increases after remodeling. The rent control law actually hurt the mobile population and new renters, while for long-time renters keeping the rent increases within limits. These new renters of low income, often at risk for homelessness, were faced with any increase the landlord could make when a unit vacated. In San Francisco, in addition, new renters were faced with an increasingly high initial outlay as more and more landlords demanded first and last month rent and a large security deposit, often totalling $2,000-2,800 (see, Baar and Keating, forthcoming, for general discussion of rent control; also Huttman and Huttman, 1986).

An early source of overall loss of units in San Francisco, including SROs, should also be mentioned. In the 1960s San Francisco led the country in urban renewal and some of this was in areas of low cost housing such as Western Addition, the black ghetto area. In the U.S., as the Fainsteins point out, this federal spending peaked in 1969 and then decreased. In San Francisco as elsewhere, due to neighborhood protests and shift in governments in Washington, rehabilitation/conservation of neighborhoods became more popular. This rehabilitation again caused the loss of low rent units, as has the considerable private gentrification in many San Francisco neighborhoods, including in the gay community in the Castro area and Duboce Park area. Victorian houses have been rescued from their run-down apartment and boarding house condition in these areas, Cow Hollow, Russian Hill area and other city neighborhoods. A recent last cause of loss of low rent units is the converison of such to office buildings, especially in the Chinatown and North Beach areas bordering on the financial district, where new buildings have very high square foot costs.

Vacancy Rate

These rates are usually used as an indicator of the supply of housing; however, they may be misleading as they do not distinguish between high rent units and low rent ones. It also can be misleading as a number of vacant units are not available for general rental. For example, in the Bureau of Census data on vacant housing units, it includes those held off the housing market (3.6 million of the 10.3 million vacant units, 1986) and even those "in the housing market" include those for sale (1.0) million): "rented or sold, not yet occupied" (0.6 milliion), as well as the 2.7 million "for rent". The Federal Home Loan Bank Housing Vacancy Survey includes *all* vacant units, as identified by postal workers.

According to the latter source, San Francisco multi-family vacancy rate doubled in the 1985 period, from 0.8% September 1985 to a tight 1.5% in September 1986. In adjacent counties it was somewhat higher, but actually declining: San Mateo county declined from 2.4% to 2.2% and 2.5% to 2.3% in Marin county (Bay Area Housing Briefs, 1987f). This is much worse than the national picture where rental vacancy rates have actually risen in 1986 (7.7% in April, 1987) and were very high in the South (10.3%); however, with a slump in apartment house building from late 1986 onward these are likely to go down (Business Week, May 4, 1987).

Starts

In San Francisco the multi-family housing starts went up in 1986, from 1217 in 1985 to 1898 in 1986. However this situation is unlikely to last because the changes in the tax laws, especially the change in the depreciation time period, have had a very negative impact on multi-unit builders' future plans, as three fourths of such Business Week surveyed builders said (40% said very negative effect). This is already shown nationally in the drop of starts, averaging only 464,000 annual rate during the first quarter of 1987, compared to a high of 1,100,000 multi-family units in late 1985 (the earlier 1980s had also had some drop in multi-unit construction). Since some experts believe multi-family unit starts should be between one million and one and a half million a year to meet demand this is low. In San Francisco it is estimated 1500 units are needed annually according to the San Francisco Residential Housing Element (1984) but in 1980-82 less than a 1000 units were started [Weeden and Linehan, 1987].

Even with somewhat higher vacancy rates in San Francisco (though still very low at 1.5%) and multi-unit starts somewhat higher, this does not effect the low rent market. As Cook in the Bay Area Housing Briefs (1987f) reports, "while the rental construction boom has increased vacancy rates (in the Bay Area) and resulted in stable advertised rents, much of the new rental housing coming on the market is unaffordable to most rental households". In other words, this building distorts the vacancy rate statistics as these new units remain empty while there is a scarcity of cheap units; the more construction, the possibility of more distortion if the new additions are not subsidized units. Cook, to back this up, states that "the Consumer Price Index surveys reveal that high levels of production may not have had much effect upon improving the affordability picture for renters in older, less expensive units. Rent levels measured across a wider spectrum of rental units show a continued, though lessened, rate of increase during the past two years. The demand for low-priced units remains undersupplied despite increased levels of rental housing" (Bay Area Housing Briefs, 1987d). (See Figure 1.)

This statement indicates the lack of "trickle down" or "filtering" process at work. While San Francisco rents have not increased in the last year, and for medium to high rent units there has been some decrease (limited by landlords' worry over inability to pull the rent back up under rent control), this has not effected the low rent market. Because rent unit operating costs have risen at a fast rate (50% faster than renter incomes in the

1976-83 period) and construction costs also risen faster (Downs, 1983) apartment house owners have been limited on how much they can reduce rents. They abandon the units first--not a common occurrence in San Francisco but certainly in Detroit, New York and elsewhere (see, Lawson, 1984).

Figure 1: Bay Area Median Rent* for Two-Bedroom Apartments

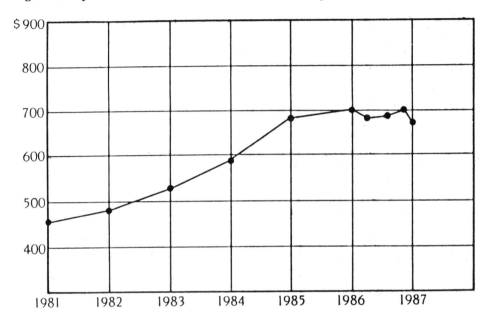

* Annual Figures are for January of each year. Sample size averaged 309 for 1981 through October 1986. 449 in January 1987. Based on sampling of rents advertised for two-bedroom unfurnished apartments in the Saturday and/or Sunday classified sections of six Bay Area newspapers: San Francisco Chronicle and Examiner, San Jose Mercury News, The Tribune, Marin Independent Journal, Contra Costa Times, and Peninsula Times-Tribune. Rents reflect the cost of renting an available apartment--not what all current renters of two-bedroom apartments are paying.

Rents and Affordability

The high cost of the new units is shown by the Bureau of Census (1984) statistic that median gross rent of units added to the stock between 1970 and 1983 was 20% higher than overall median rents, and the median income of those who occupied these units was about 25% higher. The median rent for a two bedroom apartment was $850 in San Francisco in January 1987, down from $900 in October 1986. This rent is among the highest outside of New York City. Advertised rents in the Bay Area increased 75% from 1980 to 1986 (while household incomes only increased 40%). In 1984, Bay Area rents skyrocketed 16.8%. The Census shows 41% of Bay Area renters pay over 30% of income for rent; in San Francisco it is worst. In San Francisco, the typical renter household with a 1986 median household income of $17,948 would need to pay 60% of its income to rent the median rent apartment. For Oakland/South Alameda County it was 44% and for central San Mateo County, 39% (Bay Area Housing Briefs, 1986, using U. S. Census and Urban Decision Systems data; see Table 1).

Table 1: 1986 Bay Area Rental Housing Affordability

Sub-Region	Median Household Income ($)*		Percent of Income Needed for Rent (Renter HH)
	All HHs	Renter HHs	
San Francisco	22,435	17,948	60
Oakland/So. Alameda Co.	26,002	16,901	44
Central San Mateo Co.	32,483	23,063	39
Central Contra Costa Co.	32,322	19,176	39
Palo Alto Area	33,206	22,192	38
Marin County	36,182	24,242	37
Santa Rosa Area	25,034	17,274	36
San Jose Area	33,206	22,912	34
Regional Average	*28,810*	*19,303*	*44*

* Median renter household income is based on percent of total household income as estimated by 1980 U.,S. Census, applied to county estimates of 1986 median househoild income.

Sources: Urban Decision Systems; U.S. Census; Bay Area Council.

Nationally rent burden was high for those with low family incomes (0-50% of gross annual median family income). According to a GAO study (1985), of this poverty group only 22% paid 30% or less of their income for rent, while 49% (almost six million households) paid over half their income for rent. In fact, almost a third of this poor population (0-50% of median family income) paid over 70% of their income for rent (3.7 million households). (See Table 2.)

Nation-wide, Zigas, of the National Low Income Housing Coalition, has stated that "there is absolutely less housing renting at prices affordable for low income households than there was five years ago; about half of the 8.1 million renter households that earned less than $7,300 in 1985 paid more than 30% of their income in rent" (San Francisco Examiner, April 19, 1987). The number of units renting for less than $250 per month in 1983 nationally fell to 8.8 million from 10.8 million in 1974, while the number of households with income below $10,000 (in 1983 dollars) increased from 8.9 million in 1974 to 11.9 million in 1983 (Carliner, 1987).

Table 2: Rent Burden of Households With Incomes 0-50 Percent of Area Median Family Income

Rent Burden*	1975 Housing Units (000s)	Percent of Total	1983 Housing Units (000s)	Percent of Total
30% or less	2,777	29	2,695	22
Over 30% to 40%	1,670	18	1,897	15
Over 40% to 50%	1,309	14	1,635	13
Over 50% to 60%	982	10	1,339	11
ver 60% to 70%	589	7	935	8
Over 70%	1,995	21	3,681	30
Total **	9,321	99	12,182	99

* Rent burden, or rent-to-income ratio, equals gross annual household rent divided by gross annual household income.

** Figures do not add due to rounding.

Source: U.S. General Accounting Office (1983).

The lack of such cheap units in San Francisco is verified by the situation of Section 8 eligible households. A very large proportion (60%) eligible (in possession of a certificate) have not been able to find housing units at rents (fair market rents) allowed for San Francisco by the federal government for Section 8 housing. (San Francisco Housing Authority, June 29, 1987; cf. McLeod, 1987). Section 8 hunters can only pay $765 (1987) for a two-bedroom by HUD regulations, and cannot find anything available.

Low Income of San Francisco Households

Part of the housing affordability problem as shown above is that incomes have not risen as much as rents, even though the CPI (Consumer Price Index, Bureau of Labor Statistics) shows rents rising at a slower rate than utilities and maintenance costs, and one could add construction and operating costs (Downs, 1983). (Figure 2.) In San Francisco (1985) 21.6% of the population was below the very low poverty level ($11,000 annual income for a family of four).

Figure 2: Homeowners' (a) and Renters' (b) Costs and Incomes, USA, 1973-1980
a)Homeowners

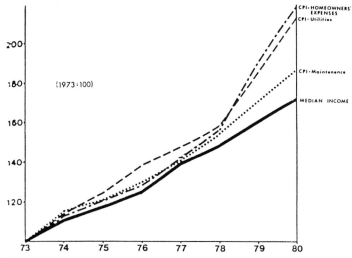

b) Renters

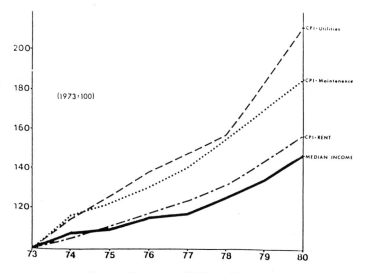

Sources: Bureau of Labor Statistics; CPI Detailed Reports.

In San Francisco, 159,840 (1985) lived below the poverty line; 8-10,000 were homeless; and 41,195 receiving food stamps (San Francisco Chronicle, November 27, 1986). For those elderly homeless or "at risk of displacement" in San Francisco, Weeden and Linehan found incomes low--46 percent on SSI ($533 a month for a single person).

Unemployment was above that of surrounding counties, especially for minorities, and wages were depressed by the influx of immigrants to work in the large service sector. Murtagh of the Ecumenical Association for Housing points out for the Bay Area (1986) a bank clerk's starting salara was only $12,000 and thus he should only pay a maximum rent (30% of income) of $300; a school secretary's was $18,000 and a school teachers $20,000, so they should pay $450 and $500 respectively, and a county sheriff (policeman) a high of $22,800 should pay $570; much more, over $30,000, was needed to afford San Francisco's median rent for a two bedroom (or a working wife was needed, as true for the large majority of home purchases in the Bay Area).

Rental Supply Increased by Home Purchase

This was true to some minor degree in1986 in San Francisco due to heavy home purchase by pent-up buyers who had long waited for interest rates to go down to the below-10 percent level they did in spring and summer 1986. Some of these were first-time buyers, baby boomers now having their own children, but many were previous homeowners upgrading. First-time buyers, with the salaries mentioned above, found it hard to enter the buying market even when the wife's income was included. With an average $166,011 sales price on San Francisco homes, one needed almost $40,000 for a down payment and closing costs, and an income of $58,003. Monthly payments on a 9.5%, 25 year mortgage would then be around $1500 a month, plus $150-200 a month property tax.

This keeps many would-be owners as San Francisco renters and they compete for the available rental units, as they do elsewhere (Harloe, 1985; Huttman, 1985). It thus makes less likely the filtering down process - in fact in San Francisco with these young families unable to buy new housing, we have the filtering-up, that is upgrading of Victorian houses. The rental supply is also not opened up as fast as in the past because the city's considerable elderly population are living longer, thus occupying units longer (Huttman, fothcoming).

Affordable Housing Supply Increased by Subsidized Housing

Low income in San Francisco in the past have benefited from various housing subsidy programs, whether public housing, Sections 236, 221(d)(3), 202, Section 8 new or substantially rehabilitated or tax exempt bond programs. Nationally, 22% of eligible low income are in units under housing subsidy programs (Carliner, 1987); one of the "at risk" groups, female headed households, is even more likely to be in subsidized units (two out of three such households live in such according to Sullivan and Damroch, 1987). A large proportion of elderly are likewise in subsidized housing (Huttman, 1975). In total three million renters were in such, over half (1.8 million) in private rental units (Harloe, forthcoming).

Figure 3: Subsidized Housing Production, USA, 1969-1984

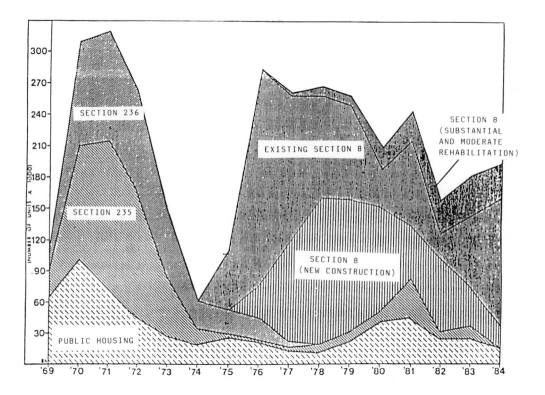

Sources: Pre-1975 data from HUD, 1979 Yearbook; post-1975 data compiled by National Low Income Housing Coalition from HUD sources.

Little new subsidized housing is being built, however, as that Figure 3 shows, from 1980 onward Section 8 new construction dropped way down as did public housing. And in 1987 Congress authorized almost no new public housing at the same time some public housing units were sold. Section 8 new and rehabilitated housing starts have fallen, from about 132,000 annually in 1980 to 15,500 in 1986 (Harloe, forthcoming; Low Income Housing Information Service, 1985). Other programs were also cut back, and the federal new budget authority (1985) a third of that in 1980; and in 1986 far below that for housing (Harloe, forthcoming).

As Pit and Van Vliet (forthcoming) point out, from 1981 on the Reagan Administration determined that housing assistance consumed too much of the federal budget. Of course, as Carliner (1987) states, outside of public housing to a minor degree, and some Section 8, these programs were not aimed at the population, mainly singles and transients, at risk of becoming homeless. In fact only these two programs were aimed at the real low income.

In addition to little new subsidized housing, some of the present units are likely to be pulled out of the market, not only by sale of public housing units, but through arrangements made with investors in the contractual agreements for their investing in and building low rent housing under Section 8 new and rehabilitation programs, Section 236 and Section 221(d)(3). The investors received below market interest rates, with the provision of having the rents of the units at levels affordable to low and moderate income households (usually moderate income) or in Section 8, to 30% of their income. To encourage private sector participation, and to reduce long-term budget expenses, project owners were given the option of ending their participation at a future date, such as prepaying their 40 year mortgage after 20 years, for Sec. 236 and 221 (d)(3). For Section 8 project owners pre-1979 contracts were for five years, and after 1979 for a minimum of 15 to 20 years (Bay Area Housing Briefs, 1987e; Huttman, forthcoming). HUD data shows for San Francisco this means 2950 units can face early prepayment or contract opt-out, many in the next five years.

Another program, the locally-issued mortgage revenue bond housing, a major source of new units in San Francisco for low income, is also being cut back under the federal tax reform law. In 1985, in San Francisco 3789 units were produced under this program and 27 of these units were for low income. Under federal regulations at least 20% must be for low income (Bay Area Housing Briefs, 1987b).

In reality the number of affordable units is not large, as also true under other programs for affordable housing heralded by the City of San Francisco government such as the hotel tax contribution ($2.8 million a year) for low income senior housing or the funds given by developers of high-rise buildings in return for permission to build (Bay Area Housing Briefs, 1987b). A little more significant may be the inclusion of low and moderate income housing (after protests by concerned groups) in several new San Francisco large developments, for example the 300 acre Mission Bay area, with 7,700 housing units, with a goal of 30 percent affordable (now judged at around $650 monthly rent) (Bay Area Housing Briefs, 1987c). It is doubtful that much of this housing will find its way to the low income "at risk of displacement" or presently homeless.

Demand for Affordable Housing in San Francisco

As the above indicates, demand is high as rents go up. San Francisco has had a major upturn in immigration in the 1980s, first from the Vietnamese refugees who made it one of their major relocation destinations, then Central American refugees, and the increasing group of Mexican immigrants; in addition it has had a heavy influx of Filipinos, of Hong Kong residents leaving before Hong Kong's British rule terminates, of Korean and Taiwanese, and earlier, of Iranian refugees. All of this has added to housing demand. The Tenderloin, the traditional location of low income singles, has been inundated by Vietnamese and other Asian families. Chinatown has continued to be very densely populated.

Demand has also come from the many baby boomers forming their own households. Likewise it has come due to the continuing high divorce rate whereby one household turns into two. Until the Aids epidemic, demand came from gays from all over the country who were seeking a more comfortable urban environment. It came from runaways who considered it a haven from their family. Even from battered women demand developed, due to shelter and counseling programs.

This high demand for affordable housing is attested to by the long waiting lists for public housing and other subsidized housing; in San Francisco these waiting lists have run as high as 5000. Another indicator of demand is the degree of doubling up, with experts saying this has greatly increased (New York Times, April 5, 1987).

The Homeless and "At Risk" Group and Housing Demand

The size of the homeless population, and the increasing number of families and non-traditional homeless in this population, indicates that demand for low rent housing can not be met in San Francisco, where it is estimated that 8-10,000 are homeless (San Francisco Mayor's Taskforce on the Homeless Survey, 1986). Most homeless are without shelter because they can not afford the rent for the unit and/or the initial housing outlay, and/or they have been evicted from their housing. In the San Francisco Weeden and Linehan study (1987) they found that of elderly homeless and the "at risk of displacement" group, the main reason for housing need was financial. The 1986 National Coalition of the Homeless in its many city study found the same. In the San Francisco study a number said they ran out of money before the end of the month, with too many bills to pay. For a number their money was decreased by medical expenses as about two-thirds of them were physical disabled (though under MediCaid and MediCare in many cases). Those who ran out of money before the end of the month. A large proportion (46% had only an SSI check of $533 and some had less than that) were likely to spend part of a month in a SRO or apartment and part homeless in shelters, or on the street. (San Francisco shelters often must turn several hundred a night away.)

For those homeless with a job, three out of five still had financial problems that brought them to shelters. This is found for women, especially those with children, and for large families. In San Francisco while those in shelters are likely male (88.8% in Mayor's Survey, 1986) and white (55.1%) and between 20 and 44, an increasing number are families and female headed households. In some areas the latter group make up half the population. Witty (1986), in her study of San Francisco homeless women over 50, found a large number; she found a non-uniform pattern of alcohol consumption with some never drinking. The National Coalition of the Homeless reports that in several states such as Illinois and Massachusetts, homeless families by 1986 made up the majority of the homeless population. They also found in their 21 city survey that the homeless population had jumped 25% from 1985 to 1986.

Homeless women and especially families are often not in the shelter statistics because the shelter does not have facilities for them. McChesney (1986) found that "during 1985 and 1986 Los Angeles County had no county, state or federally funded shelters for homeless families"; five privately funded shelters were used. They were unable to accommodate the number of families seeking shelter, and second, were quickly discharged back on the street. Some shelters did use apartments (McChesney, 1986). Some shelters, of course, are only for battered women. Besides financial reasons, a reason for being homeless is because one has left a home where one is abused, or where divorce is in process; it may even be due to financial abuse as with elderly living with relatives (Weeden and Linehan, 1987).

As mentioned earlier, homelessness may be due to discharge from a mental health facility, board and care, or from a hospital. Weeden and Linehan (1987) found this true for their elderly homeless sample. And in New York City the Project Future survey found 9% of the homeless elders could not find an apartment after hospitalization or institutional discharge, 25% were no longer welcome in shared housing, and 59% were homeless due to eviction. In the San Francisco survey by Weeden and Linehan eviction was again a major reason. At the same time they found 9.3% of their homeless had been in board and care facilities and 6.1% in medical facilities.

While affordability was the main cause of housing need of those evicted, another cause of eviction and inability to relocate in another unit was the fact of high alcohol or drug use or mental illness or other disabilities. In every study this group makes up a large part of the total population. A number of these in the Weeden and Linehan study were no longer acceptable in the family home, where there was a family. In their study 41% were in contact with a mental health provider; 41% had substance use; 35% in shelters were confused; and again over 60% had a physical impairment. This was hardly a group that could even search for its own housing or face applying for subsidized units. But it was also a group that had a 40-50% portion who might not be the type of tenant desired by landlords, thus have a hard time getting in a tight housing market.

Conclusion:. Thus, the solution to the housing of this group can not be just regular subsidized apartments; there is need for renovated SROs; for some type of mental health facility for some; and alcohol abuse programs and special housing settings.

References

Bay Area Housing Data, 1986: Bay Area Housing Data: Rent Levels. *Bay Area Housing Briefs*, December.

----, 1987a: Bay Area Housing Data: Mortgage Revenue Bonds. From Production to Affordability. *Bay Area Housing Briefs*, January.

----, 1987b: Trends and Information. *Bay Area Housing Briefs*, January, pp. 1, 3.

----, 1987c: San Francisco/The Peninsual. (Draft Ordinance on Establishing SRO Standards.) *Bay Area Housing Briefs*. February, p. 3.

----, 1987d: Bay Area Housing Data: Rent Levels. *Bay Area Housing Briefs*, March.

----, 1987e: Special Issue: Potential Loss of Substandardized Housing. *Bay Area Housing Briefs*, April, pp. 1-3.

----, 1987f: Bay Area Housing Data: Building Permits. *Bay Area Housing Briefs*, May.

----, 1987g: Trends and Information. *Bay Area Housing Briefs*, May, p. 1-2.

Baar, K. and Keating, D., forthcoming: Rent Control in the U.S. In: E. Huttman and W. Van Vliet-- (eds.): *Handbook on Housing and the Built Environment.* Westport, CT: Greenwood.

Baxter, E. and Hopper, K., 1984: Troubled on the Streets. In: J. Talbott (ed.): *The Chronic Mental Patient.* New York: Greene and Stratton.

Bingham, R., Green, R.E. and White, S.B. (eds.), 1987: *The Homeless in Contemporary Society.* Newbury Park, CA.: Sage.

Business Week, 1987: Tax Reform Hurts Apartment Building. *Business Week*, May 4, p. 28.

Campbell, K.E., 1987: *Work Experience of the Homeless.* Paper presented at the Society for the Study of Social Problems. Chicago.

Carliner, M.S., 1987: Homelessness: A Housing Problem? In: R. Bingham, R.E. Green and S.B. White (eds.): *The Homeless in Contemporary Society.* Newbury Park, CA: Sage.

Downs, A., 1983: *Rental Housing in the 1980s.* Washington: The Brookings Institution.

Fainstein, N. and Fainstein, S.S., forthcoming: Urban Renewal. In: E. Huttman, E. and W. Van Vliet-- (eds.): *Handbook on Housing and the Built Environment.* Westport, CT: Greenwood.

Garland, S. and Reilly, J., 1987: Nowhere to Go: Dilemma of the Poor in America. *San Francisco Sunday Examiner and Chronicle*, April 19, pp. 1-8.

Goode, E., 1986: Hotel Owner Ousts Homeless - Mayor Gets Him to Relent. *San Francisco Chronicle*, October 11.

----, 1986: The Filthy Hotels for the Homeless. *San Francisco Chronicle,* October 10, p. 1.

----, 1986: Why S.F. Program for the Homeless Failed to Work. *San Francisco Chronicle,* October 13, p. 6.

---- **and Hsu, E.,** 1986: San Francisco Can't Handle the Homeless. *San Francisco Chronicle*, October 15, p. 6.

Harloe, M., forthcoming: Private Rental Housing. In: E. Huttman and W. Van Vliet-- (eds): *Handbook on Housing and the Built Environment.* Westport, CT: Greenwood.

----, 1985: *Private Rental Housing in the United States and Europe.* London: Croom Helm.

Hartman, C., forthcoming: Housing Affordability. In: E. Huttman and W. Van Vliet-- (eds.): *Handbook on Housing and the Built Environment.* Westport, CT: Greenwood.

----, **Keating, D. and LeGates, R.,** 1982: *Displacement - How to Fight It.* Berkeley: Legal Services Anti-Displacement Project.

Henslin, J., 1985: *Today's Homeless.* Paper presented at the Society for the Study of Social Problems Meeting. Washington, D.C. August.

Hoch, C.., 1986: Homeless in the United States. *Housing Studies* 1, 228-240.

---- **and Huth, M.J.,** forthcoming: The Problem of Homelessness in the United States. In: E. Huttman and W. Van Vliet--, W. (eds.): *Handbook on Housing and the Built Environment.* Westport, CT: Greenwood.

Huttman, E., 1985: Transnational Housing Policy. In: I. Attman and C. Werner (eds.): *Home Environment.* New York: Plenum.

-----, 1985: *Private Rental Housing Crisis.* Paper presented at the International Ad Hoc Committee on Housing and Built Environment Conference. Amsterdam. June.

----, 1985: Policy Approaches to Social Housing Problems in Northern and Western Europe. In: W. Van Vliet--, E. Huttman and S.F. Fava (eds.): *Housing Needs and Policy Approaches in Thirteen Countries.* Durham, NC: Duke University Press.

----, forthcoming: The Elderly and Housing. In: E. Huttman and W. Van Vliet-- (eds.): *Handbook on Housing and the Built Environment.* Westport, CT: Greenwood.

---- **and Huttman, J.,** 1986: *An Economic and Social Analysis of the International Private Rental Housing Crisis.* Paper presented at the International Housing Policy conference. Swedish National Institute of Building Research. Gaevle. June.

Kain, J., 1983: America's Persistant Housing Crises: Errors in Analysis and Policy. *Annals of the American Academy of Political and Social Science* 465, 136-149.

Kasinitz, P., 1984: Gentrification and Homelessness: The Single Room Occupant and the Inner City Revival. *Urban and Social Change Review* 17, 9-14.

Koch, J.Q., 1987: The Federal Role in Aiding the Homeless. In: R.D. Bingham, R.G. Green and S.B. White (eds.): *The Homeless in Contemporary Society.* Newbury Park, CA: Sage.

Lawson, R., 1984: *Owners of Last Resort*. New York: New York City Housing Preservation Department.

Marcuse, P., 1987: Isolating the Homeless. *The Nation*, April.

McChesney, K.Y., 1986: *Homeless Women and Their Children*. Unpublished report of Ford Foundation-funded project.

McLeod, R., 1987: Rent Subsidies for S.F. Poor Often Can't Be Used. *San Francisco Chronicle*, June 29, p. 8.

Murtagh, M., 1987: Government Housing Policy: The PEA Shooter Approach. Keys to Housing. *Eucumenical Association for Housing, San Raphael, CA., Newsletter* 11, p. 2.

National Association of Home Builders, 1986: *Low and Moderate Income Housing: Process, Problems, and Prospects*. Washington, D.C.: NAHB.

National Coalition for the Homeless, 1986a: *New Survey Shows Increase in Homelessness Since 1985*. Press Relase. New York.

----, 1986b: *Suit Filed Against HHS Seeks Relief for Families*. Press Release. New York.

New York Times, 1987: Stop Homelessness Before It Starts. *New York Times*, June 2, p. 34.

O'Connell, B., forthcoming: Cooperative and Condominium Conversions. In: E. Huttman and W. Van Vliet-- (eds.): *Handbook on Housing and the Built Environment*. Westport, CT: Greenwood.

Palen, J., forthcoming: Gentrification, Revitalization, and Displacement. In: E. Huttman and W. Van Vliet-- (eds): *Handbook on Housing and the Built Environment*. Westport, CT: Greenwood.

Pit, F. and W. Van Vliet--, W., forthcoming: Public Housing in the U.S. In: E. Huttman and W. Van Vliet-- (eds.): *Handbook on Housing and the Built Environment*. Westport, CT: Greenwood.

Project FUTURE, 1986: *Project Future: Focusing, Understanding, Targeting, and Utilizing Resources for the Homeless Mentally Ill*. New York: City Human Resources Administration.

----, no date: *Senior Center Survey of Elderly Homeless*. New York: Human Services Administration (Unpublished).

San Francisco Chronicle, 1986: Survey Tells Who Is Homeless in San Francisco. *San Francisco Chronicle*. October 13, p. 7.

San Francisco Housing Authority, 1987: Phone Interview. June 29.

San Francisco Mayor's Task Force on the Homeless, 1986: *One Night Survey of Homeless Shelters*. August (Unpublished).

San Francisco Residence Element, 1984: *The Residence Element of the Comprehensive Plan of the City and County of San Francisco*. Draft for Citizens' Review. San Francisco: Department of City Planning.

Stoner, M.R., 1984: An Analysis of Public and Private Sector Provisions for Homeless People. *Urban and Social Change Review* 17, 1, 3-8.

Snow, D., Baker, S.G., Anderson, L. and Michael, M., 1986: The Myth of Pervasive Mental Illness among the Homeless. *Social Problems* 33, 402-423.

Sullivan, P. and Damroch, S., 1987: Homeless Women and Children. In: R.D. Bingham, R.E. Green and S.B. White (eds.): *The Homeless in Contemporary Society*. Newbury Park, CA: Sage.

U.S. Bureau of the Census: *Annual Housing Survey. 1981 and 1984*. Washington, D.C.: GPO.

U.S. Census, 1987: *10.3 Million Vacant Housing Units*. Press Release. March 22.

U.S. Congressional Budget Office, 1981: *The Tax Treatment of Homeownership: Issues and Options*. Washington, D.C.: GPO.

U.S. General Accounting Office, 1983: *Changes in Rent Burdens and Housing Conditions of Lower Income Households*. GAO/RCED-85-108, April 23. Washington, DC.: GPO.

----, 1985: *Changes in Rent Burdens and Housing Conditions of Lower Income Households*. GAO/RCED-85-108, April 25. Washington, D.C.: GPO.

----, 1979: *Rental Housing: A National Problem that Needs Immediate Attention*. Washington, D.C.: GPO.

U.S. Conference of Mayors, 1984: *Report to the Secretary on the Homeless and Emergency Shelters*. Washington, D.C.: U.S. Department of Housing and Urban Development.

----, 1985: *The Growth of Hunger, Homelessness, and Poverty in America's Cities in 1985: A 25 City Survey*. Washington, D.C.: U.S. Department of Housing and Urban Development. Office of Policy Development and Research

Weeden, J. and Linedan, M., 1987: *Elders and Housing Displacement*. San Francisco: University of California Institute for Health and Aging.

Witty, C., 1986: *Homeless Women: Recent Research Findings*. Unpublished Abstract of research at U.C. San Francisco.

Wright, J.D., Rossi, P.H. et al., 1987: Homelessness and Health: The Effects of Life Style on Physical Well-Being among Homeless People in New York City. *Research in Social Problems and Public Policy* 4, Spring.

PATHS IN HOMELESSNESS:
A VIEW FROM THE STREET

Dennis Culhane and Marc Fried

Home is the place we belong to, the place which belongs to us. As the stationary sphere of our most private and personal thoughts and feelings, it provides a sense of stability and security as we move about in the environment. It is a precious resource for human well-being.

To be deprived of a home, to be homeless, is to confront the overwhelming sense of being cast out and outcast, to be naked and deserted in the most profoundly social sense. Given the extraordinary human capacity for tolerating the intolerable, for coping with depletion and destitution, even this experience is sometimes moderated, albeit at the expense of many human potentials. The initial realization, however, the dawning recognition that one is homeless is a terrifying experience for many homeless people. Listen to Manny: "When I began to realize that I was actually homeless, I had no place to go, it was a shock that you could never experience without going through ... I was riding the subway back and forth, trying to figure out who was I going to see, what friend of mine was going to be up that time of the night, that time of the morning. Where was I going to get my next meal at. I wasn't used to at that time walking around two or three days without a shower. I wasn't used to looking for a place to eat. I wasn't used to wearing the same clothes. These things, when I began to smell myself, these things told me something about society. These things told me that society says, "You are now unprotected. You are now no good to us". That's what it really told me. I was so hurt, I was so damned angry, and afraid to admit that I was homeless."

Manny has been homeless in a large mid-Western city for nearly two years. As he indicates in his interview, he did not want to admit his homelessness. To admit to himself that he was homeless was to feel, as another homeless man put it, "that you are unloved, unwanted, and that no one gives a crap about you". Estimates of those who are homeless in America vary greatly and, in fact, the actual numbers may vary considerably over time. But the millions who do find themselves without a home encounter a painful experience that is often obscured in analyses, statistics, or charitable agency plans. All too often, reports focus on manifest malfunctioning as a cause or consequence of homelessness, and without adequate attention to the disastrous conditions of life on the streets. A brief review of the literature reveals this clearly.

The last five years have seen a surge in research on and observations about homelessness. Many reports have appeared in the media and have figured prominently in public debate. The image of homelessness which has been popularized in the press

(Newsweek, January 6, 1986, p. 1), and encouraged by psychiatric research (see Arce, Tadlock, Vergare and Shapiro, 1985; Bachrack, 1984; Bassuk, 1984, 1986; Bassuk, Rubin and Lauriat, 1984; Jones, 1983; Lamb, 1984; Lipton, Sabatini and Katz, 1983) has characterized the homeless as mentally disabled, disorganized persons, many of whom are castoffs of mental health systems (deinstitutionalization). While it is generally acknowledged that psychological disabilities and inadequate aftercare for mental patients account for some part of the problem of homelessness, the extent to which homelessness is primarily a mental health problem has been vigorously debated (Landers, 1987). Mental health advocates and government officials have been accused of over-stating and over-emphasizing disabilities among the homeless, or "blaming the victims", while housing advocates have been accused of ignoring the fact that the homeless "need more than homes", i.e., health services, education, domestic skills, institutional care.

But the primary focus of existing psychological and psychiatric research has been to explain homelessness by characteristics of the homeless themselves. Whether it is alcoholism (Garret, 1986), chronic psychoses (Bassuk, 1984), personality disorders (Arce et al., 1983), criminal histories (Bassuk, 1984), or abusive tendencies (Bassuk, 1986), homelessness is depicted as a consequence of the problems of homeless people. However, reported prevalence rates of mental illness vary from 20% to 91% (Crystal and Goldstein, 1983; Bassuk et al., 1984) and reports of previous psychiatric hospitalization vary from 10% to 35% (Crane, 1984; Arce et al., 1983): Such *widely* discrepant estimates raise questions about the validity of these research findings and their traditional, diagnostic focus.

Existing studies are problematic for the following methodological and theoretical reasons. (1) Sampling procedures have generally relied upon emergency shelters for men for subjects; shelters, at best, represent only a portion of the homeless population and may introduce their own bias. (2) The class bias and other diagnostic problems of professional psychiatry make the accuracy of diagnosis questionable. Yet, no studies have measured the inter-judge reliability of the diagnoses of homeless people. (3) In these reports it is widely assumed on the basis of correlational data that mental illness causes homelessness, but the hypotheses that homelessness leads to mental illness or is an intervening factor are equally plausible. (4) The deepening problem of homelessness in America among families and working people raises serious questions about the utility of formulating the homelessness debate within a professional discourse such as psychiatry which almost entirely overlooks, not only the social and economic context generally, but quite specifically the enormous costs of housing and the continuing decline of affordable housing in the United States (Even the most sympathetic of these reports, which steer clear of blaming the victim, nonetheless fail to appreciate the potent problem of affordable housing as a major determinant of homelessness). These problems not only suggest alternate avenues for epidemeological research but reveal the need for a deeper understanding of the issues involved. One critical source of information stems from the effort to enable and empower the voices of those who are themselves homeless. And it is our purpose here to allow the homeless to speak for themselves, to present their stories, so we can begin to unravel the complex paths into homelessness. Interviews have been conducted with homeless men and women who are leaders of the National Union of the Homeless, and are quoted here to create a space for the voices of those who are themselves the victims of this serious, worldwide problem.

Disruption and Loss

The literature on stress has familiarized us with the fact that the traumatic events and conditions, the undermining experiences that are encompassed within the term stress, often involve a lag-time before their effects become manifest. And in the intervening stages, many different economic, social, and psychological changes may take place which lead down the path of destitution and the loss of a home. Indeed, more than half the people we interviewed began their stories with the fact that they no longer had a home but were unable to confront the devastating reality of homelessness.

For Jim, a middle-aged man who lived in a metropolitan area in the South, "a bad divorce" began his search for a new life. "I foolishly quit my job. I had $1,500.00 with me, and I went to Miami and I figured I'd easily get a job 'cause I can type. I've done a number of jobs in my life, and I figured it would be very easy." Only able to find sporadic employment through temporary labor pools, Jim's money ran out, and he could no longer afford a week's rent for a room. All of the eight people interviewed have similar stories of a life disruption, followed by living with friends, relatives, in a car, or in cheap rented rooms, until finally money runs out. The initial disruptions were as varied as a business failure, divorce, domestic abuse, layoffs, eviction, or escaping a living situation embroiled with drugs. And, despite intense economic and personal stress, despite many courageous and many desperate efforts to keep things together, to maintain a modicum of stability, all of these men and women were swept into the streets sooner or later.

As with other stress experiences and consequences, the road to homelessness is usually a slow transformation. As one man describes it: "It was a gradual thing ... spending some period of time with friends, and really very rapidly, very quickly wearing out my welcome there. So that was a slow process, and all the time money was very swiftly moving away from me. I was spending and nothing was coming in. Looking for jobs and job interviews, and food, and trying to maintain my clothes, and plus a car."

Roger's realization of his being homeless came after months of struggling to recover from a business failure: "My business went bankrupt and my whole life fell apart. I guess there was no question, even though I started sleeping in the car, and on very cold nights staying in the Third Street shelter in New York City, I still didn't consider myself homeless until the car was vandalized, my clothes were stolen, and I was completely broke. In fact it was just such a shock that the moment that I realized that I was homeless without clothes, without any material things at all, and that I was just absolutely naked in the world ..., I ended up in Bellevue Hospital, in the psych ward there."

Another man, Richard, worked for sixteen years with a company that began farming out work to cheaper overseas labor. Consequently, Richard lost his job and became homeless. Yet, as he and the others were quick to detail, the conditions which one finds for the homeless are inadequate at best, and often cruel and damaging in their own right. Shocked by his own homelessness, now Richard faces a world of temporary labor pools, emergency shelters, long food lines, and harassment from police, thugs, and thieves. But that first, forced recognition of the very *fact* of his homelessness was most demoralizing. After working a long day on temporary labor, Richard sat down one evening in the subway to catch some sleep. "I was awakened about 2:00 in the morning", he reports, "by four policemen and two German Shepherd dogs. And I just sat down there and I said to myself, you know I did everything I was supposed to do. I went to school, I was mischievous as a child, but not a violent child. I went in the service. I came out of service. I worked. I took care of my children. Why? Why is this happening to me? And I started blaming myself for it, you know, and I felt my sanity sort of slipping away from me, because at that moment I wanted to attack the policemen and the dogs".

Initial Stresses

For most of the homeless people we interviewed, the shock of the recognition of their homelessness was so stark and sudden because they were totally unprepared for this situation on the basis of childhood or adult experience. And, in fact, the combination of events and chance occurrences could rarely have been anticipated. Manny tells about his tragic experience: "First of all, I have to say I worked from the time I knew what work was up until the time I got laid off. I used to work for a food distributor ... Two days before Thanksgiving in 1984 I was laid off. The impact ... I really hate to think about that. It was a situation that Thanksgiving time, two days away, you're all hyped up and then someone snatches the rug out from under you. I had an apartment. I was paying $400 a month rent, I had a telephone ... and a house full of furniture, a car, and I mean I had what society says makes you wealthy. And I worked hard to get it ... And when I was told that I was laid off, my American dream went down the stream. When I got back out there, in the rat race, applying for a job and putting in applications and, at the same time, trying to figure out what am I going to do with my stuff, my personal belongings. I had a ten year stamp collection. And when I seen that stamp collection disappear, I just said fuck it ...".

Richard, whose job loss we previously described when his factory declined under foreign competition, tells a similar story. "I have worked all my teenage and adult life", he says. "I never was out of work longer than a week at any time in my life". He was one of the last three people to be kept on in the factory where he worked. "And", he goes on, "at that particular time jobs just weren't there, or .. the type of jobs that was there I had no training for, even though I had a high school education. So after my employment compensation exhausted, I had to give up the apartment ... because surely welfare wasn't enough at that time ... So I went out there into Southern New Jersey ... and worked out there on the farms ... picking peaches, and then when the apple season came, I went out there picking apples. They pay you minimum wage ... You worked nine hours if you were lucky ... You have to get up 3:00 in the morning ... We'd all meet at this one place in order to catch the bus. And there you ran into a problem also ... There's one bus, and there's about 150-200 people who want to try to get on that bus. And the bus only takes between 40 and 45 people. So if you made it then, all right, so then you go to work. If you worked there nine hours, then you made thirty dollars and fifteen cents. Now if you are homeless and don't have anywhere to go, the next morning you're lucky if you got $10 or $15 still in your pocket. Why? Because you spend more money being homeless in the street. You go into a restaurant and eat and pay five or six dollars on a meal ... You cannot go in, being homeless, you can't go and buy enough food, then cook it, and what you don't eat you put away...".

And then there is Darlene. She says: "My story surrounds low-income, affordable housing and in the fact of being in an abusive situation. In 1985 I was pregnant, five months pregnant. I was ill at the time and had to be hospitalized. As she indicates later, this was due to a beating and a kick in the stomach from her batterer. "The doctors stated", she goes on, "that they didn't want me to work ... so I had to stop working ... I could no longer afford my apartment and from the hospital I went straight into a shelter ... They placed me in a battered women's shelter, which I ended up staying in ... for a total of 13 months. My son was born during that time, and I just felt so lost, so alone ... I spent six years in the army, and I've always had an excellent work history. I attended college, I was a student majoring in sociology ... I am a cosmetologist but there was nothing ... there weren't any jobs, and there wasn't any daycare in the shelter ... My son was a newborn infant, and I couldn't even afford milk, so I had to breastfeed my son".

Generally, the tragic histories have a great deal in common. In only one of these instances do we have a situation involving drugs, a pattern that may represent a sub-group quite different from those homeless people we interviewed. But even Josh's situation reflected his getting caught up in circumstances he could no longer control and finding himself gradually becoming homeless. "The guy I was sharing an apartment with", he tells us, "was always into cocaine, smoking, even before we got the apartment together. But I figured, you know, I didn't and that I could continue to not deal with drugs and cocaine. Living under them conditions I was wrong. Him, his lady, a couple of friends would come over, they would have smoke parties ... and that leads on after you get high, the fun, the activity, the women. It tends to draw you in and make you want to be a part of that. So eventually I got into it, and ... cocaine isn't something to get into because if you get into it, you'll like it ...". Homelessness, in Josh's case, was inevitable because, as he says, "Every bit of money you make is going towards getting drugs, staying high, you know, just getting high every day. You work, you live to get high tomorrow".

Life on the Streets

Living on the streets as a homeless person means spending your days - and nights - in dark, forbidding, and unforgiving passages. The initial stresses that precipitate or implement the misfortunes of homelessness are further compounded by unremitting bruises and barriers. Daytime has its massive problems. Nighttime has its terrors. For the majority who are not able to get a bed in an emergency shelter, they must develop their own means for making it through the night.

First, of course, there is the necessity of sleeping, to be capable of searching for a job or an apartment. One of the men describes sleeping on the subway. "When you get to the end of the line there's always another train waiting to go back on the other side. Go back north or south. I seen pickpockets work on the L. You pull into every station and you open up one eye because you don't want nobody picking your pocket. You ain't got nothing, it's just a thing that you would normally do. Sense of security for yourself. I've slept in the back of cars, also slept in abandoned buildings, not thinking of the danger of the roof collapsing, the dangers of the rat bite, the danger of just the walls collapsing. You know you're tired, who cares about that shit when you're tired. You just want to go in and lay down. Basically on the street sleeping in those conditions, you don't get a good two hours straight sleep. You're always waking up, you know, noise on the street, noise within the building".

Another man, Jim, describes it this way, "You're not able to sleep because wherever you sleep you're, someone is going to challenge you, even when you stay in Charity Hospital. The guard will come around and say, are you a patient here, and somehow, they'll kick you out ... You sleep in an abandoned house, you don't know if the police are going to come in and arrest you, or if some crook or robber is going to come in and hurt you while you're asleep. At least three homeless men since I've been in New Orleans have been found dead, beaten to death, in these abandoned buildings".

Richard explains that he sometimes avoids shelters, "I was opposed to going into a shelter because I had heard about shelters in the city, and I know how it's run, and I knew there was no way in hell I was going to endure that abusive treatment, inhumane treatment, that exists in these shelters ... and I couldn't see my life being dependent on someone ... So you get varied (sleep) because you sleep with fear. See, a lot of the times we are victims of being mugged ourselves because we are very vulnerable. Why are we vulnerable? Because number one we are deprived of food, we don't get the proper rest. So therefore we are weakened to whoever decides they want to mug us, or rob us, or anything. They usually hang around the welfare offices, and watch whoever comes and goes, and then they walk down a street, a dark alley at night, sometimes we ourselves are robbed ... You're living in fear of your life also, as well as your health".

But it is not only the difficulties of finding a place and a way to sleep. The same problems attend every aspect of life: eating, shelter from the elements, going to the toilet, taking a shower, finding a way to look respectable in seeking a job, and trying to get medical help.

Manny talks about trying to use the bathrooms in a local college. "We used to sneak in through the side doors. ... It's a public building but they don't want people in there who's not going to school. But ... my tax dollars helped to build that school. ... Some of us who like to clean ourselves carry some soap and a rag or something. When you get around some hot water that's the first thing you want to use. For those of them who do want to shave, they got a razor, just use the McDonald's up there. ... You can't keep yourself up, make yourself presentable even when you do go looking for jobs; you still look like a bum...".

And Richard talks about the humiliation of trying to get medical treatment. As he talks, other sources of his anger and sense of maltreatment begin to well up. "When you go to the hospital and tell them that number one, you don't have a medical card, they'll just band-aid you, give you a pill and send you back out there on the streets because, I mean, you're nothing to them ... And that's the people that turn and call us drunks. That's not really so. Sometimes people buy drinks, or buy a bottle of wine. It might be cold out there. This is the way that they get warm. They just get drunk, and there's heat in there, or just because all day long they had, all the shit they had to go through. All the elements of eating, of sleeping, just merely surviving".

It is evident that, certainly for many of the homeless, the path to functioning effectively, to getting back to a decent way of living, is fraught with myriad and often wholly unreasonable impediments. Darlene finds this to be so up to the very last. After many struggles, she finally was able to obtain a 707 housing subsidy certificate (allows people to rent housing in the private market and receive some part of their rental cost from the federal government). As she says, "... with that certificate you have to still, you have to run around the whole city and try to find some realtor or some landlord that will accept the certificate ... So I moved into (an) apartment after thirteen months of being homeless, and it was a rat infested, sleazy, rundown place. So I'm still homeless. Right now I'm homeless. I cannot accept this as being home. I'm still trying to get on my feet. I need, I don't even have forks. ... you find a place to live, then you have to find a way to survive in that empty shell of a house ... So you're still depressed at each and every angle. Where's the way out?"

Finally, Jim describes an encounter with the police which shows how the homeless continue to be exploited for cheap or free labor, subject to the whims of the police. "A van will come around and we hear the officers in the van joking that they need so many people, and this is why we're around today, and they sometimes they ask you if you have any medical problems like once I was sleeping underneath a bridge, and they came around, and they hadn't been around, I understand they hadn't been around in weeks or months, and they said, we need a lot of people to work. We need a lot of prisoners. And they ask you your medical history, whether you have any problems, and I told them I had a heart problem, but they realized I was bullshitting ... The people who seemed in good shape, they piled them in the van and took them to jail, and after that they started working

... They come up with these amazing charges and every time you see a homeless person he pulls out his arrest sheet says look what they got me on this time and everybody has a big laugh about it, but it's really frustrating and makes you just feel angry".

The threat of arrest, and the subsequent problems which that causes, such as loss of a job, or a potential criminal record, these are used as forces to continue taming the homeless, as well as fulfilling the need in the society to have certain public, menial labor done, which no one wants to do. These are among the forces that shape the social construction of the homeless and their homelessness. The very agencies that are designed to ameliorate the most urgent features of the problems of the homeless, the shelters, mainly serve to sustain the sense of degradation and powerlessness. The threat of losing a bed, and the struggle to obtain entrance to the shelters, and the dangers of victimization, help to keep the homeless docile in this site which only exacerbates their helplessness.

The Shelter System

Superficially women and families receive more consideration in their efforts to stay within shelters than do single men but, more often than not, they all share the shocking and obscene life of the temporary shelters. A phenomenon hailed as a solution by many government officials indeed is one of the cruelest forms of bureaucratic dehumanization.

Darlene, whose situation we described in earlier sections, was battered by her husband, and found herself in need of emergency shelter. Actually giving birth to her son in a shelter, without childcare available she was forced to take her newborn son with her everywhere, searching for a job, for an apartment, and spending hours in the burger King to keep warm and to breastfeed her baby. "I wasn't getting the proper care, the healthcare, or anything that I needed. The counselors, in fact, they would speak about things right in front of our faces as though we ... weren't comprehending what they would say. There was a particular incident that happened at one of the shelters, the battered women's shelters ... where the staff actually was stealing the food. Me and the other women in the household had to sneak down in the cellars after midnight and the freezers were bound with chains and we had to try to lift up that freezer to get food for that week and to feed our families that were in the shelter. The shelter providers were taking our necessities, our basic necessities, for surviving in there; they were taking our toilet tissue, our soaps, I mean everything, our deodorants, I mean you know, it's unfair. It's unfair".

The shelter system serves to ameliorate the guilt of society by its appearance of harboring the down and out, the homeless. In fact it only serves to keep people alive and communicates its message o the homeless, that keeping alive is all that can be done for them. As institutions of social control, the shelters tend to confirm people's self-blame, to increase their feelings of helplessness, and to perpetuate their powerlessness by denying virtually all opportunities to allow people to control their own lives. In the rituals of obtaining food and shelter, the homeless are forced to be utterly dependent and without a voice, often denied even the minimal chances to improve their situations.

Roger provides a graphic picture of what one can expect to see if one becomes homeless and must rely on an emergency shelter. Turned away by his brother for a place to stay, Roger tells us, "I walked to the center of the city, and met a policeman, and told him I was stranded overnight ... and was there someplace I could spend the night, because I was without funds. And he directed me to the city-run Drop In Center. And I went around and they rang the bell, and they sent me around to the back. And in the back alley, in the back of the shelter, there were about 200 people in all states, some drinking. People huddled around a can, a 55-gallon can with dropped wood fire in it. Some people at the steam vents. I mean I just couldn't believe the whole amount of people. And at some point the back door opened and a kind of man came out. He was a counselor and announced that women came in first and all the women went in and when the women went in, it was just a free-for-all. People fighting, men fighting their way in. And I went through that for three days and three nights and I just never got in ... For two nights I said I'm not going to go through this bullshit, I'm not going to be fighting no one to get inside. I also said look, they're like animals, they're fighting like animals. I'm not going through this shit, ... I won't dignify this kind of bullshit by engaging in it. But on the third night I was completely exhausted, and just decided that I was going to fight my way in. And they said women in, and after the women went in I fought my way in and went in. What I fought to get in was a basement where they had fifty chairs and as you go down the steps there's a counselor at the head of the steps that gives you a peanut butter and jelly sandwich. And you go downstairs, and at that time there was some coffee there, and they let in men and women. And there were fifty hard back chairs that you sat in all night 'til six o'clock in the morning and then they'd turn you out at six o'clock in the morning".

Tired, full of anger and shame, the homeless are pitted against one another to get even a chair in a basement on which to rest. Roger continues, "After I got a nice rest, my thing with the counselor was where can I go look for a job at, could I use this place as a reference, can I use a typewriter to type a resume, can I use the telephone, can I go out, you know during the daytime, and look for some work, and then come in at night. And people looked at me like I was some kind of weird animal from a strange planet. Absolutely not, that everything that I said was against the policies of that organization, that once I was in there I had to stay for the three days, and then be released on the third day, and then wait a week, and then I could come back again for three more days ... And that's it. People laid around for those three days, watched television, played cards, and that was essentially it".

The shelters exist as a private-public partnership, and in every city, the number of people far outnumbers existing beds. The shelters function on implicit assumptions that create invalids among those who are disabled, and downgrade the needs of those who are not disabled, but in need of assistance to locate jobs, job training and housing. By derogating and downgrading, shelter providers are exonerated from any responsibilities except those of keeping some homeless alive. But the shelter providers are merely low-level proxies for societal attitudes. In a Southern city, Jim tells us that "At the Salvation Army (they have) 200 beds, and at Baptist Mission about 300. So they've got roughly 600 beds for 4,000 homeless people." Unlike other cities, the only existing shelters actually charge people $5-$8 per night. Manny explains the role of shelters this way, "The shelter system was established to help keep you in that binding condition. *You* are there. *They're* getting paid. They don't want to see you leave. All they want is a head count ... They don't even care if that's my name ... Suppose I'm supposed to be taking medication. They should know that. Suppose I've got relatives in the south, and suppose I die. They should know that. They don't take this kind of information. All they take is a body count ... They ought to know how to identify people for what they are, and not for what they think they are ... Once there were times when I had to get up in the morning to go apply for a job and I tell them they had to wake me up at 5:00 in the morning. He oversleeps. I oversleep, and therefore I can't leave the shelter system. So then therefore I'm totally dependent on them again, as long as I keep coming to them, as long as homeless people keep going to the shelters, and as long as the shelters keep saying 'well, what else can we do?' They don't -- the shelter system do not consult homeless people for what they know their needs are. The shelter system sits there and dictates what they think the homeless people's needs are. The homeless people don't have any input, as to the rules of the shelter, what is needed in the shelter, how do we view the shelter".

Silenced, excluded, and left to fight for survival, this is the outcome of perceptions of the homeless which make them undeserving, and in characteristic fashion result in blaming the victims. In this way, the shelters and the labor market together encourage dependency upon a Band-Aid system of temporary and emergency services.

Conclusion

During the past year and even more recently than that, increased attention to the homeless has modified, without entirely altering, the stigmatization of the homeless. In focusing mainly on the language, observation, and thoughts of the homeless themselves, we have tried to fill in some large lacunae and to compensate for other reports. Frequently, the discussions by psychiatrists, social scientists, and public officials try to explain the conditions of the homeless in terms of characteristics of the homeless themselves. Much of this discussion virtually ignores the economic, social, and cultural contexts in which homelessness occurs and opts for an individualistic psychologism. The homeless and the conditions of homelessness are presented as caricatures, frozen in a space which silences them, makes them into outlandish images of tramps, bums, alcoholics and psychotics. Some meager factors that may, indeed, provide a partial accounting for some small proportion of the homeless population, are generalized beyond all warrant. Even the sympathetic discussions often view the homeless as unfortunate failures without adequately evaluating the ways in which our society facilitates the process of skidding economically, socially, psychologically. Thus, the discussion is wrapped around the homeless, to cloak them in a pseudo-explanatory otherness which ends up controlling them *and* our understanding of them.

For these reasons we have felt it essential to tell of the suffering, the anguish, and the painful realization which accompanies the paths to homelessness. In this sense, we have tried to provide a place for homeless people to contest the naming and stigmatization which silences them and to challenge the formulation of homelessness which relegate them to an undignified, dehumanized space.

Not only are the realities of homelessness graphic statements about advanced capitalist society, perhaps about all mass societies, but they point to ways in which such abuse and inhumanity is sustained. Primary among these staying forces is the language which keeps homeless people in powerless positions, which isolates them from access to gaining stability and control in their lives. Throughout the interviews there are stories of strategies used by people to survive. But time and time again, the homeless are met with the most absurd of circumstances. Trying to locate a bathroom, a place to shower, waiting four hours in line for soup and a stale sandwich: these are some of the countless examples of ways in which society encourages the demeaning and degradation of a whole mass of people who are already suffering from inadequate resources. Moreover, the care systems that society has established serve more of a function of sustaining dependency and powerlessness, than of mobilizing people for real change. Without attempting a detailed examination of the options for coping with the problems of homelessness, a brief example may help to point to one important direction.

As was stated earlier, the people interviewed for this paper are members of the National Union of the Homeless. The National Union was founded in Philadelphia in October, 1985, by homeless people, for the collective empowerment of the homeless, socially and politically. The strategy of the organization has been to disrupt service agencies, governmental forums, construction projects, and tourist districts, to call attention to the anger and militancy of homeless people. Chris Sprowal, himself homeless, and a former labor organizer, led 6,000 of Philadelphia's homeless in winning voting rights, the right to shelter, better pay and fairness from the temporary labor pools, and better access to employment training and education. After three years of sit-ins, blockades, building take-overs, and protests, Mayor Wilson Goode of Philadelphia agreed in March to give the Philadelphia Union 200 units of housing and $7.2 million.

The Union of the Homeless has now organized in 10 cities across the U.S., and claims a membership in 1987 of some 20,000 people. In each city, common themes emerge, and common political struggles. A popular tactic with the homeless has been the take-over of emergency shelters, a tactic unpopular with service providers and many homeless advocates. But the locals have maintained that the seizure of power at the shelters represents the unfettering of the population, and makes possible the movement of empowerment and social change among the homeless. In fact, two locals now run shelters, and have used them as organizing and leadership training centers. These shelters are entirely staffed by homeless people, and each offers literacy programs, job-placement programs, and community organizing classes. The Union of the Homeless is just one example of how involving victims in the challenge of their own circumstances helps to enlighten research and policy, but more importantly, it helps people to re-capture the dignity which they lose in the face of narrowly defined services and degrading living conditions.

Roger, in a deeply philosophical vein closes the issue for us: "We cannot continue to live where we have 'haves' and 'have-nots' in the wealthiest nation in the world. And we cannot continue to talk about millions of dollars going to dictatorships in other countries and building things like Star Wars and upping the arms race. We have people who live in poverty who go to bed hungry at night being born in shelters; born homeless in the richest country in the world. I don't think that we have any other choice but to be out there organizing, but to be galvanizing, but to be saying that we have to look for something that's going to work for us, we have to take government back and get it going. We have to run it on a fair and equal basis, not on your ability to have money and the whole question that we're a commodity. Homeless people have become a commodity in this country. In fact, we have become a growth industry. That alone tells me how sinister this kind of system is, that we can make a profit off the misery of homeless and poor people, and we have to change it".

References

Arce, A., Tadloc, M. Vergare, M. and Shapiro, O. S., 1983: A Psychiatric Profile of Street People Admitted to an Emergency Shelter. *Hospital and Community Psychiatry* 34, 812-817.

Backrack, L., 1984: Interpreting Research on the Homeless Mentally Ill: Some Caveats. *Hospital and Community Psychiatry* 34, 914-916.

Bassuk, E., 1984: The Homelessness Problem. *Scientific American* 251, 40-45.

----, 1986: *Characteristics of Massachusetts Sheltered Homeless Families.* Paper presented at Homelessness Conference, Harvard Medical School. Cambridge, MA.

----, Rubin, L. and Lauriat, A., 1984: Is Homelessness a Mental Health Problem? *American Journal of Psychiatry* 141, 1546-1550.

Crane, S., 1984: *Rhode Island MH-HR Department Reports on the Homeless Mentally Ill.* State Report, National Association of State Mental Health Program Directors. Washington, DC.

Crystal, S. and Goldstein, M., 1983: *New Arrivals: First-Time Shelter Clients.* New York: Human Resources Administration.

Garret, G., 1986: *Alcoholism and the Homeless.* Paper presented at the Homelessness Conference, Harvard Medical School. Cambridge, MA.

Jones, R., 1983: Street People and Psychiatry: An Introduction. *Hospital and Community Psychiatry* 34, 807-811.

Lamb, H., 1984: Deinstitutionalization and the Homeless Mentally Ill. *Hospital and Community Psychiatry* 35 (a), 899-907.

Landers, S., 1987: Homeless Families: Roots of Crisis Debated. *The APA Monitor* 18a, 4-5.

Lipton, F., Sabatini, A. and Katz, S., 1983: Down and Out in the City: The Homeless Mentally Ill. *Hospital and Community Psychiatry* 34, 817-821.

Newsweek, 1986: Abandoned: They are America's Castoffs - Turned Away from Mental Institutions and Into the Streets. Who Will Care for Them? *Newsweek*, January 6, 1986, p.1.

ABOUT THE AUTHORS

Dennis Culhane is currently doctoral candidate in Psychology at Boston College, Chestnut Hill, MA, U.S.A. He does research on social inequality and its psychological effects. He has worked with the National Union of the Homelessness for the past two years, most recently serving as the National Director of Technical Assistance and Organizing.

Jane Darke is currently a lecturer in housing, administration and policy at Sheffield City Polytechnic. She has researched, taught and written extensively on housing including an introductory text *Who Needs Housing* 1979 Macmillan (with Roy Darke) and a doctoral thesis *The Design of Public Housing: Architects' Intentions and Users Reactions* (1983). From 1983 to 1987 she worked in housing management in local authority area teams in Sheffield and Haringey, London.

Roy Darke is Director of Urban Studies, University of Sheffield. He has researched and written in the areas of housing, local government, public participation, town planning, planning theory and policy-making. His current interests in housing in the developing world was fired by recent visits to Central America and India. Recent action research undertaken includes work as principal consultant to Sheffield City Council on public participation in the central area plan and running an advisory service for community organisations seeking help with building and environmental projects.

Dan Ferrand-Bechman is Maitre des Conférences at the University of Grenoble and deputeee at the Department of Social Affairs and Employment in Paris. Her major interest is in housing problems and participation of dwellers in cities of Western Europe. She has contributed chapters to several French and English scholarly publications..

Marc Fried is currently Professor of Psychology and research professor of Human Sciences at Boston College, Chestnut Hill, MA, U.S.A. He has studied the role of the neighborhood, community life and the determinants of residential, community and life satisfactions. Along with his long-term studies of stress and malfunctioning, he has more recently become involved with the study of adult developmental changes and the social factors associated with mental disorder. He also has been examining homelessness and the dynamics of victimization.

Jürgen Friedrichs is Professor of Sociology in the Department of Sociology, University of Hamburg, and Director of the Center for Comparative Urban Sociology. He is a Senior Fellow of the Metro Center of the Johns Hopkins University, Baltimore. He has done extensive studies on urban structure and change of cities in Western and Eastern Europe, downtown development, urban unemployment (with John D. Kasarda), social ecology, and urban theory. Among the more recent publications are: *The Changing Downtown* (1987) and Large Cities in Eastern Europe (In: *The Metropolis Era*, Vol. 1, edited by M. Dogan and J.D. Kasarda, 1988). He has edited and co-authored *Urban Development in Western and Eastern Europe* (1985) and *Cities in the 1980s* (1985) He is currently working on problems of spatial effects of new technologies.

Ray Forrest, is teaching at the School for Advanced Urban Studies at the University of Bristol, Bristol, U.K. His major interest is in housing problems and housing policy. On these topics he has published several articles in international scholarly journals.

Elizabeth Huttman is Professor of Sociology at California State University, Hayward, and was formerly professor at the University of British Columbia and Visiting Scholar at the University of California Berkeley. She is co-editor of *Housing Needs and Policy Approaches: Trends in Thirteen Countries* (1985); author of *Housing and Social Services for the Elderly* (1977); *Handbook of Housing* (1988), and *Introduction to Social Policy* (1981). She has written chapters on housing in many books. She is co-organizer of the International Sociological Association Committee on Housing and the Built Environment. Her special interests are comparative housing policy and housing affordability.

Arne Karyd, master of economics and political science, is affiliated to the University of Gothenburg and the consulting organization GSU. Earlier reports and papers cover mainly various issues within the construction and housing sectors, energy conservation and planning, railway economy, and democracy within the planning process. Present work deals with the forrest industry and the cost structure in domestic air traffic.

Antonin Kerner is Professor of Economics at the Charles University in Prague, CSSR. His major fields of interest and publication are the changes in the economic structure and the role of the service sector in socialist countries, urban change, and housing policies. Among his more recent publications are *The Scientific-Technological Revolution and the Development of Services* (1975), and *Perspectives of the Service Sector* (1982).

Alan Murie is Senior Lecturer at the School for Advanced Urban Studies at the University of Bristol, Bristol, U.K. He has recently edited *Living in Bed and Breakfast: The Experience of Homelessness in London* (1987).

David C. Thorns is Professor of Sociology and Head of the Department of Sociology of the University of Canterbury, Cristchurch, New Zealand. He has done reasearch on suburbanization, urban change, and housing problems and policies in Australia and New Zealand. He has published books and written articles in several international scholarly journals. Among his recent publications is Owner Occupation, the State, and Class Relations in New Zealand (in *In the Public Interest*, edited by C. Wilkes and I. Shirley, 1983).

Wouter Turpijn is Associate Professor in urban studies, University of Utrecht, The Netherlands, Department of Urban and Industrial Studies. He is the author of books and articles on sociological and interdisciplinary reserach on urban development, renewal and maintenance; dwellers' participation and self-help housing, including e.g., self-building by dwellers and the actions of communes, dweller-organizations and squatters.

Willem van Vliet-- is an urban and environmental sociologist at the University of Colorado, Boulder, U.S.A. His research interests concern international housing, neighborhood and community planning, and the environmental requirements of women, children, and the elderly. He has contributed widely to anthologies and journals in urban studies, planning, and environment-behavior studies and is editor or co-editor of seven books, including *Housing Markets and Policies under Fiscal Authority (1987), Women, Housing and Community* (in press), and the *International Handbook of Housing Policies and Practices* (forthcoming).

Dieter Frick (Editor)
The Quality of Urban Life
Social, Psychological and Physical Conditions

1986. 17 x 24 cm. X, 262 pages. With 35 illustrations. Cloth.
ISBN 3 11 010577 2; 0-89925-095-5 (U.S.)

Hans-Jürgen Ewers / John B. Goddard / Horst Matzerath (Editors)
The Future of the Metropolis
Berlin – London – Paris – New York
Economic Aspects

1986. 17 x 24 cm. XII, 484 pages. Cloth.
ISBN 3 11 010498 9; 0-89925-096-3 (U.S.)

J. Friedrichs / A. C. Goodman et al.
The Changing Downtown
A Comparative Study of Baltimore and Hamburg

1987. 17 x 24 cm. X, 256 pages. Cloth.
ISBN 3 11 011113 6; 0-89925-274-5 (U.S.)

Richard P. Schaedel / Jorge E. Hardoy / Nora Scott-Kinzer (Editors)
Urbanization in the Americas from its Beginnings to the Present

1978. XII, 676 pages. Cloth.
ISBN 90 279 7530 2 (World Anthropology). Mouton de Gruyter

Poul Ove Pedersen
Urban-regional Development in South America. The Process of Diffusion and Integration

1975. XVI, 294 pages. With figures, maps and tables, summary in Danish. Cloth.
ISBN 90 279 7631 7; PB. ISBN 90 279 7753 4 (Regional Planning). Mouton de Gruyter

WALTER DE GRUYTER · BERLIN · NEW YORK

Genthiner Straße 13, D-1000 Berlin 30, Phone (0 30) 2 60 05-0, Telex 1 83 027
200 Saw Mill River Road, Hawthorne, N.Y. 10532, Phone (914) 747-0110, Telex 646677

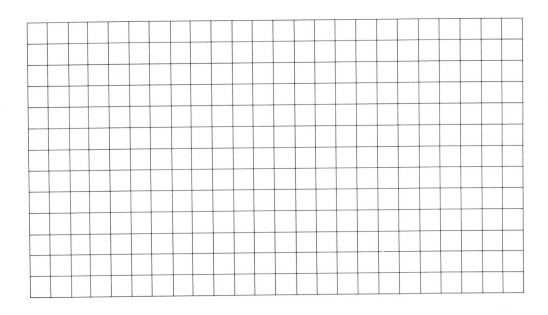

**INFORMATION
TECHNOLOGY
AND
CIVILIZATION**

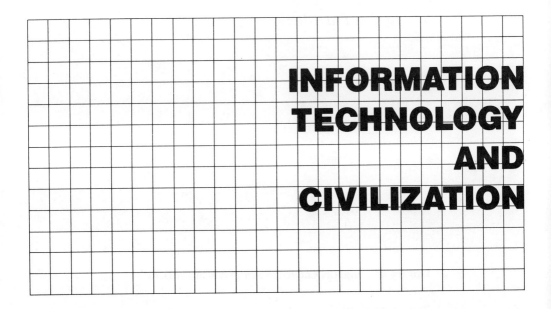

INFORMATION TECHNOLOGY AND CIVILIZATION

Hiroshi Inose
John R. Pierce

With a Foreword by Koji Kobayashi

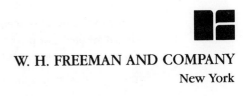

W. H. FREEMAN AND COMPANY
New York

To Mariko and Ellen

Library of Congress Cataloging in Publication Data

Inose, Hiroshi, 1927–
  Information technology and civilization.

  Includes bibliographies and index.
    1. Information science.   2. Information storage and
retrieval systems.   3. Technology and civilization.
4. Computers and civilization.   I. Pierce, John Robinson,
1910-   II. Title.
Z1001.I56   1984   020   83-20721
ISBN 0-7167-1514-7
ISBN 0-7167-1515-5 (pbk.)

1 2 3 4 5 6 7 8 9 0   MP   2 1 0 8 9 8 7 6 5 4

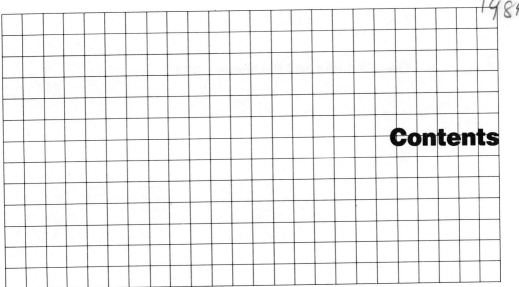

Contents

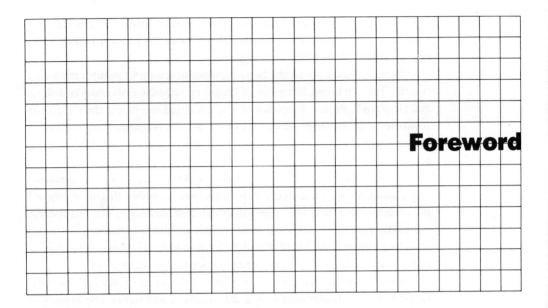

Foreword

As Chairman of the Japan Committee of the Club of Rome I am delighted to have been invited to write the foreword to this book, which is based on the report presented at the Inose–Pierce Project workshop at the club's Tokyo Conference in October 1982.

The Club of Rome, thrust into the limelight in 1972 by its first report, *The Limits to Growth,* has become well-known as an international group studying the future of mankind and the shape of modern civilization. Although the club holds meetings annually, it was not until the 1979 Berlin Conference that microelectronics was put on the agenda. As one with a long career in the electronics industry, I was a little taken aback by the idea that progress in my field might create problems of global proportions for mankind. After listening to the discussions at the conference my dismay was intensified: Most of the participants were pessimistic about the microelectronic future, believing it would create unemployment and deprive people of purposeful lives.

During the 1960s I had developed an interest in the future of civilization, especially in the trend toward knowledge and information industries. I came to believe that the development of electronics would bring about an integration of computers and communications and that information would become as important a resource for human civilization as material or energy resources. Thus, I endorsed the Japan Committee's motion to gather research reports which would accurately present the current and future social and cultural ramifications of information technology at the club's 1982 conference.

We were fortunate to get two outstanding scientists to undertake this task, Dr. Hiroshi Inose, Professor of Engineering at the University of Tokyo, and Dr. John R. Pierce, Professor of Engineering Emeritus of the California Institute of Technology. After two years of joint research they presented their report at the Tokyo Conference for discussion by participants from around the world.

The debate was a trilateral affair: the Americans and the Japanese, eager to move ahead in high-tech fields and favorably disposed toward microelectronics and the new information technology; the Europeans, culturally confident, but relative latecomers to the field and unconvinced of its benefits; and the Third World, lacking an industrial base, yet demanding that the industrialized countries transfer their technology.

Many institutions besides the Club of Rome are studying the relationship between civilization and information, and hence the impact of information technology. Information is growing in importance, both in the development of civilization and in solving the problems arising from that development. The long history of the human race shows, I believe, that mankind has achieved global dominance by using intellectual skills. It therefore gives me great pleasure that Drs. Inose and Pierce have published this volume, for I am sure it will greatly increase our understanding of the world today.

Let us not ask what the future holds in store; it is ours to build.

Koji Kobayashi
Chairman of the Board
Nippon Electric Company
Tokyo, Japan

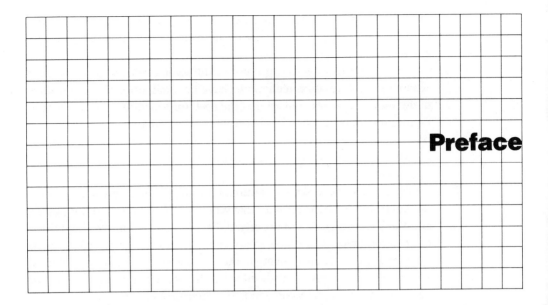

Preface

Since the invention of language, spoken and written, information has had a central place in civilization. The questions that T. S. Eliot asks in *The Rock* move us all:

> Where is the Life we have lost in living?
>
> Where is the wisdom we have lost in knowledge?
>
> Where is the knowledge we have lost in information?

To this the beleaguered data analyst might well add:

> Where is the information we have lost in data?

We cannot answer Eliot's questions explicitly. They address the human heart as much as the human mind. Yet, in a modest way, we hope that this book may help the reader to appreciate the problems that Eliot enunciates with a clearer head if not with an untroubled heart.

Whatever profound questions we may raise concerning information technology and its place in human life and society, the role played by information technology in human life is old and ever present rather than new. To provide this sense of perspective, in the first chapter we review the information technologies of the past and the roles they have played in civilization. We see that many of the problems we now face are old, and some seem eternal.

Yet, in some ways the present is different from the past. Current advances in information technology have become more than extensions of the information technologies of the past. Information technologies are rapidly merging into one common digital electronic art of tremendous power and impact. The power of this art is so great that the changes it is working and will work in our civilization are qualitative as well as quantitative.

This book addresses the nature and power of the new arts of information technology, the changes that will or may arise through this power, and the opportunities and problems that we face. No matter how powerful, information technologies are merely tools. Properly used, these tools may bring great benefit to our society; misused, they will have adverse effects. To take full advantage of the usefulness of these tools, we must understand their value and know their proper uses.

Our exposition of information technology has been drawn chiefly from the experience of Japan and the United States and of other nations with advanced technologies in the field, including European nations as well as Hong Kong, Singapore, and Taiwan. The development in Japan was entirely civilian. In the United States, military work provided the initial impetus, though we must remember that the transistor itself was a civilian development, as were early digital technology, communication satellites, and optical fibers.

Purely military technologies are not discussed in this book. Further, we can only suggest the relevance of information technology to nations of very different industrial and economic statuses. The fates of nations and peoples are, or should be, primarily in their own hands. While we can try to offer helpful information, it would be presumptuous of us to prescribe in detail for the lives of others. Factual material of the sort we present can, nonetheless, form a necessary groundwork both for initial speculations and the later development of concrete and ambitious plans.

Because today's information technology has so many aspects and serves so many functions, it is easy to miss the main features that distinguish it from important information technologies of the past. We see three outstanding aspects, interwoven rather than independent, that must be taken into account when particular consequences, opportunities, and problems are discussed. These three aspects are the convergence of modes, communities of interest, and impacts on culture.

The Convergence of Modes

In past societies, various information technologies have favored various modalities of information: printing favored written language; the telephone, the phonograph, and the radio favored spoken language and music; photography, motion pictures, and television favored visual information. Today, digital technology serves speech, sound, text, data, and graphical and pictorial displays, in a common manner and equally well, in the transmission, processing, storage, and retrieval of information. This allows a convergence of service modes in which pictures and graphs, sound, and data are used together and will be increasingly intermingled for all purposes: communication, transactions, work, information retrieval, and so on. Our success in taking advantage of this convergence of modes depends on legal and societal factors that encourage or interfere with the realization of the full potentialities of the convergence of modes already inherent in our powerful new digital technology.

Communities of Interest

In some past day, all of the inhabitants of a village may have known all that was important in their daily lives. As society has become more complex, the particular, powerful knowledge that is necessary in our technological civilization is produced, disseminated, and used through informal communities of interest made up of those interested and knowledgeable in various fields.

The convergence of modes and the associated speed, reduction of cost, and increase in power of information technology can encourage communities of interest that span many countries. Fast and economical air travel has worked together with the convergence of modes in fostering such transnational communities of interest. Such communities of interest are an inevitable outcome of the convergence of modes and the increasing effectiveness of the transmission, processing, storage, and retrieval of information. They are valuable both as a means of advancing human knowledge and as a means of illuminating and perhaps overcoming cultural biases.

Communities of interest should not be thought of as either elitist or divisive. Each of us belongs to many communities of interest—some small, such as those concerned with neighborhood affairs or with the serious pursuit of, say, general relativity, and some large, such as those concerned with national policies or with the advance of computer technology. Mutual membership in many communities of interest helps to link them more profitably to human needs and aspirations and prevents them from becoming unduly parochial or from failing to profit from activities in other areas.

Impacts on Culture

In one sense, culture embraces the whole of civilization (to which this book is addressed). In a narrower sense, we can take culture as arts and letters. Our languages, books, buildings, statues, visual arts, dance, music— all not only are influenced by economic, political, and social patterns; they have always been, and will continue to be, strongly influenced by our technologies. Powerful new information technology is bound to have a profound influence on existing arts and letters, and new information technology could lead to striking advances and bold new syntheses that will involve an interactive appreciation of artistic and literary creations.

We believe that the qualitative and quantitative effects of the impact of information technology on civilization are best thought of in terms of the three intertwined aspects we have just described. These important aspects of today's and tomorrow's information technology manifest themselves in a complex society as particular opportunities. We must make wise choices if we are to gain the full advantage of the convergence of modes, of increasingly widespread communities of interest, and of favorable impacts of information technology on culture.

We cannot make wise choices, however, without knowing something of the content and nature of today's information technology and without understanding these powerful tools. To this end, we trace the development of information technology from language in Chapter 1 and devote Chapter 2 to exploring the nature of information technology and to explaining what we can do, how it is done, and what we may reasonably expect of the future.

However, the heart of our considerations lies in the impact of new information technologies on the lives of us all. In Chapter 3 we sketch present and potential impacts in a number of areas of life: on the integration of societal activities into more widespread activities and organizations, on improvements in industrial efficiency, on improved access of the individual to information valuable in his or her life, on changes in industrial structure, and on possible improvements in the social infrastructure, including transportation, medical care, personal security, and the enrichment of culture. We also raise various problems concerning the privacy of information, the integrity of information, and the possible misuses or monopolies of information.

Several matters raised in Chapter 3 are discussed in greater detail in later chapters. Chapter 4 discusses issues of machine translation, computerized instruction, artificial intelligence, and related matters. Chapter 5 discusses the broad and fruitful relation of information technology to the arts. Chapter 6 deals with opportunities and hazards in the government's role in information technology. Chapter 7 tells us what we, the people, can gain through information technology.

Even though we have provided a chapter of summary, Chapter 8, we feel it is important to point out here some things that our study of information technology and civilization has led us to view as particularly pertinent to our discussion.

Machines in Information Technology

The most productive examples of the impact of information technology on civilization involve the use of machines as tools. When used properly, machines do the things they can do faster or more accurately than human beings, while human beings are freed to do what they can do better. In such profitable uses, how a machine accomplishes a task is quite different from how a person would do the same work. This is, of course, contrary to the use of machines to duplicate what people can do in the way they can do it.

The capabilities of human beings and machines differ profoundly. Machines can act much more rapidly than people and can take many rules into account infallibly, while people can easily sort relevant data out of complex inputs or memories. The recognition of spoken language is one example of human capabilities. Another is the ability to drive through traffic.

As digital machines—computers, if you will—become more and more capable, they will take over many tasks, or aspects of tasks, now performed by human beings. As a bird cannot fly as fast or as high as an airplane, so a man cannot compete with a bulldozer. It is foolish to try. In the arts, for example, it is quite conceivable that numerically controlled machine tools might replace the sculptor's mallet and chisel, but it is very unlikely that the computer will replace the sculptor. In a like way, computers are very useful in producing musical sounds and musical scores, but the music *composed* by computers hasn't been very interesting.

It seems inevitable that clever machines will be of great help to human beings and will benefit their civilization. However, we believe that artificial intelligence in the sense of imitating human capabilities is the wrong approach. The fruitful course is to make machines do for people those tasks at which they easily outstrip people in capability, and for people to do those things—including using and directing machines—for which they are best suited.

The proper use of machines, and simple and "friendly" interfaces between human beings and machines, are important in the present and will be increasingly important in the future.

Availability of Information

Governments gather much information that is useful to industries, businesses, scientific institutions, and other groups. Our new information technology makes it possible to disseminate such information widely and economically. Insofar as possible, useful information should be made easily available, even when the cost of dissemination is not fully covered by revenues. The citizens of a country need to know about their land.

Integrity of Information

The fabrication and misuse of information must be as old as man. Recently, the issue of privacy of information has received a great deal of attention. This issue is too narrow. A better concern is the integrity of information. Information is of value only if it informs us correctly; it can be dangerous if it does not. Thus, the source of information should be identified, and the ways data were gathered and processed should be made known. Further, the meaning of summaries or numbers derived from data should be understood. For example, GNP (Gross National Product) and prevailing wage are informative only if we know what is meant, and many people don't know.

While we favor the widespread disclosure of information, some information is of a very personal nature or is proprietary information of value to a company. Of course, pains must be taken that information of this sort be accurate. But further, the disclosure of personal information may embarrass or damage an individual. The disclosure of proprietary information may damage a company and jeopardize the livelihood of many employees. Thus, confidential information, personal or industrial, should be gathered only when absolutely necessary, destroyed when the necessity has passed, and guarded zealously while it is held.

The integrity of information, both in accuracy and in privacy, requires that data can be entered into information systems or altered only by authorized personnel and that there be an audit trail through which the person entering or altering data can be identified. In addition, the time of entry or alteration should be noted. This is an appropriate field for government action, but it is an issue that should concern professional groups and industrial associations as well. Who is to guard the guardians?

Information Glut, Information Famine, and Communities of Interest

It has been observed that the media overwhelm us with a mass of information, mostly irrelevant and some of it false, while we find it difficult to learn the particular things we need to know in our day-to-day lives. We do not believe that this is a problem that can be cured by government action. Rather, the cure lies in new technological alternatives to the mass media, alternatives that serve a multiplicity of communities of interest, some of them transnational. Alternatives to the mass media include the telephone, specialized journals (sports, financial, scientific), and access through computer terminals to a growing number of data banks and data services. As we have noted, such access can involve the simultaneous use of speech or sound, text, and graphical displays.

Standardization

Standardization—of language, of type style in printing, of paper size, of a telegraph code, of a typewriter keyboard, of weights and measures—has long been a problem. Today, a considerable degree of standardization is necessary and has been attained in international communication. The digital revolution and the incorporation of pictures, sounds, and text into a common pattern of transmission, processing, switching, storage, and retrieval of information poses new problems of standardization.

Historically, only a part, perhaps a minority, of standards have resulted from governmental or intergovernmental (say, United Nations) actions. Many standards have been adopted from the best current practice.

Governments and professional and technical organizations should work toward standards cooperatively and wisely. Restrictive or ill-chosen standards make operation costly and difficult. Standards should not be overelaborate; they should provide the minimum restraints necessary for interoperability. Further, standards should always be based on successfully demonstrated practices; they should never be adopted in the absence of actual experience.

Labor Intensiveness of Information Technology

Through LSI (Large-Scale Integration) and VLSI (Very-Large-Scale Integration), the cost of computer hardware is decreasing, and its capability and the amount of hardware in use are increasing. Consequently, the production of software is growing even more rapidly. In fact, software costs now exceed those of hardware, and the ratio of software costs to hardware costs is increasing. Computers and information technology are changing from being capital intensive to being labor intensive, though the labor required is skilled labor. This will have a considerable effect on employment patterns. The need for software can provide both at-home work and skilled work in countries that are not heavily industrialized.

Change and Infrastructure

All technologies change with time, and information technology is changing rapidly. As our technologies change, our world changes. People move from one area to another and from one occupation to another. The private sector alone cannot be expected to provide the infrastructures in rapidly growing areas. Here, as in education, police protection, and medical care, the public sector must play a role. Nor can the private sector retrain the employees of dying industries en masse so that they can find new work.

It is proper to regard the provision of adequate infrastructures, including education and retraining as a responsibility of government, but government may best fulfill its obligation in cooperation with the private sector. Support of research and of culture is a reasonable function of government. What government should not do is try artificially to preserve industries, businesses, or communities whose usefulness has vanished.

Competition, Monopoly, Regulation, and Cooperation

Competition is a wonderful force for progress. It has been essential in the growing power and decreasing cost of computer hardware. However, not all problems are amenable to solution through market forces. If they were, every country would have a multiplicity of governments, each one promising its adherents (that is, its taxpayers) the best government service for the least money.

The advantage of one interconnecting telephone system (if not one company) seems obvious. Through digital technology and the convergence of modes, the telephone will become but one small part of our electronic information resources. There will be an advantage to standardization, interconnectability, and dealing with a single source in gaining access to very powerful communication and information resources.

Monopoly is one way of providing economically a uniform, easily accessible service. With monopoly goes regulation. Yet, regulation has been more commonly used to prevent the growth of new services than to encourage change.

In the complex world of the future, information and communication will involve the gathering of information (newspapers and magazines do this, in their advertising as well as in their editorial work), the storing, processing, and retrieving of information, and the transmitting of information. All are complex, costly undertakings. What seems called for is neither monopoly (for the task is overwhelming) nor a form of competition that puts various components of information service at odds. Rather, we need cooperation in providing a unified, effective service and in some areas of research and development.

Both monopoly (for government services, at least) and competition have their strong adherents, but cooperation is regarded with suspicion by almost everyone. It is rendered difficult or impossible by both regulations and antitrust laws. Yet, we see no way in which the full potentialities of information technology can be realized without a great deal of cooperation among information providers, communication companies and equipment manufacturers, and between the public and private sectors.

Past, Present, and Future

New digital technologies are changing work and the workplace profoundly. Computer-controlled machine tools, looms, processing plants, and robots on assembly lines are carrying automation into a new era. New products rely more and more on cheap and easy-to-produce electronics and less and less on ingenious mechanisms—contrast the digital watch with clockwork. Less labor is needed to produce new goods, and there is a shift of the work force from the manufacturing to the service sector.

Computerization plays several roles in this shift. Sometimes it displaces personal service, as in automated bank tellers that dispense money. Sometimes it takes over much of the "intellectual" part of a job. At a supermarket checkout station, a terminal can read the price tags, make out the sales slip, and make change. The checkout clerk need only bag groceries and deal with unexpected events. The clerk may now approve checks, but automation of funds transfer will probably displace that function. Through computerization, a lower level of ability and training will suffice for many jobs.

For all of the citizens of advanced countries, computers and the digital arts are changing life dramatically and will change it further. Microprocessors control the functioning of microwave ovens, toasters, automobiles, television sets, home security systems, and a host of other things.

Video games, computer games, sophisticated toys, and recreational computers, all based on the digital art, are changing the lives of the young— and of many of the not-so-young. Surely, this is as powerful a force as television, and it is participatory. The child with a digital toy, game, or computer does not merely watch; he or she does something, and what he or she does can be highly educational. The child may learn words in a foreign language or learn to spell, type, program, or play intellectually challenging games, including chess. This participatory interaction with computers may lead to new forms of art. Through a connection between a personal computer (or even only a keyboard) and a data base of some sort, a child or an adult may learn what he or she wants or needs to know without having to rely on the sketchy summaries suplied by television or the bulky summaries supplied by newspapers.

We are approaching a day when a host of services, from shopping to medical care—and especially emergency medical care—will be made far more effective and efficient through computers and communication. All of this can make a better world, but it makes the world more complex in organization.

To a large extent, this new world will be created through a new digital information technology that allows a *convergence of modes,* one information technology that can serve both our eyes and our ears. The knowledge and skills of this new world will lie in *communities of interest,* many of them transnational, that are served and fostered by the convergence of modes. Our new information technology will have profound *impacts on culture*—impacts on all of our arts and letters.

Through all we have learned, we believe that the world of the future will be a new world. We observe that governments are rooted in tradition and freighted with bureaucracy. They reflect the past, and in that reflection there is much that was good in the past and much that is still good in the present. Yet, not everything from the past is appropriate to man's present civilization.

If information technology and civilization are to reinforce one another happily and productively in a better future, it must be through a gradual transition from acceptance of the past to acceptance of the present. It would be a happy thing if governments reassured us about productive, good new things and helped us to view obsolescent aspects of our society with wistfulness rather than with a desperate resistance to change.

We wish to give details of the origin of this book, and to acknowledge the invaluable help and support which made it possible. In 1980, the Japan Committee of the Club of Rome asked us to prepare a report that would explore the impact of information technology on society. While we were contemplating the work, we found that the Japan Committee of the Club of Rome was to host the annual meeting of the Club of Rome in Tokyo in the fall of 1982 and that the committee wished the report to be presented at one of the sessions of the annual meeting. As work progressed further, the suitability of the manuscript as a report to the Club of Rome became apparent to Dr. Aurelio Peccei, as well as to the Japan Committee of the Club of Rome, and so the book was issued as such a report.

The first draft of this book was written while one of the authors, Hiroshi Inose, was a Sherman Fairchild Distinguished Scholar at the California Institute of Technology in the fall of 1981; he wishes to thank the California Institute of Technology for the opportunity they afforded him to do this work. The first draft of the book was entered into the Caltech computer at the end of 1981, and copies of the manuscript were sent to a number of reviewers; the names of reviewers who sent us written comments are given in the Appendix.

We owe a great deal to these reviewers, who read the first draft of the manuscript with great care. We also owe a great deal to members of a workshop that met at the California Institute of Technology, in Pasadena, California, on June 1 and 2 of 1982. The names of the members of this workshop are also given in the Appendix. Through the comments of the reviewers and the workshop participants, our views were somewhat changed and considerably clarified. Indeed, the present emphasis of the three essential and intertwined aspects of today's information technology—the convergence of modes, the importance of communities of interest, and the impact on culture—became central to this book.

Preparation of the second draft of the book began after a day-long workshop held in Tokyo on October 25, 1982, in connection with the Tokyo Conference of the Club of Rome. The names of the participants of this workshop are also given in the Appendix. A summary was presented at a session of the Tokyo Conference of the Club of Rome on October 27, 1982.

Besides our debt to the reviewers, the workshop participants, and those who took part in the meeting in October, we wish to acknowledge the support of the Japan Techno-Economics Society and a grant from the Kikawada Memorial Foundation, which made possible the preparation of the manuscript, the essential reviews, and the workshop held in Pasadena, and which covered other expenses incurred during the preparation of this book.

October 1982

Hiroshi Inose
John R. Pierce

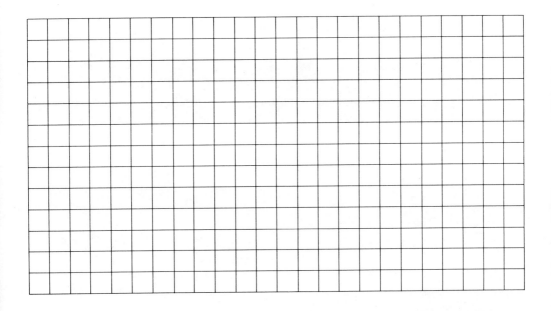

**INFORMATION
TECHNOLOGY
AND
CIVILIZATION**

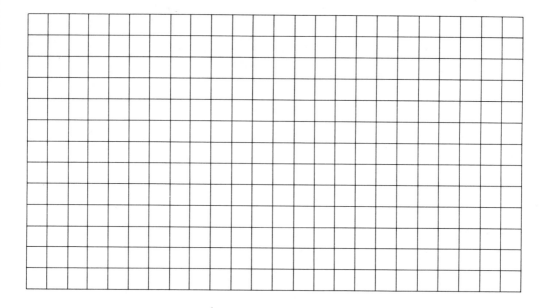

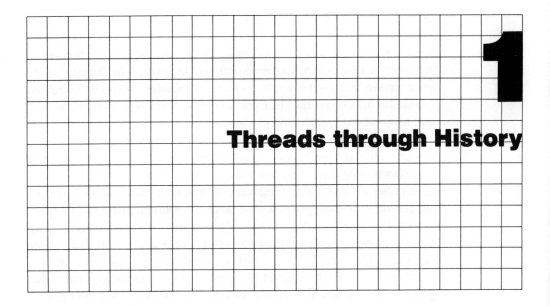

Threads through History

1-1 Introduction

Various threads run through the development of information technology as a part of civilization. These threads diverge from an origin in language. They finally come together in the present convergence of all modes of communication and information technology into one common digital art of transmission, processing, storage, and retrieval, whatever the content, whether it be sound, sight, figures, or symbols.

The first spoken language must have served all of the members of a community. It came to convey not only matters of workaday interest, but tales and legends. Wise men, storytellers, and poets shared their recollections; they formed what we may regard as early communities of interest. Initially, written language was a skill of only priests, scribes, and administrators, and it knitted together groups with religious and administrative responsibilities. In our time, written language has become almost universal, both as a tool of everyday life and as a resource of the countless communities of interest that are essential in adding to and using a body of information so tremendous that no single person, however wise, can master and use it all.

Through the entire history of information technology, language has served mankind's need for stories, for explanations, for that strange compound of entertainment, appreciation, and aspiration that we call art or culture. Some of this culture has been expressed in sights and sounds, in spectacles, in ceremony, and in music. These continue to play their part in our lives. However, with the invention of language—the human race's greatest invention—the word, spoken and written, became central to human life and to civilization. Even in ceremony and spectacle, we would feel lost without explanation or commentary.

Language, even that of simple societies, is complex beyond our conscious understanding. Its secrets lie hidden within us. The nature, growth, and standardization of language have occurred largely by common consent rather than by edict. Languages such as Latin and English emerged in their times as widespread second languages without plan if not without reason. Paper and printing, books, the postal service, radio, and television have been more powerful than goverments or academies in influencing language. The form and structure of language respond more to the medium—speech, the text of the copyist, the handwritten letter, the printed book or newspaper, radio or television—than they do to rules or dicta.

Both the use of language and society itself, its arts and its commerce, have been influenced by or have come to depend on technological advances in communication. The swift messengers of whom Xenophon wrote were necessary for the existence of the Persian Empire. The Roman postal system, called the *cursus publicus*, was a necessity of the Roman Empire. Our modern postal system has shaped literature through the popularization of letters, and it has shaped our society and commerce as well. Post office reform first raised the issue of monopoly and efficiency versus fairness.

Messengers, heralds, and postal systems are examples, as were bards and Homeric poets, of the transmission of information and of how it affects arts and commerce. Papermaking and printing are examples of the recording of information. Their effect has been prodigious. Paper made mass popular graphic art possible. Printing gave people something to read and made reading widespread. Together with postal systems, paper and printing created a world community—but a community still fragmented and slow to react.

Telegraphy, with its roots in signal fires and semaphores, linked far places instantly. But telegraphy is an esoteric art, for the initiate only. Telephony is for everyone. It has given us instant, do-it-yourself communication. Together with radio, telephony marked a departure from written language. Electricity and electronics have carried us back to the spoken word, as did the phonograph. Movies and television reacquainted us with something far older—the spectacle. Mass media—the press, radio, and television—and their they-to-us communication contrast glaringly with the me-to-thee communication of the letter and the telephone call.

At last, through the digital computer and through data services, information technology has united all media and forms of information. In the future, all will be served by the same technology, and all will be intermingled in our life, work and recreation. The threads have come together. Previously diverse problems and uses have become aspects of information technology and its service to mankind.

History tells us that these problems are old. We find the falsification of data and the violation of privacy in a novel by Dumas. The problems of standardization, so acute now, have been with us always. History tells us that much successful standardization has been based on what has already been done, not on plans for doing things, and has come about through common consent rather than through governmental edict. Deliberate attempts to force standardization do not always succeed.

1-2 Language—Spoken and Written

Whatever we may discuss that comprises information technology and civilization, we must return to language as the ultimate source. Most of what we know about civilization is expressed in language. Language can be a means of giving expression to emotions, of venting one's feelings, of deceiving, persuading, cajoling, wooing, or berating another. Even this sort of language is dependent on meaning—on the transmission of information—for much of its effect. A sigh is less than a sigh if we do not know what evoked it. A joke is not funny unless it is intelligible, nor is a curse searing unless it is understood. Meaning is central in other uses of language in connection with physical as well as mental work.

Besides having expressiveness and meaning, language has structure. All languages, those of pre-literate societies as well as written languages, are complex beyond explicit analysis. The rules of their structure and use are transmitted from parent to child in a way that we do not fully understand. Once a child acquires the smallest degree of skill in language, he or she quickly masters complex patterns of usage that the most skilled linguists have not been able to teach to machines. Our knowledge of language is hidden within us, defying deep probing. We do not know how much of our skill is hereditary, how much of it is based on the unique structure of the human brain and on our unique vocal apparatus. We do know that the results of efforts to teach language to animals are very limited, however fascinating they can be.

Human ability to acquire language appears to be greater in children than in adults, but we do not know to what extent. The ability to acquire and use language is closely linked to hearing; the congenitally deaf have far more difficulty in acquiring any use of language than do the congenitally blind.

In short, little as we know about language, we do know that it is peculiarly human, and that, even in literate societies, it is strongly dependent on speech and hearing. We know that the complex structure of language is the result of an evolutionary process rather than of design. Complex standardization is arrived at by some sort of consensus.

Indeed, language can defy conscious attempts to standardize it. The sixteenth-century salon of Mme. de Rambouillet may have been responsible for the remarkable homogeneity of French classical literature, but it led to the unrealistic emphasis on refinement and delicacy that Moliére ridiculed in *Les Précieuses Ridicules*. Richelieu's great *Académie Française* does not fare much better in protecting contemporary French from Americanisms. English classicists, from Milton through Johnson, ultimately failed in their efforts to impose Latin order on their own tongue.

Efforts to standardize language are commendable in purpose. China has a uniform written language, but it is a babble of spoken dialects. Within human memory, a person traveling a hundred miles in the British Isles could encounter a variety of seemingly unintelligible dialects. Today, in many parts of the world, language is becoming more nearly uniform—not through academies, but through radio and television and a greater mobility of the population. Mobility is the reason English became more uniform over the huge area of America than in the small expanse of Britain.

Some orderly minds seek standardization at any cost or expense of effort. Successful standardization must be based on use and experience, not on the scholarly preciosities of a Rambouillet. Useful standardization, with or without conscious encouragement, can grow out of need and usage.

Languages are becoming more standardized. Only a part of this is centralized and deliberate, such as Ataturk's introduction of the Latin alphabet in Turkey in 1928 or the simplification of Chinese characters in the People's Republic of China in 1956.

Successful efforts to provide communication among various linguistic groups have been evolutionary rather than revolutionary. The Latin that served Europe so well through the time of Newton was the result of a scholarly tradition rather than of an organized effort. Deliberately constructed languages such as Esperanto have had very limited success. Yet, new languages have appeared, have gained a considerable currency, and have then failed—Yiddish in East Europe, Pidgin in the Far East. The international language of science is not the carefully thought-out Basic English; rather, as the Dutch physicist Hendrik Casimir has observed, it is broken English. That the international language of air traffic control is a subset of English may be described better as a historical necessity than as a conclusion of standardizers.

While language remains firmly rooted in human speech and hearing, the invention of the symbols and characters of a written language around 3000 BC dramatically changed human use of language. Written language also opened the way for a series of technological advances that have revolutionized the recording, the transmission, and the processing of information.

One of the most easily seen effects of written language is that on style of communication. The *Iliad* and the *Odyssey* are magnificent examples of the traditions of a pre-literate society. Their metrical nature and their repetitive rhythmic phrases (rosy-fingered Dawn, wily Ulysses) aid recollection as well as adding poetic and dramatic effect. The poetic diction of spoken and memorized literature carried over into, and shaped, written language. Thus, simple, clear English literary prose appeared about the time of Dryden (late seventeenth century), though some personal letters were written in clear, simple English a century earlier.

The nature of written languages has had an important effect on literature. The homophonic ambiguity of Japanese written kana encouraged the allusive, punning style of medieval Japanese poetry and romances. The technologies of writing also have had a profound effect on the details and uses of written language. Parchment was an expensive medium, suitable for important documents only; the wax tablets of the Romans must have been awkward as well as impermanent. The very form of the cuneiform writing of the Near East (fourth millennium BC until second century BC) was dictated by the clay tablet and the writing stylus. The medium was cheap and more enduring than parchment or paper, but clay tablets were not suited to journals illustrated by pen or pencil drawings or by watercolor sketches, such as the journals kept by Leonardo da Vinci and by nineteenth-century scientists and explorers.

1-3 Paper and Printing

The general diffusion of written language, which is common in all present literate societies, came about through two inventions: paper and printing. Paper was invented in China around AD 105. It had reached the Near East by the end of the eighth century, and Europe by the twelfth century. One of the first European uses of paper was pictorial. Woodcuts printed on paper were widespread by the middle of the fifteenth century. What was printed? Playing cards. Madonnas and other religious figures. Pictorial representation was accessible to the illiterate poor as well as to the wealthy. Printing on paper from wood blocks and, later, etching, engraving, and lithography inaugurated a tradition of illustration, a little earlier than printing, that had a profound effect on all European civilization. The architectural handbooks of Sebastiano Serlio (1475–1554) exerted a profound influence on contemporary European architecture; the designs of Andrea Palladio (1518–1580) had an even greater influence. The woodblocks illustrating the book of human anatomy of Andreas Vesalius (1514–1564) were essential in communicating his findings.

Prints in themselves afford a limited means of communication, and we usually link paper with the printing of text. By the end of the second century AD, the Chinese had devised printing with wooden blocks, and this, together with paper, made the circulation of books far greater in China than in the West. The Chinese began printing from movable type in the eleventh century. The invention of movable metal type by Gutenberg around 1450 was facilitated by the alphabetic nature of Western text. Paper and printing made the tools of literacy cheap.

In the days of scribes and parchment, books, necessarily rare and venerable, were expensive works of art. Great pains were taken to make them beautiful through handsome lettering and illustrations. The first printed books imitated, less elaborately, the illustration and character styles of the scribes. With more and cheaper books, legibility and readability became more important than adornment and imitation of the past.

The first typeface (Gutenberg, 1456) imitated a common script that had evolved from the official script that Charlemagne had adopted for the Holy Roman Empire. As a family of typefaces, these are now called Old English or Gothic. Gothic survived in Germany for the printing of literary works up to 1940, when it was forbidden by government edict.

An early and permanent departure from Gothic was our common roman typeface, in which this book is printed. The first notable roman type was designed by Nicholas Jenson in 1470, only fourteen years after Gutenberg. Today, roman is supplemented by italic, which was introduced by Francesco Griffo around 1490 and which became a special-function typeface around 1550. In the adoption of roman and italic type we see a rapid and revolutionary change, brought about through the acceptance of the excellent work of a few fine craftsmen. Although typefaces have changed since the time of Jenson and Griffo, we recognize their roman and italic types as being much like our own. A sort of standardization has been achieved by general consent, without the work of governments or institutes.

Printing woodblocks made pictures and illustrations widely accessible. Printed books gave ordinary people something to read. Alphabetic writing made the learning of writing easy compared with the memorization of thousands of characters that the Chinese student must master.

In classical times, emperors and lesser public figures sometimes kept private journals and diaries of a sort. It appears that Marcus Aurelius wrote his *Meditations* for himself alone. In the late middle ages, perhaps through the encouragement of the availability of paper, private diaries became increasingly common.

The increasing literacy of later centuries made diaries very common indeed, and they acquired an increasing literary value, as evidenced by the diary of Samuel Pepys (kept from 1660 to 1669) and Boswell's *Journal of a Tour to the Hebrides* (1785). Japanese diarists flourished from the eleventh century on, and some of the most interesting diaries were written by women in syllabic script, which is easier and more flexible than kanji (Chinese characters). Some Japanese scholars, who were bound by custom to write learnedly in Chinese, wrote pseudonymously as women, thus availing themselves of the allusive qualities of Japanese prose and poetry.

Alphabetic writing, paper, and printing are information technologies that have made literacy widespread in our world, and they have added a host of private diaries and journals to a host of more public books.

1-4 The Development of Postal Systems

Today, one more commonly writes to another individual or to a public audience than to oneself. For this, a postal system is necessary.

In some periods of history, the only way to send letters or messages was by occasional travelers or, for government messages, by messengers or heralds. Regular, prompt, and certain transmission of messages, over distances long and short, is necessary in keeping a large country or an empire together. Herodotus and Xenophon tell us with admiration of the relays of mounted messengers who served the Persian emperor and state. Today, on the facade of the central post office of New York City, the following quotation from Herodotus is graven: "Neither snow, nor rain, nor the gloom of night keeps these messengers from the swift completion of their appointed rounds." Well, maybe.

The excellent Roman postal system, the *cursus publicus*, was the most highly developed of the ancient v. orld. Like the messengers of Persia, the *cursus publicus* served the state, though some use was made of it for private messages as the writing of letters was an important part of Roman life—for the wealthy and literate at least.

When we say that we have entered a postindustrial or information society, it may be well to note that information technology is a necessary, but not sufficient, condition for national survival. The messenger system of Persia did not prevent the fall of that empire, nor did the *cursus publicus* prevent the fall of Rome. Rather, it survived the fall of Rome, for in AD 493 this postal system fell into the hands of Theodoric, who maintained it because he found it useful. The Roman postal system gradually degenerated as the Roman roads did, for materials as well as services are essential to survival.

As a part of the developing commerce of the later middle ages, various nongovernmental postal systems evolved, such as the Germanic *Butcher Post*, founded by a corporation of butchers, and a biyearly service operated in the mid thirteenth century between the great Italian commercial centers and important annual fairs held in France.

Increased commerce, the invention of printing, and increased literacy led to the founding of various postal services, both governmental and commercial. After a period of evolution, postal service as we now know it emerged from the work of a British educator and tax reformer, Rowland Hill. In 1837, Hill published a book, *Post Office Reform: Its Importance and Practicability*. His revolutionary reforms, none entirely new, were adopted in 1840. These consisted chiefly of (1) prepayment by affixing a stamp to a letter and (2) a cheap, uniform rate (initially one penny) for a half-ounce letter addressed to any part of Britain.

Before the "penny post," charges were based on distance. The smallest charge for a letter was fourpence; the average charge was 6¼ pence. Hill's investigations showed that transit charges were an insignificant part of the total cost of handling a letter; the irrelevant charging scales based on distance required a host of clerks and inflated the cost of operations.

While the penny post that followed Hill's suggestions succeeded, it could succeed only as a monopoly. Had a competing operation been allowed to provide limited service, such as service in London only, it could have undermined the postal system by what is now called "cream skimming," leaving the provision of costly and unprofitable but necessary service to the government. This early illustration of the conflict between smallest cost to a favored few and smallest overall cost continues to plague the communication industry.

A uniform and finally worldwide postal service has contributed greatly to dissemination of information throughout the world. It has been used to favor some media over others, thus, in many countries, books can be sent at a very low rate.

Postal service popularized, and perhaps degraded, an old literary form. From the time of Cicero to the Renaissance, the writing of letters was a cultivated literary art among a small wealthy or educated minority. Letters were written with care and were read by many besides the person addressed. The *De concribendis epistolis* of Desiderius Erasmus (1466–1536) was an essential manual of his time, went through 40 or 50 editions, and was still recommended in the seventeenth century. Sixteenth- and seventeenth-century Englishmen followed Angel Day's *The English Secretary*.

Common, cheap postal service and growing literacy increased both the use and the scope of correspondence. Letters could be short and chatty, but, above all, they could be written by and about ordinary people in an everyday tone. This led not only to more widespread correspondence but also to a new literary form. Samuel Richardson's *Pamela*, written in 1739, is the first English novel that concentrated on a single action, a courtship, told in the form of a series of letters. Its influence reached far: "Ah, Richardson," a sentimental character exclaims in the first scene of Tchaikovsky's *Eugene Onegin*.

Since the advent of effective postal service, the flood of letters defies preservation. Fancied letters remain an accepted literary form. Does the writer of actual letters still have a wide public in mind? He or she must be particularly skillful and the letters particularly spicy if they are to be published and read.

1-5   From Talk to Technology

Postal systems convey letters and manuscripts from city to city and from country to country. Information, however, is not marks on a unique piece of paper—though such marks can express information. The idea that information can be carried in some immaterial form rather than by the transmission of a physical record from place to place is not new. Indeed, speech does just this, though over a limited distance. That distance can be extended by using a whistle as a signaling device or even by the production of "whistle talk" without the use of whistles. Drums have been used to communicate over longer distances.

Signal fires by night and smoke signals by day have been used to send simple messages over great distances. Along the Silk Road in central Asia, one still finds signal-fire mounds that span thousands of miles. These were built before the Christian Era to send alarms to the capital of ancient China. Although the signal fires could tell only that an enemy was approaching, they provided by far the fastest way of transmitting this vital information; the delay was only that of seeing one fire and setting another. The symbolic use of signal fires in connection with Queen Victoria's Jubilee is described by A. E. Housman:

> From Clee to heaven the beacon burns,
> The shires have seen it plain,
> From north and south the sign returns,
> And beacons burn again.

The Greek historian Polybius describes a method of alphabetic signaling by vases set in rows and columns. The idea is awkward, and the range must have been very limited in the age before the telescope.

The first effective semaphore telegraph was set up in France, following an invention made by Claude Chappe and his brother in 1791. The telegraph consisted of 120 towers spaced 5 to 10 kilometers apart between

Paris and Toulon. An operator at a tower looked through a telescope for a signal at a preceding tower. He then imitated the signal at his own tower so that it could be seen at a succeeding tower and be passed along. Fifty signals could be sent in an hour. This was 90 times faster than sending such a message by mounted couriers. The telegraph was used in 1794 to send news of French victories over the Austrians at Quesnoy and Condé-sur-Escaut. Within a decade, semaphore telegraphs had appeared in Russia, Sweden, and Denmark; eventually, in Prussia, India, and Egypt.

Those who have read Alexander Dumas's *Count of Monte Cristo* may remember that the semaphore telegraph played an important role for the count in his revenge on Baron Danglars, who had been partly responsible for the incarceration of the young Edmond Dante's (later the count) in the horrible Chateau D'If. Danglars had been speculating in bonds on the clandestine advice of M. Debary, the secretary general of the government. Some of this advice had been transmitted from Spain by telegraph. By bribing an ill-paid civil servant who operated one of the semaphore stations, the count arranged for Danglars to receive an erroneous telegraph message, which contributed to the ultimate bankruptcy of the baron.

An astute observer, Dumas included in his novels many of the foibles and failings of his time, including the smoking of hashish. His fictional account of the use of government information for private gain and of the deliberate creation (by the count) of false information raises issues that are still with us in our serious consideration of information technology and society.

The semaphore telegraph was useful, but it was too slow and costly to become a major mode of communication. Morse's electric telegraph, invented in 1835, had a rapid, widespread, and spectacular success. Morse received a government appropriation in 1843 and completed his first telegraph line, between Baltimore and Washington, D.C. (60 kilometers apart), in 1844. The use of the telegraph spread rapidly, and by the time of the invention of the telephone (1876), the telegraph as a local service had become the standard means of rapid communication within large cities. As a long-distance service, it spanned the oceans (by means of undersea cables) as well as the continents.

The success of the telegraph has lessons even for this age. Morse's telegraph was not the first electric telegraph; it was the *right* electric telegraph. Success depends not on general ideas, but on satisfactory implementations. The success of Morse's telegraph led to an international standard telegraph code, a modification of the excellent code that Morse

Transoceanic Communication

The first transoceanic telegraph cable was laid in 1857; the first successful cable in 1866. Transoceanic telephone communication is more difficult. The first transoceanic telephone cable, which used vacuum tube amplifiers and coveyed 36 two-way telephone channels, was laid in 1956. A cable using transistor amplifiers was laid in 1976; it carries 4000 two-way telephone channels.

The passive Echo balloon satellite, launched in 1960, demonstrated that voice signals could be sent coast-to-coast across the United States by satellite. The active Telstar satellite, launched in 1962, carried the first live television programs across the Atlantic. Syncom, the first synchronous satellite, was launched in 1963, and Comsat opened commercial service with a Syncom-type satellite in 1965. Today, a host of satellites carry domestic and international voice and television signals all over the world.

Laying undersea coaxial cable (Photograph courtesy of British Telecom)

Echo ballon (Photo courtesy of NASA)

Early Bird satellite under construction (Photo courtesy of Comsat)

The Soviet telecommunications satellite "Molniya-1"

himself devised. This standardization of a telegraph code was made possible because of the early and widespread success of a particular telegraph system—that of Morse—and the lack of any strong competitor. Though Morse's code is gone from wire lines, manual morse still plays a small role in long-distance radio communication.

Although the telegraph was a wonderful means of communications, it had severe limitations: It was awkward to transmit messages in nonalphabetic languages; worse, one had to learn a code in order to send or receive messages.

Bell's telephone was very different—anyone who could speak and hear could use it without training. The telephone's success was spectacular. By 1880, four years after the telephone was invented, in the United States there was one telephone per thousand people; eight years later, there was one telephone for every ten people. Now there is one telephone per person in the United States.

The invention of automatic switching in 1889 and its ultimate universal use made telephoning a completely do-it-yourself service, in which calls can be made without the intervention of an operator.

The telephone first spanned the ocean commercially in 1927, not by undersea cable (that came only in 1956), but by radio telephone, an outgrowth of Guglielmo Marconi's wonderful invention in 1895 of wireless telegraphy and his first spanning of the Atlantic with radio signals in 1901.

The telephone has had many striking effects on our society. By providing easy and rapid communication, it caused a removal of the headquarters of industries from factories to cities such as New York. Skyscrapers would have been infeasible in the days of communication by messengers; the messengers would have clogged the elevators. Yet the telephone, together with the automobile, also made satisfactory suburban life possible.

Telephone communications can be highly personal, but within a company, a telephone call is usually a bare exchange of information or the giving of orders. It has none of the trappings of "how are you" or of talk about the weather. An internal business telephone call, by being brief and to the point, saves time. For some purposes, it is better than a face-to-face meeting.

The almost universal telephone service in some nations has had a profound effect on social as well as business life. Meetings are arranged quickly with little prior notice rather than days or weeks in advance.

Social relations become more spontaneous, less formal. Communications among separated family members or close friends can be frequent without the slow interchange of letters.

What was the effect of the telephone on arts and letters? Certainly, the telephone reduced the writing of letters. Recorded telephone conversations appear to have more political or legal significance than literary potential. The telephone opened up new possibilities in the plots of plays. New and current information could be provided by a telephone call rather than transferred slowly and elaborately. Gian Carlo Menotti composed an opera called *The Telephone*. In Jean Cocteau's play *La Voix Humaine*, one character talks endlessly but movingly on the telephone. This play was converted into an opera by Francis Poulenc. For the arts, the positive influence of the telephone may be outweighed by our loss of letters. Perhaps recorded human interchange will revive as people communicate more and more by interconnected computer terminals.

In 1877, a year after the invention of the telephone, Thomas Alva Edison gave us that ingenious and unlikely invention, the phonograph. Like the telephone, the phonograph was a step back from reading and writing to listening and speaking. But the full effect of sound recording— and of the telephone as well—waited the age of electronics.

A new era in information technology began with the invention of the vacuum tube by Lee De Forest in 1906 and lasted over forty years until the invention of the transistor in 1948. The vacuum tube gave us transcontinental and transoceanic telephony. It also gave us high-fidelity recording, radio broadcasting, and television.

For electronic mass media, as for the postal system and the telephone, the evolution of service has been from the spoken word of preliterate society to the written word of literate society and then back to the spoken word—of the telephone, recorded sound, and the radio—and on again to the words and gestures of motion pictures and television.

This similarity of evolution is in form only. In substance, personal letters and telephone calls derive from day-to-day conversations. In contrast, the mass media of radio, television, and recorded sound and pictures derive from public ceremony, events, recitations, plays, spectacles, exhortations, hearings, and political speeches. Letters and phone calls are from me to thee and from thee to me. Radio and television are from them to us.

The mass media were born in the age of print as newspapers and pamphlets. At first, they expressed the views of the men who produced

Three Greats

The three great inventors of modern telecommunication were not primarily technologists. Samuel Finley Breese Morse, who invented the telegraph during a transatlantic voyage in 1835, was primarily a portrait painter and was the founder of the National Academy of Design. Alexander Graham Bell, who invented the telephone in 1876, was a teacher of the deaf; he was trained by his father, Alexander Melville Bell, who was a student of speech. Guglielmo Marconi, who invented wireless in 1895 at the age of 20, had eager genius but little training in anything. The history of information technology shows that what counts is eagerness and insight, not dull expertise.

Samuel F. B. Morse (Reproduced with permission of AT&T)

Alexander Graham Bell (Reproduced with permission of AT&T)

Guglielmo Marconi (Courtesy of the Museum of the City of New York)

and circulated them. By the end of the nineteenth century, some news-papers had achieved tremendous circulation by giving people whatever they would pay to read. The mass media had become a sort of hybrid between the information and the entertainment industries. They pre-sented a comprehensible but limited and sometimes misleading world to those—indeed, all—of us who cannot understand the real world because it is so large, complex, and distant. Today, it is hard to tell whether we live our lives in a real world or in some media construct.

The immediate impact of radio, which appeals to all who can hear, and of television, which adds gesture and spectacle to sound, has carried the mass media to new heights of impact and influence. Yet, we still rely on the me-to-thee of the telephone in dealing with the immediate, prac-tical aspects of life. In all cases, we place our reliance on the spoken word. Perhaps, in the age of computers, we may go back to the written word.

"In the beginning was the Word," Saint John assures us, but important as language is, words are not all of life. Spectacles are as old as civilization, and perhaps older; so are song and dance and all of those more personal means of communication, such as facial expression, gestures, and touch-ing. Further, we have seen that in Europe, the influence of paper was felt a little earlier through woodcuts than through the printing of text.

Subsequent advances in illustration have had profound effects in the dissemination and popularization of the arts and sciences. After the wood-cuts that served Palladio and Vesalius came engravings, first on copper and then on steel, through which fair though often inaccurate represen-tations of buildings and paintings were circulated widely. Good engrav-ings were expensive, however.

The development of lithography in the early nineteenth century cre-ated a new art in itself—bold, sometimes irreverent (as in Daumier), reproduced cheaply and in an almost unlimited number of copies. Fur-ther, lithography made it possible to print cheaply and to disseminate widely copies of paintings, including color copies.

The technology of the nineteenth century created something even more powerful than lithography, a revolutionary new information tech-nology. Building on earlier work of Joseph-Nicéphore Niepce, Louis-Jacques Mandé Daguerre, a professional scene painter, devised in 1837 a practical method for taking photographs. The consequences for human life and art have been prodigious.

The effects of photography on painting were manifold. Many painters used photographs as an aid in depicting minute detail realistically. New usages of light and shade in photographs, together with the blurring of figures in motion, may have helped to set the impressionists on quite another course. Clearly, two effects were the demise both of miniature painting and of the reproduction of paintings through engravings. An ultimate effect has been that most modern painters avoid photographic detail, though this is not true of some photorealism of the early 1970's. A very clear effect lies in the more accurate rendition of animals and humans in motion.

Eighteenth- and early nineteenth-century English sporting paintings and prints show galloping horses with legs stretched symbolically ahead and behind. Eadweard Muybridge, an English photographer and adventurer who went to California in the gold rush of 1849, changed that. Leland Stanford had bet that all four feet of a galloping horse are off the ground at the same time. He supported Muybridge's work to settle the question. Muybridge arranged twelve cameras in a row, the shutters tripped in succession by threads across the horse's path. The photographs showed that all four feet were at times off the ground, and Stanford won his bet. Muybridge's photographs did more than just settle a bet; they changed the way in which artists represented horses at gallop. Other photographs by Muybridge gave an accurate depiction of human beings performing commonplace actions.

Muybridge's photographs were also the first step that led to motion pictures (and then to television) through the work of a number of pioneers, including George Eastman (celluloid film), Thomas Edison (early motion pictures), August and Louis Lumière (the cinematograph, a motion picture projector), and a host of others. One-reelers achieved commercial success in France, England, and the United States from 1896 through 1907. Silent films spanned the years 1908 to 1929, and at the time of World War I, D. W. Griffith produced films of great scale and impact: *Birth of a Nation* (1915) and *Intolerance* (1916). The first notable European feature-length films appeared somewhat later. The German film *The Cabinet of Dr. Caligari*, produced in 1919, was outstanding. During the October Revolution, the USSR made effective use of montages of tsarist films that the new government had seized. The great French films, and those of Japan, India, and many other nations, lie largely in the era of talking pictures.

Silent films had an unprecedented international vogue. At one time, stars from many countries were predominant in U.S. films; Hollywood films and their stars were known throughout the world. Talking pictures

Vacuum Tubes

Vacuum tubes brought us the revolution of transcontinental telephony, radio, television, and computers.

The first vacuum tube was the audion, or triode, that Lee De Forest invented in 1906. The triode was improved by Irving Langmuir and Harry De Forest Arnold and was used effectively in radio during World War I. The postwar tetrode and pentode gave higher amplification. High-power tubes were developed for radio and television transmitters.

The triode and its relatives were not suited to the very short, high-frequency microwaves of radar, microwave communication systems, satellites, and spacecraft.

De Forest audion followed by its successors, ending with the pentode (Courtesy of Bell Labs)

created more of a language barrier than did silent films, although this has been overcome to a degree by dubbing in voice translations. The first successful talking films, like the first high-fidelity phonographs and sound reproduction, were an outgrowth of telephone research carried out at Bell Laboratories. From their start in 1927, talking films soon replaced silent films completely.

Television was first broadcast in England in 1929, but it did not become a powerful force until after World War II. In part, its success depended on new inventions, such as Vladimir Kosmas Zworykin's iconoscope, the

The cavity magnetron gives a powerful pulsed signal of very short wavelength and extremely high frequency. This device, at the heart of the World War II microwave radar that helped to defeat the Luftwaffe and German submarines, was invented in England. So was the traveling-wave tube, which is used as a microwave transmitter in communication satellites and far-ranging spacecraft. The klystron, invented in America, is used in powerful radars and in communicating with spacecraft, such as Voyager. The carcinotron is a newer and more efficient device.

Miniature vacuum tubes for high-frequency applications (Courtesy of Bell Labs)

A high-power, high-frequency successor of the magnetron, an experimental gyrotron made by Varian operating at 200 kilowatts and 28 gigahertz (Courtesy of Varian)

first practical television camera tube, invented in 1938. Television does not have the impact on the eye and ear of motion pictures, but it has greater immediacy in bringing into the home live spectacles, sports, political speeches and events, war, disaster, and anything and everything that people will watch and listen to, whether real or concocted. Unlike movies, television displays a modest amount of text and charts—a small concession to written language and a step toward the incorporation of written material into electronic mass media.

The vacuum tube gave us electronics. It gave us carrier telephony,

Early Digital Computers

Mechanical calculating machines were designed by Blaise Pascal (1623–1662) and Gottfried Leibniz (1646–1716). Charles Babbage envisaged a mechanical digital computer in 1835 but was unable to build an operating device. In 1880, Herman Holerith, an American statistician, devised a way to use punched cards that activated electric circuits to sort data. Card sorters developed by IBM did much early statistical sorting and business work. In 1940 George Stibitz demonstrated his "Complex Computer," a remotely controlled relay device that used binary arithmetic to make calculations that were important to electrical communication. Several other useful binary relay computers followed. Beginning in 1939, Howard Aiken constructed his Mark I machine, a decimal computer made up of relays and motor-driven elements borrowed from business machines. The

The "Complex Computer"
(Photo courtesy of Bell Labs)

or frequency-division multiplex, in which many voice signals travel on the same cable or pair of wires in different frequency ranges. It gave us time-division multiplex, in which different signals are interspersed at different times. It gave us high-fidelity recorded sound, talking pictures, and radio and television. The vacuum tube gave us sonar during World War II, and new forms of vacuum tubes gave us the invaluable radar that played a critical role in the defeat of both the Luftwaffe and Germany's submarine blockade in the North Atlantic.

The vacuum tube also gave us the first fast electronic digital comput-

first vacuum tube computer, ENIAC, was completed at the University of Pennsylvania by J. Presper Eckert and John W. Mauchly in 1946. In 1947, John von Neuman had his revolutionary idea of stored program control, which was demonstrated on a computer called the EDVAC. Earlier computers were controlled by keyboard or by programs stored on punched paper tape.

Mark I (Photo courtesy of Harvard University)

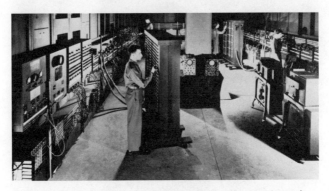

ENIAC (Photo courtesy of the University of Pennsylvania)

er, the ENIAC, built in 1946. The digital computer is proving to be a fateful step in a shift—small as yet—from the spoken language of the early electronic age to the written and symbolic world of computers and data.

Versatile as vacuum tubes were, they were limited compared with the transistor (invented in 1948 by Bardeen, Brattain, and Shockley), and the marvelous world of integrated circuits that followed. You can put one vacuum tube in your pocket. A pocket calculator, whose integrated circuit chip contains thousands of transistors and other solid-state devices, is smaller and lighter, batteries and all.

The Impact of Solid-state Devices

For their operation, vacuum tubes make use of electrons "boiled off" into a vacuum from a red-hot cathode. Solid-state devices make use of electrons that occur naturally in very pure semiconductors, such as silicon and germanium, to which minute quantities of another element, called a dopant, have been added. Amplification in a solid-state device was first demonstrated by Bardeen, Brattain, and Shockley with their invention of the transistor in 1948. Today, tens or hundreds of thousands of transistors and related devices are incorporated on one small chip of silicon a few millimeters square. Such large-scale integrated (LSI) and very-large-scale integrated (VLSI) circuits handle digital—that is, on-off—signals, and they are the tool of an all-embracing digital revolution. Their power is shown in the fact that today's battery-powered scientific hand calculator is more powerful than the ENIAC, the huge first vacuum tube computer, and by the decreased size of the memory of the ESS switching system as it was converted from magnetic storage to LSI.

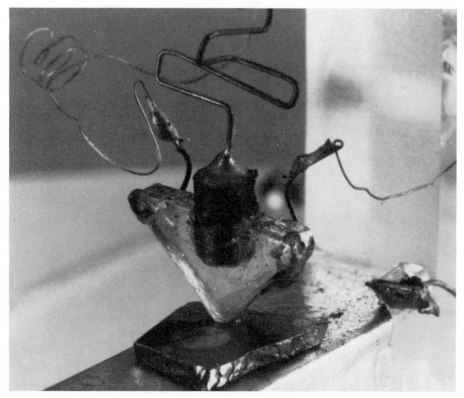

In 1947, the first transistors were large and cumbersome. (Photo courtesy Bell Labs of AT&T.)

In 1981, this solid-state computer memory chip from IBM could store 288,000 bits of information in this small area.

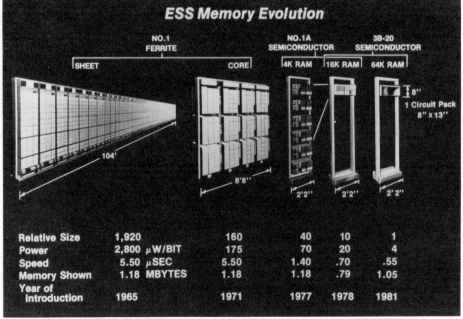

ESS Memory Evolution

| | NO.1 FERRITE | | NO.1A SEMICONDUCTOR | | 3B-20 SEMICONDUCTOR |
	SHEET	CORE	4K RAM	16K RAM	64K RAM
Relative Size	1,920	160	40	10	1
Power	2,800 μW/BIT	175	70	20	4
Speed	5.50 μSEC	5.50	1.40	.70	.55
Memory Shown	1.18 MBYTES	1.18	1.18	.79	1.05
Year of Introduction	1965	1971	1977	1978	1981

Reduction of the size of computer memory elements through solid-state technology (Courtesy of Bell Labs)

1-6 Concluding Remarks

We can regard all of human communication as supported by some sort of information technology. Language, spoken and written, is the greatest invention and the central part of information technology for communication, but other things, ranging from gestures to spectacles, also have important roles.

Various technologies have been built around or adapted to various modes of communication: letter writing and postal systems; paper and the widespread dissemination of graphic art; printing and the publication of books, journals, and newspapers; the telephone; sound recording, radio, motion pictures, and television; and, finally, computers and computer-accessible data bases. Technology has made change possible—or, indeed, inevitable. Human beings have made the changes, going where they could and where they would.

Early technologies of communication and information were disparate in nature. Some, like woodcuts, served pictorial representation. Some, like printing and telegraphy, favored written language. Others, such as the phonograph and the telephone, favored spoken language. Photography favored attitude and gesture, as did the silent movies.

Today's electronic technology is providing a common technical basis for all modes of communication. The same coaxial cables, optical fibers, microwave radio relay systems, and communication satellites that transmit thousands of telephone messages by carrier telephony are also used to transmit telegraph, data, and television signals. More and more, all sorts of communication signals—data, voice, and pictures, including pictures of earth seen from space and of far planets seen from spacecraft—are converted into the digital form of off-on pulses for transmission, switching, recording, and retrieval. The variety of modes of communication has become subject to human use and regulation, a mere aspect of the use of a common digital technology of transmission, processing, switching, storage, and retrieval.

In our present digital technology, all of the historical threads of communication technology have come together and are inextricably entangled. All signals travel over the same circuits and are used in conjunction with one another. The person at a keyboard may be generating or editing text, preparing a manuscript for publication by photocomposition (typesetting is obsolete), commanding a computer to perform an arcane calculation, searching data bases for information, performing a banking transaction, making an airline reservation, or playing a game.

As the various threads of information technology come together, so do the problems of the past. One of these is the problem posed by our multitudinous languages. Other problems include the violation of privacy and the outright theft of information, as in the use of data present in various files for personal gain, and also the falsification of data, as depicted in Dumas's novel. Another is the problem of a monopoly making the overall cost of service low versus fairness in giving the lowest rate to those whom it costs least to serve. Another is the eternal problem of evolution versus revolution: Shall we expect to progress through the gradual refinement and adaptation that have been characteristic of language, publishing, and the postal service, or will we see a series of unpredictable, revolutionary inventions like the telegraph, the telephone, radio, radar, communication satellites, the transistor, integrated circuits, and pocket calculators?

Prominent among our questions concerning the future is that of standardization. Without standardization, the world would be an inoperable chaos of incompatible equipment, systems, and services. There are, in different countries, three different television standards, and conversion among these is awkward. Yet, it is also unfortunate and awkward that the low definition of the standard used in the United States was chosen at a time when the electronic art was much more primitive. Perhaps, despite present standardization, a new standard with higher definition will emerge as a luxury option in cable television and then became a de facto standard.

What can history tell us about standardization, which is so serious and central a problem today? Standardization can come about in various ways. Languages, spoken and written, are standardized through an evolutionary process. The information technologies of radio and television and the greater mobility provided by air travel and automobiles have helped to standardize spoken language. Contrast this with organized attempts to standardize language, such as that by the French Academy, which have had only modest success. The standardization on a narrow range of roman and italic typefaces in printing occurred spontaneously within a few decades of the invention of printing by Gutenberg. Napoleon succeeded in making the metric system the standard in Europe. Was his success the result of overwhelming force, or was it, perhaps, because there was no way of reconciling the similar but not identical feet and pounds of various countries? We suspect the latter.

Information Theory

Claude Elwood Shannon's *Information Theory* (he called it "A Mathematical Theory of Communication"), published in 1948, is a landmark in understanding certain physical limitations in the process of communication. Shannon describes the amount of information as the amount of choice the sender exercises in generating a message or the amount of uncertainty on the part of the recipient as to what message he may receive. Shannon's elementary measure of amount of information is the bit, a binary choice, such as the uncertainty as to whether a flipped coin will land heads or tails. The information rate of a message source, such as speech or text, is measured in bits per message or bits per second. The capacity of a communication channel—even an imperfect channel that sometimes gives errors—can be measured in bits per second. Shannon shows that if the information rate of a particular information source is less than that of a particular communication channel, messages from the source can (in principle) be so encoded that they can be sent over the channel with an error rate less than any prescribed value, however small. Information theory is important because it tells us what we can and cannot do, because it gives us deep insight into the process of communication, and because it gives clues as to how to make better communication systems.

Shannon's theory says nothing about the meaning or content of information. It deals only with the amount of information, measured in terms of choice in the generation of a message and uncertainty as to what message will be received.

While an existing calendar was successively reformed under a Roman emperor in the mid first century (the Julian Calendar) and under a pope in the late sixteenth century (the Gregorian Calendar)—a reform not adopted in Russia until the revolution—the French Revolutionary Calendar perished, perhaps for reasons of religion or tradition, or perhaps because month names such as *Brumaire* ("Fog," beginning October 22) and *Frimairee* ("Sleet," beginning November 21), which admirably suited the weather in parts of France, didn't apply in other European countries.

International morse code was an adaptation and elaboration of the telegraph code that Morse himself invented.

In the early days of telephony, the practices of the American Bell System were copied elsewhere and hence served as a standard. Growth of information technology in other countries and a repressive antitrust policy in the United States weakened Bell's international position. Today, standardization is carried out or attempted through several international bodies, including the CCITT (a committee of the International Telecom-

munications Union of the United Nations) and the International Standards Organization, and by kindred organizations in many countries.

While standardization is essential to the proper functioning of international technology, overelaborate standards or ill-advised standards can inhibit progress and raise costs. The best standards arise from a sort of mutual consent among those who build and operate information equipment and systems. History teaches us that standards should be no more specific than necessary to assure compatibility of services and that standards should always be based on successful, operating hardware and systems and never on conjectures about things that have not been built and tried.

At any time in history, information technology is what it is and not what people dream of or what they would like it to be. This makes it important to understand our present capabilities, the tools actually at hand, and the true state of the art, which we shall explore in the next chapter.

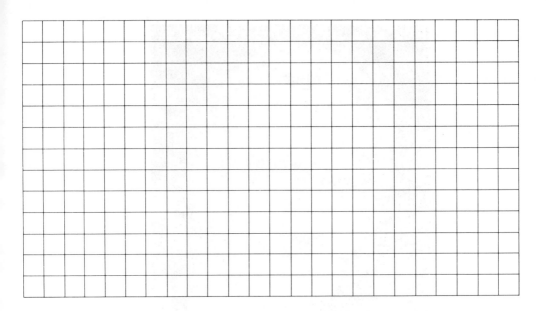

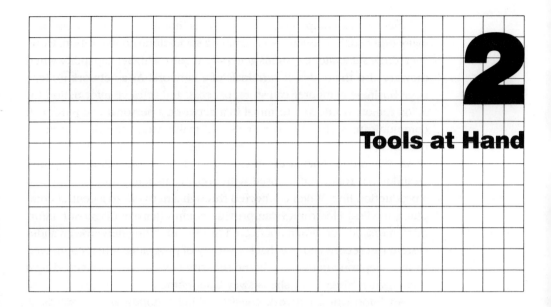

Tools at Hand

2-1 Introduction

What can information technology contribute to civilization? Only those things that it provides tools for—that is, only that which is within the state of the art, within our demonstrated ability. Thus, understanding the state of the art and the lines along which development can proceed are of crucial importance.

Naturally, the present state of the art is our best guide to what we will be able to accomplish in the near future. Unpredictable new discoveries and inventions may shape the far future, but their effects will be delayed by the processes of development, manufacture, and marketing. What we have—or can have—today is our most reliable guide as to what we will have tomorrow.

Through rapid and sustained technological innovation during the past century, we have acquired many entirely new information technologies. The pace of change will be intensified in the years ahead. We can see that even the technologies we know now will, by the end of the century, drastically change the whole picture of information technologies and services.

As utilized in our society, information technologies either form stand-alone systems or networks. Business computers, industrial robots, medical electronics equipment, audio systems, home security devices, and many other such technologies can have a stand-alone configuration. However, these stand-alone systems generally acquire a higher capability when they are also the nodes or terminals of a network. As a network node, a large business computer can store, process, and retrieve information for many remote users. As a terminal in a network, a personal computer can communicate with other terminals and make use of the diverse information resources provided by larger computers in many different locations. When coordinated through a network by a controlling computer, an industrial robot can be used with greater efficiency and flexibility in a production line. When connected through a network to a central computer, medical electronics can provide comprehensive diagnostic information to a doctor. When connected to a broadcasting network, an audio system can record and play back a variety of programs. When connected to the telephone network, a home security device can be checked by a homeowner when he or she is away from home.

An information network consists of links, nodes, and terminals. A great variety of technologies have been devised to meet ever-increasing and -diversifying demands for links, nodes, and terminals. Links of an information network can be either wires or radio waves. Coaxial cables are used for high-capacity wired links, spanning continents and the oceans. A modern coaxial cable with a bandwidth of 60 megahertz can carry the speech of more than 10,000 individuals or 800 megabits of data per second. Optical fibers offer a revolutionary advance in wired links because of their extremely broad bandwidth and low attenuation.

Microwaves, or very short radio waves, are used for high-capacity radio links for terrestrial and satellite communications. A modern communication satellite can carry more than 20,000 speech signals or several television programs. Three geostationary, or synchronous, satellites suffice to relay messages to most of the habitable parts of the earth. Radio waves of lower frequencies are extensively used for television and radio broadcasting. Radio waves are an indispensable medium for mobile communication. Ships can now use satellites to communicate and to obtain weather maps. A system known as cellular mobile communication permits automobile drivers to communicate not only with each other but also with anyone else through access to the public telephone network.

Nodes of an information network can perform a variety of functions. A large computer provides information processing for hundreds of terminals simultaneously. A data base that is used to store and update a large amount of information provides information retrieval to scientific and business users through remote terminals. Switching systems on various scales provide interconnection between a very large number of telephones and terminals for ordinary conversation and for data communication. A large telephone switching system can connect several tens of thousands of speech channels simultaneously. Modern data switching systems permit computers and terminals of different specifications to communicate with each other by transferring a number of message blocks called packets. A switching system for mobile communication tracks the movement of cars from one cellular service area to another and automatically maintains connection. A television or radio station produces a larger variety of programs that are disseminated by radio waves and over coaxial cables. An information retrieval service known as videotex provides day-to-day information retrieval to the general public.

Terminals of information networks perform an even greater variety of functions. In addition to telephones, teletypewriters, and radio and television receivers, many different types of terminals are being more widely used. Microprocessors, memories, keyboards, and television screens allow users to carry out word processing, text transmission, and on-line computing and file access from such terminals. These capabilities are broadly referred to as intelligence, and terminals having them are called intelligent terminals. Facsimile terminals permit users to transmit copies of original documents quickly through a sophisticated redundancy-reduction or data-compression technique. A request for videotex information is entered using a keypad (a small handheld keyboard), and the response is displayed on a television screen. Some terminals have character- and speech-recognition capability.

Increasingly, information networks are becoming entirely digital in order to take full advantage of the great reduction of cost and improved reliability of digital hardware and the high efficiency and versatility of digital techniques in transmitting, switching, storing and processing information in different forms. Digital technology allows centralized monitoring of network traffic as that traffic goes on (real-time monitoring), dynamic routing of overload traffic, error detection and correction, automatic diagnosis, and reconfiguration of computers. It also permits switching for rerouting in case of failure, as well as other techniques that significantly improve reliability and maintainability. Various protective means, including encryption, are now making information systems more secure against intentional or accidental disturbances.

This chapter outlines the state of the art of information technologies by discussing some of many significant topics. The information technologies we have at hand are extremely powerful tools. When properly used, these tools will provide many benefits and much impetus to the progress of civilization. When misused, however, they may cause adverse effects in our society. A basic understanding of information technologies and the state of the art is therefore crucial if we are to understand and solve today's problems and foresee impacts on the future.

2-2 Transcending Geographical Distances

Today, more than 400 million telephone sets scattered around the world can be connected arbitrarily and almost instantaneously through a worldwide telephone network that includes ocean cables and communication satellites. Radio and television broadcasting networks provide the peoples of the world with on-the-spot news reports, entertainment, and educational programs through more than a billion radio and television receivers. The peoples of the world can now understand each other better, without delay and without moving physically over long distances. They can also share a variety of information resources, regardless of where individuals or resources are located. Among the variety of technologies that are permitting us to transcend geographical distances, satellites and optical fibers are perhaps the most outstanding in their present and potential impacts on human activities.

Communication satellites have given us one world through instant television news and by access to remote places by telephone. They are an amazing and gratifying example of the contributions of space and microwave technologies to civilization. The idea of communication satellites was first put forward about 39 years ago by Arthur C. Clarke. The Echo balloon passive communication satellite was launched in 1960, 24 years ago. Telstar, which first carried television across the ocean, was launched 22 years ago. Syncom, the first synchronous satellite (one that maintains a constant position in relation to the earth), was launched 21 years ago. Early Bird, or INTELSAT I, the first commercial satellite, was launched 19 years ago. INTELSAT I could provide 240 two-way telephone circuits or 1 television channel. Today, one INTELSAT satellite (INTELSAT V) provides 12,000 telephone circuits plus 2 television channels, and INTELSAT VI will have a still greater capacity.

Selective coverage by special antennas aboard modern communications satellites, such as the Galaxy models: Each Galaxy has 24 transponders. *Galaxy I* was launched on June 28, 1983. It is owned by Hughes Communications, and is used to distribute cable television programs. (Photo courtesy of Hughes Aircraft Company)

Communication satellites are microwave repeaters that receive signals beamed at them from one point on the earth's surface and transmit an amplified signal back toward earth, where the signal can be received at one or several locations. Use of such satellites requires large dish-shaped antennas, ranging from a few meters to 30 meters in diameter. Such antennas can be used on ships but not on airplanes or automobiles, so at present, highly effective mobile satellite communication is limited to maritime use. Designs have been proposed to allow satellite communication with planes and cars, but economic and regulatory problems have thus far prevented implementation.

The initial use of communication satellites was to provide television and telephone links across oceans. They have been particularly important for telephone communication to countries not reached by submarine cables. Before communication satellites, the internal communication systems of such countries were linked to other countries only by shortwave radio, which provided limited and fragile service. Satellites have proved very useful in regional and domestic communication as well.

INTELSAT is owned and operated by the International Telecommunications Satellite Organization, of which 109 nations are members. Member countries own their own earth stations. In the United States, COMSAT (Communications Satellite Corporation) is the designated signatory of INTELSAT. The organization owns 12 satellites used in international communication. It also provides domestic communication service in 26 countries. The INTELSAT system has 398 earth stations with 329 antennas located in 148 countries. In provides about 30,000 two-way telephone circuits that are leased full time and a great deal of occasional television and other communication services. The owners' investment in INTELSAT is about $1.24 billion, and the yearly revenues are about $300 million.

The Soviet bloc countries are not members of INTELSAT; they are served by an organization called INTERSPUTNIK, which provides international and domestic service. However, several of these countries have stations operating in the INTELSAT system.

In 1976, 1977, and 1983 Indonesia launched three Palapa satellites, which provide communication among the islands of that country.

Canada has a Telesat system, with four satellites, that provides a large amount of communication in southern Canada as well as links to the sparsely settled Northwest Territories.

The United States has many domestic satellites: 2 Westar (Western Union) satellites, 3 Satcom (RCA) satellites, 4 Comstar satellites (launched by COMSAT General and leased to AT&T), one Telstar (AT&T) satellite, and 2 SBS (Satellite Business Systems) satellites. (SBS is owned jointly by COMSAT General, IBM and Aetna Life & Casualty.) A good deal of the capacity of these domestic satellites is used in carrying programs to a number of cable television systems in various parts of the country. They are also used to send the copies of printing plates of national newspapers and journals to various parts of the country, where the issues are printed locally. They provide a great deal of point-to-point telephone, data, network television, and facsimile transmission and are used for conferences linked by closed-circuit television. Domestic satellites are particularly useful when there is unusually high but transitory regional traffic or when

The SBS telecommunications satellite, launched November 15, 1980, from Cape Canaveral, Florida: The first of a series of three, the satellite was built by Hughes for Satellite Business Systems to provide secure voice, video teleconferencing, data, and electronic mail services to U.S. businesses. The powerful satellite has two concentric cylindrical solar panels, which open out in space from about 3 meters to nearly 7 meters high, to double the spacecraft's solar power generating capacity over many previous satellites. (Photo courtesy of Hughes Aircraft Company)

other communication facilities go out of service, because satellites can be used to provide circuits between different points at different times. The SBS satellite system is designed primarily to provide private networks for large organizations that have multiple, dispersed locations.

The MARISAT system, developed by COMSAT General, launched three satellites in 1976. These provide leased circuits to the U.S. Navy and provide voice and telex service to 468 terminals on ships flying the flags of 40 nations. INMARSAT, an international counterpart of INTELSAT, started operation in 1982, with the commercial transponders of these MARISAT satellites. Since then they have employed the capacity of the maritime frequency transponders on the MARECS and INTELSAT V satellites.

Syncom, which was launched in 1963, weighed only 36 kilograms (79 pounds). INTELSAT V weighs 1012 kilograms (2231 pounds) and has over 50 times the communication capacity of Syncom. In part, progress in satellite communication has come about through an ability to launch larger, heavier, and more complicated satellites. It also has come about through the exploitation of newly available frequency bands. Early satellites used a 6000-megahertz uplink frequency and a 4000-megahertz downlink frequency, with a total bandwidth of 500-megahertz.* Some new satellites also use a 14,000-megahertz uplink frequency and a 12,000-megahertz downlink frequency, with a 500-megahertz bandwidth. It is expected that in the future, a 30,000-megahertz uplink frequency and a 20,000-megahertz downlink frequency will be used with a 2500 MHz bandwidth, although signals in these frequency ranges are weakened by heavy rain. The effects of rain can be overcome to some extent by using two earth stations separated by a few miles; it is unlikely that heavy bursts of rain will occur at both simultaneously.

The antennas of the earliest satellites, such as Telstar, sent microwave power out in all directions; consequently, only a little of the power reached the earth. The receiving antennas of these satellites were likewise not focused on the earth. Today's advanced satellites have narrow antenna beams that cover the disk of the earth for handling light traffic and still narrower beams aimed at particular densely populated areas to handle heavy traffic. Also, advanced satellites can make separate use of the two different possible polarizations of radio waves and thus double the number of circuits that can be provided in a given band of frequencies.

Frequency modulation was used in early satellite communication and

---

*One megahertz (1 MHz) equals 1 million cycles per second.

Part of an HS 376 antenna system, mounted in a radome atop a Hughes facility, undergoes antenna pattern measurements. Communications satellite antenna systems are designed to produce shaped beams to cover specific patterns of receivers and transmitters on earth.

is used to carry most present traffic. However, frequency modulation is giving way to digital transmission, which is more efficient when one satellite repeater must handle traffic originating from several earth stations. Digital transmission is also well adapted to switching messages aboard satellites, which seems sure to come in the future.

It is uncertain whether or not satellites will have a very substantial use in direct broadcast of television to homes. Comsat General plans to launch satellites for direct broadcast in the United States. The Japanese have a satellite that has been used for experimental broadcasts to homes, and they have developed effective home receiving equipment. However, the number of people in Japan who do not receive television by other means is small and decreasing. Experiments with direct broadcasting to homes have been motivated in part by a legal obligation of Japan to reach all citizens with broadcast television. The experimental NASA ATS-6 satellite was used to broadcast to Indian villages educational information, which the government found difficult to convey in other ways. The number of programs that can be sent to a home by satellite is small compared with the number that can be sent by cable, and there is no way to supply local news, weather, or advertising in television via satellite.

The total satellite communication capacity that can be made available depends on the total microwave bandwidth assigned for this use and on how many satellites are put in orbit around the equator. Large, highly directive earth antennas allow close spacing of satellites; small earth antennas require larger spacing between satellites. INTELSAT satellites can be spaced as close as 3 degrees apart, allowing 120 positions around the equator. COMSAT and Canada have been spacing domestic satellites 3 to 4 degrees apart. The United States Federal Communications Commission has specified a 2-degree spacing for domestic satellites, with a few exceptions for early satellites.

At present, the greatest technological uncertainty concerning communication satellites is how future satellites, which are getting larger and heavier, will be launched. Past civilian satellites have been launched with such vehicles as Delta, Atlas Centaur, or Ariane. The U.S. plans to rely on the manned space shuttle to launch future satellites.

Certainly, satellites can provide a great deal of communication capacity between many locations on earth. This capacity can be established very rapidly, regardless of the distance between locations to be linked. One need merely launch satellites and establish earth stations. But the potential satellite communication capacity is limited, in contrast to the potential capacity of signals that travel without mutual interference on cables, wires, or as light waves through transparent optical fibers. Moreover, satellites cannot provide millions of independent circuits directly to homes and offices. On the other hand, mobile services cannot be provided by wire, cable, or fiber. We may expect a very rapid growth in satellite communication in the future, but we may expect a very rapid growth in other modes of communication as well.

Lightwave transmission via highly transparent optical fibers promises

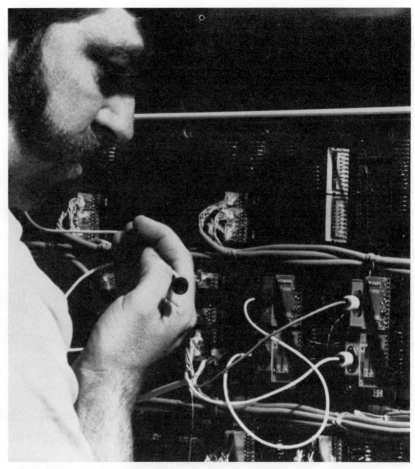

A Bell System local and toll digital switch: The cables contain lightguides that carry signals through the switch. (Photo courtesy of Bell Labs)

to have a revolutionary effect on all communication, whether over long, intermediate, or short distances. At present, it is in an early stage of use. The first applications were in interconnecting communication centers a few kilometers apart and in interconnecting the component units of computer systems and digital communication systems. At present, a 3200-km system is being installed in Saskatchewan, and transoceanic undersea cables are planned.

Lightwave communications systems transmit all signals digitally,

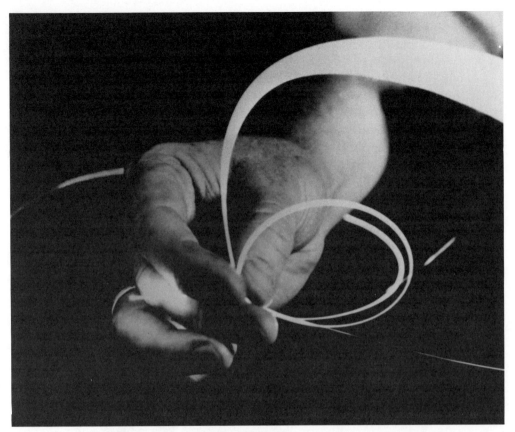

Glass fiber used to transmit light signals (Reproduced with permission of AT&T)

whether the signals are television, voice, or data. This is partly because of a general trend in the whole communication industry toward digital communication. Partly it is because the properties of the fibers themselves—and, more especially, the properties of the devices used to generate and receive light signals—are best adapted to digital operation.

In 1968, it was conceived that it should be possible to make very pure transparent fibers with so low an attenuation (loss of light) as to allow communication over considerable distances with little loss of power. In 1970, the first low-loss fibers were produced. These fibers could deliver a least 10 percent of the signal over a distance of a kilometer (a loss of

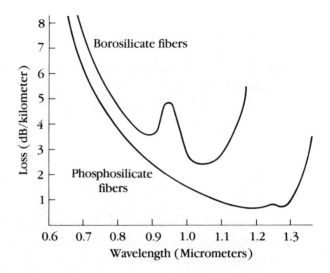

Figure 2-1 Signal loss in fibers (expressed in decibels per kilometer) decreases as the wavelength increases in the range shown. The upper curve represents loss in the type of fibers used in Chicago and currently in production; the bottom curve, the lower loss achieved in a newer fiber that will soon go into production. (Courtesy of Bell Labs)

less than 10 decibels per kilometer). Other research in the United States, Japan and elsewhere has resulted in the production of fibers of lower losses. Figure 2-1 shows a plot of loss versus wavelength of the light used. At a wavelength of around 1.3 micrometers (1.3 millionths of a meter, in the infrared), the loss can be less than 1 decibel per kilometer.

In addition to the optical fiber, a working lightwave communication system must include a device for generating light, a device which can be controlled by an electrical signal, and a device for turning received light signals into electrical signals.

Light sources are semiconductor lasers, which generate a single frequency and a single mode or spatial distribution of light, and LEDs (light-emitting diodes), which generate a narrow range of frequencies and a broader spatial distribution. Lasers can be used with single-mode fibers, through which the light travels in a unique pattern, with all parts of the pattern traveling at the same speed. LEDs are used with multimode fibers, through which a light pattern travels in a complex way, with its different parts moving at slightly different speeds. Thus, in multimode fibers, fed by LEDs, the signals that are initially very short pulses of light spread out as they travel (this is called dispersion). This limits the distance over which they can be sent and still be received accurately.

The devices used to convert the received light pulses into electrical signals are called photodiodes. A particular type now used is the PIN diode (the acronym comes from *P* semiconductor layer, *I*ntrinsic semiconductor layer, *N* semiconductor layer).

Early lasers, LEDs, and photodiodes worked at wavelengths around 0.8 micrometers, for which the attenuation of the best fibers is around 3 decibels per kilometer; actual fibers in a cable have an attenuation of around 5 decibels per kilometer. Later work has produced lasers and LEDs that operate at longer wavelengths, for which the attenuation is lower, and LEDs and PIN photodiodes for operation at 1.3 micrometers now seem practical. It is possible to send a single-mode signal 160 kilometers between repeaters at a rate of 420 million bits a second. Single-mode fibers can actually be used at pulse rates up to several thousand million pulses per second. It is not yet clear what pulse rates will be most advantageous.

Lightwave communication over optical fibers has many advantages. The fibers are electrical nonconductors, so unintended currents cannot flow along them between apparatus that they interconnect. This is advantageous in interconnecting complicated, computerlike equipment; fiber interconnections will be widely used for this reason alone. Immunity from electrical interference makes possible a very low frequency of errors in lightwave transmission systems.

The greatest advantage of optical fibers is their low attenuation. While the attenuation of wires and cables can be low at low frequencies, the attenuation goes up rapidly as the frequency or bandwidth is increased. This makes it difficult and expensive to provide individual broad-band communication paths to offices and homes. Optical fibers promise to make this possible and also to make medium-haul and long-haul broadband communication cheaper. We have already noted the 3200-km system for Saskatchewan. There are definite plans for a transatlantic lightwave cable that would use multiple single-mode fibers to carry 36,000 simultaneous telephone conversations—three times the capacity of one of the INTELSAT satellites in use in 1982. The cable is to be put into service in 1988 at a cost of $230 million. A cable linking the mainland United States to Hawaii is also contemplated.

Another advantage of optical fibers is their small cross section. This makes it possible to increase communication capacity in cities by substi-

New lightwave telephone cable (right) compared with coaxial telephone cable (Photo courtesy of Bell Labs)

tuting fibers for wire cables in existing ducts. In addition, their light weight makes it possible to string high-capacity circuits from poles.

An early disadvantage of optical fibers was their considerable cost compared with pairs of wires. However, in 1981 Northern Telecom of Canada estimated that the installed cost per 2-way circuit mile for fiber, for a comparable capacity, to be 20 percent less than for copper. Eventually, the preferred individual circuit to an office or home will not be a pair of wires, but rather a broad-band optical fiber capable of transmitting two-way television along with voice or data.

Even if the cost of optical fibers falls drastically, fibers will not cause the instant revolution that communication satellites did. Launching a satellite and constructing a few earth stations establishes communication to remote areas very quickly. Setting up an earth station can enable a cable television system to pick up programs from a central location. The full exploitation of lightwave communication will mean routing fibers to millions of locations most of which are already served by existing wire pairs. This will take time, and it would be very expensive even if the fibers themselves were to cost nothing.

For these reasons, and also because the technology is in an early and evolving state, the first applications have been modest—the interconnection of existing telephone communication centers a few miles apart in a number of metropolitan areas. A typical pulse rate is 44.7 million pulses per second per fiber, and a typical cable has 12 fibers bound together in one plastic tape and 12 tapes (144 fibers) per cable. The installation of fibers for such uses is progressing rapidly. In 1981 in the United States, over 15,000 miles of fiber was installed. It is universally recognized that in the long range, the potential of optical fibers is enormous. Research and development are going forward at a rapid pace around the world.

2-3 An Integrated Digital World

Technologies for transmitting, switching, processing, and retrieving information are increasingly becoming digital and are being combined to form an integrated whole. Analog signals, such as speech, visual patterns, or the outputs of various sensors, are converted to digital signals. At the far end, digital signals are converted back to analog signals to be heard through telephone receivers, displayed on cathode-ray tube (CRT) screens, or recorded on paper. Characters are converted into digital codes by the manipulation of keyboards and, at the far end, are converted back to characters to be displayed on a screen or printed on paper. While in its digital form, information is switched through communication networks, processed by computers, and stored for information retrieval.

One of the typical examples of such integration is on-line banking systems. In the old days, when files were kept in individual branch offices of a bank, a customer who wished to withdraw money had to go to the branch office where he or she had deposited it. In today's on-line banking systems, files are stored and updated in a centralized data base. By using a machine that is connected to the center, a teller in any branch office can find a customer's balance, give the customer money, and update the balance, which is part of the data base. The customer can also get a limited amount of cash instantly at any time by inserting a card in a cash-dispensing machine, which is connected by a telephone line to the centralized data base.

On-line reservation systems, which are used by airlines, railroads, hotels, and other businesses, work in a similar fashion. In a department store or supermarket, a cashier can identify a commodity by using a light pen, which is connected to the point-of-sales terminal (cash register), to scan code bars printed on the commodity. The terminal then prints a detailed sales slip and transmits the sales information to a central computer. When a customer uses a credit card, the point-of-sales terminal also reads the credit card and sends the information for verification. The central computer, with its data base, makes use of the information from point-of-sales terminals for accounting and inventory-control purposes.

Automobile manufacturers have even more sophisticated information systems. In accordance with the information sent from each dealer's terminal, central computers update production plans for various models with certain options, order components and parts from subcontractors to be delivered in exact quantities and at the right times, schedule the distribution of components and parts along production lines, and communicate with industrial robots and assembly workers.

The invention of transistors and the remarkable progress of solid-state circuit technology that followed brought about the revolutionary change in information technology. Such important inventions as pulse code modulation (PCM), described below, and digital computers were made practical and useful through the high performance and low cost of solid-state devices.

Before the advent of pulse code modulation, modern high-speed information transmission was based on an analog technology. In this technology, electrical signals are analogs of speech sounds; the electric voltage changes in accordance with changes in air pressure in the sound waves produced in speaking. Many such individual speech signals are transmitted over a single wire or channel by modulating a number of carriers of different frequencies.

Carrier telephony of this sort is known as frequency-division-multiplex (FDM). At present, FDM systems can carry as many as 10,800 speech signals or several television signals over a single coaxial cable, or 12,000 speech signals plus 2 television signals over a single satellite microwave link. Analog modulation is also employed in broadcasting radio and tel-

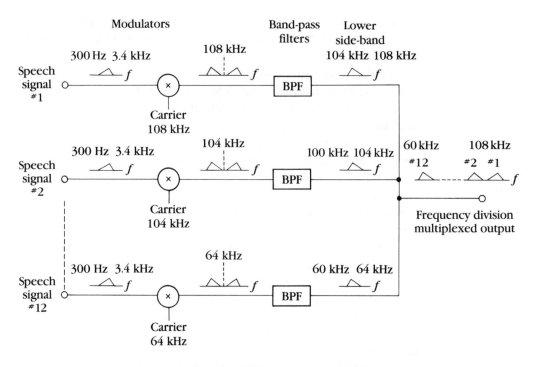

Figure 2-2 Principle of frequency-division-multiplexing (FDM): Twelve speech signals, each occupying a bandwidth of slightly less than 4 kHz, are applied to the modulators. The output of a modulator, which is the multiplication of the speech signal and the carrier, consists of an upper side-band and a lower side-band, which are centered around the carrier. The outputs are then fed to the band-pass filters that select only the lower side-bands. A combination of 12 lower side-bands occupies the band from 60 kHz to 108 kHz. The combined signal, which is called a group, is further combined with four other groups to form a supergroup of 60 speech signals, and five supergroups form a master group of 300 speech signals. (In the Bell System, ten supergroups form a master group of 600 speech signals.) As many as 10,800 speech signals can now be frequency-division-multiplexed and transmitted over a coaxial cable. (Source: Inose, *Digital Integrated Communications Systems*)

evision programs. Another analog system is space-division-multiplex (SDM) telephone switching—a new name for the old telephone switchboard, where individual signals are carried by separate wires.

Pulse code modulation is a digital technology. It is characterized by three processes: sampling, quantizing, and coding. In sampling, an analog

Subsets

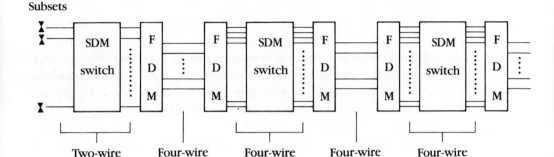

| Two-wire base band | Four-wire carrier transmission | Four-wire base band | Four-wire carrier transmission | Four-wire base band |

Figure 2-3 Network with FDM transmission and SDM switching: When frequency-division-multiplex (FDM) is used for transmission, modulated and multiplexed speech signals have to be demultiplexed and demodulated before being switched by a space-division-multiplex (SDM) switch, and after switching, they have to be modulated and multiplexed to be transmitted. The repetition of the procedure results in an accumulation of noise (caused by the modulation and demodulation) as well as an increase in cost. A pair of wires from a subset transmits the speech signal two ways and hence are called the two-wire base band lines. After being switched, the speech signals are modulated and frequency-division-multiplexed at the transmitting end. The carrier transmission path is one way, so two pairs of wires are required to transmit and receive a signal. Such a path is called a four-wire path. At the receiving end, the speech signals are demultiplexed and demodulated and enter the SDM switch over four-wire base band trunks. (SOURCE: Inose, *Digital Integrated Communications Systems*)

speech signal is sampled periodically in order to find its instantaneous amplitude. In quantizing, the sample amplitude is assigned to one of many small ranges of amplitude, and so the continuous range of amplitudes is represented approximately by a number of discrete amplitudes. In coding, each discrete amplitude is represented by a sequence of off-on electrical pulses that represent the quantized amplitude derived from the analog signal.

A technique known as time-division-multiplex (TDM) is employed in transmitting many speech signals encoded by PCM. The period of sampling, which is typically 125 microseconds, is divided into a number of time slots, and one of the encoded speech signals is carried within each of these time slots. Carrier telephony by PCM-TDM can carry as many as 5760 speech signals over a coaxial cable or a microwave link.

One of the benefits of PCM is its immunity to noise through the use of simple devices called regenerative repeaters. A regenerative repeater identifies the presence or absence of a received pulse and then transmits a new, reshaped, retimed, noise-free pulse. By using a sequence of regenerative repeaters, the original speech quality can be retained even when transmitted through noisy channels over long distances. Digital transmission with remarkably low error rates thus becomes possible. Because of the complexity of the circuitry that performs sampling, quantizing, coding, and multiplexing, PCM-TDM systems became practical only after the advent of transistors and integrated circuits.

Despite PCM-TDM systems having been successfully introduced for speech transmission, existing space-division-multiplex systems have remained dominant for telephone switching. As a result, at the input of each switching node of a network, FDM or TDM signals must be demultiplexed and demodulated or decoded in order to provide individual speech signals to be SDM switched; at the output, the individual speech signals must be modulated or encoded and multiplexed so that they can be transmitted by an FDM or PCM link. This is not only costly, but, it also

Figure 2-4 Principle of time-division-multiplexing (TDM) and pulse code modulation (PCM): A pair of switches at the transmitting and receiving ends rotate in synchronism across 24 contacts, to each of which 24 individual speech signals are fed (a). The instantaneous amplitudes of the speech signals are repeatedly sampled as the switch rotates (b). The sampled speech signals in the form of the pulse amplitude modulation (PAM) are combined to form time-division-multiplexed (TDM) signals (c). The TDM-PAM signals are then quantized (d) and coded (e). In this illustrative example coding into four bits is shown. The PAM sequences, i.e., 113, 52, 119, 58, and 151 millivolts, are divided by the quantizing step of 10 millivolts into 11, 5, 12, 6, and 15 steps, respectively (d), and are converted into four-bit binary codes, 1011, 0101, 1100, 0110, and 1111, which represent decimal numbers 11, 5, 12, 6, and 15 (e). The truncation error in the quantizing process is called the quantizing noise. In practice, seven-bit coding is generally employed to reduce quantizing noise to less than 1 percent. The framing pulse shown in (e) is inserted to tell the receiving end when the next sampling interval begins. The number of time slots in a sampling interval ranges from 24 to 5,760. (SOURCE: Inose, *Digital Integrated Communications Systems*)

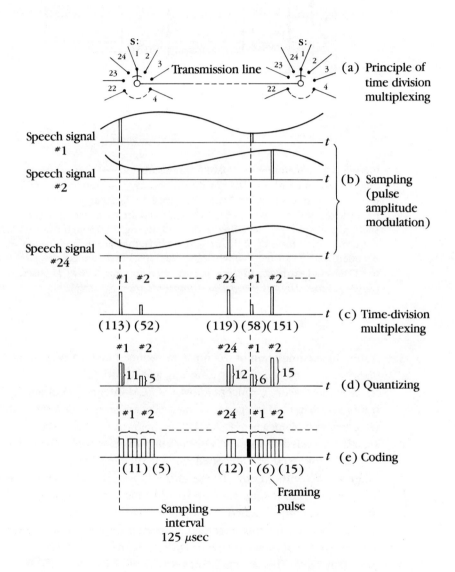

(a) Principle of time division multiplexing

(b) Sampling (pulse amplitude modulation)

(c) Time-division multiplexing

(d) Quantizing

(e) Coding

Subsets

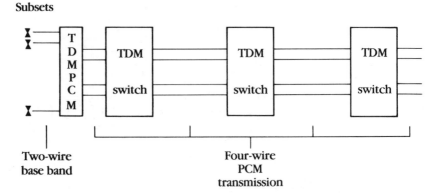

Figure 2-5 Network with TDM-PCM transmission and TDM switching: When time-division-multiplex (TDM) by means of pulse code modulation (PCM) is used for transmission and switching, the speech signals are encoded and multiplexed at the entrance of the network and are then transmitted and switched, without any decoding or demultiplexing, all through the network until they reach the exit of the network, where they are demultiplexed and decoded. Except for the two-wire base band lines that connect the subsets to the TDM-PCM terminal, all transmission paths are four-wire PCM buses. (SOURCE: Inose, *Digital Integrated Communication Systems*)

results in accumulation of the noise introduced in each process of modulation and demodulation or encoding and decoding.

For this reason, a concept known as PCM-integrated communication has emerged. In PCM-integrated communication, transmission and switching are integrated by means of PCM-TDM techniques. In such a system, speech signals are coded and time-division-multiplexed at their points of origin and demultiplexed and decoded only at their points of destination. In other words, without any change in their form, speech signals in coded and time-division-multiplexed form not only are transmitted over the links but also are switched at the nodes. This prevents the quality of a speech signal from being degraded, no matter how many links and nodes are involved in its path. It also provides circuits for data transmission at low error rates. This arrangement also drastically cuts down the cost of the network by avoiding modulation (or coding) and demodulation (or decoding) at each link and by replacing inefficient SDM switches at each node.

The mainframe of this IBM 3081 processor complex (the cabinet with two doors, at the rear) consists of a number of modules that carry highly integrated circuit chips. This mainframe contains some 20 modules in a volume close to one-tenth of a cubic meter. Each module consists of up to 133 chips, which are mounted on a board, 9 centimeters on a side, having 33 layers. A module contains more than 45,000 logical circuits—equivalent to an IBM 370/148 computer. Covered hermetically by a metal plate and filled with helium gas, a module is cooled by circulating water. (Photo courtesy of IBM)

The concept of PCM-TDM switching was strengthened by the invention of time-slot interchange, which made it possible to switch the speech signal from one time slot to another by using temporary memories. The fact that PCM-TDM switching requires a large amount of memory delayed its full-fledged introduction until medium-scale and large-scale integrated circuit technology had drastically cut the cost of memory circuits.

It was digital technology that first made the integration of transmission and switching of information possible in telecommunication. However, the benefits of digital technology are many, and this integration is but one of them.

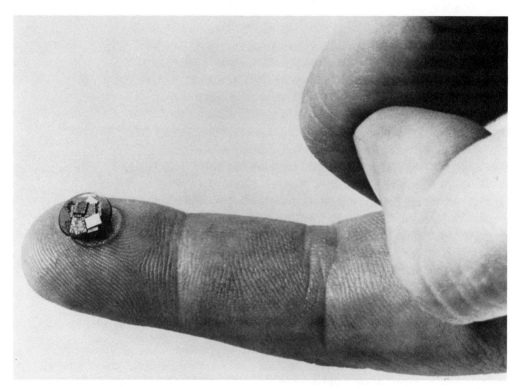

Silicon chips in a contact lens (Photo courtesy of Philips)

First of all, digital circuitry provides a drastic reduction in hardware cost, extremely high reliability and maintainability, and substantial savings of space, material, and energy. At present, progress in large-scale integrated circuit technology is reducing both the cost of digital hardware and the failure rate of components by more than an order of magnitude each decade. Digital circuitry permits the extensive use of automatic diagnostic techniques and thereby drastically reduces repair time and maintenance costs.

Digital systems with more than 100,000 components are now operating almost trouble-free, with a total estimated down time of only a few hours over 20 years. More than 10,000 components may now be mounted on a chip of some 30 square millimeters and consume very little material and electric energy. Chips with hundreds of thousands of components will be common in the near future.

Secondly, digital techniques enhance transmission capability. Extremely broad-band transmission media such as optical fibers are now available, but their transmission characteristics require the noise immunity of digital techniques in order to fully realize their capability. A digital technique known as time-division-multiple-access (TDMA) provides more efficient use of a satellite link in communicating with a number of earth stations than does a frequency-division counterpart. Subscriber lines that receive very low levels of use can be made more efficient by digital multiplexing, which sends many messages over one link, thus using more of the available capacity of these channels. Data of various speeds can be transmitted much more efficiently by digital transmission than by its analog counterpart. Speech, data, and visual signals for customers, as well as control and supervisory signals for setting up and releasing connections through the network, can be transmitted by digital techniques in a unified form.

Thirdly, digital techniques permit sophisticated signal processing and efficient signal handling. Coding of analog signals permits the use of digital processing to drastically reduce redundancy, and the use of inexpensive microprocessors provides opportunities for more sophisticated processing, for example, pattern recognition. Digital information can be temporarily stored without distortion in digital memories, which are rapidly becoming inexpensive. Such temporary storage permits more efficient use of network facilities and provides a variety of benefits, such as refreshing the image on the screen and converting signals to different speeds (part of what is called buffering). Above all, digital communication provides better interfacing between computers and terminals.

In contrast to speech communication, which requires a negligible transmission delay that can be provided by so-called circuit switching, data communication generally permits some delay in data delivery. Taking advantage of this fact, data communication employs another form of switching, known as store-and-forward switching, a predecessor of systems that switch packets of information. Messages are generally divided into a number of message blocks. By keeping message blocks waiting until a path to the destination becomes available, higher usage of facilities is attained.

Circuit switching is also used in connecting terminals to the computer by means of a switched telephone network. The use of acoustic couplers, which convert binary data into audible tones, provides four-wire connection through the switched telephone network.

The concept of data communication has now been extended further

New computer-based, mobile, digital telephone networks provide advanced communication capabilities. Such new systems are more flexible and powerful than larger systems based on older technology. (Photo courtesy Philips)

to provide communication between remote computers. A network with a number of computers at its nodes permits users to gain access, by way of their terminals, to any one of the computers in the network. This provides the benefit of sharing hardware, software, data bases, and other information resources.

Among such information resources, data bases are outstanding in the sense that they provide information selected to suit users' needs through information retrieval. Four major functions—transmission, switching, processing, and provision of information—are thus combined to give an integrated digital world.

As the needs of society for information and information-related services become more diverse, the concept of an integrated-service digital network (ISDN) is emerging. The capacity of digital technology to handle information in various forms and to provide diverse services in a unified manner is a crucial factor because, although the amount of information to be carried by each individual service may be small, the aggregate demand is very large.

2-4 Pervasive Computer Power

While inflation is pushing up the prices of almost all commodities, computers are getting cheaper year after year. This is partly due to rapid technological innovation, but more significantly, it is due to the exploding demand for computers in a great variety of activities. As we find numerous electric motors in our homes, the use of computers is now expanding into almost all aspects of our lives. Unlike electric motors, whose designs and uses have changed little over decades, computers are in a process of dramatic evolution. Knowledge of the trends in computer technology is therefore crucial if we are to understand their societal implications.

Until a few years ago, the distinctions among computers, minicomputers, and microprocessors were clear. A typical computer used a 32-bit word, had a main memory of up to 16 megabytes (where one byte corresponds to eight bits or one character), and was capable of processing a few million instructions per second (MIPS). It had a sophisticated operating system that could process a number of programs concurrently, provide virtual memory space larger than that of a physical main memory, and enable the implementation of a large variety of sophisticated application programs, including a data base management system (DBMS) to allow retrieval and updating of information from data bases, and a time-sharing system (TSS) to provide interactive communication with a large number of terminals simultaneously. It had a variety of language processors to allow users to write their programs more easily by using high-level languages.

A typical minicomputer used a 16-bit word, had a main memory of up to 256 kilobytes, and was capable of processing up to a few tens of thousands of instructions per second. It had a much simpler operating system and a few language processors.

A typical microprocessor used either a 4-bit or 8-bit word, had a main memory of up to 64 kilobytes, and was slower and far less capable than a minicomputer.

The rapid progress of digital integrated circuit technology brought about a drastic change. In the early 1970's, less than 5000 transistors of a 4-bit microprocessor were mounted on a chip of 5 millimeters on a side. In the mid 1970's, about 10,000 transistors for an 8-bit microprocessor were mounted on a chip of similar size. By 1980, 16-bit microprocessors, with more than 20,000 transistors mounted on a slightly larger chip, appeared on the market. Chips with hundreds of thousands of transistors are close to being available.

A 32-bit microprocessor mounted on a single chip has appeared. This has been incorporated in a computer with a main memory of up to 2.5 megabytes and a fast disk of 10 megabytes or more. This means that a microprocessor is superseding conventional minicomputers and coming close in power to the large computers of several years ago. Some microprocessors will be designed to be fully compatible with large computers so as to make use of the enormous bank of software products already in use on large machines. At present, the computer based on the 32-bit microprocessor costs several tens of thousands of dollars, but within a few years such powerful microprocessors may cost only a few thousand dollars, about a hundredth of the cost of a present large central processor with similar capability.

Mass production and mass consumption helped to bring about a drastic cost reduction in microprocessors. A 4-bit microprocessor that cost a few hundred dollars in the early 1970's is now available for a few dollars. As a result, microprocessors are becoming more common and are being employed in almost all spheres of human activity, whether or not this use is immediately evident. A large number of 4-bit and 8-bit microprocessors of newer generations are now used as versatile controllers for machine tools, automotive engines, and business machines as well as in many other applications.

Microcomputers that include microprocessors, floppy disks, keyboards, displays, and printers are now used not only for personal computing and entertainment but also for business purposes, and these are supported by a variety of software packages. Personal computers are also used as on-line terminals when supplemented by appropriate interfaces or as word processors when supplied with an appropriate software package. Operating systems with various application programs are now available for microcomputers. The most popular language for microcomputers used to be BASIC, but more powerful languages are now emerging for 8-bit and 16-bit microprocessors.

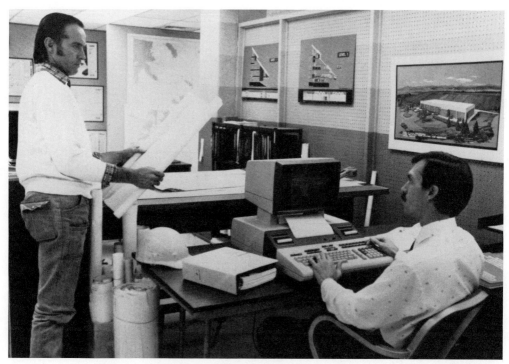

Desktop computers in daily work: This system brings computer power and graphics into the workplace for engineering, construction, and technical work. (Photo courtesy Hewlett-Packard)

Besides microprocessors, another significant trend in computer technology is the introduction of supercomputers. Unlike large-scale general-purpose computers, which are designed mainly for business applications, supercomputers are special-purpose computers for scientific applications that deal, in particular, with large matrix arrays. Examples of uses for such supercomputers include solving equations of fluid motion on a very large scale for weather forecasting and for other fluid-dynamics studies, analyzing models in nuclear physics, making computer-aided tomograms, exploring for oil resources, and cracking cryptograms. To improve accuracy or extend coverage, the number of rows and columns in the matrix arrays treated by such computers is being increased. Doubling the number of rows and columns quadruples the number of elements in a two-

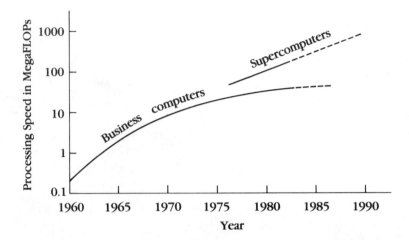

Figure 2-6 The processing speed of large-scale business computers used for scientific calculations is less than 30 million floating point operations per second (30 megaFLOPs), with special software and in multiprocessor configurations. Special-purpose computers known as supercomputers attain processing speeds of 100 megaFLOPs or more through a high degree of parallelism. The ultimate target of supercomputers is 1000 megaFLOPs.

dimensional array and increases by eight times the number of elements in a three-dimensional array.

Since most scientific calculations are done with floating decimal point arithmetic, the capability of a supercomputer is expressed in FLOPS, that is, the number of floating point operations per second. Since the mid 1970's, powerful supercomputers that can attain a maximum throughput of 100 megaFLOPs or more have appeared on the market. A large-scale general-purpose computer can attain a maximum throughput of only 30 megaFLOPs, even when special software for array processing is implemented.

Some supercomputers are built as stand-alone systems. Special hardware known as an array processor may also be attached to a large-scale general-purpose computer to form a supercomputer, allowing it to perform many operations at once (parallel processing). Some consist of a very large number of processors. The ultimate target of supercomputers is now seen as 1000 megaFLOPs. Supercomputers with 200 megaFLOPs or more will soon appear on the market.

Still another significant trend in computer technology is progress in information-storage devices. Storage devices are categorized as one of two types, a main memory (high speed) and a file (large capacity). For a large-capacity main memory, integrated circuit chips that consist of field-effect transistors (often called MOS transistors) are used almost exclusively. A main memory chip with a capacity of 64 kilobits and an access time (time required to read and write) of some 100 nanoseconds has been available on the market since 1980. The capacity may soon be enhanced to 512 kilobits and the speed to 50 nanoseconds. These chips are assembled to form a main memory with a total capacity of up to 64 megabytes. Since a main memory is slower than a fast central processor, another memory, known as a cache memory, is used for buffering purposes. A cache memory employs very fast bipolar transistors similar to those used for a central processor. A cache memory has an access time of less than 30 nanoseconds and a capacity of several tens of kilobytes.

Files employ magnetic recording. A thin layer of iron oxide is coated on the surface of a disk or a tape. When a disk or a tape is driven under a recording electromagnet, known as a recording head, magnetic dipoles in the surface layer are aligned in either of two directions in accordance with the directions of the recording head.

Files chiefly use magnetic disks, with magnetic tapes for backup. The storage density of magnetic disks has been enhanced significantly by the improvement of layer materials and of technologies for reducing the gap between the polepieces of a head as well as the gap between the heads and the disk surface. The storage density of a commercial disk was 4000 bits per inch on each track in the mid 1970's, 8,000 bits per inch in the late 1970's and 12,000 bits per inch in 1981. Track density has been increased as well. Studies on a somewhat different recording technique known as perpendicular magnetization indicate that the storage density may be further multiplied more than fivefold. A magnetic disk with a storage density of 12,000 bits per inch has a capacity of 2,500 megabytes.

Any bit on a disk surface is accessible by the rotation of the disk and the movement of an arm on which the read and write heads are mounted. Because the disk and arm are mechanically driven, the access time of a magnetic disk is approximately 100,000 times greater than that of a main memory and is in the range of 20 to 100 milliseconds. However, the storage cost per bit is only a hundredth of that of main memories.

A simpler and smaller version of a magnetic disk, known as a floppy disk, has become available. This consists of a thin Mylar sheet with an

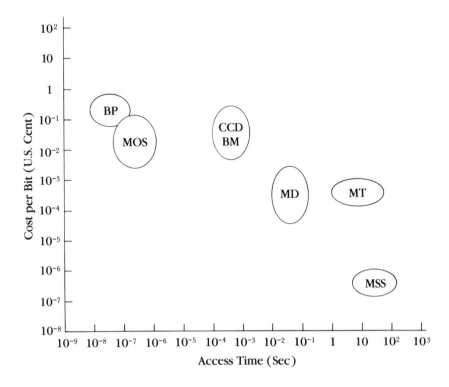

Figure 2-7 Computer storage cost and access time ranges of major storage devices for computers are shown conceptually. Integrated circuit chips employing bipolar transistors (BP) are the fastest and most expensive and are used as cache memories that interface with a fast central processor. Chips employing MOS transistors (MOS), an order of magnitude slower and cheaper than BP, are used as main memories. The rest of the storage devices are much slower and cheaper than these two and are used as file memories where very large storage capacity is required. Magnetic disks (MD) are mainly used for files, with magnetic tapes (MT) as backup. Due mainly to the extensive technological innovation in MD, cost ranges of MD and MT now overlap, although the Mass Storage System (MSS) which is a modified form of MT, is much cheaper (but slower). Charged coupled devices (CCD) and bubble memories (BM) are prospective alternatives for MD, although these are presently more expensive. Generally, cost decrease of such electronic devices as BP, MOS, CCD, and BM is much faster than that of such mechanical devices as MD, MT, and MSS because of rapid innovation in integrated circuit technology. As a result, the present hierarchy of memories (i.e., BP for cache memory, MOS for main memory, MD for file, and MT for backup, in descending order of cost and speed) will undergo significant changes.

iron oxide coating. A floppy disk with a diameter of 8 inches can store a few megabytes, and a minifloppy disk with a diameter of 5¼ inches can store up to 1 megabyte. Since a floppy disk rotates at slightly more than one-tenth of the speed of a magnetic disk, its access time is several hundred milliseconds.

A typical magnetic tape with a storage density of 6250 bits per inch has a capacity of up to 150 megabytes. Since a magnetic tape works like an audio tape, stored information is accessible only sequentially. A modified form of a magnetic tape, known as the Mass Storage System, has a honeycomblike container, each cell of which accomodates a magnetic tape cartridge with a capacity of 50 megabytes. Magnetic tape cartridges are carried mechanically and brought to a read-write mechanism one after another. One unit contains some 700 cartridges and has an access time of 15 seconds.

Attempts have been made to replace magnetic recording with a completely electronic device. Devices known as CCDs (charged coupled devices) and bubble memories have been developed. These devices have access times ranging from 100 microseconds to several milliseconds, thus they are faster than magnetic disks. However, the present cost per bit for CCDs is almost 100 times higher than that for magnetic disks.

As we look at various areas of computer application, a significant trend, sometimes referred to as mechatronics, is generally found. Computers and mechanical systems are being rapidly integrated in office machines, machine tools, vehicles, cameras, and many other devices. Further, computerized industrial robots are revolutionizing manufacturing processes. Industrial robots, when used for welding, die casting, spray painting, transferring, and other highly repetitive jobs, work faster, more reliably, and better than humans. The robots relieve human workers of monotonous labor and remove them from dangerous or unhealthy working environments. Robots also can work while hanging from supports or in cramped quarters that human workers could scarcely endure. The versatility that minicomputers and microprocessors provides is changing a robot from a special-purpose machine to a general-purpose machine. A group of microprocessors permits a robot to perform coordinated multiple movements. A number of computerized robots along a production line can be closely coordinated by a robot that transfers tools and gives instructions. Some advanced robots are now acquiring visual and tactile capabilities that enable them to assemble components and inspect products.

One of the major problems in computer technology is the rising cost of software development and production. While hardware cost is decreasing rapidly through the progress of integrated circuit technology, software cost is increasing sharply, because demands for more sophisticated and diversified types of software are continuing and because software development and production is done mainly by humans, whose wages are increasing. Several techniques, including structured programming, yield a considerable improvement in software productivity. Yet, it seems that there is a long way to go before dramatic improvements in software development, production, and testing can be attained. In view of the fact that microprocessors are being used in an increasing variety of applications, it appears that tremendous effort will be required to produce the great many programs needed for specific applications. It must be pointed out that unless extensive innovation is accomplished in the development, production, and testing of software, computer industries will turn into labor-intensive industries.

Another problem associated with computer software is the patent and copyright protection of software. Generally, patent protection has been given to hardware-oriented inventions. Since an algorithm has been considered similar to a mathematical formula or a law of nature, a software-oriented invention that permits a particular algorithm to be executed by a general-purpose computer has been ruled as having no patentable novelty. This is a sort of discrimination against brains in favor of brawn. It prevents software producers from openly marketing their products; rather, they tend to keep software as a trade secret. In view of the rapid proliferation of microprocessors, however, it has become increasingly difficult to prevent the theft of software. In some countries, an amendment of copyright law has been made, or is in progress, that allows specific programs to be copyrighted. However, copyright protection is not effective enough, as shown in previous instances involving books and journals. Perhaps the most effective way of protecting microprocessor-oriented software is to sell large quantities at a price so low that theft is not worthwhile.

One encouraging factor is the increasing use of firmware. Firmware is a specific program built into a microprocessor or an attached read-only memory (ROM). Although a microprocessor is a general-purpose computer, when firmware is built in it performs a specific function. If the function is identified as novel, the firmware may be patentable. Firmware also makes it difficult for pirates to copy the program.

2-5 Information Utilities

Utilities such as electricity, gas, and water support our day-to-day life. By hooking up an appliance and turning a knob, we obtain light, heat, or water or get some work done in our homes. In an age when our lives increasingly depend upon information, we need utilities that process information in ways we specify and that provide information we want to acquire, regardless of where we are. Computer networks and data bases are now providing such conveniences, which are becoming necessities. These networks and data bases have come to be known as information utilities.

Computer networks, which in their experimental stage were private networks employing leased analog lines, are now capable of utilizing public digital data networks that provide digital circuit switching as well as store-and-forward switching, with data rates up to 48 kilobits per second.

A digital data network provides simultaneous connections between a number of terminals and computers. The terminals and computers so interconnected by means of a digital data network constitute an integrated whole, that is, a computer network. A terminal of a computer network may have access to any of the computers within the network if it is authorized to do so. A computer serves a terminal on the network by performing computation, retrieval of information, and so forth in accordance with the request of the terminal; therefore the computer is called a host for the terminal. The host permits the users of a terminal to share such diversified resources as special-purpose hardware and software and general- and special-purpose data bases covering diversified disciplines. If it is authorized to do so, a computer may have access to any other computer within the network. The benefits of computer-to-computer connection include load sharing, function sharing, and emergency backup.

Connection of a terminal or a host to a digital data network requires an appropriate interface. Interface is a rather broad and somewhat vague concept of an intermediate entity between two systems. It includes hardware as well as software. The hardware interfaces for a terminal and a host are often called a terminal interface processor (TIP) and a front end processor (FEP), respectively. In either of these cases, a software interface is a set of rules specifying the operation of the interface hardware.

The interface between a digital data network and a host or a terminal

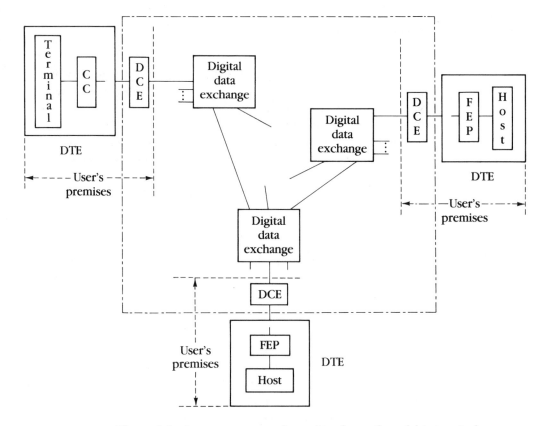

Figure 2-8 A computer network consists of a number of data terminal equipment (DTE) and a digital data network. A DTE may be either a terminal or a computer that is connected by way of an interface to the digital data network, which consists of a number of digital data exchanges interconnected by digital transmission links. The gate of entry to a digital data network is called a data circuit terminating equipment (DCE) and is generally located at a subscriber's premises. (SOURCE: Inose, *Digital Intergrated Communications Systems*)

has been standardized and divided into four levels, namely, physical interface, electrical interface, link-level protocol, and network-level protocol, in accordance with CCITT* Recommendation X.25. The physical interface specifies mechanical connection, and the electrical interface specifies voltage level and duration of signals. The link-level protocol specifies the

---

*International Consultative Committee for Telegraph and Telephone, a committee of the International Telecommunication Union (ITU)

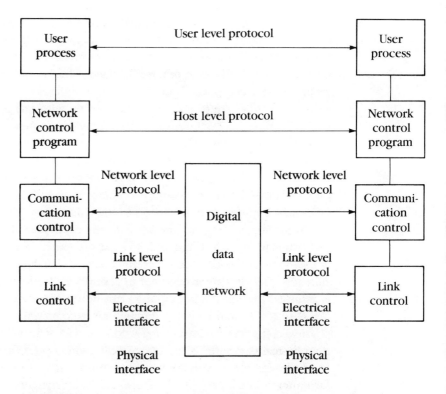

Figure 2-9 In a computer network, a set of rules called a software interface, which specifies the operation of the hardware interface, is required. The rules are called protocols and generally form a hierarchical structure. (SOURCE: Inose, *Digital Integrated Communications Systems*)

procedure for controlling data transfer over the link connecting the digital data network with a host or a terminal. The network-level protocol specifies the method of controlling data flow through the digital data network.

For computer communication as a whole, several additional protocols exist, and these form a hierarchical structure. Generally, a host or a terminal interface processor has in its operating system a module called the network control program (NCP). The procedure for communication between NCPs is called the host-level protocol. A user process (or application program) of a host also communicates with a user process of another host through the user-level protocol. In the case of terminal-to-host communication, the user process on the terminal side may be the user, who manipulates the terminal.

Considering the fact that a great variety of specifications exist on computers and terminals, it is quite difficult for a computer network to permit arbitrary connection between all of them. This leads to the perplexing—indeed, awesome problem of standardization. Suppose that there are n different computers and m different terminals in a computer network. If all these are to communicate directly with one another, $(n + m)(n + m - 1)/2$ different interfaces must be implemented. If n and m were both equal to 10 (a very modest number for the whole world), the number of interfaces required would be 190. Even if each of the terminals communicated by way of an intermediate computer, $nm + [n(n - 1)/2]$ interfaces would be required, or 145 in the case of 10 different computers and 10 different terminals.

In an effort to deal with the problem, the concept of virtual computer and virtual terminal has emerged. A virtual computer or a virtual terminal is a standardized computer or terminal having well-defined protocols at all levels. This computer need not necessarily exist physically. Rather, it is assumed that existing computers can be programmed to emulate it, that is, to act like it. If a physical computer is to communicate with another physical computer, the interfacing is done by way of the virtual computer. If a physical computer is to communicate with a physical terminal, the computer interfaces with the virtual terminal, and the virtual terminal in turn interfaces with the physical terminal. This arrangement reduces the number of interfaces to be implemented to $n + m$—only 20 if the whole world had 10 different computers and 10 different terminals.

The realizability of this concept depends on the possibility of standardizing a virtual computer or a virtual terminal that is an acceptable if not equal distance from all existing and upcoming computers or terminals. If such a standardization is settled upon, it seems likely that all computers will be able to emulate the standard because of the power of these machines. Terminals, in general, have less intelligence, so their interfacing must be done by some intermediate entity, including a terminal interface processor.

A number of protocol hierarchies, known as network architectures, have been developed by manufacturers in accordance with their own specifications. Much effort toward standardization has been expended on the international scene. For instance, the open system interconnection (OSI), which is under consideration by the International Standards Organization (ISO), consists of seven protocol layers, namely, physical, link, network, transport, session, presentation, and applications, in ascending order of the hierarchy. Necessary and sufficient standardization of these protocol layers, avoiding pitfalls as well as duplications, is essential in establishing a realistic and useful hierarchy of protocol.

Digital circuit switching of data is generally made compatible with digital circuit switching of speech, which employs time-division-multiplexing. In order to carry a speech signal, an 8-bit time slot that repeats 8000 times per second is used in every frame. In each time slot, 6 bits are used to carry data. If such a time slot is used in every frame, data can be transmitted at 48 kilobits per second. If such a time slot is used once in every 5 frames, data can be transmitted at 9.6 kilobits per second. If such a time slot is used one in every 20 frames, data can be transmitted at 2.4 kilobits per second. Thus, the system can handle data of various speeds as if they were pulse code modulated speech signals. A data switching system of this sort has shorter connection and disconnection times than a digital telephone switching system, because the conversation period for data is much shorter than that for speech. Once a connection is set up, digital circuit switching provides a dedicated physical path that permits uninterrupted data flow, and thus it is suitable for transferring a large amount of data continuously.

Store-and-forward switching in digital data networks is known as packet switching. A message is broken up into a number of message blocks of fixed maximum length, and a header that includes the destination address is attached to each message block to form a packet. The packet is routed through the network on a store-and-forward basis. A physical path is used only when a packet is actually transmitted. This makes packet switching suitable for such sporadic (or "bursty") and interactive uses as time-sharing systems and on-line file access.

The use of packet switching for speech communication is also envisaged because pauses in telephone conversation take as much as 50 percent of the time, and speech interruption as much as 25 percent. However, the existence of a variable store-and-forward delay in packet transmission requires a delay adjustment before speech packets are delivered to talkers.

Packet switching services are divided into two categories, namely, datagram and virtual call services.

The datagram service is the simplest and the most fundamental among a variety of possible services provided by packet switching. Packets from a source, each of which is associated with the destination address, are entered into the network and are delivered to the destination in an order that may be independent of the order of entry. At the destination, therefore, the packets received must be sequenced by the user to reconstruct the original message. Also, the user must detect the loss of an offered packet since delivery is not guaranteed. The concept is similar to that of public parcel services, in which several packages accepted at the same time are not always delivered to their destination simultaneously.

The concept of virtual call service, on the other hand, is similar to that of circuit switching. In the case of circuit switching, a physical path is established before data transfer; in the case of virtual call, a specific plan for the path (called a logical path) is set up prior to data transfer. Packets carrying data are transferred over a physical path that is specified by the logical path. In setting up a logical path, several packets that carry no data are sent back and forth. These are known as call supervisory packets. At the end of the data transfer, the call supervisory packets are again interchanged in order to release the logical path. During the data transfer phase, virtual call service performs packet sequence control as well as packet flow control. Sequence control is done by numbering the data packets being transferred over each logical path so that the packets can be delivered in the proper order and lost packets can be identified.

Figure 2-10   Digital circuit switching of data is generally made compatible with that of speech. A digital speech switching system employs time-division-multiplexing where, typically, 24 speech signals, each of which is coded into 8 bits, are aligned in 24 time slots that make up a frame of 125 microseconds. To be compatible with this, a digital data switching system employs a data frame of 2.5 milliseconds, which corresponds to 20 frames (a). 6 out of 8 bits per time slot are used to carry data. If a time slot is used once in every data frame (or 20 frames), data can be transmitted at a data rate of 2.4 kilobits per second (b). If a time slot is used once in every 5 frames, data can be transmitted at 9.6 kilobits per second (c). And if a time slot is used in every frame, data can be transmitted at 48 kilobits per second (d). A time slot that includes 6 bits of data is called an envelope (e). Since 6 out of 8 bits are used to carry data, the data rate is 6/8 of the inherent speed of a time slot, which is called the bearer rate. When terminals are not synchronized with the clock of the system, several samples of an unsynchronized data bit are transmitted as if it were a sequence of synchronized bits. For instance, an unsynchronized data bit with a data rate of 200 bits per second is sampled 12 times and transmitted as if it were a sequence of 12 synchronized bits. Synchronized and unsynchronized data with a variety of speeds are thus transmitted and switched in a manner similar to speech. (SOURCE: Inose, *Digital Integrated Communications Systems*)

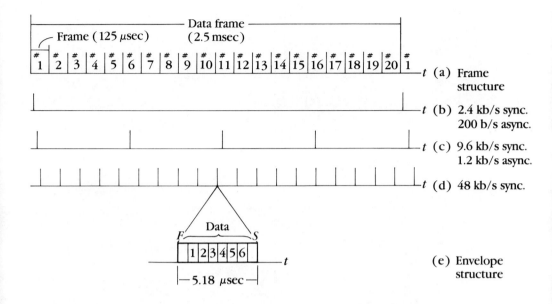

(a) Frame structure

(b) 2.4 kb/s sync. 200 b/s async.

(c) 9.6 kb/s sync. 1.2 kb/s async.

(d) 48 kb/s sync.

(e) Envelope structure

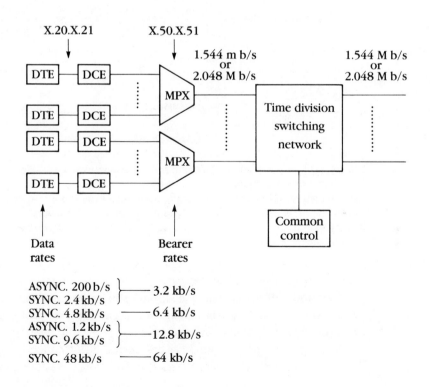

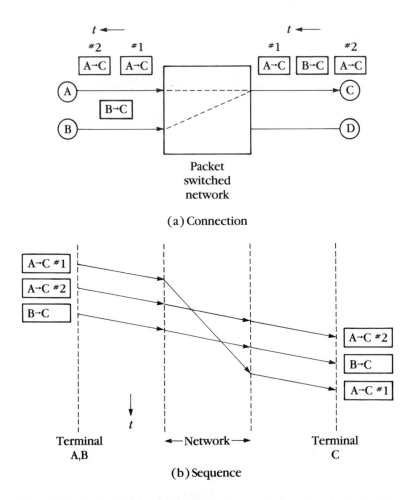

(a) Connection

(b) Sequence

Figure 2-11 Packets in the datagram service are delivered to the destination in an order that may be independent of the order of entry to the network. Some computer users prefer the datagram service because the restrictions on the use of the network are minimal, and the connection time of terminals is shorter than that of the virtual call service. (SOURCE: Inose, *Digital Integrated Communications Systems*)

Flow control is used to manage the rate of packet flow between the network and a terminal (or a computer) in order to avoid network congestion and terminal overloading. At present all public packet switching systems provide virtual call service.

Reduction of transmission cost has been a major concern in organizing computer networks because transmission cost has not decreased as

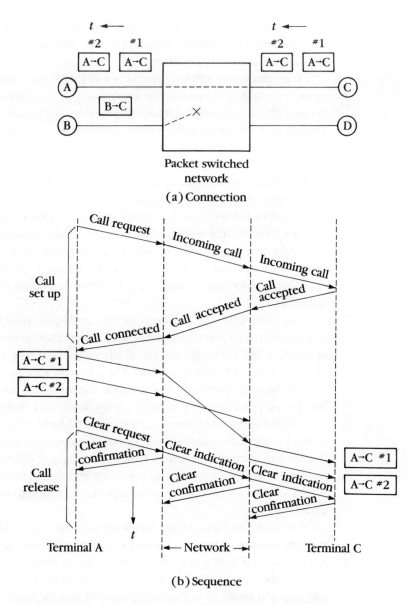

(a) Connection

(b) Sequence

Figure 2-12 Virtual call service is, in a sense, similar to circuit switching. Prior to the transmission of data packets, packets known as call supervisory packets are sent back and forth to set up a logical path. At the end of data transfer, the logical path is released by interchanging supervisory packets. Since virtual call service is capable of controlling the packet sequence as well as the packet flow, all of the public packet switching systems prefer it to datagram service. (SOURCE: Inose, *Digital Integrated Communications Systems*)

fast as computer cost. Efforts have been directed toward two major areas: long-distance transmission, which is costly, and subscriber loop transmission, which is very inefficient.

A geostationary satellite provides a revolutionary medium for this purpose in that it eliminates the significance of terrestrial distance and permits direct access to and from computers and terminals scattered over a broad area. Packets may be transmitted from the ground to the satellite via a common radio channel on a random-access basis and sent back from the satellite to the ground via another radio channel in a broadcasting mode. This is a typical example of a packet radio system, the concept of which originated with the ALOHA system.

Satellites, however, are not an indispensable medium for packet radio systems. The ALOHA system used terrestrial radio channels to connect terminals on the Hawaiian Islands to a computer center in Honolulu. Induction wires and other media may also be used for the purpose by using low-power radio transceivers for fixed or mobile computers and terminals.

The same principle has been further applied to wired communications known as local area networks, such as the Ethernet system, in which computers and terminals are physically connected to a common wire installed within a building or plant. The common wire may be extended outside the user's premises. The transmission media for this purpose may be twisted pairs of wires, coaxial cables, or optical fibers. Distributed control of a common channel employing broad-band cable loops laid out within plants, offices, large aircraft, or ocean liners could drastically reduce the amount of copper required. Other advantages of distributed systems over centralized systems are that the costly investment for central control is unnecessary at the time of initial installation and system expansion is easier.

One of the major problems associated with the original ALOHA scheme was the overlap of packets, known as packet collision. Because packets are transmitted from a number of terminals in a completely unsynchronized manner, packets sent from different terminals may overlap fully or partially and result in transmission error. When the overlap occurs, the terminals retransmit packets until they are free of overlap. Several techniques have been developed to improve the situation. A technique known as the slotted ALOHA avoids partial collision of packets. For a terrestrial radio or cable system in which propagation delay is much smaller than the packet transmission time, another technique, known as carrier sense

Networks and terminals allow distribution of work stations. This photograph shows the Intel NDS-II connected through an Ethernet system to allow development and management of complex projects through a system of terminals spread over various locations. (Photo courtesy of Intel)

multiple access (CSMA), has been developed. In this scheme, each of the terminals sharing a channel controls its packet transmission, so as to avoid collision with packets from other terminals, by sensing the carrier. This technique increases the maximum throughput to more than twice the value of the slotted ALOHA.

The needs for file-oriented data processing appeared in the late 1950's, when sophisticated software known as an operating system was developed to control computer operation. A data management function was

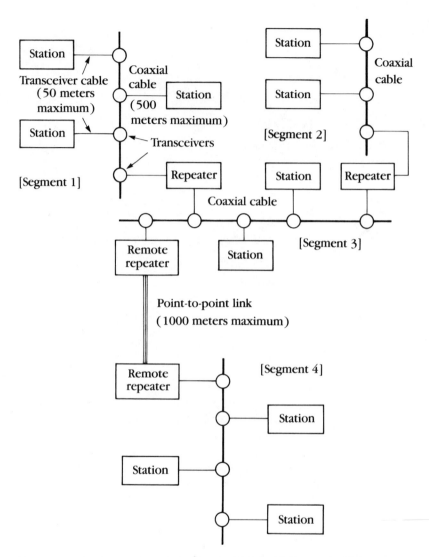

Figure 2-13   A typical example of local area networks is the Ethernet. Although the concept is along the lines of the ALOHA system, the Ethernet employs coaxial cables, rather than radio waves, that form a branching, nonrooted tree. Carrier sense multiple access (CSMA) technique is used; this increases the maximum throughout to more than 80 percent of the channel capacity.

Up to 100 data stations are connected by way of transceiver cables and transceivers to a coaxial cable that extends up to 500 meters. The maximum permissible length of a transceiver cable is 50 meters. A group of stations connected to a common coaxial cable is called a segment. A number of segments are connected by way of repeaters. To connect a remotely located segment, a point-to-point link is used that has remote repeaters at its ends. The maximum permissible length of a point-to-point link is 1000 meters.

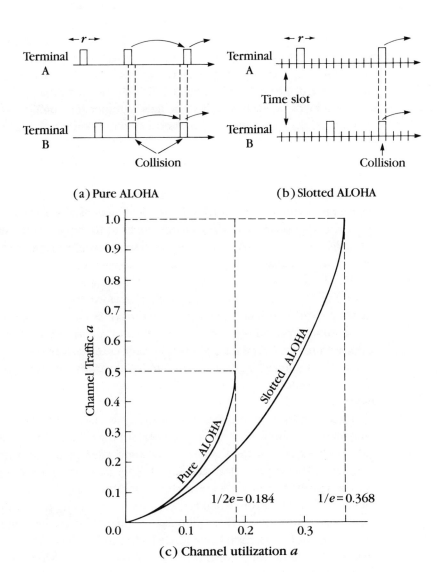

(a) Pure ALOHA   (b) Slotted ALOHA

(c) Channel utilization a

Figure 2-14 Packet collision in pure and slotted ALOHA schemes: Terminals of the original ALOHA system transmit packets randomly, and hence the packets sent from different terminals may overlap fully or partially (a). To avoid repeated overlap, the interval of packet transmission is randomized at each terminal. To avoid partial overlap, another scheme, known as the slotted ALOHA, synchronizes packet transmission so that each packet is accommodated within a distinctive time slot (b). While the maximum possible throughput of the ALOHA system is about 18 percent of the theoretical upper limit, that of the slotted ALOHA is twice that (c). (SOURCE: Inose, *Digital Integrated Communications Systems*)

implemented as an important part of the operating system to provide users with a capability of organizing, maintaining, and accessing their own files. As data processing became increasingly file oriented, handling of a number of individual files became more difficult and inefficient. As a result, the concept of organizing individual files together for commonly controlling and sharing data emerged. Such a system is known as a data base system.

A data base system consists mainly of a data base, a data directory, and a data base management system. A data base is generally defined as an organized group of files, the contents of which are highly structured in order to permit efficient retrieval and updating of data. A data directory is a sort of dictionary that maps a user's query to the specific data stored in the data base. A data base management system is sophisticated software that controls the data base by referring to the data directory.

The benefits of sharing a data base will be jeopardized if no appropriate measure is taken to protect data. Therefore, two measures, data access control and data integrity control, have been introduced. Data access control provides privacy protection and security. Access control locks are provided for data, and unless a user enters an appropriate key, reading or modifying the data is prohibited. Some users are provided with keys that permit them only to read the data. Others are permitted to read and modify.

Data integrity control maintains consistency of data by checking validity, controlling concurrent operations, and performing failure recovery using audit trails. Data validation is performed right after each transaction is completed. Data types, value ranges, and other parameters are validated by means of check programs. Concurrency control is necessary to protect data from possible errors when two or more users intend to modify the same data simultaneously. For this purpose, a data base system generally has two types of locks, namely, exclusive lock and share lock. An exclusive lock is to prohibit other concurrent transactions from having access to the data and is used when the data is to be modified. A share lock permits other concurrent transactions to read the data but not to modify it. A lock is generally effected immediately before the execution of a transaction and released right after the execution. To insure integrity of data, a lock should preferably be in effect to cover an entire transaction. However, if a transaction consists of many actions, this will reduce concurrency of operation. Optimum use of locks is therefore an important factor in the design of a data base system.

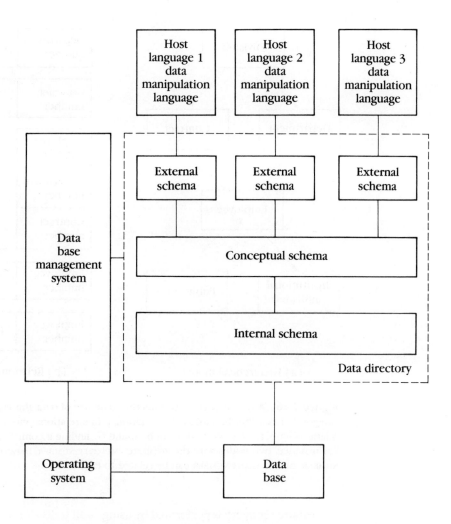

Figure 2-15 Conceptual structure of a data base system: A data base system consists mainly of a data base, a data directory, and a data base management system. Generally, a data directory consists of three layers—an external schema, a conceptual schema, and an internal schema—for the purpose of making the physical structure of the data base and the user's application program independent of each other. A data base management system needs the assistance of an operating system to control a physical data base. It also needs support programs (not shown) for initialization, reconfiguration, monitoring, and failure recovery of a data base system. In some cases, no distinction is made between a data directory and a data base management system, and they are considered an integrated entity.

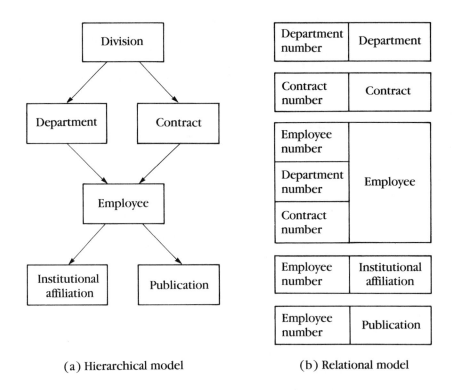

(a) Hierarchical model   (b) Relational model

Figure 2-16   A data model represents the structure of data and is generally categorized as either hierarchical or relational. In a relational model, the relationship between two nodes can be found by finding a common attribute. For instance, two nodes with the attribute EMPLOYEE NUMBER, DEPARTMENT NUMBER, or CONTRACT NUMBER can be related to each other.

Failure recovery is performed by using audit trails stored in magnetic tapes and disks. If a failure happens when a transaction is being executed, the execution rolls back to the beginning of the transaction by using the audit trails stored on a magnetic disk. Sometimes, the execution has to roll back to the very beginning of an application program that consists of a number of transactions. In a catastrophic failure, in which a part of the data base is lost, the data base is reconstructed by using the audit trails stored in magnetic tapes.

The structure of a data base is represented by a data model. A data model is often formed as a hierarchical tree, in which a node represents data and a link indicates the relation between data. Another data model,

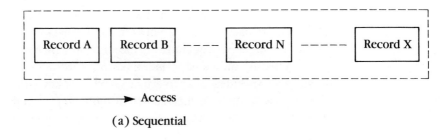

Access

(a) Sequential

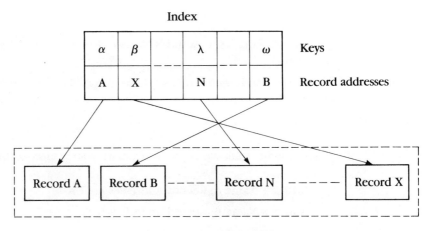

(b) Indexed sequential

Figure 2-17 Data base organization: The simplest way of organizing a data base is to write and read records sequentially. None of the previous records can be deleted or modified, and a new record can only be added at the end of a sequence of previous records. This method has been used since earlier days, when a magnetic tape was the only recording medium. Data in magnetic disks are organized either sequentially or randomly. Randomizing is done by means of a mathematical transformation that converts keys or attributes of data into record addresses. The transformation function is known as the hashing function. The simplest (and most classical) method of conversion is the use of an index. Generally, an address is given to a block of records in order to limit the table size.

known as a relational model, represents the data and their relationships without using links.

A data base is physically organized in several ways. The simplest among these, in use since magnetic tapes were first used as storage media, is to arrange records sequentially (where a record is a set of data items, such as author's name, title, key words, and publisher's name). To improve accessibility, indexed sequential organization, in which a specific record is approached by means of an index has been introduced for magnetic disk storage. An index is a table that converts a key (an attribute of a record) to an address of the record. In bibliographic retrieval, several indices have been used that employ such attributes as author's names and key words as keys. As a simplified example, let us use the following bibliographic records:

Record Address A: Author's Name α, Key Word a, Title; Publisher's Name

Record Address B: Author's Name β, Key Word b, Title; Publisher's Name

. . . .

A set of indices known as an inverted list is structured as follows:

Author's Name α: Record Addresses A, C, K

Author's Name β: Record Addresses B, G

. . . .

Key Word a: Record Addresses A, H, K, N

Key Word b: Record Addresses B, L, P

. . . .

An inverted list permits identification of record addresses by means of attributes. It also permits the user to find the address of the specific record of the book written by the author α with the key word a by using the intersection of the record addresses A, C, K and A, H, K, N. An inverted list, however, occupies considerable storage capacity, and for such applications in which updating must be done frequently, the maintenance of the inverted list becomes quite difficult. In some data base systems, therefore, inverted lists are prepared for some but not all of the attributes.

For such purposes as maintaining data bases locally, permitting smooth expansion, saving communications cost, and increasing overall reliability, distributed data base systems have been under development. Problems associated with a distributed data base system include communication

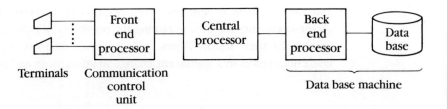

Figure 2-18 Data base machine: A specialized machine that is sometimes called a back end processor may be connected to a central processor to perform data base control exclusively. A data base system that consists of a back end processor and a data base is known as a data base machine. A back end processor may consist of a conventional minicomputer with an appropriate interface or of a number of microprocessors to provide parallel processing in close association with specially designed magnetic disks or high speed sequential memories, such as charge coupled devices (CCD).

and coordination between data bases so as to make distribution invisible to users. Another recent development of interest is the separation of the data base control function from the central processor by the introduction of a specialized computer known as a back end processor.

Data bases play a major role in the selective dissemination of information. They also provide the convenience of retrospective search through archives for specified information. Unlike information processing, which performs processing in accordance with a given program and given data, information retrieval provides whatever information the user needs. To accomplish this, a very large amount of information must be collected, entered into data bases in machine-readable form, and retrieved and updated in a precise and efficient way.

Bibliographic retrieval for scientific and technological information plays an indispensable role for professionals in carrying out their work. Business users now rely heavily on commercial credit information and market quotations for stocks, commodities, and foreign exchanges. Data services for the users of home computers have appeared. These services are increasingly provided over telephone lines by information vendors, who have access to a number of data bases owned and updated by providers of information.

Data bases also provide seat reservations, telephone directory assistance, credit card verification, and other services over telephone lines. In some instances, the request is entered through push-button telephone and the response is sent back by computer-synthesized speech. Telephone companies are now exploring the possibility of providing a retrieval service for their Yellow Pages. Such a service to users, if permitted by law, could result in a significant change in advertising and purchasing.

2-6 Toward the Office of the Future

The age of the Dickensian clerk has long passed. Huge stacks of files have been replaced by a few floppy disks. Messengers who carried documents and oral messages are being replaced by facsimile and teletext. No longer do documents have to be edited and rewritten in longhand; this can be done on a word processor much faster and more neatly. Information technology is now bringing a revolution not only to work in offices but to the whole business of publication as well.

Facsimile machines can transmit and record as hard copy a large variety of images, including printed pages, handwritten documents, and diagrams. A typical facsimile device scans sequentially the brightness of an image along lines an eighth of a millimeter apart by using a number of tiny photoelectric converters that form part of an integrated circuit chip. This scanning generates an electrical signal. The signal is then transmitted over communication lines. At the receiving end, the image is printed on a paper electrostatically, thermally, or by other means. The electrical signal can be an analog signal that represents halftones in the original image; these can be reproduced in a hard copy, with accuracy depending upon the type of recorder.

Because neighboring picture elements are much alike, differences of neighboring picture elements are taken, along either one dimension or two, to reduce redundancy in the transmitted signal. By doing this, the time for transmitting an ISO standard A4-size document over a telephone channel can be reduced from six minutes to three minutes.

Though facsimile can be used to transmit halftone pictures, its major purpose is to transmit black-and-white patterns, such as characters, letters, and diagrams. These picture elements are either black or white, and sequences of black elements and of white elements alternate. In transmitting such sequences, a redundancy-reduction technique known as run-length encoding is used. The number of successive black elements or white elements in a sequence is counted. The counts are then converted

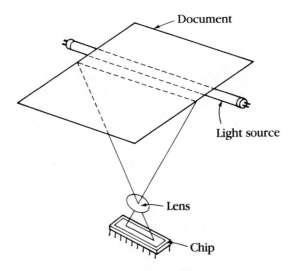

Figure 2-19   Photoelectric conversion for facsimile transmission: An integrated circuit chip that contains as much as 1728 sensor cells is used for converting an optical image of a document into electrical signals. An optical system focuses the image of a document on to the chip. The outputs of the sensor cells are sequentially scanned to be transmitted. Metal oxide semiconductors (MOSs) or charge coupled devices (CCDs) are used for the chip.

to a particular set of code sequences, known as the Huffman code, in which shorter codes are assigned to the counts that appear more frequently. This method of digital facsimile cuts down transmission time for a typical document over a telephone channel to about 10 seconds. It also permits digitized facsimile signals to be temporarily stored in a buffer until a communication link becomes available or until the recipient wants to receive them. While the signals are stored in a buffer, format and speed conversion are made possible for interfacing with recorders of different standards. Digital facsimile known as CCITT G-3, which uses encoding schemes somewhat different from the original Huffman encoding, is now available on the market.

Facsimile can transmit better-quality images faster when wide-band channels are employed. Newspaper companies use wide-band facsimile in transmitting original make-up pages to local centers to be printed and distributed. Facsimile can be piggybacked on a television signal to allow

Figure 2-20   Run length coding for facsimile: A sequence of black or white picture elements is represented by terminating codes (a) and make-up codes (b). If the number of picture elements in a sequence, that is, the run length, is less than 64, it is represented by a terminating code. If 64 or more, it is represented by a make-up code and a terminating code. For instance, white run lengths 15 and 530 are represented by 110101 and 011001010100111, respectively. In the latter case, the first eight digits (01100101) are the white make-up code for 512 and the last seven digits (0100111) are the white terminating code for 18. When all the sequences of black and white picture elements in a line are encoded, the code for end of line (EOL) is added. The same code is added before the first line of a page. Shorter codes are assigned to run lengths that statistically appear more frequently.

White Run Length	Codes	Black Run Length	Codes
0	00110101	0	0000110111
1	000111	1	010
2	0111	2	11
3	1000	3	10
4	1011	4	011
5	1100	5	0011
6	1110	6	0010
7	1111	7	00011
8	10011	8	000101
9	10100	9	000100
10	00111	10	0000100
11	01000	11	0000101
12	001000	12	0000111
13	000011	13	00000100
14	110100	14	00000111
15	110101	15	000011000
16	101010	16	0000010111
17	101011	17	0000011000
18	0100111	18	0000001000
19	0001100	19	00001100111
20	0001000	20	00001101000
21	0010111	21	00001101100
22	0000011	22	00000110111
23	0000100	23	00000101000
24	0101000	24	00000010111
25	0101011	25	00000011000

26	0010011	26	000011001010
27	0100100	27	000011001011
28	0011000	28	000011001100
29	00000010	29	000011001101
30	00000011	30	000001101000
31	00011010	31	000001101001
32	00011011	32	000001101010
33	00010010	33	000001101011
34	00010011	34	000011010010
35	00010100	35	000011010011
36	00010101	36	000011010100
37	00010110	37	000011010101
38	00010111	38	000011010110
39	00101000	39	000011010111
40	00101001	40	000001101100
41	00101010	41	000001101101
42	00101011	42	000011011010
43	00101100	43	000011011011
44	00101101	44	000001010100
45	00000100	45	000001010101
46	00000101	46	000001010110
47	00001010	47	000001010111
48	00001011	48	000001100100
49	01010010	49	000001100101
50	01010100	50	000001010010
51	01010101	51	000001010011
52	01010101	52	000000100100
53	00100100	53	000000110111
54	00100101	54	000000111000
55	01011000	55	000000100111
56	01011001	56	000000101000
57	01011010	57	000001011000
58	01011011	58	000001011001
59	01001010	59	000000101011
60	01001011	60	000000101100
61	00110010	61	000001011010
62	00110011	62	000001100110
63	00110100	63	000001100111

(a)   Terminating Codes

64	11011	64	0000001111
128	10010	128	000011001000
192	010111	192	000011001001
256	0110111	256	000001011011

continued

Figure 2-20 *continued*

320	00110110	320	000000110011
384	00110111	384	000000110100
448	01100100	448	000000110101
512	01100101	512	0000001101100
576	01101000	576	0000001101101
640	01100111	640	0000001001010
704	011001100	704	0000001001011
768	011001101	768	0000001001100
832	011010010	832	0000001001101
896	011010011	896	0000001110010
960	011010100	960	0000001110011
1024	011010101	1024	0000001110100
1088	011010110	1088	0000001110101
1152	011010111	1152	0000001110110
1216	011011000	1216	0000001110111
1280	011011001	1280	0000001010010
1344	011011010	1344	0000001010011
1408	011011011	1408	0000001010100
1472	010011000	1472	0000001010101
1536	010011001	1536	0000001011010
1600	010011010	1600	0000001011011
1664	011000	1664	0000001100100
1728	010011011	1728	0000001100101
EOL	000000000001	EOL	000000000001

(b) Make-up Codes

users to receive hard copies of news and other information via a recorder attached to a home television receiver through an interface unit. Some postal services now provide facsimile transmission between end offices. Known as electronic mail service, such service alleviates physical transportation to a considerable extent, although copies must still be delivered to the recipients.

Teletext is an offspring of telex. It transmits characters in coded form from one terminal to another. Since the information is in digital form, it can be buffered to take advantage of buffering benefits, as in the case of facsimile. A list of buffered messages is provided to a recipient, who can choose urgent messages and read them first. This is known as mailbox service and is of considerable convenience, especially in business. Teletext in combination with word processing is especially useful in business. A variety of intelligent terminals that have such features are now appearing on the market.

Word processing is perhaps the most significant among office automation technologies. Personal computers and small business computers have acquired word processing capability. This permits users to write, edit, justify, modify, and store text by keyboard and screen. The typical stand-alone word processor of 1983 provided 64 kilobytes or more of main memory area for this purpose and two floppy disks. This permits word processing to be done over several successive pages. Some word processors are connected on-line to a minicomputer or a large-scale computer to provide a much more sophisticated processing capability as well as access to much larger files. In Japan, where thousands of different characters must be dealt with, the introduction of word processing was slow at first. However, word processors are now available that are capable of interactively converting an input message entered by Kana (syllabic) characters into Kanji (ideographic) characters.

Not only does word processing help users to write text, but it also permits users to write a large number of personalized letters easily by merging the text file with name and address files. When word processing is combined with teletext, such letters can be sent automatically to a large number of recipients.

Office automation systems that integrate facsimile, teletext and word processing with copying machines, document files, and private automatic board exchanges (PABXs) are now appearing on the market. Floppy disks have become the most popular medium for filing documents. Microfiche sorters and magnetic disks have also been used to some extent. Video disks, which have a direct-read-after-write (DRAW) capability, will soon follow and will allow users to write their own files on the disks. When combined with a bibliographic data base and facsimile, video disks will be able to provide hard copies of original documents to remote terminals on request from users. An integrated office automation system can thus generate, process, document, store, retrieve, and transmit text in a variety of forms in close association with the use of telephones.

Electronic publishing systems are now emerging. Text that is edited by word processing and artwork that is optically read and converted into digital form are combined by a composer to form a page, which can then be printed by an electronic printer. This eliminates typesetting, plate production, and printing on a printing press. Bound reports that have the quality of published books can be produced. Some newspapers are already being produced in a similar way. Updating for late editions is done more quickly, and printing is done locally by sending an image of composed pages to local centers through high-speed facsimile and by adding some locally composed pages.

A concept known as an electronic journal is also emerging. A manuscript is prepared by word processing and submitted by teletext to an institution. The institution transmits the text to referees via an electronic mailbox system, and the referees review the manuscripts and return their comments and suggestions to the institution. The institution then compiles the referees' comments and suggestions and transmits them to the author. After the author has made corrections and changes to the satisfaction of the referees, the final manuscript is stored in a permanent file. The institution then announces the publication of that paper to its members, who may read the paper on their own screens. Should such systems prove to be economically feasible, the process of printing may be eliminated in the publication of journals.

2-7 Information for Everyone

Until recently, those who lacked computer terminals or the knowledge of how to manipulate computer terminals were unable to gain access to data bases. Teletext and videotex now promise to give them access by the addition of interface units to their television sets. The major difference between teletext and videotex is that in the former, information is disseminated one way, whereas in the latter, information is provided through two-way interactive communication.

In teletext, texts as well as some graphics are converted into digital signals and are transmitted during the time between sweeps of television image (the vertical blanking period). A large number of digital signals that represent news, stock market quotations, entertainment, travel, and other information are transmitted sequentially. A user specifies the information he or she needs by means of a keypad, and the interface unit picks up the corresponding pages from the television signal and stores them, one after another, in the refresh memory used to refresh the images. The contents in the refresh memory are then read out and displayed on the television screen. Since the teletext information is piggybacked on a television signal, care must be taken not to interfere with the main program. Therefore, only a few lines of vertical blanking signal are used to transmit teletext information. This limits the amount of information that can be provided. Generally, it takes 10 seconds or longer for a page to appear after a request has been entered. Teletext has been experimentally transmitted at high speed using broad-band cables or full television channels. Teletext transmission by a narrow-band wire has also been used to provide information locally.

In videotex, digital signals that represent texts and graphics are modulated onto a voice-band carrier and transmitted over a telephone network. By manipulating a keypad, a user sends a request for needed information to the data base center. The information retrieved by the center is stored in a refresh memory in the user's interface unit and is displayed on the television screen. A voice-band channel between a user and the center is divided into two subchannels, one wide and the other narrow. The wide channel carries videotex information and the narrow one carries user requests. A videotex page, which typically consists of 24 lines of 40 characters each, can be displayed within a few seconds after a request is made.

Wide-band services similar to videotex have been tried experimentally or are being planned. These systems provide moving pictures, voice, facsimile, and other services in addition to text and graphic pages over broad-band cables or optical fibers. The high cost of such services makes them unsuitable for the general public. For business purposes, however, these services may make their way in association with the introduction of intelligent private automatic board exchanges and office automation equipment. Some experimental systems employ sophisticated interfacing units at users' premises that include microprocessors, character and pattern generators, and other components.

One of the problems of teletext, videotex, and other such services is standardization. A user may wish to use one interface unit to receive both teletext and videotex services. An information provider may wish to sell information through the videotex services of several countries. To do so, standards must be agreed on for display format and transmission, nationally as well as internationally.

In some systems, a text page is displayed in 24 lines of 40 characters each; in others, in 20 lines of 32 characters each. An alphabetical character is displayed by either 5-by-7, 6-by-10, or 8-by-12 dot matrices. In a Japanese system, where thousands of complex kanji and kana must be displayed, a character is presented by a 10-by-15 dot matrix. A graphic pattern is displayed in some systems by a mosaic and in others by a combination of geometric primitives. In still other systems, a graphic pattern is expressed by 204-by-248 or 960-by-1280 dot matrices (the latter for a high-resolution television screen). In some videotex services, information to viewers is sent at a data rate of 1200 bits per second; in other systems, at 3200 bits per second. The requests from users are entered at different speeds, ranging from 50 bits per second to 100 bits per second.

Another problem is public acceptance of such services. To meet the diversified needs of users at a reasonable cost, a great many different information providers must be motivated to take part. Users and information providers may be concerned about privacy issues. Manufacturers must be interested in providing inexpensive interface units and other accessories that the general public can afford.

There is a shortage of available radio frequency bands and a degradation of television picture quality owing to multipath reflection in urban areas. These conditions have led to a rapid increase in availability and use of cable television in recent years. In the United States, 35.7 percent of the households with television are served by cable television, and the percentage is increasing. Cable television provides not only rebroadcast of radio wave television programs but also a variety of local television programs, movies, and still pictures. By employing wider-bandwidth cables, cable television can provide a greater number of television programs simultaneously.

Some cable television services now have two-way capability, with a narrower bandwidth allocated for requests by keypad. One of such services provides, in addition to 10 broadcast television channels and 6 local television channels, a great variety of videotex-type information over 4 television channels.

Nationwide broadcasting of a large number of television, movie, and teletext programs by a powerful satellite permits local cable television services to receive these programs selectively and, by adding their own programs, to serve a variety of needs of local communities. When optical fibers are used for this purpose and a large number of data bases are made accessible, an unprecedented impact to our society may literally be brought home.

The effects of video packages will be as great as that of cables. Videotapes are rapidly becoming popular, and video disks are now entering

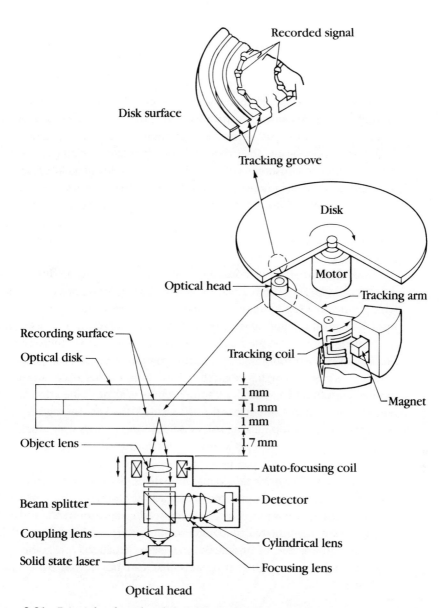

Recorded signal

Disk surface

Tracking groove

Disk

Motor

Optical head

Tracking arm

Recording surface

Optical disk

Tracking coil

1 mm

1 mm

1 mm

1.7 mm

Magnet

Object lens

Auto-focusing coil

Beam splitter

Detector

Coupling lens

Cylindrical lens

Solid state laser

Focusing lens

Optical head

Figure 2-21 Principle of a video disk: A binary datum is stored as the presence or absence of a tiny pit (0.8 micrometer in diameter and 0.2 micrometer in depth) along a helical groove engraved on a disk surface. Ten billion bits of information can be stored in a disk surface 30 centimeters in diameter. Since two disk surfaces are sealed together with a spacer and protective coating, a disk plate can store up to 20 billion bits or some 2 billion characters. An optical head, mounted on a tracking arm precisely controlled by servomechanisms, keeps track on the groove with an accuracy of less than 0.1 micrometer. The optical head consists of a solid-state laser and an optical system. Fully powered, the solid-state laser can record pits on a disk surface. For reading, the laser is underpowered. Reflection of laser light from the disk surface is conveyed to a detector by way of a beam splitter in the optical system, and the presence or absence of pits is identified.

the market. The impact of video disks will be particularly significant because of their enormous storage capability and low cost. A video disk stores information in tiny pits (about 1 micrometer in diameter) made by a high-power laser beam. The information can be read out by a weaker laser beam. Copies of consumer video disks, which are for playback only, can be made as easily as phonograph records and therefore have the advantage of economy of scale. A 30-centimeter video disk can accomodate an entire movie program (1½ to 2 hours), several television programs, or digitized high-quality stereophonic sound programs (*compact disc recording*).

Modified versions of consumer video disks, known as direct-read-after-write (DRAW) video disks, are also appearing for document files and computer files. The system has a high-power laser diode that enables a user to record his information on a video disk, which can be used as a document file. Such a video disk can store as many as 2000 megabytes of information, corresponding to an entire volume of the Encyclopedia Britannica. Access to any information recorded in a video disk can be had within a fraction of a second. Although access time of a video disk is only about one-tenth that of a magnetic disk, a video disk has a storage capacity similar to that of a top-ranking magnetic disk, and it costs very much less. The video disk, therefore, is a prospective mass-storage media for computer files and, in particular, files for a very large data base.

As mass media, video tapes and video disks may compete to a certain extent with radio wave and cable broadcasting. However, these may also complement broadcasting by providing a detailed and uninterrupted original program, unmutilated by commercial messages and unhampered by the rigid time frame of broadcast television. Broadcast programs may become digests of original programs that can be viewed from video packages.

2-8 For Highly Reliable and Secure Services

Almost all aspects of societal activities are now highly dependent on telecommunications, computers, and other information systems. If information systems fail or seriously malfunction, the societal activities lose support, and this may sometimes result in uncontrollable chaos in society as a whole. To bear fully these ever-increasing societal responsibilities, information systems are being organized and operated so as to maintain an extremely high reliability.

Information that is crucial for privacy and even necessary for secrecy of legal persons and governments is increasingly being handled by information systems. Hence, society is becoming seriously concerned with the possibility of leakage, destruction, theft, or abuse of the information handled by information systems. To minimize such possibilities, information systems are being organized and administered so as to attain the maximum possible degree of security.

Information systems are subject to a variety of disturbances, both external and internal to them. External disturbances range from such physical factors as electrical noise, supply voltage instability, temperature change, vibration, and shock to such human factors as operator's mistakes, vandalism, and unauthorized access by outsiders. Internal disturbances range from chance and wear-out failure of components to hardware and software design errors not detected by testing.

The system abnormality caused by these disturbances is either an instantaneous malfunction that recovers without repair or a permanent malfunction that requires repair. The former is called an error; the latter, a failure.

An error is detected by adding some redundancy to the information being handled. The simplest example is the parity check. Alphabets, numbers, and other symbols are converted into 7-bit codes for information transmission. For the purpose of error detection, another bit is added to the 7-bit code to make the mark count odd. This additional bit is called vertical parity. Message blocks, each of which is composed of a number of 8-bit characters thus formed, are transmitted one after another over a communication link. To enhance error-detection capability, each message block generally contains, at its end, a block-check character (BCC) to make the mark count of elements in a block even. This is called horizontal parity. At the receiving end, a mark count of each character and of the elements of all characters in a message block is performed, and if the former result is even or the latter result is odd, the receiving end requests the retransmission of the message block. By adding more redundancy, an error can be automatically corrected without retransmission. A large variety of error-detecting and error-correcting codes have been developed and are in use to provide various degrees of error-protection capability. Error protection is also provided for information storage and processing. As an example, redundancy of 8 bits is added to 64 information bits when storing them in a computer memory. This permits single-error correction and double-error detection.

To reduce failure of an information system, several measures have

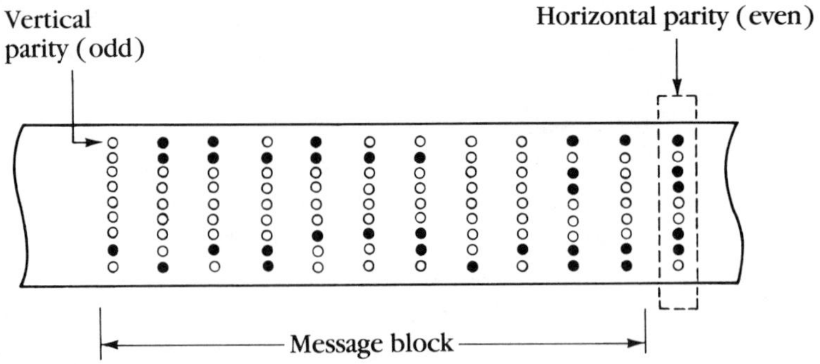

Figure 2-22 Vertical and horizontal parities: For the purpose of error detection, one bit is added to the 7-bit code for information transmission. Mark or space of the added bit is chosen so as to make the mark count over 8 bits odd. This additional bit is called the vertical parity, because the eighth element for this bit is added vertically on a perforated tape. Transmission disturbances that change the mark count from odd to even (such a change is called parity violation) can be detected at the receiving end. However, disturbances that cause no parity violation, such as two changes from space to mark, cannot be detected.

To enhance the error detecting capability, each message block generally contains a block-check character (BCC). The BCC may be extended to a block-check sequence (BCS), consisting of a few characters. The horizontal elements of the BCS represent the least significant digits of the binary count of the horizontal marks of the information characters. A more sophisticated BCS, known as the cyclic redundancy check (CRC) sequence, is also used to provide an extremely high degree of error protection. (SOURCE: Inose, *Digital Integrated Communications Systems*)

been taken. In the area of device technology, extensive studies on physical phenomena of device failure have contributed significantly to improved device structure and fabrication techniques. The progress in large-scale integrated circuit technology under strict quality control has drastically reduced device failure. Air conditioning, shock absorption, supply voltage stabilization, electrical noise shielding and other techniques have contributed to improved environmental conditions. As a result, the failure rate of a solid-state device has fallen during the past two decades from the order of 10^{-6} per hour to 10^{-9} per hour.

In the area of systems technology, redundancy techniques have been developed to keep a system operating when some part of its subsystem has failed. Automatic diagnostics and plug-in repair techniques have reduced the repair time for complex systems remarkably.

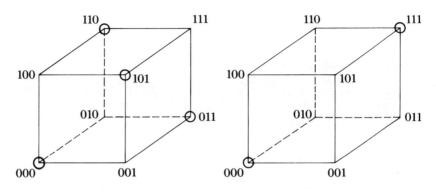

(a) Error detecting code   (b) Error correcting code

Figure 2-23 Error-detecting and -correcting codes: The eight corners of the cube represent eight possible combinations of 3-bit codes. (a) If four combinations—namely, 000, 011, 101, and 110—are used to carry information, a single error that turns a 0 to a 1 or a 1 to a 0 changes them to one of the four unused combinations. This permits single-error detection. The rightmost bit in each combination is the parity bit to make mark (1) count even.

(b) If only two combinations—namely, 000 and 111—are used, single errors can be corrected automatically, because 000 can change only to 100, 010, or 001; and 111 only to 110, 101, or 011. This also permits detection of double errors, but not correction.

In general, to correct a single error, m bits in n-bit codes must be used for redundancy, where

$$n \leq 2^m - 1$$

This indicates that for large values of n, redundancy addition becomes relatively less significant. For instance, $n = 3$ and $m = 2$ in the case of (b), but for $n = 127$, $m = 7$. In practice, 8 bits are added to 64 information bits when storing into a memory.

Curves showing failure statistics of a system over time generally have a bathtub shape. In the early stage of operation, system failure is large, mainly due to incomplete hardware and software design and to inferior components not detected during testing. Design modification and component changes (debugging) reduce the system failure rate to a steady value. While a system is in its useful life, the failure rate stays almost constant. During this period, failures occur at random, and maintenance action can be taken only after the occurrence of a failure. This is called a posteriori, or emergency, maintenance. When a system is in operation beyond its useful life, wear-out failure of components becomes dominant,

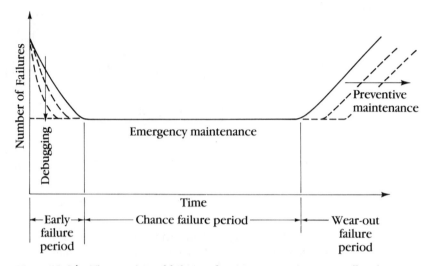

Figure 2-24 The number of failures of a system over time generally takes a bathtub shaped curve. Like that of human beings, mortality of a system is higher in the system's infancy, which is called the early failure period. The mortality also rises in the system's old age, which is called the wear-out failure period. The period between the two is the useful life of the system. During the useful life, failures occur at random; therefore, the useful life is called the chance failure period.

and the system failures tend to increase. To extend the system's useful life, aged components must be replaced before they wear out and result in system failure. This is called preventive maintenance.

While in its useful life, a system can be assumed to have a constant failure rate or a constant mean time between failure (MTBF), which is the inverse of the failure rate. If the value of the MTBF is not large enough, a redundant configuration is employed. Reliability theory tells us that if two systems run in parallel, the MTBF of the total system increases by 50 percent; if two systems assume a standby configuration, with one operating and the other standing by, the MTBF of the total system increases by 100 percent.

When a redundant configuration is used, a repair action further increases the MTBF of the total system. The measure of repair action is the mean time to repair (MTTR). According to reliability theory, the MTBF of a parallel system is

$$\frac{3}{2}(\text{MTBF}) + \frac{1(\text{MTBF})^2}{2(\text{MTTR})}$$

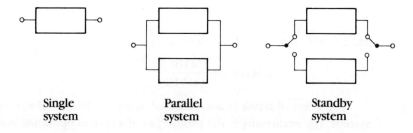

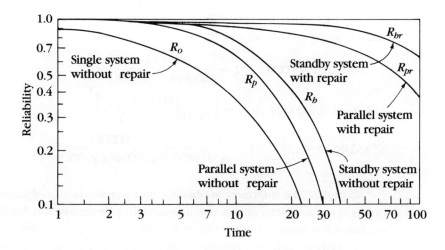

	Mean time between failure (MTBF) (hours)	Stationary availability (percentage)
Single system	10	95.24
Parallel system	115	99.77
Standby system	220	99.88

Figure 2-25 Reliability improvement of parallel and standby systems by repair: Some information systems are required to operate for longer than a certain period without stopping. The reliability of a system is the probability that the system keeps on operating for longer than a given period. The graph indicates how reliability is improved by parallel and standby configurations and by repair. MTBF and MTTR of a system is assumed as 10 hours and 0.5 hour, respectively. The improvements in the MTBF and the stationary availability of the total system by redundant configuration and repair are summarized in the table.

and the MTBF of a standby system is

$$2(\text{MTBF}) + \frac{(\text{MTBF})^2}{(\text{MTTR})}$$

The effect of repair is also reflected in the availability of a redundant system. The availability is the probability of a system operating normally at a given time. It is a function of time, but it generally has a time-independent value when the system is in stationary state. Theoretical results indicate that stationary availabilities of a single system, a parallel system, and a standby system are as follows:

SINGLE SYSTEM $\quad 1 - \dfrac{(\text{MTTR})}{(\text{MTBF}) + (\text{MTTR})}$

PARALLEL SYSTEM $\quad 1 - \left[\dfrac{(\text{MTTR})}{(\text{MTBF}) + (\text{MTTR})}\right]^2$

STANDBY SYSTEM $\quad 1 - \dfrac{(\text{MTTR})^2}{2(\text{MTBF})^2 + 2(\text{MTBF})(\text{MTTR}) + (\text{MTTR})^2}$

Shorter MTTR improves availability, and a redundant configuration brings about a significant increase in availability. By means of redundant configuration and appropriate repair, availability of a highly reliable information system such as a real-time computer or a telephone exchange now exceeds 99.99 percent. This can be interpreted as corresponding to a total downtime of less than 10 hours over a period of 10 years.

It is clear that the MTBF as well as the availability of a redundant system is improved if the MTTR is shortened. In a complex information system, a significant part of the repair time is spent in trouble-shooting. Once a card board that contains the component in failure is located, it can be replaced almost immediately by plugging in a new card board. For this reason, sophisticated diagnostic techniques have been developed. Generally, a large amount of diagnostic software is used that feeds diagnostic inputs to the system, observes its outputs, analyzes symptoms, and locates failure. Sometimes, the hardware configuration is modified to simplify diagnosis. Typically, one card board out of thousands can be located in less than 10 minutes with a success rate of more than 90 percent.

As hardware is becoming extremely reliable, attention is increasingly directed toward software reliability. Software failure is caused almost solely by some incompleteness that was not found by testing or debugging. The incompleteness ranges from a simple coding error to a very complicated mistake or misunderstanding in software design. Various techniques have been developed to avoid design and coding errors and to make testing and debugging easier and more nearly complete. The techniques include flow-charting, documentation, structured programming, modularization, and automatic program testing. Yet, software is less reliable than hardware, because it is produced predominantly by human beings who make mistakes more often than machines do.

Various techniques have been developed to provide secure information systems. In Section 2-5, we noted how data bases are protected from possible theft, inconsistency, and loss resulting from unauthorized access, concurrent modifications, and system failure. Similar protection has been provided to various sorts of computer-based information systems. Yet, information systems are still vulnerable to thieves. For instance, a microwave link can be intercepted by a highly sensitive receiver from a distance of a few kilometers, with very low probability of being detected. Interception of a satellite link can be made anywhere. Wiretapping can be done very cheaply to any lines and trunks, although the risk of being detected is higher. A magnetic disk pack or magnetic tape may be stolen or copied by breaking in or bribing.

To enhance security, encryption is an indispensable tool. Encryption is a process of converting an intelligible text into seemingly random sequences that are unintelligible to humans or computers. The conversion is done by applying a number of mathematical transformations, such as transposition and substitution of text symbols. The particular mathematical transformations to be applied to an original text are specified by a cryptographic key. If the key is known, the original text can be reconstructed by applying inverse mathematical tranformations. If the key is kept secret, no outsider can decrypt the text. In sending encrypted information, the sender secretly passes the key to the receiver. Although keys are kept secret, the mathematical transformations are not. For instance, the Data Encryption Standard (DES) of the U.S. National Bureau of Standards gives the algorithm for mathematical transformations which is now implemented on a large-scale integrated chip.

Another cryptographic system of interest is the public key system which uses two keys, namely, the encryption key and decryption key. The two keys are related, but it requires an enormous amount of computing time to distinguish them. Therefore, one of the two can be known to the public while the other is kept secret. This avoids the need of the conventional system for secretly passing the key from the sender to the receiver. A text to be transmitted is encrypted by an encryption key, which is known to the public; at the receiving end, the text is decrypted

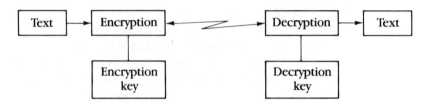

(a) Conventional system

(b) Public key system

Figure 2-26 Encryption systems can convert an intelligible text into seemingly random sequences through mathematical transformations specified by a secret key. Decryption is performed by applying inverse mathematical transformations to the encrypted text. The key must be transmitted secretly over a very secure channel (a).

A public key system (b) uses two keys, an encryption key and a decryption key. It is extremely difficult to distinguish one from the other. One of the two keys can be made known to the public while the other is kept secret.

only by the owner of the corresponding decryption key, which is kept secret. Although a public key system avoids secret key delivery, it requires larger memory space and is slower in operation than a conventional system.

2-9 Concluding Remarks

We have described some of the significant aspects of the state of the art of information technology that have been and will be used as powerful tools to enhance civilization. These tools already permit diversified types of information to be transmitted, switched, stored, processed, and retrieved in large quantities, at enormous speeds, and regardless of geographical locations. The prime mover is digitization, which will further provide an integration of information in various forms, a drastic reduction in hardware cost, and extremely high reliability, maintainability, and security as well as highly sophisticated information handling.

If these tools are properly used, our societies will be more closely knit, and our industries will be able to attain higher productivity and provide more knowledge-intensive products. Our societal infrastructure will be strengthened, traditional culture will be preserved, and new culture will be created. Above all, the integration of various forms of information and of ways for handling them will enhance the convergence of modes, in which traditionally isolated modes of human activities and services are merged together. Taking advantage of the convergence of modes, many communities of interests will be enhanced and new ones will be created, and, through this, civilization will flourish.

However, information technologies are no more than tools of human beings. We should know how to use these tools properly, aware of the consequences of their use and misuse. We also should know what can be done and what cannot be done by these tools. Further, we should be aware of the need to adjust the societal framework to maximize benefits and minimize negative consequences.

As a result of the extensive use of these tools, privacy may be infringed in a closely knit society, unemployment may result from automation, malfunction of information systems may endanger our property and life, some cultural patterns may become extinct, and existing regulatory measures may hamper the convergence of modes. An overview of these problems will be undertaken in the next chapter.

REFERENCES

H. Inose. *An Introduction to Digital Integrated Communications Systems*. University of Tokyo Press, Tokyo, 1979.

J. Martin. *Telecommunications and the Computer*. 2nd ed. Prentice-Hall, Englewood Cliffs, N.J., 1976.

Microelectronics, A Scientific American Book. W. H. Freeman and Company, San Francisco, 1977.

J. R. Pierce and E. C. Posner. *Introduction to Communication Science and Systems*. Plenum Press, New York, 1980.

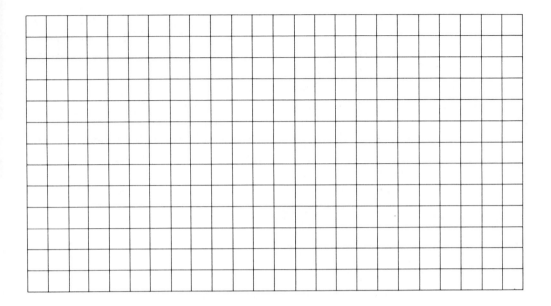

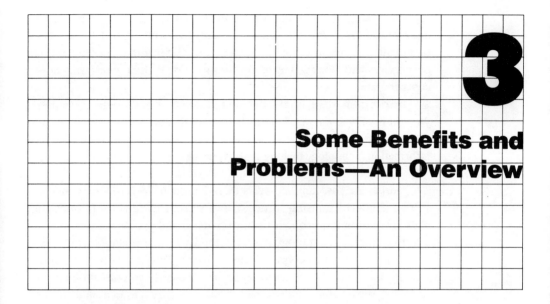

Some Benefits and Problems—An Overview

3-1 Introduction

In Chapter 1, we reviewed briefly the information technologies of the past and some of the effects that these technologies had on the world. What humans can do is constrained by the capabilities of their technologies. Yet, they can use their technologies in various ways—some beneficial, some detrimental to their security and their satisfaction with life.

It is both fruitless to ask for things that our technologies are powerless to supply and foolish not to take advantage of our technological capabilities. That is why we devoted the previous chapter to an extensive discussion of what our information technology can do and how it does it. Chapter 2 paints in some detail a realistic picture of the extent of information technology and indicates how the capabilities of this technology will grow in the near and the foreseeable future. It is an explication of our tools. Our real interest in tools is in learning what they enable us to do. Using our tools, what kind of world can we build? What opportunities lie before us? What problems may we encounter? What hazards may we face?

In later chapters, we will discuss in considerable detail the relation of information technology to several aspects of civilization, considering separately language and learning, arts and letters, the interrelation and interaction of information technology with government, and, most important of all, what information technology can do for, and to, people in their perception and knowledge of the world and in their work and home environments.

Before embarking on the detailed discussions of these later chapters, we will review some general issues that are frequently raised concerning information technology and the world and also point out some effects of information technology that, we believe, have received insufficient attention.

During the past hundred years there has been a revolutionary increase in our ability to transmit, process, and store, and retrieve information. This revolution has brought us both benefits and problems.

Information technology has integrated activities that in the past were often functionally or geographically separate. This has permitted sophisticated functions to be performed more efficiently and has allowed geographical separation of individual activities that are part of a single unified project. However, societal activities that are closely knit by information technology may be vulnerable to misuse of, or accidental or intentional leaking of personal information, which infringes on privacy. Such activities are also vulnerable to destruction of data, to errors introduced in data, and to breakdowns or malfunctions of information systems. Further, effective integration may not be possible if technological standards do not permit adequate interfacing.

Information technology can help to change the present industrial structure of mass production and consumption to a structure that consumes less material and energy and produces fewer things—but things—that have greater values added. Further, the productivity and working conditions of traditional industrial sectors can be improved by the use of information technology. However, changes in the industrial structure can lead to a loss of jobs in traditional areas and a shortage of workers in emerging industrial sectors.

Information technology promises to improve such services as medical care and transportation, making it possible to provide them efficiently and at less cost. However, in such areas, the same information-based technology may endanger human life if it does not work reliably. It may also infringe on privacy if security measures are inadequate.

New information technology permits the integration of various information services that are now provided separately. Such integration, known as the convergence of service modes, can provide users with diversified information more effectively and at less cost. But, if we are to take full advantage of the convergence of service modes, present regulatory policies must be changed. Moreover, appropriate measures are needed to avoid concentration of control over a number of media and to alleviate uneven distribution of information resources among countries and districts.

Information technology can provide a powerful tool for understanding and preserving the human cultural heritage and for enhancing the cultural creativity of mankind. Information technology can help a community to learn about the cultures of other communities; this, too, has advantages and disadvantages. Communities can enrich their cultures by selectively introducing elements from foreign cultures. However, communities can lose their cultural identity and be overwhelmed by outside influences.

This chapter gives a brief overview of some of the societal benefits and problems that are associated with new capabilities of information technology. Later chapters will discuss selected areas in greater depth.

3-2 Integration of Societal Activities

Human society and civilization developed through an intuitive and inherent desire to integrate the activities of individuals and thus acquire knowledge and skill for the betterment of life. Tribal villages, city-states, kingdoms, empires, and republics were formed to promote the integration of societal activities.

In ancient days, the means of societal integration included roads and coastal navigation networks. Pilgrims on foot, traders with wagons, messengers on horseback, and warriors on chariots traveled the Appian Way, the Silk Road and other great thoroughfares. The Greeks, the Phoenecians, and the Vikings, under sail and by oar, dominated the Mediterranean and North seas, enriching themselves and devastating others.

The integration of our modern society is supported by the transportation network, the power network (carrying electricity and liquid, gas, and solid fuels), and the information network. The flow of passengers and freight, the flow of energy, and the flow of information through these networks combine the activities of individuals in diverse locations into an integrated whole. The information network is the most vital. It is indispensable in our society and it plays a controlling role in regard to all other networks.

The convenience of information networks has stimulated rapid growth of complex activities, and these, in turn, have made increasing demands on the networks. This positive feedback will be intensified in the years ahead. Let us consider only a few examples. The demand for toll telephone service is estimated to increase by at least 15 percent per year. Taking into account the rapid growth of data communication and other communication demands, the present communication network may be required to double its capacity in less than 5 years and quadruple that capacity in less than 10 years. The growth rate of intercontinental telephone calls is estimated to be even greater. If the present estimates of a 30-percent increase per year holds, the intercontinental communication network may be required to double its capacity in 3 years and quadruple it in 6. The demand for on-line computers is increasing at an annual rate of more than 60 percent; this would quadruple the number operating in less than 3 years.

The information network is making it possible for an industry to control its inventory and production at widely dispersed locations continuously by computer, in accordance with sales over an ever-greater geographical area. Such continuous control allows what is called real-time operation. In banking, similar networks provide on-line services to customers while allowing for control of lending and other financial operations in accordance with the bank's assets and liabilities as tracked by a central data base. In electric power networks, generators are controlled in real time to meet changes in demand and to generate and distribute electric energy most economically. Thanks to such networks, engineers or scientists may work at home by using their terminals, which give access to the large computers and data bases of the company; much waste of time and energy in commuting to and from an office can thereby be avoided. A man or woman can use a computer terminal at home to produce computer software. This opens up important possibilities for part-time work and sharing of household duties.

The integration of activities that information technology allows is of benefit, not simply to large corporations, but also to individuals and small enterprises. This technology allows such activities carried out over a wide geographic area to be integrated into a single functional enterprise. It allows the resources of computers located elsewhere to support local activities. Data bases linked by a network can be distributed for easier maintenance and updating by local specialists. Still more broadly, the individual user at a terminal can connect with these computers and data bases as if they were on his or her own premises—surely a great benefit to individuals and small operations.

Governments also benefit from the integration of activities provided by information technology. Statistics covering agriculture, industry, finance, education, environment, health, and other areas can be collected easily and comprehensively from all over the country. Data bases that store these statistics provide the government with a large variety of economic and social indicators, which, in turn, permit the government to adjust its policies more sensibly and adaptively by using computers. The government can also use these data to aid law enforcement by detecting dubious financial dealings, repeated patterns of crime, false income tax statements, fraudulent driver's licenses, and so on.

Here we clearly see the dangers as well as the benefits of the integration of activities. Recall what the Gestapo did without benefit of computers, a data base, or a modern communication network. Are present governments reasonable enough to avoid such abuse of our personal data? People in modern society, especially those living in large metropolitan areas, prefer to live unnoticed by others and to enjoy freedom of speech while being protected by privacy and anonymity. If a citizen knew that all details of his behavior were recorded in government data banks, he or she might well worry about the use, abuse, or leakage of that information. Will mass media, armed with the right to know, obtain private data from the government and publicize it? Will a competing company, by claiming freedom of information, gain access to financial and technological secrets of an enterprise and endanger its existence and the livelihood of its employees? Not only private persons, but corporations or other enterprises, may feel that they are under excessive control and are vulnerable to the leakage of information. It is proper to be concerned about corporations, because the potential financial losses of a corporation may be far larger than those for individuals, and damage to a single corporation can damage many individuals, not just one.

If a government wished to gain full advantage of the benefit of information technology in this respect, it would have to enact and effectively enforce a series of legal measures that would protect the privacy of individuals and enterprises while maintaining reasonable freedom of access to the information collected by the government itself. And its information technology should make use of all practical measures to protect information from leakage, corruption, and destruction. Even with the best of intentions and the greatest of efforts, this will not be easy to achieve.

The reliability of information systems is also vital. Information technology is drawing us toward a tightly linked, highly complex, and vital organization. No matter how complex the technology becomes, it must continue to work smoothly in order to fulfill its functions—functions vital to our social and economic well-being. As we indicated in previous chapters, these systems overall and their hardware in particular are remarkably reliable, but still greater reliability should be sought, particularly in software systems.

Standardization of technological specifications in terms of hardware as well as software also deserves careful attention. Without this, integration to form networks cannot be accomplished, because interconnection of equipment of different makes and models will be either impossible or uneconomic.

Systems are being integrated not only within nations but also among nations and across and between continents, knitting societal activities together on a global scale. The benefits and problems of this integration are of worldwide importance and concern.

3-3 Change in Industrial Structure

The industrial structure of our society has undergone many changes in the past. Most changes were evolutionary, but some have been large and sudden—depending on the technological innovations that caused them. These changes in industrial structure have allowed society to support an ever-increasing population and to meet an apparently limitless desire for a better and more convenient way of life.

The Industrial Revolution, which originated in the late eighteenth century in England, provided steam engines, spinning machines, power looms,and other useful machines and thereby greatly reduced the effort required in production. Mass production, which was established in the early twentieth century in the United States, followed the Industrial Revolution and provided customers with wide-ranging products that were uniform in quality and lower in cost. The principle underlining the present industrial structure is economy of scale. Every industrialized nation in the world now consumes a great deal of energy and raw materials and produces a very large quantity of products for domestic consumption as well as for export.

To promote the sale of consumer products, which were saturating the market, the concept known as planned obsolescence was introduced. This encourages consumers to buy the latest models and sell or discard still usable older ones. Industries flourished, unemployment was reduced, and economic growth was sustained in the industrialized world.

Some of the developing countries quickly followed this pattern of industrialization; they are now known as the newly industrialized countries (NIC). However, most of the developing countries remained suppliers of energy and raw materials and buyers of industrial products.

Toward the end of the 1960's, citizens became increasingly aware of the seriousness of environmental disruption and pollution, which were to a large extent attributed to mass production and mass consumption. Free and inexpensive access to energy and raw materials was a thing of the past, both because of the competitive effects of increased demand and because natural resources are unevenly distributed on earth. Developing countries became increasingly reluctant to sell natural resources. The oil crises of the 1970's were decisive signs of these developments. Since the mid 1970's, economic growth has faltered, and high levels of inflation and unemployment have coexisted. Competition in the international marketplace has been intensified almost to the point of unrestrained conflict.

It has become clear that the present industrial structure, which was based on mass consumption of energy and raw materials and mass production and consumption of products, needs to be adjusted to alleviate the difficulties described above. Consumption of energy and raw materials should be reduced, and productivity of labor and capital should be increased in traditional industrial sectors, including the iron, steel, and chemical industries so vital to society. Similar improvements are necessary in productivity in agriculture and the distribution of agricultural products, which are also vital for human survival. Beyond this, more emphasis should be placed on high-technology products, because these consume less energy and raw materials and have higher values added.

Information technology will play a major role in reaching these ends. Information technology, including process control computers and industrial robotics, reduces the consumption of energy and raw materials, enhances the productivity and performance of conventional industrial products, and relieves workers from unnecessary monotonous labor.

A robotlike "hand" is used to insert and remove cassettes from tape decks in a quality-control check. (Photo courtesy of Philips)

Information technology, including meteorological satellites and computers for weather forecasting as well as computerized distribution systems, helps to improve the productivity of agriculture and the distribution of agricultural products. Knowledge-intensive products and systems, including computers, telecommunications equipment, numerically controlled machine tools and microprocessor-oriented equipment, which are based on information technology, save energy and raw materials, and they have higher values added than conventional industrial products.

However, a change of the industrial structure presents problems. Whenever structural changes in industry have taken place, workers in traditional industrial sectors have become obsolete and have lost their jobs, while newly emerging industrial sectors have suffered from a shortage of workers. A change to an information-oriented industrial structure can be no exception. Skilled workers, such as those doing routine machining jobs in industrial plants, may lose their jobs because of the increasing use of process control computers and industrial robots. General office workers without special talents may also lose their jobs because of the rapid penetration of word processors and other office automation equipment. Changes in distribution channels may cost jobs in various areas, for example, food production and distribution. On the other hand, enormous job opportunities will be created in the area of software production, since much new software is needed to improve productivity in traditional industrial areas and to support knowledge-dependent products and services. No matter the extent of machine support in this effort, this software is ultimately written by human beings, and the need is immense. Education and training, which allow a smooth shift of the labor force from decaying to emerging areas, are crucial for such a change in industrial structure.

Another question arises: Can developing countries adopt such structural changes in their industries, or can such changes in developed countries benefit developing countries? It seems clear that developing countries need information technology for efficient development of their natural resources and for enhancing the productivity of their agriculture as well as of their industries. It also seems clear that, in view of the enormous amount of software needed for the informatization of industries, software production has to be shared on an international basis. In particular, programs for specific applications have to be produced locally to meet end users' needs which differ in many respects among differing societies. Some developing countries, where wages are relatively low and job opportunities for educated people are insufficient, may have an advantage over some developed countries, where wages are high and people are not motivated to promote structural changes in industry. In fact, quite a few newly industrialized countries have been very active and successful in the area of software production.

Implications of information technology for industrial structure, if correctly understood, may hasten the arrival of the developing countries among the ranks of the developed. Indeed, if the developed countries do not correctly perceive the technical possibilities, they may join the ranks of the underdeveloped.

3-4   Strengthening the Societal Infrastructure

The present industrial pattern of mass production and mass consumption stimulated rapid urbanization. A large portion of the population drained from rural areas and concentrated in metropolitan districts as people pursued better job opportunities. The results were the environmental disruption of urban sprawl near large cities and the increasing abandonment of remote rural villages. The pace of urbanization was so fast that the deployment of societal infrastructure was unable to catch up, and the quality of life in metropolitan districts was degraded. In rural areas, where the population steadily decreased, societal infrastructures, such as medical care, were lost. Such tendencies have been observed throughout the world. Rapid industrial expansion in developed parts of the world and the population explosion in developing countries have been major causes.

A strengthening of societal infrastructure is urgently needed. We seem called on to build a heavenly welfare society on the earth without the assistance of an almighty god. However, our resources in money and manpower are quite limited, especially at a time when most countries— except those rich in oil—have been suffering from stagnation. We must use our limited resources at the highest possible efficiency if we are to realize anything approaching this goal of paradise on this sinful earth— indeed, if we are to avoid sliding to a situation more closely approximating purgatory, or even hell.

Here again, information technology can play a significant role. Let us take emergency medical care as an example. Success depends almost solely on how quickly proper medical treatment, including surgery if necessary, can be provided to a patient. Sometimes, however, an ambulance takes a long time to arrive at the site of need and then has to go from one emergency hospital to another in order to find specialized doctors on duty. In addition, the facilities and paramedics of the emergency hospital are not always in readiness for the doctors to provide proper medical treatment.

An emergency medical information system can be of great help in such situations. It quickly locates the nearest ambulance and directs it to the site via radio telephone. Paramedics on board the ambulance report the patient's injury or symptoms to the center, which immediately determines which hospital to direct the ambulance to by consulting a computerized table that stores, in real time, information on emergency hospitals in the area, including availability of doctors, paramedics, and facilities.

The center relays information about the patient's condition to the doctors so that they will be ready to provide proper medical treatment immediately upon the arrival of the ambulance.

Without a system like this, a much larger number of ambulances, doctors, paramedics, and medical facilities must be available around the clock in order to provide a similar level of service. This is a direct increase in productivity. It may also be noted that an emergency medical information system provides better service because, without this, delay in treatment or even improper treatment is more likely. The system also improves the lives and productivity of doctors and paramedics, who, instead of idly standing by in their clinics and hospitals, could relax in their homes and dormitories or be engaged in productive work of lower priority until summoned by an emergency call.

A computerized road traffic control system is another example of efficient improvement of an infrastructure. By means of a very large number of detectors, the amount of vehicular traffic in a complex road network is measured and sent over communication lines to a central computer. The central computer analyzes the data and, in accordance with the changes of traffic pattern, directs the local controllers at each of the intersections of the road network to switch traffic lights in such a way that the total travel time of vehicles within the road network is minimized. Basically, this is accomplished by controlling traffic lights in favor of more heavily traveled routes. As a result of such control, significant reductions in travel time, fuel consumption, air pollution, and driver fatigue have been reported, as vehicles in heavier traffic flows are permitted to pass several intersections without stopping or with less acceleration and deceleration. The system also increases the traffic capacity of the road network under control, thereby saving the cost of expanding roads and avoiding community conflict that might arise through such expansion.

Air traffic control systems are still another example. A radar system detects a number of aircraft en route or around an airport and, with the help of transponders on board and computers on the ground, displays on its cathode-ray tube the image of each aircraft along with a tag that indicates the aircraft's speed, altitude, and flight number. Using this display, a traffic officer can direct each aircraft in his flight area to maintain a proper speed, altitude, and distance from other aircraft. The system not only improves safety but also allows more efficient use of the flight area. By adjusting flight schedules and speeds, the system can also reduce stackups above the airport and thereby help to save energy.

Although these examples are only a few out of many, they clearly tell

Computers are a vital part of air traffic control systems. (Photo courtesy of U.S. Federal Aviation Administration)

us that information technology results in significant savings in money and human effort while providing better services.

Information-oriented infrastructure also must meet demanding requirements. First, it must be extremely reliable, as in the example of air traffic control systems. It also must be extremely secure. For instance, the benefit of an emergency medical information system would be greater if the system could have access to data bases that stored patients' medical records, as such access improves the speed and accuracy of diagnosis. But here, people must become concerned about abuse or leakage of information. Would competitors steal one another's medical records and use them to jeopardize their rivals' political or corporate futures? A doctor may worry that information on certain cases might be stolen and used in malpractice suits.

Likewise, a computerized road traffic control system would be upgraded if the central computer could trace and guide each vehicle from its origin to destination to provide the shortest travel time. The drivers might then fear that the traffic police will make use of the computer trace and automatically give them tickets for speeding or other violations. A sales company may suspect that the activities of its sales vehicles are known by its competitors through leakage of information.

3-5 The Convergence of Service Modes

As a result of rapid innovation in information technology, a variety of information services that traditionally have been considered separate are becoming increasingly similar. This trend is often referred to as the convergence of service modes. If we look back in history, we see that this is not a new phenomenon. As we have seen in Chapter 1, postal service is a convergence of services that were previously provided by heralds, couriers, and messengers. The use of such technological innovations as horse-drawn wagons, trains, and trucks stimulated the convergence and enhanced the economy of scale of the postal service, as did the ingenuity of the policy makers who provided a single service with a distance-independent rate.

As we have seen, telecommunication and information-processing services have already merged to provide data communication or on-line processing. The benefits of such systems as on-line banking, airline or train seat reservation, emergency medical information, and traffic control were brought to our society by this natural and inevitable convergence of service modes.

The telecommunication common carrier now provides facsimile communication service, in which customers can either use their own terminals or lease them from the common carrier. The postal service also provides electronic mail service, in which one post office, upon receipt of a sender's letter, transmits it by facsimile to the post office closest to the receiver. In the latter service, documents must still be transported physically between customers and post offices, but both types of service will soon merge in some form so as to transmit copies of documents more rapidly between customers.

Videotex of telecommunication service and teletext of broadcasting service both display still pictures on customers' television screens. The difference is that in videotex, pictures are provided selectively upon the customer's request via telephone lines, while in teletext, pictures are carried one way over radio waves or coaxial cables for the customer's choice. The difference may become less significant as cable television systems acquire two-way capability.

Newspaper, book, and journal publishers increasingly use word processors, computerized typesetting, text transmission, and facsimile transmission. In fact, by using a text-editing program and computer composition, anyone can now prepare reports in good form without going through a publisher. Newspapers are now exploring the possibility of facsimile delivery to their customers by means of a subchannel piggybacked on a television channel. Information vendors who provide data base retrieval service to their customers are expanding their repertoires by adding news reports. Libraries are also providing bibliographical-information retrieval. Eventually, they will provide copies of book and journal pages by facsimile. By that time, newspaper, book, and journal publishers will be able to provide similar services.

It is clear that by the extensive use of information technology, capabilities of all sorts of information services are enhanced. In particular, traditionally nonelectronic services, such as postal service, newspaper, book, and journal publication, and libraries, are acquiring capabilities they never had before and thereby tend to merge together with the traditionally electronic services, such as telecommunication, information processing, and broadcasting.

The benefits of the convergence of service modes are that it brings economy of scale and that a variety of information can be provided in various forms through a variety of media. The high cost of information collection, processing, and creation in the forms of data bases and audio and video programs can be shared by users of a number of media. More communities of interests of smaller scale can be served by providing the specific information they need. However, the convergence of service modes presents some problems.

One such problem is regulation, as the convergence is dismantling barriers between traditionally regulated and unregulated services. For instance, data communication or on-line processing is a result of convergence between telecommunication, which is regulated, and information processing, which is unregulated. If a user of a data communication system instructs the computer to process information and forward the results to another user, this may seem to be an extension of information processing. If, on the other hand, a user instructs the computer merely to store information and forward it without any processing to another user, this may seem to be an extension of telecommunication known as message switching.

Here, questions arise as to whether an information processing firm that provides message switching should be regulated or whether a common carrier that is a regulated monopoly can enter the information-processing business in which firms are unregulated and competing. This is one of many examples that make it difficult for policy makers to keep abreast of the rapid progress of information technology. Unless the policy makers have foresight and wisdom, the merit of the convergence of service modes will be totally lost.

Another problem is the danger of centralized control of various media. A conglomerate that owns newspaper companies, book and journal publication companies, radio and television stations, and computerized information vendors would be able to utilize its information resources very efficiently, take advantage of the complementary characteristics of various media, and provide information to match its customers' needs at low cost. However, the conglomerate might use its influence to control public opinion by providing biased information through a variety of media. Such multiple control of media might have a significant influence if the conglomerate had a nationwide network of operation and few major competitors who held different views. Clearly, the worst case is that in which the conglomerate is part of a totalitarian government and is given a complete monopoly.

Still another problem arises from the fact that information resources are unevenly distributed on the earth. The success of information services that take advantage of the convergence of service modes depends almost solely on the quantity and quality of the information they can provide. However, it is not easy to collect, accumulate, update, and distribute information. Hence, the supply of news reports in the world is, to a large extent, in the hands of five major news agencies, AFP, AP, Reuters, Tass, and UPI. The majority of data bases for bibliographical retrieval and other purposes are in the United States. In general, we find more information resources in developed countries than in developing countries and more in large metropolitan districts than in remote rural districts. This brings about differences in the ease of access to information resources in countries and districts. If the convergence of service modes is left solely in the hands of market forces, more information will be collected and distributed in developed countries and in large metropolitan districts, rendering them even more information rich, and the rest of the countries and districts even more information poor.

3-6   The Enrichment of Human Culture

As we have seen in Chapter 1, since ancient times, information technology has provided humans with a great many tools useful in developing their cultures. Such ancient technologies as recording characters on paper, printing copies of these records, and distributing the records and copies by mail have stimulated creative authors to write letters, diaries, and books of great literary value. Likewise, technological progress in musical instruments and painting materials have helped composers and painters to create their masterpieces.

The invention of cinematography brought a new genre for theatrical arts by providing diversified ways of expression and presentation, including special effects and animation, which are now being further enhanced by the use of television and computer animation. The phonograph permitted musicians to capture their best performances. Such innovations as high-fidelity amplifiers, long-playing stereophonic records, optical sound tracks, magnetic tapes, and compact disks, as well as the videotapes that followed, improved the performance and convenience of audio and image recording.

By means of audio and image recording, we now can appreciate performances of virtuosi and great actors, living or dead, at any time and at any place. For the first time in human history, the performing arts have been made potentially immortal. People in the future will be able to see all sorts of performing arts, from our time and onward, by means of film, tape, and record libraries. These media also provide opportunities to record languages, dialects, folk melodies, festivals, religious rites, and other activities of various communities.

Today we can see sculptures of Assyrian, Persian, Egyptian, Greek, Roman, Hindu, and Chinese deities, kings, and warriors; transcripts of ancient bibles and sutras, such as the Dead Sea Scrolls; original manuscripts written by great authors; and the great paintings of all ages. Because many such cultural artifacts of great anthropological value are disappearing, it is clear that information technology has a great contribution to make in preserving the human cultural heritage.

X-ray photographs, carbon-14 analysis, and other information technologies tell us how ancient sculptures and paintings were made, reveal their ages, and establish their authenticity. Curators and art historians are acquiring powerful tools for better understanding and evaluating the fine arts and archeological objects and are thereby finding better ways to preserve them. Information technology has also provided a powerful tool to linguists and music theorists in understanding the principles underlying languages, musical structures, and sounds.

Emerging information technology is providing artists with new means of expression. Serious composers and listeners are increasingly paying attention to electronic musical instruments and computer-synthesized musical sounds. Producers of television programs, motion pictures, and stage performances are rapidly introducing computer-graphics, lasers, holograms, and other special effects, not only in science fiction dramas, but also in more serious productions. Computers are helping architects and industrial designers, by providing structural analyses and animated graphics, to implement their ingenuity without sacrificing practicality. Computers are also assisting fashion designers in laying out forms and patterns through interactive graphics.

Information technology has been very useful and will be even more useful to humans in learning about the cultures of different communities. However, exposure to different cultures brings both advantages and disadvantages. It helps one community to understand the cultures of others, and by selectively borrowing from these, a community will be able to enhance its own culture. If, on the other hand, one community is exposed to a powerful culture and absorbs it without discrimination, the cultural identity of that community will be lost. This is particularly true when a remote rural community is suddenly exposed to an advanced civilization. Because of the conveniences it provides, an advanced civilization may quickly overwhelm the community, and the traditional culture of the community may be lost. In the past, we have seen many instances in which an advanced civilization was successfully adapted by a number of communities and flourished through the endogenous efforts of such communities. However, we have also seen other instances in which the introduction of advanced civilization merely caused chaos or complete loss of identity. Thus, an effort should be made to strengthen the endogenous culture of individuals and communities and to maximize the profit and minimize the loss due to such interaction.

3-7 Concluding Remarks

In this chapter, we have described benefits and problems that have been brought to our society by unprecedented capabilities of information technology in respect to the integration of societal activities, the change in industrial structure, the strengthening of societal infrastructure, the convergence of service modes, and the enrichment of human culture.

Among a large variety of societal impacts of information technology, the most vital are those that affect human identity. Typical examples are the impacts on the languages and means of learning on which human identity and culture depend. Another emerging impact that is becoming increasingly significant is that on arts and letters. These topics will be dealt with in chapters 4 and 5.

Market forces have played and will continue to play a major role in promoting and bringing into use the capabilities of information technology for the betterment of human life. However, there are some areas in which market forces are weak or do not function properly. Protection of privacy and security, establishment of optimum regulation of information services, standardization of hardware and software, and implementation of societal infrastructure are typical examples of such areas in which the intervention and assistance of the government are required. These and other topics will be discussed in Chapter 6.

Whether or not market forces and governments function properly, the people of the world today face enormous opportunities and problems. The formation of a great variety of communities of interests, the creation of vast employment opportunities in the area of software production, and the conveniences for home life and work are examples that can benefit people. The difficulty of obtaining needed information, the displacement of the labor force through automation, and a lack of proper evaluation of service quality are examples of impacts that confuse people. Chapter 7 deals with these topics.

REFERENCES

"Communication." *Scientific American* 227, 3 (September 1972).

Ithiel de Sola Pool, ed. *The Social Impact of the Telephone*. MIT Press, Cambridge, 1977.

G. Friedricks and A. Schaff, eds. *Microelectronics and Society: For Better or For Worse.* Pergamon Press, Oxford, 1982.

H. Inose. "Planning for Information Oriented Society in Japan." *Journal of Information Processing* 1, 1 (April 1978):3–13.

H. Inose. "Road Traffic Control with Particular Reference to Tokyo Traffic Control and Surveillance System." *Proc. IEEE* 64 (July 1976):1028–1039.

Sean MacBride. *Many Voices, One World.* Report by the International Commission for the Study of Communication Problems, UNESCO, Paris, 1980.

S. Nora and A. Minc. *L'informatization de la Société.* Editions de Seuil, Paris, 1978.

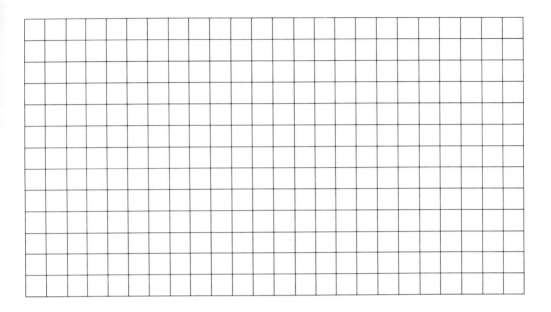

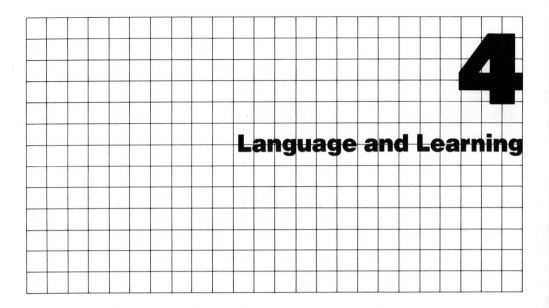

Language and Learning

4-1 Introduction

Language is central to human civilization, thought, and technologies. It is mankind's most astonishing invention. Yet, we cannot trace it to an inventor or even to a single cultural source. Today, more than 3000 languages and a much larger number of dialects are spoken, representing a large variety of cultural backgrounds of the people who speak them.

Major languages (those spoken by more than 100 million people) number less than 15, and only English, French, Russian, and Spanish, and in some instances Chinese and Arabic are generally acknowledged by international organizations as official languages. Documents are issued and simultaneous interpretation is provided in these official languages. Speakers whose native tongues are not one of the official languages must be bilingual if they are to speak in any one of them, or they must make use of a simultaneous interpreter, who translates their native tongues into one of the official languages. As social and economic activities in the world become more closely knit, inconveniences of language barriers are felt increasingly, and misunderstandings owing to language barriers are mounting.

Some of the languages spoken by minorities will soon become extinct, as rare species die out, because of the difficulty in communicating with the rest of a highly interdependent world. As telecommunications and broadcasting in major languages continue to cover more and more of the earth, we may expect the variety of today's languages and dialects to decrease rapidly. Languages will be lost, and with them will be a significant loss of the human cultures of which these languages and dialects are a vital part.

Information technology provides a means for preserving dead languages—thus protecting rare species from oblivion—and also for lowering language barriers. Cassette tape recorders, pocket-sized and battery powered, can be carried by linquists into the most remote rural areas to record local languages and dialects that face extinction, just as movie cameras and videotape recorders help anthropologists and artists to record the ways of life and cultures of rare communities.

Electronic language laboratories and computer-aided instruction systems can help minorities to learn one or more major languages while preserving their own. If its cost is low enough, machine translation of simple, straightforward text may help to lower language barriers, especially when the process can be adapted to the vocabulary and sentence structure of a particular body of material (for example, the technical manuals of one firm) or when the material to be translated can be written in a form that is easy for the machine to translate.

However, languages are products of the most sophisticated intellectual activities of human beings whose behavior we do not understand well and will never understand completely. It is impossible to translate mechanically a text in unrestricted natural language into another natural language by using dictionaries and grammatical rules alone. Natural-language text is meaningful only to those who speak the language, and only those who understand a text can translate it sensibly and effectively. A machine translates some sentences accurately into a closely related language, but machines also make false or unintelligible translations. Some texts can be translated by any bilingual informed person because they say things that any informed person can understand. Some texts can be translated only by an expert in a field. Language is an area in which information technology can accomplish much through a well-thought-out interaction between machines and human beings. Human beings are best at some tasks, machines at others, and a wise combination can be very powerful. This chapter will describe the difficulties and possibilities of information technology in dealing with languages and learning.

4-2   History of Machine Translation

Machine translation is one of the oldest dreams of information technology. Warren Weaver, an insightful and perceptive scholar, and A. Donald Booth loosed this demon in the computer world in 1946. The Association for Computational Linguistics, a respectable professional organization, was originally named the Association for Machine Translation and Computational Linguistics when it was formed in 1962.

In the 1960's, machine translation seemed just around the corner. In fact, the United States Air Force was paying for a translation project in which a computer converted large amounts of Russian technical literature into a form that a bilingual editor could turn into an awkward translation. Nonetheless, in 1966 a study of the National Research Council of the (U.S.) National Academy of Sciences concluded that machine translation was not yet a fact and that there was not likely to be a generally useful machine translation until a computer could "understand" a natural-language text. What went wrong?

In brief, when simple machine "dictionary look-up" produced ambiguous, unreadable texts, the proponents of computer translation turned to grammar for a cure. They found that existing grammars were not helpful. In fact, they found that no attainable grammar cured the persistent ills of machine translation—inaccuracy, ambiguity, and unreadability. As Victor H. Yngve wrote in 1964:

> Work in mechanical translation has come up against a semantic barrier.... We have come face to face with the realization that we will only have adequate mechanical translation when the machine can "understand" what it is translating and this will be a very difficult task indeed.... "Understand" is just what I mean.... Some of us are pressing forward undaunted.

The search for a syntactical cure for the ills of machine translation led to a reexamination of syntax. In *Syntactic Structures*, Noam Chomsky proposed to find a grammar—that is, a set of rules for associating words with one another in sentences—that would, in principle, make it possible to program a computer so that it could generate any grammatical sentence and never generate an ungrammatical sentence. By a grammatical sentence, Chomsky meant a sentence acceptable to a native speaker. To this end, Chomsky proposed a new grammatical concept: the transformational grammar.

Chomsky's work was important in two ways. It led a number of linguists, Yngve among them, to try to produce transformational grammars of English. This work produced grammars that became larger and larger and less and less intuitive; moreover, none of the grammars produced could generate all grammatical sequences and no ungrammatical sequences.

Another outcome of Chomsky's work was to inspire certain psychologists, notably George A. Miller, then at Harvard, to do experimental work on human response to language. At first, this line of inquiry seemed very fruitful; as it proceeded, however, it became more complicated and less clear in implications, except for one—the importance of meaning in communication.

4-3 Language and Meaning

Chomsky proposed as a criterion for a sentence's being grammatical that it be "acceptable to a native speaker." When, in fact, naive native speakers are asked whether or not a sentence is grammatical, they frequently declare it to be ungrammatical unless it makes sense to them. Conversely, ingenious people will spontaneously and gleefully invent tortured circumstances in which a seemingly meaningless or ungrammatical sentence will actually be acceptable to a native speaker. We are inclined to reject "I is a boy," but what would our reaction to be if we were visiting a school in which all the children were assigned pronouns rather than called by their names?

Indeed, whether or not a sentence is grammatical or meaningful seems to depend ultimately on the ingenuity of the person who puzzles over it. Even then we are left with Weaver's exception:

> Similarly, anyone would agree that the probability is low for such a sequence of words as "Constantinople fishing nasty pink." Incidentally, it is low, but not zero; for it is perfectly possible to think of a passage in which one sentence closes with "Constantinople fishing," and the next begins with "Nasty pink." And we might observe in passing that the unlikely four-word sequence under discussion has occurred in a single good English sentence, namely the one above.

Weaver therefore stresses meaning and effectiveness in communication. We find this search for meaning and effect outside the laboratory both in the myths and magic of antiquity and in our own daily experience. We are able to find meaning in text or speech even when the text is corrupt or the speech scarcely audible.

William James observed this truth in 1899:

> When we listen to a person speaking or read a page of print, much of what we think we see or hear is supplied from our memory. We overlook misprints, imagining the right letters, though we see the wrong one; and how little we actually hear, when we listen to speech, we realize when we go to a foreign theatre; for there what troubles us is not so much that we cannot understand what the actors say as that we cannot hear their words. The fact is that we hear quite as little under similar conditions at home, only our mind, being fuller of English verbal associations, supplies the requisite material for comprehension upon a much slighter auditory hint.

This passage from James gives us a strong clue to understanding where the meaning of language really resides. It is useless to seek the meaning or utility of a book between its covers or the intent or effect of a speech in the sounds that are uttered. A textbook on physics or mathematics exists in the context of the physics and mathematics of its time. It is not a complete exposition of the physics or mathematics it is intended to teach. Such a text is addressed to a person who already knows a language, something about the world and something about physics and mathematics. It is intended to enable the person to learn, understand, and use knowledge, skills, and insights that the author has acquired. Taken out of its environment of language, such a textbook would be completely unintelligible. Taken out of its environment of physics or mathematics, such a textbook might be interpreted symbolically, construed as magic, or dismissed as boring nonsense.

Our everyday communication has meaning in a much more restricted context. An order on a battlefield communicates only to a soldier who knows the situation, and the situation cannot be recreated by an examination of the words uttered. Phrases passed back and forth in a discussion may earn John Doe a raise or cost him his job, but the phrases have meaning only with respect to what those who are discussing Doe already know about him. Communication takes place only between persons within a common context; in this context they may share a common aim, a common problem, a common curiosity, a common interest. In other words, they must share a community of interest that is important or fascinating to both (or all).

The process of communication is not one of imparting entire areas of knowledge or of drastically changing views. That is the process of education or training, which makes use of communication but goes far beyond communication as we commonly construe it. Communication in everyday use is a process of adjusting understandings and attitudes, of making them congruent, or of ascertaining how and where they agree or disagree. A common language is of extreme advantage in our efforts to communicate, but it is not so important as a community of interest and some degree of common understanding.

Yet, if we had everything—or almost everything—in common, no communication, or very little communication, would suffice. That is the case with certain animals, such as bees. The need for communication arises because something unguessable must be imparted concerning our understanding or actions. A little must be added to what we already know or as a basis for modifying what we would otherwise do. It is this element of the unguessable that Shannon, in his mathematical theory of communication (information theory), made quantitative with his definition of entropy. And it is the unguessable (and surprising) that is an essential part of communication, as opposed to the mere repetition of gestures, incantations, or prayers.

Meaning can exist only through what we have in common in our lives, minds, and language. It is in our concern for what we share that communication takes place. We cannot be certain that reassurance will be offered, and we are upset if it is not. We are excited by a new discovery or by a tidbit of gossip about someone we love or hate. We spring to a task that we understand and that we feel impelled to undertake. And, as we have observed, we continually search for meaning, whether or not meaning is there.

It is a mixture of surprise and the search for meaning in a familiar context—the English language—that lends charm to Shannon's statistical words *grocid, pondenome, deamy*. They are so like English that we wonder what they mean, or perhaps we sense some elusive meaning or connotation. It is our straining toward some such extraordinary context or meaning that gives charm to computer-produced "poems," such as those of Marie Borroff:

The river
Winks
And I am ravished.

Dangerously, intensely, the music
Sins and brightens
and I am woven.

These poems are not so much out of the world as enticingly on the fringes of it.

We are challenged by what seems almost within our comprehension, but we reject or are bored with things that completely elude our grasp. Using computer-generated patterns, Bela Julesz of the Bell Telephone Laboratories has shown that a given degree of mathematical order or redundancy (in the sense of information theory) can be detectable or undetectable to the eye, trained or untrained. For human beings, mathematical order is orderly only if they see it as being orderly. Here is one difference between the problems of human communication and Shannon's mathematical theory of information, a difference which Shannon himself recognized.

The information theorist asks: What is a general measure of order, or rather of disorder, in a message source, and how can I take advantage of the order that is there in transmitting messages from the source efficiently? To do this, one must adapt the communication equipment to the order that lies in the source. Our eyes, ears, and brains, adapted as they may have been through evolution, are with us throughout our lives. We can make use of order only if we can perceive it. Some order we can learn to perceive; some must escape our senses, to be detected only through statistical analysis.

Artists and musicians who have been inspired by information theory have sought to produce works with an optimum combination of order and randomness. Such a criterion antedates information theory. Beethoven is said to have declared that in music, everything must be at once surprising and expected. That is appealing. If too little is surprising, we are bored; if too little is expected, we are lost. Communication is possible only through a degree of novelty in a context that is familiar.

Music communicates at once by reassurance and by surprise, but we can be neither reassured nor surprised by what passes unnoticed. Sir Donald Tovey, the British composer and writer, characterized certain contrapuntal devices as "for the eye only" and so implied that they must go unheard and unappreciated by the listener.

Order undetected is order in vain. One contemporary composer, Gerald Strang, has said that much random music and much mathematically organized music sound alike—uniformly gray. This would indeed be the consequence of an order undetectable by the ear and brain.

Let us return to the very challenging problem of using the computer as a general means for translating from one language to another. Certainly, computers can be very helpful in translation. Increasingly, text to be translated is available in machine-readable form. This means a computer can display the text to be translated on a television-like screen along with translations of technical terms. This display of the text can be extremely helpful. In some translation services, the material to be translated arrives in machine-readable form on computer tapes, and the edited translation drives an electronic photocopying machine. During the process of translation and the production of a document in the target language, nothing is written on paper, and there is but one keyboard operation—that of the translator at the text-editing console. The provision of specialized technical dictionaries that ensure an accurate and uniform translation of technical terms, even when several translators work on the same document, is very important. Further, translation by rote is certainly possible; that is, the headings and explanatory notes accompanying a data base can be stored in several languages so that an interrogator can get the data in a specified language.

In some cases, automatic language translation has gone beyond this. One example is the translation of material written in a specialized sublanguage; thus, a Canadian system called METEO successfully translates English meteorological bulletins into French. This is possible because such bulletins are written in a very simple language or jargon. It is only occasionally that the machine translations need any correction.

Machine translation has been used successfully by Xerox in translating technical manuals from English into other languages. This proved to be possible only when the manual was written in simple, short sentences with a restricted grammar and when the use of homonyms (words with the same spelling but different meanings) was avoided or when only one meaning was allowed. With these restrictions on the original text, about 80 percent of the translated text was acceptable, and the rest could be corrected by bilingual experts in less time than it would have taken to translate the whole text.

During the years 1970-1973, a machine translation system called LOGOS II was developed in the United States and used by the armed forces to translate 100 technical manuals, with a total of 5 million words, from English into Vietnamese. It is said that only about 20 percent of the translated material had to be postedited and that the translations were satisfactory. A system called LOGOS III is now available, and other machine translations are in limited use.

Machine translation systems commonly display on a screen both the text to be translated and a provisional translation, which the translator can edit by means of a keyboard. Changes in word order are often needed in order for the translated sentence to seem natural. Sometimes the machine translation is either unintelligible or wrong, and the translator must start from scratch. With such translation systems, translators work faster than they do with pen and paper, but much of the gain is through text-editing features and a machine-readable source of text, which replace the slow process of writing, editing, and performing multiple keyboard operations.

What will be the future use of computers in translation? Certainly, computers will be used more widely in text editing and in providing dictionaries of technical terms that are tailored to the area of the text to be translated. Currently, there is considerable enthusiasm for full machine translation. EUROTRA, a European Community activity, plans to spend $25 million over 5 years; the support will be distributed over many countries. Machine translation work is under way in Canada at the University of Montreal, in France at the University of Grenoble, in the United States at the University of Texas, and, no doubt, at other places. At least three American firms and one Canadian firm market machine translation systems that include highly useful features, such as text editing and text scanning for new technical terms.

We have noted that in 1964, Victor Yngve asserted that in order to translate well, a computer should understand what it is translating. Various attempts have been made to allow a computer to understand text, chiefly for reasons other than translation. In the work of Roger Schank and Robert Abelson and their colleagues at Yale, the computer is provided with "scripts" describing types of news events, such as earthquakes, explosions, protests, and seizures. This has enabled it to read teletypewriter news stories, to summarize them in several languages, and to answer questions posed in natural language. The program is at the moment ambitious in scope but primitive in results. It is perhaps too early to assess the practical application of the approach for translation or for other purposes. Certainly, the knowledge of the world that has been put into the computer is far less than the knowledge of some machine or product that the writer of a "hard" book has.

So far, the actual use of full machine translation has been rather small. In part, this may be because some systems require costly large computers and costly, complex software. In part, however, it has been because results have been uncertain. For many years, machine translation experts have supplied excellent examples of the full machine translation of technical text. User experience tends to make one less sanguine. Xerox uses a system that is "capable" of full translation and which has produced some excellent "examples," yet, in practice, Xerox found it advantageous to write the manuals that are to be translated in a very restricted subset of English. For reasons given above, we cannot expect machines to produce a good rendition of an arbitrarily chosen text into another language. The prospects of machine translation are brighter when the nature of the input text is controlled or is at least taken into account (through special dictionaries and rules that apply for the subject area of the text to be translated).

Certainly, machines can translate material that is in a very small, simple subset of a language—weather reports, for example. Presumably, machines could translate the restricted subset of English used by air traffic controllers—a very simple set of words, phrases and sentences that are used continually by a limited number of trained experts and by no one else. It should not be too difficult to supply a machine with adequate knowledge of this small piece of the world. However, such a very limited sublanguage is not difficult to learn as a part of training for the job.

4-4　Computer-Aided Instruction

This brings to our attention the successful use of computers in teaching language and, indeed, in teaching other things.

There is a great deal of rote learning and practice in learning a language. Many students do essentially the same thing over and over again. Learning a language foreign to the land in which it is taught, however, is treacherous. Reasonably fluent teachers may give poor guidance concerning usage and worse guidance concerning pronunciation. It seems clear that languages—and especially spoken languages—should be taught, directly or indirectly, by native speakers, yet this is not common. Perhaps the computer can make it common.

The computer-aided teaching of language has its roots in two earlier ideas. One is the language laboratory, equipped with recorded speech and means for the student to record his or her own voice. Such a language laboratory can be of great help in learning a language well.

The other ingredient in computer-aided instruction is programmed learning, an idea advanced around the mid 1950's by B. F. Skinner, an American behavioral psychologist. The central idea of programmed instruction was step-by-step learning, in small steps, with the student being rewarded or otherwise reinforced for giving correct responses.

Early programmed instruction was accomplished by means of crude machines that presented short sections of instructional material to which the learner responded. It was soon found that the same process could be carried out by means of booklets or workbooks.

Early instructional programs were linear, meaning that each student went through the same sequence of steps. In branching programs, a student who responds incorrectly is referred to supplementary material, which, when mastered, will lead the student back into the original course of instruction. It is somewhat awkward to put branching programs into workbook form, for any particular student will receive a book that contains far more than he or she will use.

Experience with programmed instruction showed the preparation of satisfactory programs to be exceedingly time-consuming. Ideally, a set of objectives must be arrived at: What do we expect the student to be able to do after instruction? Then, tests through which we can see whether or not the objectives have been attained must be devised. Certainly, instructional programs have to be tried out over and over again before they become satisfactory. Thus, the preparation of useful instructional programs can be justified only when many people will learn the same very valuable thing and, especially, where alternative means for learning are unsatisfactory.

This is so in learning a foreign language. Learning a language (or a subset, as in the case of air traffic controllers) can have great commercial value. What must be learned is the same for everyone. Truly adequate human instruction is very expensive, and, especially in teaching spoken language, adequate instruction simply may not be available.

One computer-aided instruction system, the PLATO system, is marketed in the United States by Control Data Corporation (CDC). PLATO offers a number of language courses. Hazeltine has planned to market the Piccit system developed at Brigham Young University. However, a more widespread approach has been to develop computer languages, software,

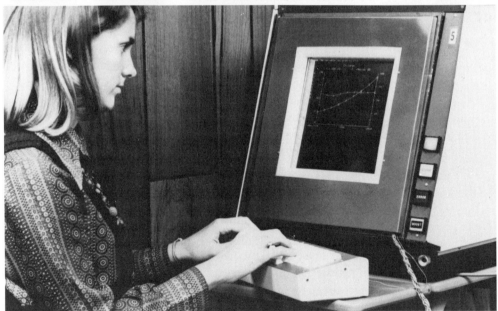

Computer-aided foreign language instruction, showing the Kanda system in use in Japan and the PLATO system developed at the University of Illinois, Urbana. (Photo courtesy of Computer-Based Education Research Lab, University of Illinois.)

and, sometimes, hardware that can be used by others in computer-aided instruction. IBM has been active in this area, as have Professor Richard Brandt, of the University of Utah, and Professor Alfred Bork, of the University of California at Irvine.

In the United States, there is already a very substantial use of computer-aided training in industry and in the armed forces. The computer has sometimes been used merely to analyze test data and recommend the course of further instruction. Dr. William L. Maloy, of the Naval Education and Training Command, calls this program, which was inaugurated in 1974, computer-managed instruction. In the Navy, computer-managed instruction is used in the simultaneous training of 25,000 sailors and 10,000 students each year. Some computer-aided instruction is used, and expansion through the use of microprocessors is planned.

Computer-aided instruction can be cost-effective in industry and in the armed forces, because the student's time must be paid for and the trainees must be taught effectively in order to do the work they are paid for. For general education, computer-aided instruction has not yet been proved to be cost-effective, though a good deal of instruction at college level has been carried out through PLATO and other systems.

So far as we know, the only strictly commercial success of computer-aided instruction has been at the Kanda Foreign Language Institute in Japan. Kanda uses equipment developed by Toshiba in teaching the employees of various firms fluency in a foreign language, an extremely valuable skill.

The approach of Seymour Papert, of the Massachusetts Institute of Technology, has been very different. In experiments that have involved about 10,000 children, Papert has had the computer, in essence, teach access to itself. The children learn a simple but powerful language called LOGO. This enables them to use the computer, for example to produce attractive and complex graphics and to experiment with music and musical sounds. This opens up to the children a world of structured thought and behavior in the course of an activity that is both pleasant and rewarding—although rather expensive.

Papert sees this approach, coupled with home microprocessor-based computers, as providing a means of educational training in many important areas of life and work, ultimately in developing as well as in developed countries. He feels that this will become feasible because the cost of small computers is falling so rapidly.

What Papert has shown so far is that when young children are provided with good equipment and talented and sympathetic teachers, they

Many computers teach children computer programming under the guise of other instruction or game playing. (Photo courtesy of Atari)

can learn programming skills and enjoy it. This is important because computers and their capabilities will play an increasing part in the world. But perhaps more children will learn more from the ever-increasing number of inexpensive microcomputers and computer games than through Papert's orderly approach. Perhaps children will teach themselves and the world how to learn through the use of computers.

Let us return to the consideration of natural languages. While machine-aided translation will be of increasing utility, for many uses it is best and most effective for people to learn a new language or a subset of a language, such as the English used by air traffic controllers. Computer-aided instruction can be effective in such learning. It seems to us that for some purposes, computer-aided instruction in languages or in subsets may be more useful than attempts at machine translation.

4-5 Computer Languages

Early work on machine translation led to deep investigations of the syntactical structure of languages. This was not lost; it helped to give us computer languages with more orderly and sensible structures. Early FORTRAN compilers parsed computer programs by brute force and awkwardness. Compilers for today's computer languages (a compiler translates programs written in a language, such as Pascal, into machine instructions) are simpler and more effective because the syntax of today's computer languages is orderly and sensible. Thus, useful machine translation of programs between good, modern computer languages has become possible (if not infallible), and it appears that we are on the verge of machine production of compilers for well-defined computer languages.

Such work on computer languages has made it much easier to devise powerful new languages for special purposes and to get them into operation on a variety of computers. One example is the LOGOS language that Seymour Papert has used in teaching children to use computers constructively.

4-6 Recognition of Spoken Language

The problems encountered in machine translation are closely related to those encountered in trying to make a "voice typewriter," which will turn spoken language into text.

We almost never enunciate certain words we speak, for example, *a*, *and*, and *the*; further, other words are inadvertently slurred. As William James noted, when a person hears a word (or sentence) he or she hears it with the mind's ear, supplying deficiencies. This has been proved by replacing the sound of one letter (a phoneme) with noise. The listener reports hearing both the noise and the sound of the letter.

At present, computers can transcribe into text only small vocabularies of spoken words or simple sentences covering a limited area they have been programmed to deal with, such as chess moves or travel reservations, and even this is not cheap or easy. Thus the voice typewriter lies far in the future, if anywhere. For most purposes, keyboard input will be fastest and best for some time, while commercial word-recognition systems have limited and special uses—usually in circumstances in which the task is such that a person's hands are busy.

The recognition of spoken words may be advantageous in languages such as Japanese and Chinese, for which keyboards are terribly complicated.

4-7 Character Recognition

Computer recognition of the characters and words printed, typed, or handwritten should be much simpler than the recognition of spoken words. In the 1960's and even in the 1970's, a good deal of effort was devoted to computer reading of text.

Computer reading of text was intended partly as an aid to the blind, and such work has continued. However, machines that read aloud have proved to be very bulky and costly. They might perhaps be used in producing audio cassettes from books, but can they compete in cost and effectiveness with human readers who are available in abundance? For direct use by the blind, simpler devices like the Opticon, which produces from printed text sound patterns that are interpretable by a trained blind person, seem preferable.

Some character-reading devices were intended to produce a machine-readable transcription of typescript, with the idea that it would be cheaper to get material into a computer (for editing, typesetting, or filing) by using a cheap typewriter rather than an expensive computer keyboard terminal. The fall in the price of computer terminals ended this approach. Character reading of ordinary text does have some use in connection with revision of old books and documents.

Optical reading of special characters is convenient for some purposes, such as checking out items in a supermarket or sorting business mail. For such purposes, the best approach seems to be the use of some code that a machine can read easily and accurately, such as the uniform product code (a sequence of parallel lines of various widths and spacings). Reading of special numerical characters imprinted on checks is commonplace.

Character recognition of carefully drawn handwritten characters has found a place in Japan, where both keyboards and printing are complicated because of the thousands of Chinese characters that are in common use.

4-8 Keyboards and Nonalphabetic Languages

We have seen that word recognition and character recognition may be most favorable for nonalphabetic languages, such as Japanese and Chinese, for which the use of keyboards is difficult.

Several means have been tried for keyboard inputting of such languages. One early way to input Chinese characters made use of keys representing the various strokes used in writing the characters, and these strokes were typed in the proper order that is taught to all Chinese. When the description of the intended character was ambiguous, all possible characters appeared on the screen and the operator could choose the one that was intended. A more recent approach is simply to number the characters and have the user learn the numbers; this is the traditional approach used in telegraphy.

Some Japanese words are written in an alphabet of syllabic kana characters and some as kanji ideograms. The words written in kanji can be spelled out in kana, but the same kana spelling will be used for several kanji characters. In recent Japanese keyboard input devices, in case of ambiguity all possible kanji characters are displayed and the operator chooses one. The machine remembers the choice and uses it thereafter unless instructed otherwise.

4-9 Computational Linguistics

Machine translation and the recognition of spoken words or even of text are only a part of a broader field, called computational linguistics. Those who work in this field would like computers to *understand* documents much as a person would, fitting the contents into a larger frame of reference. The machine could then produce abstracts, answer specific questions, and alert particular users to new information. It could, in short, act as a librarian and counselor. We have already cited the work of Schank and Abelson in this field.

Further, computational linguists have proposed the machine generation of documents. On demand, the computer would translate stored or newly acquired data into an account of the mechanics of auto repair or of medical diagnosis, prescription, and counseling of a patient.

As an extreme example, some envisage natural-language processing as an integral component of a robot that communicates in English (or Japanese or Dutch).

4-10 Artificial Intelligence

Research in artificial intelligence (generally called AI) flourishes in many universities. In good universities, it has generally attracted bright students; thus, an indirect product of artificial-intelligence research has been good students who have done well after graduation. Another indirect product has been novel and good computer languages, such as LISP. The direct product of AI has been somewhat disappointing. Algebraic and mathematical programs, such as the Massachusetts Institute of Technology's MACSYMA (now available in a modified form on microcomputers), are wonderful and useful, but many AI purists do not consider these to be mainstream AI, and several programs of this sort have been written by non-AI people. Chemists have written elaborate and subtle programs to deduce the structure of complex organic molecules from x-ray diffraction patterns. Edward A. Feigenbaum of Stanford University has produced a number of "expert" programs. These include a knowledge base derived from an expert and heuristic procedures for its use in accomplishing a task. DENDRAL analyzes mass spectra and produces highly probable molecular structures. MYCIN prescribes antibiotics for certain diseases. The Digital Equipment Corporation uses an expert program that includes all its catalog information in configuring computer systems.

The sterility of much work in AI has been in part a result of choice of goals and projects. Some goals and projects have proved too difficult. For instance, in theorem proving, AI programs have proved lots of theorems but have found few that were both new and interesting. Some projects have proved difficult but trivial in outcome—for example, piling colored blocks on one another when so commanded in common English text, a terribly difficult but highly specialized achievement. Sometimes, very good software and hardware has proved better than involuted subtlety. The world-champion computer chess player was produced by Kenneth Thompson, who is not an AI specialist, and it succeeds partly because of its excellent special-purpose hardware.

Many experts in artificial intelligence have been unaware of advances in really complicated machines, such as the nationwide automatic telephone switching system in the United States. The autonomous operation of the Viking Orbiter for over two years during the Viking Extended Mission went unnoticed in AI circles; yet however simple and stupid this spacecraft was, it was the first autonomous robot to live long and do something useful. And, it was born in space; its autonomous features were programmed in after launch.

AI should not be confused with robotics. Crude, unintelligent robots that can be "trained" to do spot welding and painting are invading automobile assembly lines. Their performance will improve through more subtle control by computer programs.

A number of AI specialists insist that their work will give insight into human thinking, but behavioral biologists appear to be far ahead of them in sound and surprising results.

Perhaps the term *artificial intelligence* is unfair to computers. From the very first, computers have performed many tasks far better and faster than humans. It may be that classifying the performance of some complex tasks as "intelligent" misses the real point—that computers are best used for doing things that they are best at, and humans are best used for doing things they are best at. Certainly, the number of things that computers do better than humans grows continually.

4-11   Concluding Remarks

What has come of all of this, besides much hard work?

Intellectually, the most important outcome has been the growing awareness, during the sixties, that words, sentences, conversations, documents, and books do not stand alone, an observation made much earlier by William James. Language has meaning only in connection with the sort of information about the world that we all have in our minds when we read or listen. Marvin Minsky calls such contexts *frames*. Thus, experimental systems can understand natural languages to the degree that they have built into them an adequate description of some part of the world, whether it be an artificial world of colored blocks, a world of ships, locations, and cargos, or a world of typical news stories.

We have seen that a fruitful outcome of machine translation was the production and manipulation of better computer languages. What of other aspects of computational linguistics?

Computers can do many useful things without understanding the text that they process. Thus, they routinely hyphenate words, correct spelling, and call attention to split infinitives, excessive use of the passive voice, and repeated cliches.

In many information services, complexities of computational linguistics can be avoided. Thus, in existing commercial systems for the retrieval (not the understanding) of information from the technical and scientific literature, much confusion is avoided by having different data bases for different areas of knowledge. These can be queried by means of lists of key words that are supplied for each data base. The key words can be combined; for example, *analysis* and *molybdenum* can be combined to locate procedures for analysis for molybdenum. Ordinarily, a keyboard, perhaps at a remote location, is used to locate a desired document, and a copy of the document is mailed to the user.

Some existing systems generate understandable material from raw data by simple programs. For example, the Educational Testing Service, which administers the Scholastic Aptitude Tests, uses a computer to fill in forms from raw test scores. These forms are easily read and understood, and this approach could be carried further to produce reports in the form of personalized letters, if that seemed worthwhile.

Humanists, historians, and other scholars are among those most deeply involved with the study of language in the form of text. All have profited greatly from information technology—chiefly from such rather simple functions as text editing, the handling of large files (as in archeological work), word searches in making indices, and the reproduction of surrounding context in producing concordances or in printing out of variations in textual criticism.

It is interesting to compare the optimistic tone of an earlier book, such as *Computers in Humanistic Research* (1967), with the more recent sober assessment in Susan Hockey's *A Guide to Computer Applications in the Humanities* (1980). By 1980, it had become clear that gross statistical features of language could establish authorship only under favorable circumstances. Problems and errors have plagued programs designed for more subtle analysis of text, such as those designed to find root words by removing suffixes (finding *search* from *searching*) and those that seek sound patterns. More and more reliance has been placed on an interactive relation among text, computer, and scholar, with searches and other arduous but clearly defined tasks done by the computer and final decisions made by the scholar.

Today there are many monuments to the computer analysis of text, including musical scores. Idiosyncrasies of various composers have been found and verified. The authorship of each of the Federalist Papers (written anonymously by Alexander Hamilton, James Madison, and John Jay) has been determined. An index citing *every use of every word* in Vergil has been produced. Information technology has increased the scope of what the scholar *can* do, but it does not solve all problems nor tell us what is worth doing.

Among the powerful tools that the computer makes accessible to the scholar are cluster analysis and multidimensional scaling. These techniques make it possible to establish orderly relations among objects, whether they be manuscripts, sounds, or trees, on the basis of properties that they share in different proportions. Such properties may be word usage, definable features of instrumental sounds, or chemical components in the sap of a tree.

The computer has also been used as an aid in classifying a key geometrical pattern—the spirals of Japanese rooftiles—and so finding the date of manufacture.

Research in automatic language processing continues. The aspirations of the sixties have been modified through a realization of the importance of meaning, including a picture of the world—a "script" or a "frame"—to any interpretation of text, and by a new sense of the importance of an easy interaction between man and machine.

Growing in part from such research (but perhaps more from better and cheaper technology), there is an increasing use of computers in providing highly useful functions: the production and editing of machine-readable text, text searching, photocomposition for the production of documents and books from machine-readable text, and retrieval by simple key-word on-line searches from various large data bases. The chief practical outcomes of character recognition have been the devising of and use of machine-readable numbers on checks and the uniform product code.

Nonalphabetic languages, such as Chinese and Japanese, cannot be entered easily by keyboard. Here, for some uses, special complex keyboard systems compete with the recognition of carefully drawn characters or even of spoken words.

REFERENCES

Translation

ALP Systems, 750 North 200 West, Provo, Utah 84604.

David Burden. "Natural Languages Automatically Translated by Computer: The SYSTRAN II System." *Computers and People*, May-June 1981.

Martin Kay. *The Place of Men and Machines in Language Translation*. Xerox, Palo Alto Research Center, 1980.

Richard I. Kittredge. "The Development of Automated Translation Systems in Canada." *Lebende Sprache* 26, 3 (1981).

LOGOS Development Corporation, 2 Low Avenue, Middletown, N.Y. 10940.

Max Morton. "Electronic Data Processing in Language Translation." *Earthspeak*, Agnew-Techtran, Winter 1981.

National Academy of Science. *Language and Machines, Computers in Translation and Linguistics*. National Research Council Publication 1416, Washington, D.C., 1966.

J. R. Pierce. *Man, Machines and Languages*. IEEE Spectrum, July 1968.

Weidner Communication, Inc., 1673 West 820 North, Provo, Utah 84601.

World Translation Co. of Canada, Ltd., 220 Laurier Avenue West, Suite 740, Ottawa X1P 5Z9 Canada.

V. K. Yngve. "Implications of Mechanical Translation Research." *Proceedings of the American Philosophical Society* 108 (1964):275–281.

Information Theory

J. R. Pierce. *An Introduction to Information Theory*. Dover Publications, 1980.

C. E. Shannon and Warren Weaver. *The Mathematical Theory of Communication*. University of Illinois Press, Urbana, 1959.

Computers and Learning

Robert S. Hart, ed. "The Plato System" and "Language Learning." *Studies in Language Learning* 3, 1 (Spring 1981). Language Learning Laboratory, Champaign-Urbana, Ill.

Elizabeth R. Lyman and Deborah H. Postlewait. *Cerl Plato Catalog*. University of Illinois, April 1980.

Seymour Papert. *Mindstorm; Children, Computers and Powerful Ideas*. Basic Books, 1980.

Computers, Language, and the World

Gary G. Hendrix and Earl D. Sacerdoti. "Natural-Language Processing, the Field In Perspective." *BYTE*, September 1981.

Marvin Minsky. "A Framework for Representing Knowledge." In *The Psychology of Computer Vision*, ed. by Patrick Wilson. McGraw-Hill, 1975.

Roger Shank and Robert Abelson. *Scripts, Plans, Goals and Understanding*. Erlebaum Associates, 1977.

Artificial Intelligence, Pro and Con

Avron Barr and Edward A. Feigenbaum, eds. *The Handbook of Artificial Intelligence*. Heuristic Press, 1981.

Joseph Weizenbaum. *Computer Power and Human Reason*. W. H. Freeman and Company, San Francisco, 1976.

Computers and the Humanities

Edward H. Bowles, ed. *Computers in Humanistic Research*. Prentice-Hall, Inc., Englewood Cliffs, N.J., 1967.

Computing in the Humanities. Proceedings of the Third International Conference on Computing in the Humanities. University of Waterloo Press, 1977.

Susan Hockey. *A Guide to Computer Applications in the Humanities*. Johns Hopkins University Press, Baltimore, Md., 1980.

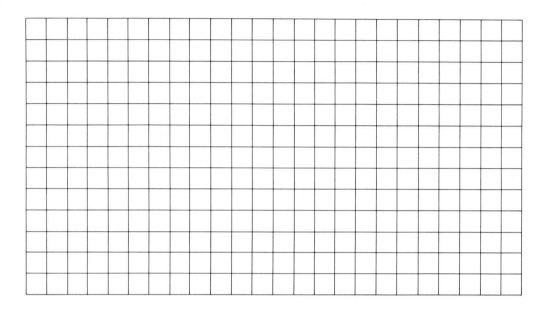

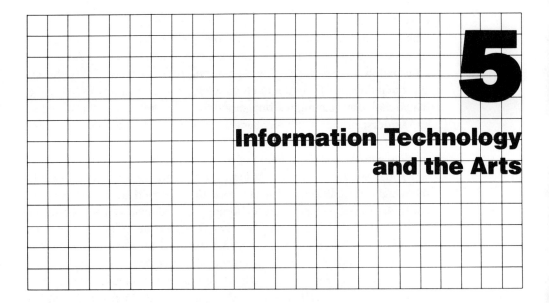

Information Technology and the Arts

5-1 Introduction

Culture is in some ways a synonym for civilization. In this sense, it embraces all we do and the ways in which we do it. In this broad sense, the whole of this book is about culture. Yet, we recognize an area of taste, design, artistic creativity, and appreciation that is connoted when we use the word *culture* in a narrower sense—the sense of arts and letters. It is with culture in this sense—a powerful subset of human activities—that this chapter is concerned.

Culture so defined has technological aspects that reach back to mankind's earliest days. Rhyme, rhythm, and melody, in chants and poetry, allowed people to memorize long and beautiful stories at the beginning of our cultural tradition. They can be found in the songs of Homer and in similar works from other cultures. Even the vividness of poetic imagery can be thought of as another way of strengthening the memorability of such songs. Thus, the techniques used to aid memory and expression— information technology of the oldest sort—are an intimate part of the arts.

Although we think of the arts as preserving traditional themes and techniques, artists have always been quick to exploit the advantages of new scientific and technological developments. We are not so much interested here in the use of scientific methods for determining the authenticity or origin of a specific work through carbon dating, chemical analysis, or x-ray examinations; rather, we are concerned with the influence of information science and technology on the production of art. Traditionally, the influence of science and technology has been largely an influence of materials and techniques, but sometimes it has been one of knowledge and understanding of the mechanical properties of materials and structures, of representation in perspective, and of the physical properties of musical sounds and the relation of these properties to what we hear.

Today we see in the arts at least three contradictory forces. One is the weight of tradition, classic and realistic. A second is a revolt from, or contradiction of, science and technology—an almost frenzied desire of artists to be themselves, to be different, to set a tone, to play freely with whatever they find about them without the need to take the elements of science, technology, or popular culture on their own terms. In a third, small area of the arts, some artists have found that anyone who understands technology well enough to use it easily and effectively has at his or her disposal a tool of revolutionary potentialities.

5-2 Architecture and Sculpture

In the cornices of Greek temples, we see representations in marble of the sort of wooden pins that held earlier Greek structures together. Yet it is clear that the physical quality of marble and techniques for cutting it give these temples their unique character. In contrast, the Roman Pantheon is an expression of the properties of concrete—as is much fine contemporary architecture.

Thus, in architecture, stylistic design has been much influenced by materials as well as by tradition. Skyscrapers became possible through structural steel, and they ultimately outgrew gothic and other early stylistic influences. There is another side to design—how to make creations structurally sound. Here, early builders relied on rules or precedents, with greater or lesser success. Structurally, St. Paul's Cathedral in London is ridiculously overdesigned; the Cathedral of Notre Dame in Chartres skirts on the edge of the impossible. Today, those who work out the structural designs of buildings, or bridges, or aircraft for that matter, have access to computer codes for structural analysis. This does more than

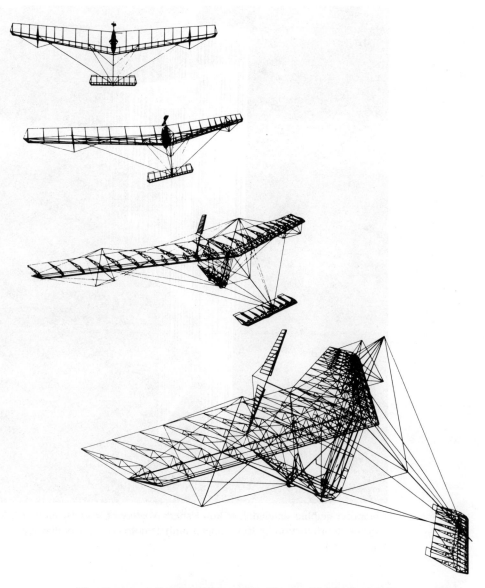

The *Gossamer Condor*, winner of the Kremer Trophy for human-powered flight, is modeled using GRAPHICS/1000-II. Computers played an important role in designing the airfoils and in many other aspects of the design of this vehicle. (SOURCE: Chris Nemeth, Paul Lionikis, and Professor Charles L. Owen, Institute of Design, Illinois Institute of Technology; photo courtesy of Hewlett-Packard)

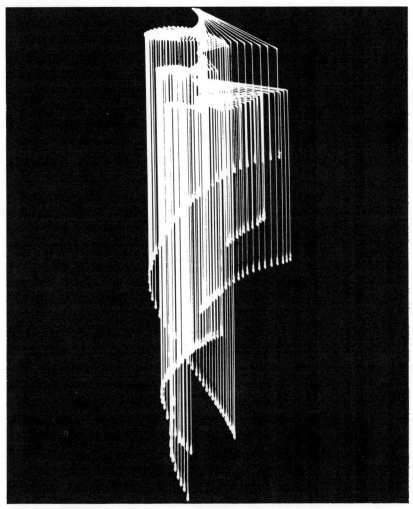

Computer graphic simulation of Rob Fisher's *Northern Lights*, by Frederick R. Stocker. Reproduction by Jack Klingensmith. (Photo courtesy of Playboy Enterprises)

merely save time and labor: It saves so much time and labor that many designs, rather than merely one or two, can be explored.

How innovative and brave has this made architects and other designers? At the Massachusetts Institute of Technology, Nicholas Negroponte has shown how one can simulate, on a video screen, a drive through the town of Aspen, Colorado, perhaps in search of the proper site for a building. The succession of streets traversed is under the control of the viewer—the remote traveler, if you will. Today, this is a heady but expensive experience; but, as Negroponte has said, one of his aims is to serve executives and generals.

Perhaps we have in such work a marvelous beginning with a bright future. Most architects and designers haven't been very innovative. Early architects struggled to make buildings stand up. Today, most architects are designers rather than engineers. They rely on engineers to make buildings stand up, and engineers can make almost any building that architects specify. Some architects seem to be little more than exterior decorators.

Yet, in building, economic forces have become very powerful. It is here that the exploration of structural design by computer can have—and sometimes does have—a real impact on buildings, as well as on aircraft and other machines.

Traditionally, sculpture and ornament have been linked with architecture. Computers have indeed been used in the design of modern decorative sculpture; Rob Fisher's hanging *Northern Lights*, in the Atrium of the Playboy Casino in Atlantic City, New Jersey, is an example. We may see progress in a somewhat different direction. Today's technology makes mass production cheap, while individual craftsmanship is painstakingly slower and increasingly expensive. Here, information technology offers a truly astonishing resource—numerically controlled machine tools. These can produce three-dimensional objects, including friezes and statues, from numerical specifications produced by designers. The production of numerical specifications of three-dimensional objects can be greatly aided by the use of computer graphic's terminals for computer-aided design.

How much sculpture and ornament has been produced using numerically controlled machine tools? Little as yet, but the potentialities seem almost limitless.

5-3 Paintings and Drawings

Like architecture and sculpture, two-dimensional representation has been strongly influenced by both science and technology. Greek and Roman artists painted with wax; medieval artists in tempera. The influence of such media is apparent in the results. The great flexibility of oil paint as a medium made new and different effects possible in Renaissance and post-Renaissance paintings. Woodblock printing and, later, lithography made inexpensive, popular art possible, and we noted in Chapter 1 the revolutionary and almost contradictory effects of photography on art. These effects have been admirably expounded in *Art and Photography*, by Aaron Scharf.

When one considers the potential influences of information technology on design, an obvious application is the production of intricate, abstract designs—designs outdoing the sort of florid, mechanically engraved borders that are characteristic of American currency and stock certificates. Indeed, the career of John Whitney, a talented cinematographer, illustrates an evolution in the production of abstract designs in motion from the use of electromechanical equipment constructed from World War II surplus military servomechanisms to computer-produced images.

A central problem of abstract design is the necessity that a design exhibit both organization and surprise. The moving eye must find things that are both expected and surprising. Complete surprise is meaningless and boring. Complete predictability is monotonous and boring.

A. Michael Noll was one of the first to incorporate both order and random choice in computer-produced designs. He produced quite handsome designs consisting of linked straight-line segments of random lengths and directions confined within a rectangular border. In another approach he caused a computer to imitate, with a random element, a drawing by Piet Mondrian. He then conducted an experiment in which a number of people were shown both the original and the computer-produced imitation but were not told which was which. Most of those who professed to like modern art preferred the computer-produced imitation. They thought that it had been produced by an artist because it seemed the less mechanical of the two drawings. The computer has also been used widely to distort simple manmade designs in order to give them variety.

In 1975, Compagnie IBM France produced a wonderful volume, *IBM–INFORMATIQUE*, No. 13, containing a host of fine illustrations of the works of computer artists (including Noll) and some illustrations of utilitarian computer graphics designs.

In its early stages, computer graphics could produce only simplified line drawings. Because of this, and because of an early awe of machines and respect for the abstract and mechanical, the first uses of computer graphics were of the sort we have described. Computer graphics have advanced startlingly since their inception and can now be used to pro-

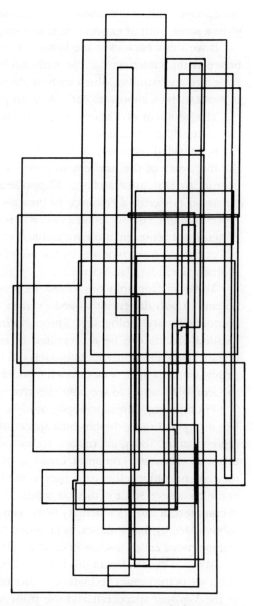

Vertical-Horizontal No. 3, by A. Michael Noll, 1965. In this picture, one of the two coordinate values (*X* or *Y*) was changed from one point to the next along a continuous line. The change alternated between the *X* and the *Y* values. Otherwise, the positions of the points were chosen at random with a uniform probability density. (© A. Michael Noll, 1965)

duce images, still or in motion, that have a sort of magic realism that truly gives a sense both of expectedness and surprise.

If we think back over the history of art, we find a striking contrast between the effectiveness, the naturalness, and the illusory effects of sculpture and painting. Much early sculpture looks essentially "correct" to modern eyes; almost no early Western painting does.

The problem of illusory two-dimensional representation of three-dimensional figures and scenes is difficult. In his early years, Vincent van Gogh struggled arduously to master the laws of perspective. Yet, it was the discovery of the mathematical laws of perspective in the fifteenth century by Florentine architect Filippo Brunelleschi that gave European artists so powerful a resource in creating an illusion of imitation and representation. Further, contributions of science and technology to two-dimensional representation are testified to by Albrecht Durer's drawing of a perspective machine and by the use of the camera obscura by artists, probably including Jan Vermeer.

Today, photography has solved the problem of representing existing objects in two dimensions—and even in three—through stereoscopic photography and holograms. Through cinematography and television, existing objects can be represented in motion. Through trick photographic and electronic effects, models can be made to seem real, and live people can appear to walk through model buildings. One need only view the *Star Wars* series to see how effective such technology can be.

Photography, cinematography, models, and special effects easily translate a physical three-dimensional space into a striking two-dimensional representation. Today, information technology offers something far beyond this—the accurate computer creation of perspective views of three-dimensional objects that exist only in the human mind and the memory of the computer. Some of this has appeared in television commercials and in commercial and documentary films. Sometimes, such creation has been subtly aided by mathematics, as in Benoit Mandelbrot's use of mathematical functions called fractals in creating plausible, fantastic landscapes.

Many of the readers of this book will have seen, during the television coverage of the Jupiter and Saturn encounters, the magnificent animations of the *Voyager* spacecraft and the planets and satellites it passed. The celestial bodies and the spacecraft in those animations were computer constructs produced by James F. Blinn of California Institute of Technology's Jet Propulsion Laboratory. They were based on information derived from photographs of planets and moons and on engineering drawings and

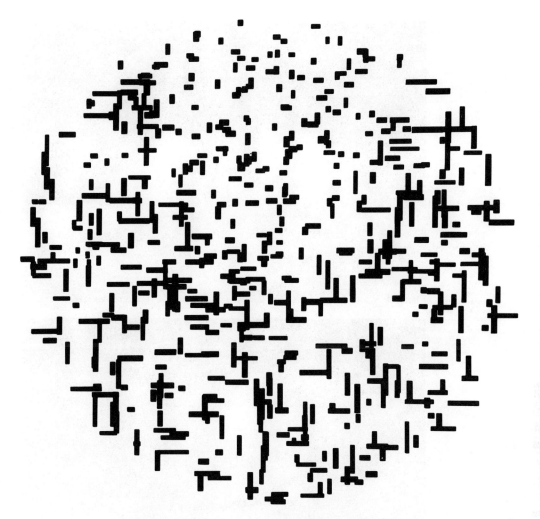

Composition With Lines, by A. Michael Noll, 1965. This picture was generated by a digital computer using pseudorandom numbers with statistics approximating a Mondrian painting. (© A. Michael Noll, 1965)

specifications for materials used in the spacecraft, down to the color of the paint. The artistic effect was that everyone in the audience participated in the exploration of the solar system. Space exploration was no longer the prerogative of a few astronauts; it became an experience for all television viewers. What they saw was true and real in the sense that

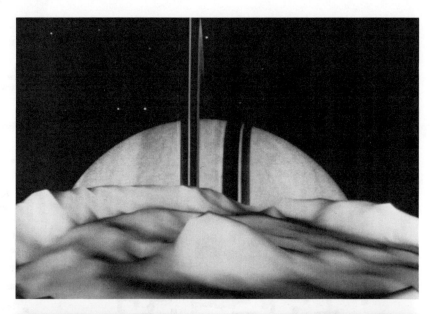

(a) Synthetic view of Saturn from the surface of the innermost large moon Mimas: The large crater discovered by *Voyager I* is in the foreground. The rings of Saturn appear vertical since we are near the equator of the moon. (Photo courtesy of Jet Propulsion Lab, NASA) (b) View of Saturn as seen by *Voyager II* near the time of closest approach.

scientific data are true and real. Emotionally, the experience was art. In content, it was a representation—not completely accurate, for no representation is—of scientific fact.

Here, through information technology, we have a linking of science and art such as that in the wonderful sixteenth-century woodcuts that illustrate Andreas Vesalius's treatise on anatomy.

5-4 Ballet

It might seem unlikely that ballet should be influenced by information technology. A little reflection makes it clear that the adaptation of ballet to the motion picture screen is one example of such influences; the airy hippopotami that perform the "Dance of the Hours" in Walt Disney's *Fantasia* is another. In a small way, other influences have been at work.

In 1967, A. Michael Noll, of Bell Laboratories, produced a computer-generated movie in which simple stick figures moved and whirled in a random dance, never, however, colliding or straying offstage. R. J. Lansdown, a British architect and secretary of the Computer Arts Society, has done much more complex work in the generation of dances. His procedure includes a vocabulary of body positions and movements; a grammar used in order to produce allowed sequences; a presentation, which is the production of a score either in ballet notation or as a sequence of computer-drawn sketches; and a selection process, which may be random or involve human choice. Lansdown has used his methods not only to produce dances but to stage sword fights and slapstick, custard-pie routines. More recently, others have attached apparatus to dancers that record their movements, which can later be reproduced in animation on a video screen.

5-5 Music

Music is another art in which information technology has been applied with startling and gratifying effectiveness. As in the case of the graphic arts, an early approach was to use the computer as an aid in organizing music—in composing music, if you will. This followed a venerable tradition of music with a chance element, from the music that Mozart com-

Six frames from a three-minute movie produced by a digital computer program by A. Michael Noll: The program specified the size and motion of each stick figure. Each frame was automatically drawn on a CRT and photographed by a 16mm movie camera. Choreographers could create dances by interacting with a video display. (© A. Michael Noll)

Figure 5-1 Taking a cue from the art of animation, J. Lansdown used the computer to prepare story boards—key frames showing the main positions of a dance in sequence. The dancers carry out the "in-betweening," the linking movements between one key frame and the next. The information included in the key frames includes timing counts, which were derived from an analysis of the music.

posed using the random rolling of dice as part of the process to the aleatory music of John Cage.*

Inspired by examples of stochastic text given in Claude E. Shannon's *A Mathematical Theory of Communication* (1949), J. R. Pierce, around 1950, produced (without the aid of the computer) a number of random, chorale-like compositions. About the same time, David Slepian, a math-

---

*"Aleatory" appears to be a mistranslation from the French mathematical term *aleatoire*. The proper English rendering is "stochastic."

ematician at Bell Laboratories, produced a number of musical compositions in various styles.

With the advent of the computer, mechanical musical composition
was carried further. L. A. Hiller, Jr., and L. M. Isaacson incorporated in
their composition program most of the traditional rules of first-species
counterpoint and, within these constraints, allowed the computer to choose
notes at random. This resulted in *Iliac Suite for String Quartet*, published
by *New Music* in 1957. This composition is harmonious, but the music
wanders, and so does the listener's attention.

James Tenny and others have attempted a more sophisticated interactive use of the computer in composition, in which the composer specifies the general course and gross details of a composition and the computer and chance are used to fill in the fine details.

What is perhaps the most sophisticated experiment in computer composition of music was carried out for scholarly rather than artistic reasons.
In 1976 B. Lindblom and J. Sundberg published an analysis of the structure
of a number of Swedish folk tunes. They sought and expressed structure
by means of a generative musical grammar based on the work of Noam
Chomsky. In order to verify their analysis, they used a computer to construct folklike melodies that exemplified the structural organization they
had deduced. These computer-produced tunes are said to sound much
like true Swedish folk tunes.

The ultimate fate and value of the computer in musical composition
is still in question, but there can be no doubt that the computer has great
musical value, both in the production of musical scores and in the generation of musically useful sounds that could not be produced by any
other means. As in the graphic arts, the emphasis in the use of information
technology in music has shifted from machine invention to machine
execution.

The computer production of musical scores is an obvious and natural
application of computer graphics. Musical typesetting is extremely labo-
rious and expensive. Some publishers of contemporary music have used
hand-drawn scores of less than satisfactory quality. Music-publishing houses
bear the cost of maintaining a tremendous inventory of seldom-per-
formed works.

It has been demonstrated by Leland Smith, of Stanford University, and
by others that the information for producing a musical score can be put
into a computer using a conventional computer keyboard and that computer graphic output can produce scores of fine quality. Further, when a
score is stored in digital memory, it can be easily corrected or edited,

RANDOM

Figure 5-2 *Random Choral*, by J. R. Pierce

and instrumental parts can be extracted from an orchestral score and printed separately. A revolution in music publishing seems possible. For inventory, the music publisher could store scores in digital, machine-readable form rather than as printed scores. Modern graphics reproduc-

Figure 5-3 Computer-generated Swedish folk tunes, Op. 1 (From B. Lindblom and J. Sundberg, "Toward a Generative Theory of Melody," Speech Transmission Laboratory, Royal Institute of Technology, Stockholm)

tion and binding techniques would allow the printing of actual scores on demand. This revolution hasn't yet happened.

Another revolution has occurred only recently—the preservation and reproduction of musical sound without degradation. Analog recordings of magnetic tapes or cassettes, optical tracks, and phonographic disks are limited and impermanent. Early digital recordings of sound on magnetic tape were bulky and costly, and digital recording was at first used for the production of phonograph records rather than as a medium for home sound systems. A new technique for recording digitally on optical disk has now provided at moderate cost permanent records of sounds with an extremely high signal-to-noise ratio.

While musical scores and the reproduction of musical sounds have become essential to music, the substance of music is sound and hearing. Music as sound and relations among sounds has been profoundly influenced by science and technology. The Greeks based their musical scale on the relation between the lengths of vibrating strings and the pitches produced. Galileo and Mersenne related pitch to frequency of vibration. In *On the Sensations of Tone as a Physiological Basis for the Theory of Music*, Helmholtz made a profound study of musical sound.

To hear the organized sounds of music, we must have sources of sound. Music itself is not material, but musical instruments are. Improvements in orchestral instruments have played a large part in the development of music. Early brass instruments lacked valves, and it was difficult to play a chromatic scale upon them. Early reed instruments had a smaller dynamic range than today's instruments do. Flutes have a greater dynamic range and a more varied tone quality than do recorders. The modern piano has a greater dynamic range than the piano of Mozart's day and far more expressive qualities than the harpsichord.

We have seen that computers can be used to generate images of objects that exist only in the human mind and the memory of the computer. In a similar way, computers can be used to generate sounds that do not exist until they finally emerge from a loudspeaker driven directly or indirectly by the computer output. In principle, by tracing out a waveform, a computer can generate any possible sound. In practice, a computer can generate any sound that a composer is talented and clever enough to specify.

Since 1960, when the computer production of musical sounds was first demonstrated at Bell Laboratories, the digital generation of new musical sounds and their skillful use in new music has advanced prodigiously. Computer music in this sense is seriously pursued at hundreds of centers, chiefly the musical departments of universities. The works of John Chowning at Stanford, Jean-Claude Rissét at the University of Aix-Marseilles, Barry Vercoe at the Massachusetts Institute of Technology, Richard Moore at the University of California at San Diego, and various composers who have worked at Pierre Boulez's IRCAM (Institute for Research and Coordination of Acoustics/Music) in Paris are outstanding. Rissét's "Little Boy Suite" appeared on a Decca record, *The Voice of the Computer*, and his "Mutations" appeared on a Musique Française d'Aujord'hui record, *Rissét-Mutations*. Chownings excellent *Turenas, Stria*, and *Phone* have not been commercially recorded. George Lucas, of *Star Wars* fame, is supporting work on the digital generation of sound for its possible impact in the movies.

Computer music meetings are held annually in several countries. There is a quarterly, *Computer Music Journal*, and several books about computer music have been published; but computer music can be properly evaluated only by hearing it, not by reading about it.

Computer-produced sounds have a challenging new feature. The link between composer and audience through performers and mechanical instruments has been eliminated. Will performers and their instruments vanish in the future? Not likely. But through the use of computers, talented composers will continue to produce new and appealing sounds and attractive and novel music.

5-6 An Interactive, Integrated Art?

In the eighteenth century, opera involved far more than music and some acting; it was an integration of many arts, stage machinery, and pageant as well as music. Some years ago, one of the authors saw a wonderful reconstruction of such a performance in a marvelous production of Handel's *Il Pastor Fido* at the Drottingholm Court Theater near Stockholm. The cast was young, handsome, and magnificently costumed. At times the actors walked in processions across the stage to charming instrumental music. The stage machinery, though a little creaky, changed a palace into a forest before the eyes of the audience as rows of columns at each side of the stage rotated on vertical shafts, becoming trees. In the last scene, a goddess duly descended, at the rear of the stage, seated on a crescent moon.

In the nineteenth century, Richard Wagner strove mightily in his music dramas for a union of poetry and music. The nineteenth-century theater sought a union of word, sight, and sound in elaborate stage effects, including waterfalls and chariot races. In our day, such spectacles have been displaced by motion pictures and television.

Interaction has been an increasing trend in our century. In some museums, people are encouraged to handle objects and to operate technological devices. Some artists have produced objects that must be handled or touched in order to appreciate them. And who has not marveled at the intensity with which children, and adults as well, exercise their skills at Pachenko, pinball machines, and—here we come to a new point— video or computer games? Do we see here the early stages of a new art form?

We have noted that computer animation is becoming important in television advertising. Both the Walt Disney Studios and Lucasfilm Ltd. have used computer animation in making motion pictures; such animation is not interactive. But the computer animation used in flight trainers *is* interactive—what the student sees depends on what he does. Interactive training devices are intended for instruction, not for artistic appreciation. Still, might not interactive computer graphics become a new art form?

Today many computer enthusiasts play computer games. In *Adventure*, the player is confronted with various opportunities and hazards, and what happens to him next, good or bad, depends on the choice he or she makes and inputs to the computer. In *Adventure* as it is now played, situations are presented as text on a video screen, and the player keys in his or her choices as text. As the power of computer graphics increases, it should be possible for situations to appear as animated color presentations on a computer screen and for the player to interact with the scene so presented by using controls similar to those of an automobile, tank, or spaceship or by firing imaginary weapons. Indeed, video games have already gone far in this direction.

We know of enthusiastic people in a large communication company who believe that interactive computer games, presented via common-carrier communication lines, will be a highly marketable product, and they have made considerable progress toward producing such games. According to these people, the games will present the player with realistic scenes and sounds, including music in connection with some scenes. The player may play in some instances against a computer and in other instances against another person at another video console. How far is it from such games—if indeed they come to be—to an art form in which one's appreciation involves wandering through imaginary milieus created by the artist and taking one's own path through a world created by an artist-programmer?

The idea of such interactive computer games as we have presented it may seem novel, but it has in it many elements of the artistic experience of wandering through a wonderfully designed garden or of going to the proper place at the proper time to view the moon or to watch fireflies. Indeed, it is not far away from our common experience of wandering through a favored city or museum.

We see that interactive art is not new in essence, but computer-produced interactive art could be very new in both accessibility and impact. It could be instantly available in one's home, either by a communication channel or on a video disk, and it could offer a range of visual and auditory experiences that would be out of this world—though not necessarily better than reality. Will we have such interactive computer art? If so, when will we have it? How good will it be? All depend on both the state of the computer art and the abilities of computer artists.

5-7 The Future of Information Technology and the Arts

From the work we have reviewed, it is clear that technology has always had a decisive influence on the arts. Information technology is a powerful technology, and its influence is bound to be powerful.

From what we can see, the most likely impact of such technology is that of a tool in the hands of the artist. The computer can allow the architect (or other designer) to explore extensively appearance, structural soundness, and cost. Computer graphics can be used to create still or moving images of objects that exist only in the memory of the computer—and the mind of the artist. In principle, numerically controlled machine tools can be used to fashion individual sculpture and ornament. Computers can be used to produce, manipulate, and reproduce musical scores. Digital technology can be used to record and preserve music with unprecedented quality and permanence. Computers can be used to create wonderful musical sounds that never were—sounds that may change the very nature and organization of music. And computers might be used to organize all of these into a new interactive art.

Information science can extend the capabilities of the artist in producing works of arts. The impact of information technology in the analysis of art and in the possible replacement of the creator of art is not at all clear.

We have lived through an era of almost complete divorce between "serious" art and science. In art, the guru replaced the sage. Artists have sought inspiration by turning inward or to other cultures. They have invoked chance and numerology. They have abandoned both the romanticism of the nineteenth century and the rational inquiry that persisted through Goethe and Helmholtz. When artists have dabbled in technology, the results have often been without insight, like a child's banging on the keys of a piano.

Today, some artists, especially musical artists and composers, are exploring the potentialities of information technology very seriously. Perhaps a new era is at hand.

References

Benoit B. Mandelbrot, *The Fractal Geometry of Nature*, W. H. Freeman and Company, San Francisco, 1982.

Kellog S. Booth. *Tutorial: Computer Graphics*. IEEE Computer Society, 5855 Naples Plaza, Suite 301, Long Beach, CA 90803, Spring 1979.

The Computer Music Journal. MIT Press.

Computer Pictures. A Journal.

IBM–INFORMATIQUE, No. 13. Compagnie IBM France, 1976.

IEEE. *Computer Graphics Journal*.

John Lansdown. "The Computer in Choreography." *Computer*, August, 1978.

Ruth Leavitt, ed. *Artist and Computer*. Harmony Books, New York, 1977.

Leonardo. *International Journal of the Contemporary Artist*, Pergamon Press, Oxford.

B. Lindblom and J. Sundberg. "Generative Theories in Language and Music Descriptions." *Cognition* 4 (1976): 99–122.

Max V. Mathews. *The Technology of Computer Music*. MIT Press, Cambridge, 1969.

Page, Computer Arts Quarterly. Computer Arts Society, John Lansdown, Secretary, 50151, Russell Square, London XC1 BJX.

J. R. Pierce. *An Introduction to Information Theory*. Dover Edition, 1980. Chapter XIII, "Information Theory and Art."

John R. Pierce. *The Science of Musical Sound*. Scientific American Books, 1983.

C. Roads, J. Snell, and J. Strawn. *Computer Music*. MIT Press, 1982.

Aaron Scharf. *Art and Photography*. Penguin Books, 1979.

Siggraph '82 Art Show. Catalog with essays and illustrations.

H. Von Foerster and J. Beauchamp, eds. *Music by Computers*. Wiley, New York, 1969.

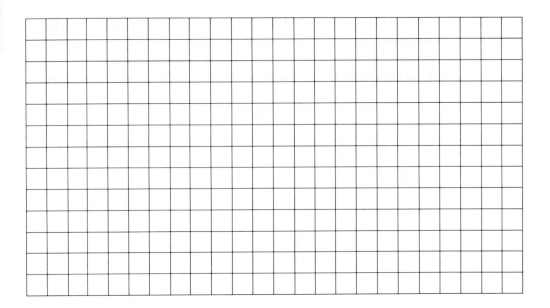

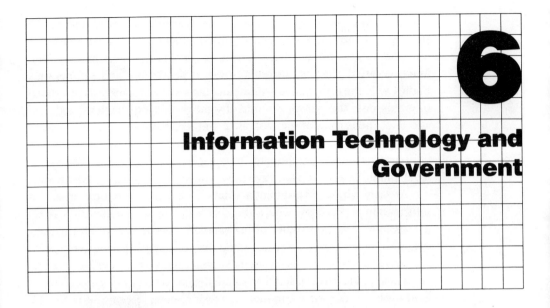

Information Technology and Government

6-1 Introduction

The relation of government to information technology and civilization is only a small part of overall government activities. We do not describe here the aspirations of nations or heads of state, nor matters of defense, nor even the gamut of social and cultural activities. We shall deal with some of these indirectly, but only as these areas necessarily come to our attention in dealing with matters that involve information technology and civilization directly.

Whether or not market forces are officially recognized, in all nations they have played—and will continue to play—a major role in advancing information technology and in enhancing the quality as well as the quantity of information-oriented products and services. Even in nonsocialist economies, there are areas in which market forces are weak or do not function satisfactorily. Therefore, government can—and should—play a leading role in these areas by providing assistance, removing impediments, and coordinating related activities, always in concert with market forces and always helping, not hindering, so as to maximize the benefits of information technology to society while keeping its negative impacts as low as possible.

The means by which public ends are accomplished differ tremendously among countries. In some countries, most authority and action stem from central government. In others, many of the most important functions of government are at a state or even a local level. Many public functions are carried out through private organizations and autonomous bodies, as in the licensing of artisans and the setting of standards by unions or guilds, or in the self-supervision of some professions, such as medicine and law. The setting of technological and industrial standards is carried out by private organizations in many countries. In this chapter, the word *government* should be thought of as applying to all bodies, central or local, public or private, that have the authority to deal with public needs.

Areas in which government assistance is crucial are basic research in information technology, where the cost and risk are rapidly increasing, and assurance of availability of information resources and information-oriented societal infrastructure, where market forces do not function.

Areas in which the government should remove impediments are the regulation of information services where the convergence of service modes is in progress and the promotion of greater social responsibility for the protection of privacy and the great need for security.

Government should work for closer coordination of basic research in universities, in government institutions, and in industrial laboratories. The competitive and cooperative aspects of information services should be carefully balanced so as to utilize limited resources of money and human energy efficiently. Standardization by governments or industrial associations should be encouraged in order to ensure the maximum compatibility of equipment consistent with future progress of information technology. Information suppliers and vendors should be organized to promote the flow of information while ensuring its integrity. And all of the above activities should be carried out in concert with the rest of the world.

This chapter explores the problems government faces in connection with information technology and describes the role that the authors hope the government will play.

6-2 The Support of Research and Development

Governments in many countries support research and development in information technology in various ways. They provide almost all the research funds available to universities and government institutions in these areas.

Governments also help to support research and development activities in industries through purchases of high-technology products and through research contracts, low-interest loans, and tax incentives. Some governments promote collaboration between universities, government laboratories, and private industries by providing financial or other assistance to joint projects.

Research and development in information technology are becoming extremely costly and risky because of the technological alternatives to be explored and because of the increasing complexity and scale of these technologies. Industries with information-oriented products increase expenditures for research and development year after year. Major industries in the world are now spending as much as 5 to 10 percent of their sales for research and development. However, the government expenditure in support of research and development tends to remain unchanged or even to decline because of severe constraints on national budgets. As we see it, the government share of this effort is diminishing.

Nevertheless, there are important areas in which the government must play a major role. Basic research is one of these areas. Because of increasing cost and risk, industries tend to invest most heavily in applied research and development rather than in basic research, while universities and government institutions continue to suffer from a shortage of financial support. The government should encourage industries by sharing the cost and risk of basic research and should reactivate basic research at universities and government institutions. In particular, due attention should be payed to supporting basic research activities in small- and medium-sized high-technology firms, from which many useful innovations have come and where the hazards as well as the rewards of risk taking are particularly large.

The government should also promote closer cooperation between universities, government institutions, and industrial laboratories in carrying out basic research in information technology by organizing and partly financing joint projects. This helps academia to confront reality and helps industry to draw wisdom from academia. In a few industrialized countries, small- and medium-sized high-technology firms have been in close contact with academia and have thereby contributed significantly. Such association should be introduced and enhanced in many other countries by the removal of organizational and societal constraint where necessary.

There are many areas in which market forces do not necessarily function to promote research and development. Societal infrastructure is one typical area. As pointed out in Section 3-4, information technology will help significantly in strengthening the societal infrastructure. However, this area is not very lucrative for industry, because the beneficiaries generally cannot pay the cost. Government initiative in research and development will be particularly important in these areas, even where commercial ventures may later play an important role. If important areas, such as agriculture and mining, lag in productivity, the government should help them by supporting appropriate research. Better information on weather or on geological structures may lead to higher productivity. Research and development for the informatization of such sectors should be promoted by the government when internal motivation is not strong enough. Considering the fact that information technology is an indispensable tool for extending knowledge and developing and conserving the culture of human beings, the government should also pay more attention to research and development in this area.

On the other hand, the government should be very careful in supporting industries where market forces are strong enough, because such support may hamper free competition in the marketplace and may be wasteful as well.

6-3 Regulation

The organization of society is based on rules—some agreed upon, others more formal and enforced by governmental action—to protect the society from adverse activities. Codes of ethics, constitutions, and laws have been issued from time to time. An early and fundamental set of laws is the Code of Hammurabi, issued by the great king of Babylonia around 2000 BC. The inscription of this code was found on a block of black diorite in 1901. The Code of Hammurabi is of particular interest because of its relation to technology. Specifically, it includes liability clauses and penalties to regulate house builders. These same regulations might have remained effective throughout the 2000-year span of the Babylonian Empire, since in ancient times, technological innovation was not as rapid as it is today.

 In the present world, technological change is often so fast that policy makers cannot understand its implications and adaptively change their regulatory measures. In the area of information technology in particular, where the pace of technological innovation is accelerating and where the convergence of service modes is in rapid progress, policy makers have difficulties in modifying their regulatory policies. In Section 3-5, we outlined one such example in connection with the convergence of telecommunication and information processing.

One of the fundamental problems in regulatory policy making in a rapidly changing technological and societal environment is how to protect the interest of the public while attaining the maximum possible freedom for private citizens, corporations, and other entities.

Telecommunications and the use of radio waves have been regulated to effectively utilize limited resources for the benefit of all citizens equally and without discrimination. Postal service and telecommunication are also regulated for the protection of privacy, whereas newspapers, journals, books, motion pictures, and radio and television programs are under far less regulation in most of the democratic countries (except for pornography, violence, and the like), in order to encourage a free flow of information and to ensure freedom of expression and the right to know.

The principle may be basically correct. The problem is that when the convergence of service modes is rapidly dismantling barriers between traditionally regulated and unregulated services, it is increasingly difficult to observe this principle. Specifically, the convergence of modes leads to the need to reorganize regulations. Without such reorganization, the benefit which information technology is bringing cannot fulfill the diversifying needs of our society; it becomes impossible to decide who can provide which service under what regulation.

Telecommunication service has been provided in almost all countries under national or regional monopoly and under tariff control by the government. The reason is that if telecommunication service is left entirely in the hands of market forces, service in pursuit of profit tends to concentrate in large cities and heavily populated districts rather than in remote, rural villages and sparsely populated districts. Lower rates and better service will be available in the former, whereas the latter will suffer higher rates and less service and, ultimately, no service at all. To avoid this, unified tariffs must be set so that each citizen, regardless of where he or she lives in a country, can receive the same basic level of service under the same rate structure.

To maintain the service, an operating agency (or common carrier, as it is often called) has to subsidize its loss in remote villages and sparsely populated districts by its profits in large cities and heavily populated districts. Hence, national or regional monopoly has been granted to the common carrier to prevent competition known as cream skimming. Cream skimming in profitable areas makes it difficult for a common carrier to subsidize its loss in less profitable areas.

Let us go back to the example in Section 3-5, the case of message switching. If message switching is considered a part of telecommunication service, information processing firms may be regulated or may possibly be prohibited from providing message switching. If, on the other hand, message switching is considered part of information processing service, the common carrier may be permitted to provide information processing service or may be prohibited from doing so in order to avoid competition with information processing firms.

The views of policy makers in the world are now split, reflecting the situations in their own countries. In some countries, in particular where the common carrier is one of the government sectors or is owned by the government, message switching by information processing firms is prohibited or regulated, while information processing by the common carrier is permitted with certain restrictions. In other countries, where common carriers are privately owned and where antitrust and competition are considered of prime importance, message switching by information processing firms is permitted, while information processing by common carrier is prohibited. While no single solution has been found, it is clear that neither of the above solutions is ultimately satisfactory, because each jeopardizes the benefit of convergence of telecommunication and information processing services.

We now arrive at issues of competition. If information processing firms are permitted to provide message switching service and the common carrier is permitted to provide information processing service, can they compete properly and thereby bring better services to the public? Probably not. Because common carriers are huge entities that provide basic telecommunication service (as telephone and other traditional telecommunication services are called) under regulated monopoly, they may be able to subsidize their information processing service by the profits they gain through basic telecommunication service. Then how about separating message switching from basic telecommunication service and permitting the information processing firms and the common carriers or their subsidiaries to compete? Some may still argue that competition will be hampered because, to provide value-added services as message switching and related new services are called, transmission facilities have to be leased from the common carrier.

Puzzled policy makers may then think that basic telecommunication service should be deregulated so that such service can be provided by others, including information processing firms and their subsidiaries. This brings the dispute back to its very beginning: Can we leave all telecommunication service solely in the hands of market forces and yet ensure that basic telecommunication service will be provided equally everywhere in a country? And what service is basic—that which our parents had, that which is common now, or that which our sons and daughters will demand? Policy makers are facing an enormous Gordian knot that even an Alexander the Great might find difficult to cut in twine.

This is only one of the many problems that policy makers are facing. Another is the use of an additional channel piggybacked on a television channel. There is no serious problem if the additional channel is used to supplement the main television program by making it stereophonic or bilingual or by superimposing characters relative to the main program, perhaps for use by the deaf. If, however, the additional channel is used independently of the main television program, questions arise as to whether the intent of the main program is violated by an additional program that may express different views. If a newspaper company is permitted to use the additional channel for facsimile delivery, will this be considered control of multiple media? Under what condition can the user of the additional channel be licensed?

Broadcasting satellites present still another set of problems. Traditionally, the relaying of television programs from a key station to local distribution stations is regulated as a part of telecommunication service. Now, a broadcasting satellite provides television programs to be received directly by television viewers by means of rooftop antennas. If a local broadcasting station received the programs from the satellite by means of a large antenna (which ensured better quality) and distributed them, would this violate the traditional regulation? In a country where telecommunications, radio wave broadcasting, and cable broadcasting are under separate regulation, how can policy makers regulate a television network that consists of a key station that transmits a variety of programs over a broadcasting satellite and a number of local stations that selectively receive these programs and distribute them over cables? How about a new information vendor that provides a variety of audio, data, and video information by way of a satellite for direct reception and local distribution?

The answers to most of these questions remain to be worked out. What is clear now is that the present regulatory framework is far less than adequate to keep up with the increasing pace of innovation in information technology and the diversifying needs of our society, and that a thorough understanding of technological and societal implications is urgently needed so that policy makers can update the regulatory framework effectively.

6-4 Competition and Cooperation

Basically, competition in the marketplace brings benefits to society. In fact, since the regulation on the connection of user-owned terminals to the telecommunication network was removed or alleviated, a great variety of terminals with higher performance and lower cost have appeared on the market. Although this is due in part to the emergence of microprocessors, it should be acknowledged that the deregulation of so-called foreign attachments stimulated competition in the marketplace and thereby brought into use private automatic board exchanges (PABXs) with new business features, word processors with text-transmission capability, facsimile terminals of various speeds and time-sharing system (TSS) terminals for switched connection over telephone and data networks.

Competition is good when the competing parties have sufficient resources of money and manpower. Competition, however, leads to a poorer result if the resources available to the competitors are limited or scarce. Telecommunication service, which requires enormous resources for research, development, implementation, and operation, may be one of the examples of the latter category. If a number of firms freely compete in basic telecommunication service in one country, resources available in that country may be divided up, and as a result, the firm that provides the cheapest and worst service may survive, only to show that Gresham's law is still valid. The resources available differ from country to country. Some policy makers may think that their countries can afford such competition and avoid catastrophe. Others may not. There may be no single solution to this problem.

Competition also presents problems for broadcasting services. In countries where public broadcasting coexists with commercial broadcasting, it has become increasingly difficult to keep public broadcasting competitive. This is particularly true for a public broadcasting agency that supports itself solely by subscription fees because it wants to avoid government intervention in programming. The fact is that the subscription fees of a public broadcasting agency cannot keep up with inflation, while the income of commercial broadcasting companies surpasses inflation because of the shift of advertising from nonelectronic to electronic media. It seems clear that an unsubsidized public broadcasting agency can no longer compete effectively with commercial broadcasting companies. Should nongovernmental public broadcasting be left to fade away? Probably not.

Some policy makers may then think that the government should collect charges from commercial broadcasting companies for the use of radio waves (as it traditionally does in cases of private use of public properties) and use the money to subsidize public broadcasting. Commercial broadcasting companies may naturally object to this as an abuse of power, and the public broadcasting agency may also be reluctant to receive such support because of fear of possible government intervention in its programming.

What is clear at this point is that although competition is a very powerful driving force, it is not the only tool for the betterment of our society. Another tool to which we must pay more attention is cooperation. Cooperation may play a more important role than competition where resources are severely constrained. Instead of dividing up limited resources, competing parties may be able to share the resources through appropriate cooperation in accordance with their objectives, functions, and localities. Cooperation between common carriers and information processing firms in setting up joint ventures may better promote value-added telecommunication service in its research, development, implementation, and operation. Commercial broadcasting companies may contribute funds, in accordance with their own will, in setting up a nongovernment foundation to support a public broadcasting agency without any strings attached.

However, cooperation is very difficult to accomplish because of the conflict of interest between participating public agencies, private companies, and government sectors. Antitrust laws, which have a dominant power in most of the industrialized countries, often work to against cooperation. Powerful insight, motivation, and enthusiasm on the part of government as well as among participating parties are necessary to bring an appropriate balance between the competitive and cooperative aspects of converging information services.

6-5   Standardization

When human beings began to trade goods, they realized that "measuring others' corn by their own bushels" did not work. Measurement is one of the earliest examples of standardization in human society. In the past, a number of standards have been established for a great variety of items and procedures, ranging from utensils in a farmer's kitchen to protocols at a royal court. Such standards permit societal activities to be carried out smoothly.

Standardization has proved to be a very difficult task. As we have seen in Chapter 1, many attempts at standardization failed because of their impracticality. Some standards were found useful, and some of them still survive. The metric system is one example, despite the fact that its basic unit of length has been found to differ from the one forty-millionth of the circumference of the globe it was originally intended to represent.

As modern technology has been rapidly introduced into society, and as societal activities in the world have been more closely knit, a number of international standards have been established. In the area of information technology, the IEC (International Electrotechnical Commission), which recommends standards for electrical equipment and components, was founded in 1906 by Lord Kelvin and others. The ITU (International Telecommunication Union), which recommends standards for telegraph, telephone, data, and radio wave communication was founded in 1865 as the International Telegraph Union. The ISO (International Standards Organization), which recommends standards for everything else, including computers, was founded in 1946.

By virtue of the efforts of these international organizations, all telephones in the world can be connected to each other and television programs can be exchanged by broadcasters throughout the world. However, this does not mean that there is only one standard for telephone systems or for television systems. Rather, the world now has a few different standards for these systems that reflect locality and evolutionary process. These standards are made compatible in order to make interconnection possible. Compatibility is achieved by an interface that converts from one standard to another. Interface units can be very simple or very complex, depending on the difference of standards. If we have n standards to be made compatible, we generally need $n(n-1)/2$ interfacing units of different types. Having one standard is clearly the best; a few may be tolerable if compatibility can be attained easily, but having many leads to disaster.

Standardization of the hardware and software of information technology is extremely important because telephone sets, terminals, transmission lines, and switching centers are always connected in networks, and, increasingly, computers and data bases are connected to such networks. To permit information to be transmitted and received between these network components, interfaces should be agreed upon, clearly defined, and as simple as possible.

Standardization is very difficult for a number of reasons. First, the pace of innovation in information technology is very fast. A standard set too early may jeopardize future innovation; set too late, it never becomes operational. Second, standardization is required to cover not only hardware but also software, that is, computer programs and the like. A very large amount of software at each switching center has to be standardized in order to attain economy of scale and ease of maintenance. To permit communication between terminals and computers, a software standard known as a communication protocol has to be implemented. Generally, to operate and to interconnect equipment that has higher intelligence, more software has to be standardized.

Third, new products tend to have diversified specifications, since they are designed by competing private industries. This makes it particularly difficult to establish a single standard in such areas as computers, terminals, and video packages, where market forces are powerful and new technologies are continually emerging.

Fourth, conflicts of interest may occur between countries or groups of countries in trying to establish a single standard. For instance, three standards—namely, NTSC, PAL, and SECAM—exist for color television broadcasting. This results in the use of complicated interfaces for format conversion when an exchange of programs is required. For the digital hierarchy for multiplexing digital signals, three standards exist, which may require costly interfaces for future interconnection. But settling on a single standard would benefit some more than others, so there are problems of fairness and politics in addition to the technical side of these issues.

Standardization in information technology requires a great deal of collaboration and compromise between governments, common carriers, and industries in the world. It also requires a thorough understanding of the state of the art as well as a far reaching insight into the future by all the participants, not only those from governments, common carriers, and industries, but also those from academia and those who represent users. Governments should assist and encourage, not hamper, cooperative activities to bring better standards to the world. What is encouraging is that despite two world wars and other international conflicts in the past, the standardization activities of the world have continued and are even accelerating in recent years. Standardization is perhaps one of very few areas of international activity in which countries, industries, and individuals of diversified backgrounds and interests can think and act constructively and cooperatively for the good of humanity.

6-6 Information Supply and Distribution

As we have seen, the repertoire of information services has been extended from the transmission and switching of information to the processing of information and, then, to the providing of information. In other words, new information services have much affinity with broadcast service, in which the quality and quantity of the information to be provided is the most crucial factor for success or failure. Information collection, processing, and formation, however, require a great deal of effort.

For instance, a data base for bibliographic information retrieval requires that many scientific papers be collected from many professional journals over many years, abstracted and indexed, entered through a keyboard into a computer store in machine-readable form, retrieved upon request, and updated in accordance with new issues, corrections, and other changes. Very few professional institutions can afford to do this by themselves, especially when the information has little commercial value. Therefore, building such data bases requires government assistance, at least until the data base becomes commercially valuable.

Various sectors of the government collect enormous amounts of data for their administrative use. These data are invaluable as industrial, agricultural, economic, and social indicators for businesspeople, economists, sociologists, and many others. In some countries, where a freedom of information law has been enacted, the government data have been made available to the public to the extent that no infringement on privacy and national security occurs. This not only promotes economic and societal progress in broader terms but also encourages information services to use government data by sorting, merging, collating, and processing to fit their customers' needs. In other countries, however, the governments seldom provide the data they own to the public, so that information services suffer a serious lack of materials. Considering the fact that economic and societal activities are increasingly information oriented, governments should be urged to provide their data to the public as much as possible in order to promote economic and societal progress and to help information services sustain their businesses. Considering the importance of the integrity of data, governments should also agree to validate their data as accurately as possible and to make quotations as detailed as possible. For the same reason, information services are required to be very careful in processing data so as not to provide biased or erroneous data to the public.

Information is an invisible commodity. Like visible commodities, it requires an appropriate distribution mechanism in order to reach end users. The government, therefore, should assist information vendors in developing their distribution channels through computer networks, videotex, teletext, and other means. Those who provide information should permit information vendors to have access to their information resources without hindrance. Government assistance seems desirable and necessary for the dissemination of scientific and technological information, which has little immediate commercial value but is of decisive importance in extending knowledge.

The government should also provide assistance for the formation of information resources for education and improved welfare. For instance, computer-aided instruction (CAI) systems require that highly sophisticated teaching programs be produced by close collaboration between experienced educators and talented software producers. Therefore, the government should assist and encourage highly experienced educators to become familiar with computer usage and thereby better cooperate with software producers.

As described in Section 3-5, information resources, especially information in machine-readable form, are unevenly distributed on earth. As a result, many countries suffer from a significant imbalance in information flow, with larger inflow and smaller outflow. The governments of such countries may think that the flow should be brought into balance by restricting inflow through a custom duty or other barriers. This, however, is not the right solution, because such action makes such countries even more information poor. Rather, the government should exert more effort to build up its own information resources so as to increase the information flow out of the country.

Information flow into a country may be disturbed if that country has no privacy-protection law, because countries supplying information may feel that the privacy of their people may be infringed in that country. The government of such a country is therefore urged to enact a protection-of-privacy law (or laws for different areas of application) together with a freedom-of-information law, in concert with other countries, so as not to obstruct information flow, which is vital for the progress of mankind. It may be worth noting that the Organization for Economic Cooperation and Development (OECD) and the Council of Europe have agreed on guidelines on the protection of privacy for the framing of national polices and legislation in a harmonized way.

6-7 Informatization

As we pointed out in Chapter 3, information technology is a powerful tool for enhancing societal infrastructure, revitalizing traditional industrial sectors, extending knowledge, and enriching human culture. However, private sectors are generally incapable of paying the cost for the implementation and operation of such information-oriented systems. Beneficiaries of societal infrastructure generally take the benefits for granted and are reluctant to bear the cost—or are incapable of doing so.

Thus the government should provide financial support for information-oriented societal infrastructure, not only for its development, but also for its operation. The government should be aware of regional differences in the need for such infrastructure, and should distribute systems properly. The government should also encourage local communities and professionals to participate actively in implementing and operating the societal infrastructure so as to service the community better.

The government system itself is a most important societal infrastructure. Tremendous amounts of statistics that have been collected independently in many government sectors often overlap and are sometimes found to be inconsistent or misinterpreted. A very large number of documents produced for administrative purposes are validated, circulated, and filed inefficiently and inconsistently. Administrative information tends to circulate through the government system with much delay, and delay hampers decision making. The government should make full use of information technology to make its own system more comprehensive, more efficient, and less costly.

The success of the information-oriented infrastructure depends on the existence of a powerful telecommunication network that can provide telephone service and data services nationwide and also in remote rural areas. Government can therefore foster the expansion and evolution of the telecommunication network.

The government should also assist traditional industrial sectors in improving productivity and working conditions by use of information technology. The need for assistance seems greatest in such industrial sectors as agriculture, in which market forces are an inadequate stimulus of innovation and upon which the basic needs of human survival are so dependent. For many other industrial sectors, where automation by means of industrial robots and process-control computers is displacing skilled workers and where needs for software are rapidly increasing, the government should provide assistance for continuing education and retraining to provide a smooth shift of the displaced work force to information-oriented jobs.

In view of the fact that the number of qualified scientists and engineers is quite limited and that the knowledge gained in the past is quickly becoming obsolete because of the rapid progress of information technology, it is particularly important to have a comprehensive system for continuing education so that scientists and engineers can keep up with their arts over a lifetime. However, continuing education has been provided mainly by large industries. Small industries—and large industries that are in financial difficulty—cannot afford to support continuing education. The government should therefore encourage universities and other educational institutions to provide continuing-education programs on the campus or on industries' premises by providing financial and other assistance.

Last, but not least, the government should increase its financial support to the use of information technology to extend and preserve our scientific and cultural heritage. Research activities in astronomy, geophysics, oceanography, biology, and all areas of the natural sciences should be encouraged by adequate financing and by establishment of information-oriented research facilities. Research institutions and museums for archeology, anthropology, and the arts should be armed with information technology so as to better understand and preserve invaluable cultural gifts from our ancestors. Artists should be encouraged to use information technology in their work. Researchers in natural sciences, social sciences, and humanities should be provided with ample information resources through sustained government support in building and updating data bases for a great variety of disciplines.

6-8 Societal Receptivity

When Prometheus stole fire from heaven and gave it to mankind, Zeus sent Pandora to earth with her box of evils. Since then, human beings have used fire in many ways to improve their way of life. However, the evils that escaped from Pandora's box have crept into the human mind and have led to the abuse of that tool, fire, to devastate civilization. Like fire—and like all other technologies—information technology is a tool. It is a powerful tool, the extent to which is is used for the good or for the bad of humanity is up to human beings themselves.

In the past, possibilities of abusing technology were often overlooked. Technologists tend to look for the potential for use rather than abuse, and social scientists and humanists have found difficulties in understanding implications of technology in general. The public has been reluctant to admit that the human mind can be infected by the evils that crept out of Pandora's box. Technology assessment was an important step toward clarifying the situation.

Through the joint efforts of technologists and sociologists, technology assessment analyses all the conceivable positive and negative impacts of a technology and provides alternatives to alleviate the negative impacts. Unfortunately, technology assessment does not always provide reasonable alternatives, because the options that alleviate negative impacts of a technology sometimes diminish its positive impacts. Let us take a very simple and years-old technology, a knife, as an example.

A knife has many positive uses, but it also has definite negative potential. When put to evil purpose, a knife may hurt or kill someone. Were the public to feel that the technology of knives was incomplete and unacceptable because of its potential negative impact, what sort of acceptable technological solution might be found? Would it be possible to pick up unusual activity occurring in the mind of a knife owner by using a lie detector, an encephalograph, or some other electronic instrument, and, by using a microprocessor, find evil intent and then electronically lock

informatization of societal infrastructures to attain more efficient use of monetary and human resources in the world. However, the government should be very careful in supporting a particular industrial sector where market forces are powerful, because this may disturb free competition in the world market.

When a government restructures its regulatory policy, it should consider compatibility with the regulatory policies of other governments so as not to disturb the international flow of information. The government should encourage cooperation of information services not only within its country but also in the international scene, especially in the use of domestic and regional satellites. When assisting standardization activities, the government should encourage all the participating parties to settle, if possible, on a common standard, and it should urge its public and private sectors to conform with the standard so as not to hamper the international flow of goods and services.

When assisting the formation of data bases and information-distribution mechanisms within its country, the government should cooperate with other governments to increase and balance the transborder information flow. The government should enact freedom-of-information laws and protection-of-privacy laws in conformity with those of other governments so as to increase international information flow while protecting the privacy of the people in the world. The government should provide technology and experience to other governments for promoting scientific knowledge and preserving cultural heritages.

The prime mover for the progress of the world is fair competition and thoughtful cooperation among countries. Information technology provides unprecedented means of mutual understanding and thereby promotes cooperation among world communities. In the present world of mutual dependence, governments should thoroughly understand the implications of information technology and fully utilize its benefits for the betterment of world society.

6-10   Concluding Remarks

We have described the problems that governments face in connection with information technology and civilization, and we have identified areas where the initiative and assistance of governments are called for.

The issues of information will remain politically charged, not only concerning accessibility, security, and integrity, but also in issues of relative allocation of resources. It is to be hoped that governments guided by communities of interest will make wise choices. Indeed, it is plausible that governments will survive, changed or unchanged, as they cope, successfully or unsuccessfully, with a real world in which information technology is an increasingly powerful force and resource.

The government should provide support in promoting basic research and in implementing information resources and information-oriented societal infrastructure. The government is responsible in setting rules for the protection of the privacy, security, and integrity of information as well as in adaptively restructuring regulatory measures on information services in accordance with technological innovation and societal needs. The government should encourage industries to promote standardization and distribution of information and to share cooperatively limited human and monetary resources for research. Government intervention should be made with a full understanding of international implications.

Perhaps a government or its equivalent may not be able—or should not be expected—to play exactly the role described in this chapter. In some countries, it has been a tradition to avoid government intervention to the greatest possible extent. Yet, it is clear that quality of life cannot be improved by depending solely upon market forces and private efforts. In some countries, governments are already overloaded with responsibilities. Bureaucratic systems may perform poorly and merely provide empty plans or impractical and sometimes stifling regulations. Adequate government involvement should be determined in accordance with the cultural, technological, and societal background of a country. This chapter may be used as a checklist for such purposes.

REFERENCES

Convention for the Protection of Individuals with Regard to Automatic Processing of Personal Data. Council of Europe, Strasbourg, 1981.

Guidelines on the Protection of Privacy and Transborder Flows of Personal Data. OECD, Paris, 1981.

Innovation in Small and Medium Firms. OECD, Paris, 1982.

Technical Change and Economic Policy. OECD, Paris, 1980.

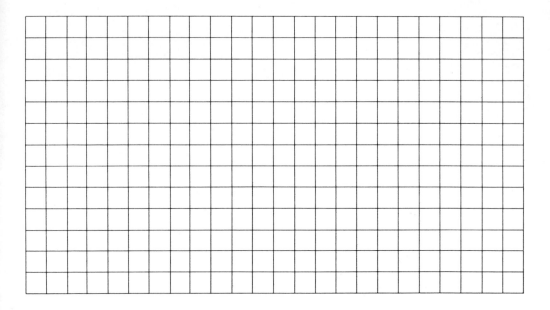

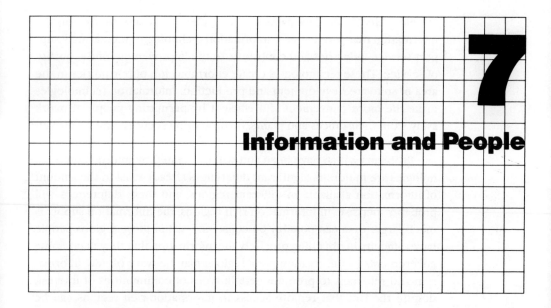

Information and People

7

7-1 Introduction

Modern information technologies bring great benefits and yet pose great problems. The benefits and problems are not new, nor is the fact that new technology should prove a mixed blessing. If we look back through history, we find instances in the past in which our ancestors viewed new developments with a mixture of pleasure and dismay. What is significantly different today is that modern information technologies have been—and will continue to be—so powerful that their benefits and problems are unprecedented and involve us all on a global scale. Perhaps these are at once the best of times and the worst of times.

One outstanding benefit of information technology that we see is the strengthening of a great variety of communities of interest. Improved technology allows formation of many new, smaller communities of interest, and it also allows existing, larger communities of interest to attain a transnational character. The high motivation of common interests, combined with ease of communication, allows such communities of interest to be extremely flexible and productive; thus, they may contribute more to scientific, technological, and artistic progress in a greater number of areas than formal or governmental organizations do.

New electronic data bases provide selective access to the specific information that people need. Information technologies increasingly support service industries and contribute to the improvement of the quality of service. These technologies create enormous job opportunities in the area of software development and production. Information technologies make life more convenient and efficient by permitting people to work away from their offices and plants, by promoting security, and by providing everyday conveniences.

Problems which have been and will be created by information technologies are multifold. Significant differences already exist in the amount of information available in different regions, and these differences will probably increase. In information-rich regions, the information supply is much larger than can possibly be consumed, yet in these regions people have difficulty in obtaining precisely the information that they need. Some governments in information-poor regions may be wary of new information and reluctant to promote certain types of communities of interest, despite the fact that remote access to information-rich regions can be made by means of low-cost terminals.

People are confused by enormous floods of data. They are concerned about the validity and interpretation of data and have difficulty in obtaining understandable, informative summaries. Data bases are a powerful tool for solving this problem; yet, for data base services to be available to everyone, tremendous efforts must be expended in collecting, entering, collating, updating, and coding (for retrieval) very large amounts of data.

In some developed countries, a majority of the labor force already works in service industries. Yet, performance evaluation in these industries has been difficult. In particular, the quality of service provided by information technologies is not easily evaluated. In the information industry itself, which is a labor-intensive service industry because of the cost of software, no appropriate way of evaluating a software product is yet known.

While information technologies provide significant job opportunities in software production, these same technologies may result in considerable displacement of labor through automation and in saving of labor, both in manufacturing and in commerce. Transition of the labor force from old jobs to new jobs is not generally easy, and it is made less easy if trade unions are rigidly organized by craft and if insufficient retraining facilities are provided.

We are in a transitional stage. For people who wish to use information technology to shop, to learn, or to entertain themselves, neither sophisticated software nor a sufficient amount of information is yet available. So it is now that we must explore the benefits and problems of this technology with the intention of finding ways to promote benefits and alleviate problems. This chapter deals with such exploration.

7-2 Information Explosion and Information Dearth

In some parts of the world, a great deal of information is gathered and made available in various forms every day. The amount is so enormous that even a Gargantua might hesitate to ask a Pantagruel to learn everything. In other parts of the world, very little information is generated or made available. People there are as information hungry as an Edmond Dante's in the Chateau D'If. It is clear that in the present world, an information explosion and an information dearth coexist. Information technology has promoted the dissemination of information; yet, because of economic, political, religious, ideological, educational, and other reasons, there are large differences among regions in the amount of information available.

If we look at the situation in terms of electronic information facilities, North America, Europe, Japan, and the Soviet Union, whose combined population is less than 30 percent of the world's, own 91 percent of the telephones, 83 percent of the radio receivers, and 89 percent of the television receivers of the world. As to other media, these areas also generate a large proportion of information: newspaper circulation, 78 percent; book titles published, 83 percent; cinemas, 88 percent; and pieces of mail, 95 percent. More than 80 percent of the data bases that are accessible to the public are in the United States.

Undoubtedly, these figures suggest how geographically uneven information resources and distribution channels are, with less than 30 percent of the world's population exposed to a glut of information while the rest of the population goes information hungry. As we look at the statistics in terms of media, we find that in recent years, the annual growth rates differ significantly with respect to media: telephone, 6 percent; television receivers, 8 percent; radio receivers, 6 percent; book titles, 2 percent; and pieces of mail, 1 percent; with newspaper circulation and cinemas

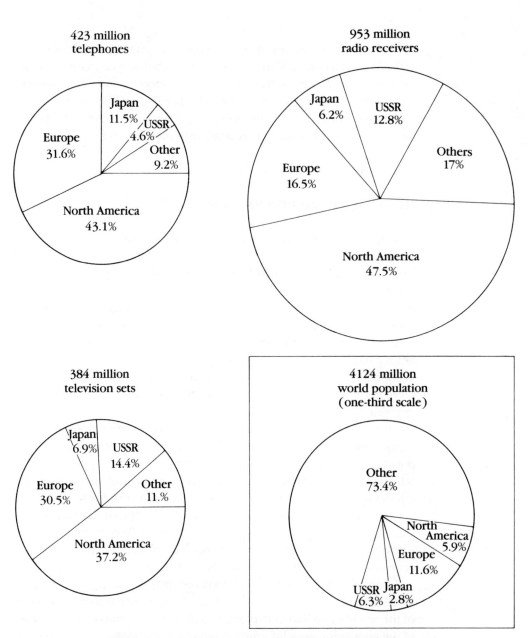

423 million
telephones

953 million
radio receivers

Japan
11.5%
USSR
4.6%
Other
9.2%
Europe
31.6%
North America
43.1%

Japan
6.2%
USSR
12.8%
Others
17%
Europe
16.5%
North America
47.5%

384 million
television sets

4124 million
world population
(one-third scale)

Japan
6.9%
USSR
14.4%
Other
11.%
Europe
30.5%
North America
37.2%

Other
73.4%
North America
5.9%
Europe
11.6%
USSR
6.3%
Japan
2.8%

Figure 7-1 World distribution of telephones, radio receivers, television receivers, and population: The area of the sectors is proportional to the numbers represented, except for the world population chart, which is reduced to a one-third scale. (SOURCE: *1977 Compendium of Social Statistics,* United Nations)

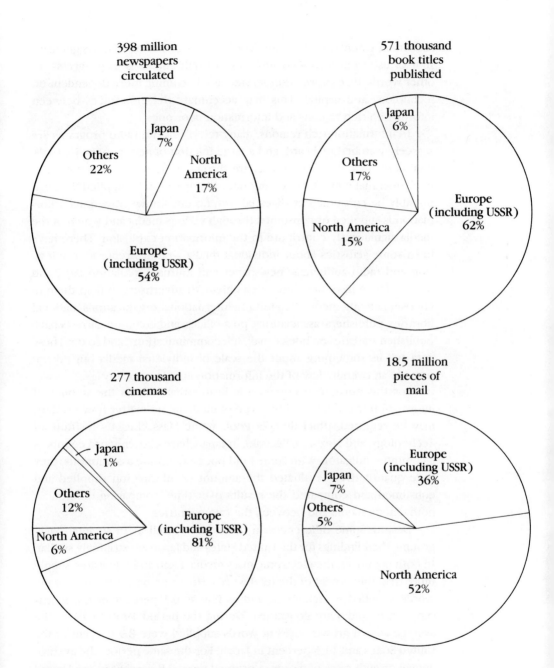

Figure 7-2 World newspaper circulation, book titles published, cinemas, and pieces of mail, 1974. (SOURCE: *Statistical Yearbook 1978*, United Nations)

remaining essentially constant. These statistics tell us that a significant shift of use from nonelectronic to electronic media is in progress—in other words, that information services are becoming more dependent on technology and capital. This may accentuate the imbalances between information-rich regions and information-poor ones.

In information-rich regions, many television and radio programs are scarcely watched or heard, and a large fraction of newspapers, journals, commercial catalogs, and books are thrown away unread. People intuitively feel that a much larger amount of information is supplied than can possibly be consumed or digested; yet, no one knows how much information is supplied or consumed through various media and which of the media significantly contribute to the information explosion. There have been some statistics about individual media—ratings reports on television and radio audiences, newspaper and journal circulation data, and others. These have been provided chiefly to advertisers to help them in choosing among media. In addition, international organizations, national libraries, publishers' associations, post offices, and common carriers have published statistics on books, mail, telecommunications, and so on. These data tell us something about the scale of individual media but do not provide an overall view of the information flow in a society.

For this purpose, a common indicator that reflects the amount of information irrespective of the type of medium, no matter how crudely, may be required. Ithiel de Sola Pool, at the Massachusetts Institute of Technology, and Nozomu Takasaki, in Japan, have chosen word counts as a common indicator. With some bold but unavoidable assumptions, they have quantitatively evaluated the amount of information supplied and consumed and compared the results over time, comparing differences both among media and between the two countries.

Despite some differences in definition as well as in societal background, their findings for the United States and Japan are strikingly similar. In both countries, the electronic mass media, radio and television, supply more than 95 percent of the total words. However, only 1 percent of the words supplied by television and as few as 0.1 percent of the words supplied by radio are consumed. During the period 1960 to 1975, the average annual growth rates of words supplied were 8.9 percent in the United States and 11.5 percent in Japan. For the same period, the average annual growth rates of words consumed were 2.8 percent in the United States and 3.3 percent in Japan. These studies have revealed many other interesting findings. In all, it may be observed that, taking into account

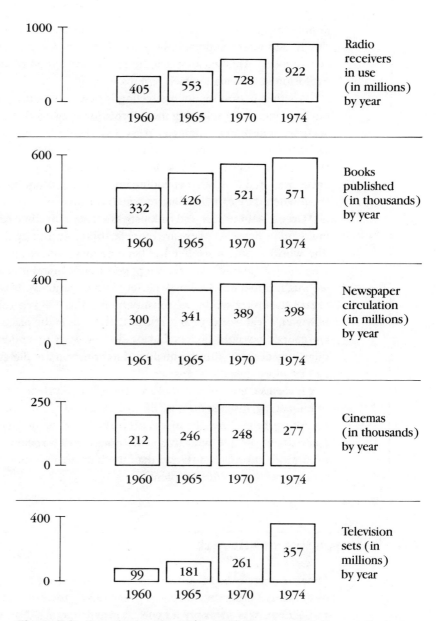

Figure 7-3   Growth of media, 1960–1974. (SOURCE: *1977 Compendium of Social Statistics*, United Nations; *Statistical Yearbook 1978*, United Nations)

population growth, per capita information consumption is increasing very slowly, and information supply grows three times as fast as information consumption. This must contribute to the perception of an information explosion in information-rich regions.

Another reason for such a feeling is that information consumers do not have means for selecting the information they need and for acquiring accurate information they can trust. One may find that nothing useful was gained through buying and reading a best-selling book or that the facts and figures in one book directly contradict those of another. Audiences are often frustrated at finding no television programs of interest to them when they can find time to watch the screen.

Greed, self-interest, and callousness account for some failures of communication; however, there are other factors contributing to such failures. The world in which we live has become increasingly opaque and overwhelmingly complex. We cannot possibly understand it in the sense that we might understand a small, closely knit community. If we do not disregard the larger world, we must perceive it as it is represented. Is this, however, a real world, or is it a myth that stands in the place of something we cannot possibly understand or do not wish to understand? These questions dealing with the quality of information are difficult to address and far more difficult to answer.

It seems common that those with special knowledge, be it of science or publishing, distrust mass media presentations of their own fields while accepting the pictures the media present of other fields. Here, knowledge feeds doubt. People who live in information-rich regions may become even more information thirsty than the information poor. Like Tantalus, they starve in the midst of plenty.

7-3 Communities of Interest

Mount Parnassus had two summits. One, consecrated to Apollo and the Muses, was a center for lovers of poetry and music; the other, dedicated to Bacchus, was probably a center for gastronomes. Naraka, the Hindu Hell, was believed to have 28 divisions—for liars, drunkards, cow killers, and so forth. People congregated in accordance with their interests or were concerned about falling into the abyss as a result of their evil deeds, regardless of their nationality. People in the present world share a variety of interests or concerns, and these are so serious that they often transcend national boundaries. A group of people who share a common interest or concern is known as a community of interest.

Human communication takes place within a community of interest. People think and act within that community, and they communicate in moving others toward or away from what they regard as appropriate thoughts and actions. Only certain information is relevant communication within a given community of interest because only certain information is appropriate, makes sense, and will be understood.

In a simple society—an isolated band or a village with a subsistence economy—a community of limited size and complexity provides a community of interest common to all. Speech is adequate communication here. The family or the clan may be a subset of a community of interest. Other places, other people, and other times must somehow be taken into account in myth and custom. Nonetheless, to a degree, all of life (that is, all that is noted) is accessible and intelligible to all members of the community.

Our world has outgrown the reach of the voice or the comprehension of any one mind. It is divided into countless communities of interest. Increasingly, these communities are intellectual rather than geographical. A physicist or a banker or a chess player may have more in common with a colleague in a foreign land than with a next-door neighbor.

Our multiple communities of interest and the institutions that serve them overlap. Such communities of interest grow from natural interests rather than from any elitism. The shared interests are diverse and varied. Each individual belongs to many communities of interest, and these multiple memberships provide natural and valuable paths of interchange among the many communities of interest that are essential to our civilization. A mathematician may be interested in the stock market and in riding a monocycle. An engineer may be interested in poetry and archeology. A farmer may be interested in science fiction and in local politics. That a person is a member of many communities of interest makes him or her no less real; rather, it makes the person a valuable link in society. Clearly, such communities of interest could not exist without proper communication channels.

Information technology plays a complex role in our complex way of life. In so serving us, the various information services interact in many ways with the people they serve. Some forms of information services support almost all communities of interest, ranging from the individual and the family to large business and cultural organizations. The postal service and telecommunication service are among these, with telecommunication playing a large and increasing role. In many countries, there are more local telephone calls per person than pieces of mail per person, and the rate of increase for telephone messages is faster. Toll telephone calls are increasing faster than local telephone calls, and overseas telephone calls are increasing even faster than toll telephone calls. In such statistics, we see a society in which both human relations and business transactions are proceeding on shorter and shorter time scales. Life has become less leisurely, less planned, more immediate. The increases in toll telephone calls and overseas telephone calls also tell us that communities of interest are becoming more far-flung.

Some modes of information service support only specific communities of interest. Books are among these. Nothing matches the diversity of books. With rare exceptions (the Bible and the Koran among them), each book reaches only a small fraction of the total population. Yet a successful book may reach a large fraction of those deeply interested in a particular area or subject, be it yoga, tennis, hieroglyphics, or general relativity. A successful book can blanket the real community of interest with from a few thousand to tens of thousands of copies. A book can serve a narrow community of interest, for example, the worldwide community of specialists in some field of science. This has been particularly true since the use of text editing and computer-aided composition have become available; these can provide excellent print without the elaborate or costly procedures of traditional publishing.

In general, periodical publications must have a substantial readership in order to survive. Nonetheless, the number of periodicals has been increasing slowly but steadily. This increase reflects a growth in the number of communities of interest of substantial size. No comprehensive

Figure 7-4 Electronics and information technology have changed the use of our leisure time. (a) Time spent reading and watching television, by education level, 1965–1966. (b) Books published in the United States, by selected fields, 1950–1975. (c) Changes in favorite leisure activities in the United States over 40 years. (SOURCE: *Social Indicators*, 1976, 1979, U. S. Department of Commerce)

(a)

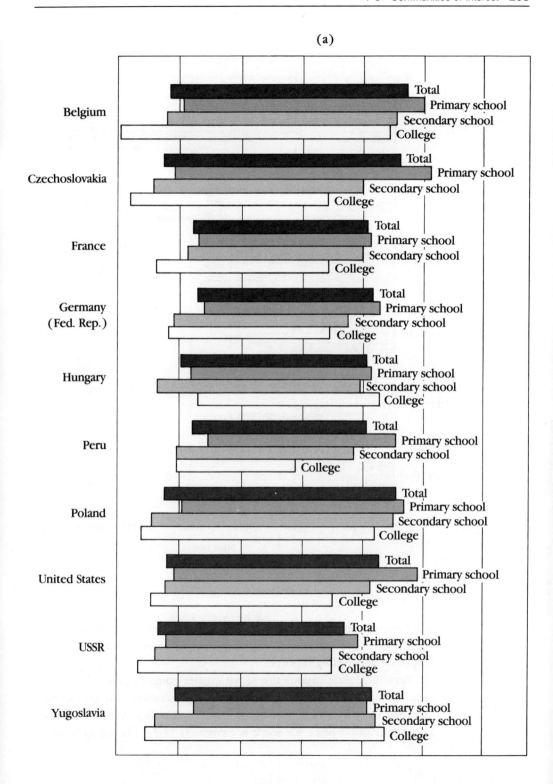

(b)

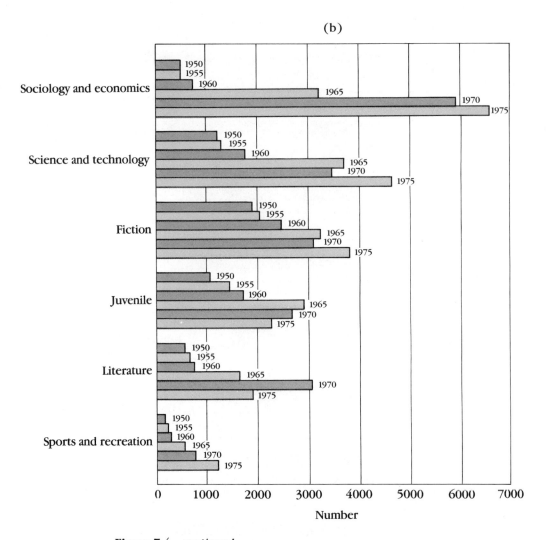

Figure 7-4 *continued*

statistics are yet available that cover all sorts of periodicals, ranging from popular weekly magazines to a great variety of commercial catalogs and corporate accounting reports.

Periodical publications also serve smaller communities of interest. A large number of highly specialized periodical publications, weekly, monthly, quarterly, or yearly, are appearing, particularly in business and technology. The subscription price for some is extremely high; this seems to show

(c)

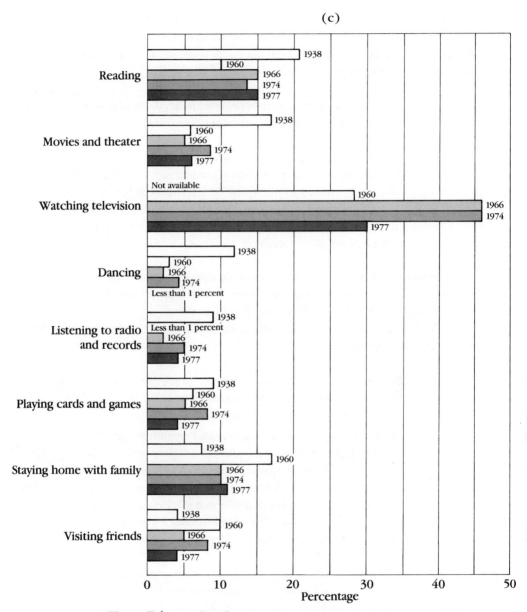

Figure 7-4 *continued*

that they serve particular communities of interest better than more general financial or technical journals. Enormous numbers of club and society bulletins and the like, many formerly typed on mimeographed, are now

DATA BASES

There has been large growth in computer-accessible data bases, particularly in the United States, and these data bases are listed in various directories. Some criteria for including data bases as computer accessible are those given by Cuadra Associates in their *Directory of Online Databases**:

1. It must be available *online* (i.e., not just available in computer-readable form) for use in an interactive mode.
2. It must be available to the public, or to organizations that can establish their eligibility through subscriptions or membership.
3. It must be accessible through an online service organization that is connected to one or more international telecommunications networks and/or to networks (including direct long-distance communication systems) that serve one country or a limited set of countries.

As of Summer 1983, indices for worldwide data bases listed about 1750 data bases that meet these requirements and about 260 on line services through which various combinations of these data bases can be reached.

Data bases can be conveniently categorized as they have been in the *Directory of Online Databases**:

REFERENCE DATABASES. Refer or "point" users to another source (e.g., a document, an organization, or an individual) for additional details or for the complete text.

Bibliographic. Contain citations and, sometimes, abstracts of the printed literature, e.g., journal articles, reports, patents, dissertations, reference proceedings, books, or newspaper items.

Referral. Contain references and, sometimes, abstracts or summaries of non-published information. Generally refer users to organizations, individuals, audiovisual materials and other non-print media, for further information.

SOURCE DATABASES. Those that contain complete data or the full text of the original source information.

Numeric. Contain original survey data and/or statistically manipulated representations of data. Are generally in the form

---

*From *Directory of Online Databases,* Vol. 4, No. 3, Cuadra Associates, 1983, pp. 7–8. Reprinted by permission of Cuadra Associates.

of time series, which represent measurements (e.g., tons or dollars) over time for a given variable (e.g., production or shipment statistics for a given product or industry).

Textual-Numeric. Are generally databases of records that contain a number of data elements or fields with a combination of textual information and numeric data, including those databases with dictionary or handbook-type data, typically of chemical and physical properties.

Full Text. Contain records of the complete text of an item, e.g., a newspaper item, a specification, or a court decision.

Many of the most useful data bases operate in conjunction with the mails. A key word search can be made from an on-line terminal, and titles and, sometimes, abstracts can be examined. Articles or reports of interest can be ordered through the terminal and be delivered by mail.

Data bases serve a large number of communities of interest and are maintained by a host of governmental, institutional, nonprofit, and commercial organizations. They provide a great variety of information, such as access to publications in various fields from a wide variety of journals, books, and reports; indices covering both domestic and international company, product, and industry information; dissertation indices; lists of foundation grants; specific, detailed information important in law, medicine, and other fields; and all sorts of numeric statistical data and physical and chemical handbook-type data.

One good way to get an impression of currently available data bases is to examine a comprehensive directory. As these directories are published periodically, dates of publication are not given in this listing.

Computer-Readable Data Bases
Knowledge Industry Publications
701 Westchester Avenue
White Plains, New York 10604

(The above publication is prepared by Coordinated Science Laboratory of the University of Illinois).

Directory of Online Databases
Cuadra Associates, Inc.
2001 Wilshire Boulevard
Santa Monica, California 90403

Encyclopedia of Information Systems and Services
Gale Research Company
645 Griswold Avenue
Detroit, Michigan 48226

Data Bases In Europe
Aslib
3 Belgrave Square
London SW1X 8PL England

increasingly prepared in good form using word processors and offset printing. Facsimile and teletext help smaller communities of interest to disseminate copies of documents faster without physical delivery. A teletext message or a digitized facsimile message can be temporarily stored and then forwarded upon a user's request. This function, known as mailbox service, together with quick production of hard copies at the receiving end, provides significant convenience to highly specialized communities of interests, especially in business and technology.

Perhaps the most drastic change in serving specialized communities of interest is the use of data bases. Chemical Abstracts, Inspec, Medlars, and other bibliographic data bases are providing bibliographic retrieval service to chemists, physicists, computer scientists, electrical engineers, medical doctors, and other professionals. These data bases selectively disseminate current information in a users' specialized field. They also provide retrospective search, over a period of a decade or more, upon the request of users. The information provided is the secondary information, namely, the title and abstract of an article, the author's name and affiliations, and the journal name and issue. In some cases, the information also indicates where copies of the article can be found. Some services will also supply a copy on request.

In the United States, data bases accessible by telephone connection serve home computers. These services supply subscribers with weather reports, stock market reports, and airline schedules and even give mailbox service.

Unlike periodical publications, which disseminate secondary information covering broad areas, data base services are capable of selecting secondary information in a very narrow area in accordance with key words specified by users. About 1750 data bases for science and technology are in public service. These provide information on spectroscopy, crystallography, and many other fields.

For business purposes, data base services are available that provide such information as credit ratings and market quotations for stocks, commodities, and foreign exchange rates. Upon request, videotex provides the general public with a great variety of information, including news reports, listings of current theatrical, concert, and movie performances, stock market quotations, weather reports, shopping guides, listings of community events, quizzes, and even seat reservations. With the spreading of such data base services, our information-rich Tantalus will be able to selectively grasp the clusters of fruit he needs and scoop what he needs from the rivers of information that flowed around him but did not slake his thirst.

The rapid progress of communication and transportation services has significantly stimulated the growth of many communities of interest that have an international or transnational character. Some of these are growing more powerful—or at least more active and visible—than governments in some areas. Might certain of these communities play a constructive role like that of the community of women in Aristophanes' Lysistrata, who stopped the Peloponnesian War by refusing to engage in sex?

Powerful communities of interest that are known as nongovernmental organizations (NGOs) now play a significant role in consulting, advising, and sometimes criticizing governments and intergovernmental organizations. In the area of information, for instance, the International Federation for Documentation (FID), the International Federation of Library Associations and Institutions (IFLA), the International Council on Archives (ICA), the International Federation of Information Processing (IFIP), the International Council on Scientific Unions (ICSU), and many others are known for their outstanding achievements and contributions.

In contrast to a government, which tends to form a jealous community of interest, nongovernmental organizations of a transnational character are communities of interest generally free from political philosophies and therefore often better at getting things done. While governments may boycott the Olympic games and exclude unpopular governments from international activities, the nongovernmental organizations tend to foster friendships and mutual understanding within their communities of interest and, in so doing, contribute to progress and the stability of the world.

As society becomes even larger and more complex, the problem of communicating within communities of interest becomes progressively more difficult. At times, some governments may wish to make society simpler and more uniform through centralization and drastic restrictive legislation concerning whatever may be deemed to be antisocial, unfair, or simply unpopular or different. Other governments may wish to make communication operate meaningfully and effectively by pushing power toward communities of interest, whether intellectual, technological, or cultural.

Long before governments take deliberate steps in this latter direction, communities of interest will have multiplied, differentiated themselves, and, in many cases, transcended geographical or national bonds. Information technologies are stimulating a drastic reorganization of world communities in a way that we have never seen before.

7-4 Knowledge, Information, and Data

In Delphi, at the foot of Mount Parnassus, there stood a famous temple of Apollo. Priestesses in the temple gave many oracles so ambiguous and obscure that they were often seriously misleading. Philip of Macedon was a victim of them. At the time of his Persian expedition, he received an oracle: "The ready victim crowned to death before the altar stands." He thought the "ready victim" was the King of Persia, but it was actually himself. Another oracle of fame was: "You shall go shall return never you shall perish by the war." This may either mean "You shall go, shall return, never you shall perish by the war" or "You shall go, shall return never, you shall perish by the war." The dismayed Christian Emperor Theodosius finally silenced the oracle in the fourth century AD.

Our modern oracles can be equally ambiguous or misleading. One might think that the gross national product (GNP) measures the amount of something (indeed, of something useful) that was produced. Wrong. The GNP is actually computed from expenditures for goods or services, however frivolous or unproductive. Thus, if the government stored surplus apples, the cost of doing so would be part of the GNP. If the apples rotted and had to be buried, the cost of so disposing of them would be part of the GNP. The unemployment index may count workers as unemployed if they worked in factories for less than half a year, but some of them might have worked on their own farms during the rest of the year. People might think that prevailing wage meant something like median wage, but it often means the union wage. Are data, even those published by governments, accurate? If accurate, do they really tell us anything meaningful? No wonder T. S. Eliot wrote in *The Rock*:

Where is the Life we have lost in living?
Where is the wisdom we have lost in knowledge?
Where is the knowledge we have lost in information?

To this it seems pertinent to add:

Where is the information we have lost in data?

There is much reason to be wary about both the validity and interpretation of data. Some data, for instance, those in the International Critical Tables, tell who made the physical measurements cited. A concerned user can go back to the scientific literature to decide whether the data should be trusted or can even repeat the experiments and calculations to verify the numbers given. This is an ideal of verifiability that should be aimed at. However, many other data come from unknown sources or in a form in which it is impossible to investigate their validity. These data lose some credibility because of the obscurity of their origins.

People want to obtain proper and accurate information in the right amount—not too much, not too little. They may wish either to obtain comprehensive, informative summaries, some of which might almost be called knowledge, or to acquire selectively detailed information, some of which might be original data. Increasing use is being made of data bases to meet such demands. Some data bases, notably bibliographic retrieval services, selectively provide information summaries, such as titles and abstracts of current scientific papers as well as of back numbers, in response to users requests. Some other data bases provide business people, scientists, and engineers with various indicators and original data in numerical form. Still other data bases, typically videotex, provide ordinary people with information to serve day-to-day needs. Data for these services must be collected, collated, compiled, and processed in a timely way and with care to assure its authenticity and validity. As pointed out in Section 6-8, in connection with protection of privacy, all data should be provided with source quotations, audit trails, and the identities of persons who control the files.

Usefulness of data base services depends not only on the quality but also on the quantity of information that can be provided to users at a reasonable cost. In particular, videotex and similar services, which are aimed at nonspecialists, require the participation of a wide range of information providers, including news agencies, publishers, libraries, advertisers, and travel agencies and their sustained efforts in creating, expanding, and updating their data bases.

Information providers do not know what kind of information their users really want to receive and how much their users or clients are willing to pay. Pilot experiments have been found useful in stimulating and estimating the interest of information providers as well as users. Experiments show that current information providers cannot afford to provide as much information as users need, and therefore users are reluctant to pay any significant amount of money for such services. Not only

Some Canadian residents can receive text and graphics on an ordinary television receiver equipped with a decoder. Here, a Manitoba resident uses the Telidon teletext to check the local weather forecast. This Telidon is connected to a fibre optics field trial network. User surveys indicate a preference for interactive services, as contrasted to viewing of extra entertainment programs. (Photo courtesy of Elie-St. Eustache Trial)

news and other real-time reports, but also games, puzzles, and quiz programs quickly become obsolete; so information providers have to continually produce new programs even before their investments have been paid off. It appears that information services for the general public can succeed only by operating on very large scales.

For information to reach users with the right content in the right form at the right time, information vendors should work closely with information providers to ensure adequate distribution channels to consumers. This includes unobstructed access to major data bases and the use of unified or compatible data base access commands.

Communities of interest and nongovernmental organizations should initiate, continue, and expand their efforts in collecting, abstracting,

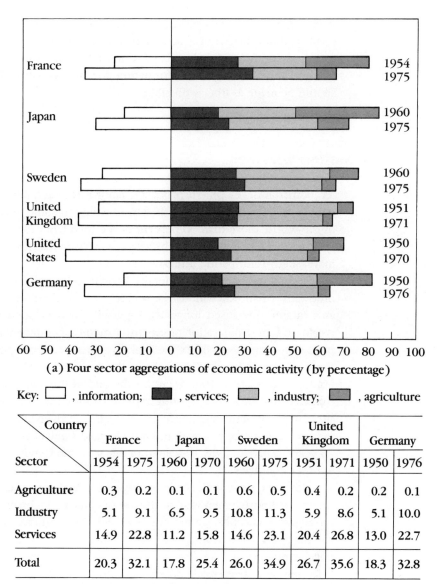

(a) Four sector aggregations of economic activity (by percentage)

Key: ☐ , information; ■ , services; ☐ , industry; ▨ , agriculture

Country Sector	France		Japan		Sweden		United Kingdom		Germany	
	1954	1975	1960	1970	1960	1975	1951	1971	1950	1976
Agriculture	0.3	0.2	0.1	0.1	0.6	0.5	0.4	0.2	0.2	0.1
Industry	5.1	9.1	6.5	9.5	10.8	11.3	5.9	8.6	5.1	10.0
Services	14.9	22.8	11.2	15.8	14.6	23.1	20.4	26.8	13.0	22.7
Total	20.3	32.1	17.8	25.4	26.0	34.9	26.7	35.6	18.3	32.8

(b) Information occupations by sector of origin (by percentage)

Figure 7-5 (a) In the time spans shown, the economic activity of these countries has shifted from manufacturing and agriculture to services, and activity related to information has increased in agriculture and industry as well as in services. (b) The table shows the role played by information in each of these areas. (SOURCE: *Electronics and Telecommunications Technologies: Impact on Employment, Growth and Trade,* Vol. I, OECD, ICCP Series No. 6, Paris, 1981)

indexing, entering, and updating specific information in machine-readable form. Without their efforts, no meaningful data bases to serve their interests could be formed and updated. Considering that these communities of interest span the world, information flow across national boundaries should be made as free as possible.

7-5 Information Services

As industrial development proceeds, labor forces are shifted from agriculture to manufacturing and then to services. In some developed parts of the world, more than 60 percent of the total labor force is in service industries. And, as we have observed, service industries are becoming increasingly information intensive.

Service industries are generally known to be more costly and less productive than other industrial sectors. Let us take medical service as an example. Increased longevity, especially in developed parts of the world, and the proliferation of expensive medical equipment are resulting in an ever-increasing cost of medical care. In some developed countries, the cost now exceeds 5 percent of the gross national product and is predicted to exceed 10 percent by the end of the century. It has been reported that in France, despite rapidly rising costs, productivity, measured in terms of the number of patients who are given medical treatment per medical doctor per year, has not changed significantly over the past 20 years. If productivity is defined in this way, the trends may be similar in other countries.

However, if we look at the quality of medical care, there has been a significant improvement due to the use of clinical biochemical analyzers, cardiograms, encephalograms, computer-aided tomograms, artificial hearts and lungs for use during operations, and many other technologies. Diagnosis is quicker and more accurate. Sophisticated operations and other treatment have been made possible. As a result, many patients have been cured who would otherwise have died.

Some may argue that the rising cost of medical care is due chiefly to the fact that some medical doctors prescribe too much medicine and make excessive and unnecessary use of expensive medical equipment and procedures, and some patients make excessive and unjustifiable use of the medical care system. However, doctors are supposed to follow the

Information technology and medicine: A computer is used to process information in an x-ray tomography device. Computers are used to store, retrieve, and send information as well as to sort and analyze symptoms. (Photo courtesy of Philips)

Hippocratic code of ethics, with a duty to preserve life, and there is no substantial evidence that the majority of medical doctors and their patients are ethically corrupt.

Most of the extra money spent on medical care does go toward improvements in quality. Yet it is very difficult to evaluate the skills of experienced and inexperienced doctors in diagnosing and treating patients with sophisticated medical equipment. Thus, no appropriate indicator has been found to accurately reflect improvement in the quality of medical care, which, to a large extent, has been brought about by information technology.

In banking services, it has been said that no significant reduction in the number of employees has been observed as a result of the introduction of on-line banking systems. However, these systems have made it possible for customers to deposit or withdraw money at any branch of a bank. Further, the financial operations of the bank have been made more efficient through knowing liabilities and assets on a real-time basis. Again, no appropriate indicator reflecting such benefits is yet known.

As information technologies have been introduced into service industries, new services have been made possible, services that had been absolutely impossible before. These new services often absorb employees who are displaced as a result of improvements in productivity in existing services. Such mechanisms are not well understood, despite the facts that service industries have already become the largest industrial sector in many countries, that productivity of and employment in service industries are at stake, and that information technologies are playing an increasingly indispensable role in these industries.

The computerized information industry itself is on the brink of turning from a capital-intensive manufacturing industry to a labor-intensive service industry. Hardware costs for information systems are decreasing drastically because of progress in microelectronics technology. Software costs, on the other hand, are increasing steeply because of diversification and sophistication in hardware use and rising wages. No efficient way of automatically producing and testing software is yet known. If these trends continue, software cost may exceed 90 percent of the total cost of an information system before the end of the century.

The computerized information industry is an unprecedented type of industry because it was born a highly capital-intensive industry and will mature into a labor-intensive industry though the labor required is knowledge intensive. This may present an interesting subject of study for economists. However, nothing has yet been written on the evolutionary mechanism of the information industry.

Labor intensiveness presents many problems. Some of these are labor issues, which will be described in the next section. Another problem is the evaluation of software products. As software cost is becoming the major cost of information systems, the evaluation of software and its costs will become as significant for producers as for users. Can we evaluate a software product by simply counting the number of program steps? Definitely not, because inexperienced programmers write software with more steps than experienced programmers do. If software is paid for in terms of program steps, software houses may employ inexperienced programmers in order to reduce wages and to increase income. In general, clever programmers will make more money as owners or part-owners of small software houses than they will as employees of large organizations. Yet,

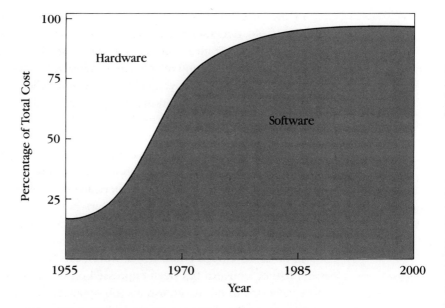

Figure 7-6   Computer users' costs, known and anticipated, 1955–2000.
(SOURCE: Worldwide Semiconductor Industry, 1977)

as in the case of medical doctors, evaluation of the skills of experienced
and inexperienced programmers is very difficult.

Simple services provided by doormen and porters can be rightly
rewarded by paying tips. Sophisticated services provided by information-
oriented professionals are too complicated and expensive to allow any
simple and just system of payment.

7-6   Labor Issues

Copyists in the fifteenth century might have looked at Gutenberg's printed
books with dismay and thought that their jobs were disappearing. Manual
workers in the early nineteenth century destroyed many power looms
and spinning machines, outraged to think that the machines were taking
their jobs. Nevertheless, technological innovations have provided opportunities for civilization to flourish and have stimulated economic growth
that reduced or eliminated unemployment.

In the past, whenever changes in industrial structure took place, workers in old, declining industries lost their jobs, and newly emerging industries suffered from a shortage of workers. Workers in old industries either reacted violently and rejected new industries in vain, or they seized upon the job opportunities provided by new industries.

The present change in industrial structure, which has been brought about to a large extent by information technology, is no exception. Concerns have been expressed in some developed countries about the adverse effect of microelectronics on employment. This is based partly upon the significant number of the skilled labor force having been displaced by automatic weaving machines and numerically controlled machine tools. It is said that not only blue-collar workers but also a large number of general office workers may lose their jobs as a result of the extensive use of word processors and other office automation equipment.

In other developed countries, however, this has never been a major issue. Rather, concern has been expressed on the availability of a labor force sufficient to fill the enormous job opportunities for software production. Some developing countries, where wages are relatively low and job opportunities are inadequate for educated people, are now becoming aware of the prospects of the software market.

At this time, views are split among countries, reflecting their societal and industrial backgrounds. In a society where trade unions are rigidly organized by craft, where workers are hesitant about changes in traditional jobs, and where no adequate retraining facilities are provided, a shift of the displaced labor force to the new job opportunities may not be easy. In particular, when the majority of workers to be displaced are aged or at a low educational level, adaptation to new jobs may be difficult. In a society where the necessity of software production is not well understood and where software industries are in an early state, the creation of new jobs may not be sufficient to accommodate the displaced labor force. In other societies, where trade unions are flexibly organized, where workers are interested in new jobs, where on-the-job training is extensive, and where software-related industries flourish, a shift of the displaced labor force may be easier.

Whatever view one takes, changes in the workplace seem to be inevitable. Because of the remarkable progress in microelectronics technology, significant changes are occurring in industrial products, business machines, and consumer products. Mechanical components are being rapidly replaced by electronic integrated components, as in digital watches.

Analog systems are quickly replaced by digital systems, as in process control and instrumentation. Special-purpose machines are being replaced by general-purpose machines, as in numerically controlled machine tools. What is commonly observed is the need for an enormous amount of software due to the increasing use of computers and, in particular, rapid proliferation and penetration of microprocessors into diversified areas of industrial, business, and societal activities.

As a result, the knowledge and skills required for engineers and technicians in manufacture and for dealers and users are shifting from analog to digital and from hardware to software. Software houses and systems houses are emerging quickly to meet the demand for sophisticated application programs and systems engineering in diversified areas of applications. In manufacture, assembly is becoming less significant compared to the fabrication of integrated electronic components. Users in industries are no longer manipulating simple tools but are programming and monitoring complex machines. Mass-distribution channels are emerging in the area of watches and cameras and are making the craft of watch repair by retailers into a dying art.

The above trends have positive as well as negative impacts on employment. Demands in manufacture for engineers and technicians specialized in digital and software technology are increasing rapidly; they are needed to strengthen research, development, design, production, and testing of microprocessors and microprocessor-applied products. Software houses and systems houses, as well as distributors and users, are recruiting a large number of software engineers and technicians for systems engineering, development, production, and the testing of application programs.

On the other hand, the fact that some microelectronics-applied products are pushing conventional products out of the market and are causing drastic change in distribution channels indicates a considerable reduction in employment in these sectors. Automation and labor saving in manufacturing brought about by the use of computers may have the most aggravating impact on employment. Automation in the distribution and business sectors may also have significant impact on employment.

Those who have undertaken the painstaking work of writing software, and those who rightly understand the implications of the rapid proliferation of computers in diversifying areas of application, may intuitively feel that new job opportunities for software production outweigh the opportunities that are closed off as old jobs are lost. In fact, some estimates

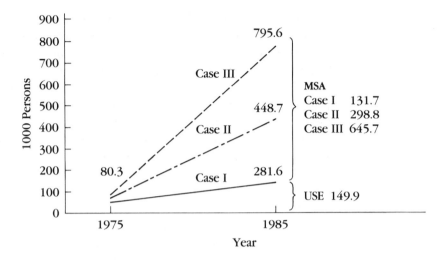

Figure 7-7 A Japanese study forecasts an increase of software engineers in Japan for the period 1975–1985 to be between 201,000 and 715,000. Annual growth rate of users' software engineers (USE) is estimated to be 12 percent, whereas annual growth rate of manufacturers' software engineers (MSE) is estimated to be 35 percent (Case I), 25 percent (Case II) or 15 percent (Case III). Even by the lowest growth estimate, a significant shortage of software engineers seems to be inevitable. (SOURCE: *Microelectronics, Productivity and Employment,* OECD, ICCP Series No. 5, Paris, 1981.)

and speculations supporting such a conclusion are given elsewhere; yet no one can predict the exact figures. What is clear at this moment is that extensive education and training should be provided for the younger generation to undertake software development and production and that sufficient continuing education and retraining should be provided for existing engineers and technicians so that a smooth shift from old jobs to new jobs can be made.

The continuing education and retraining that are crucial for a smooth shift of the labor force may sometimes be beyond a private company's capability. This education should be done with public support, where necessary, through the mobilization of universities, colleges, and vocational schools, as described in Section 6-7.

Retraining older workers is not an easy task, yet it is an inevitable task because of increased longevity and changing demography. One encouraging factor is the enormous popularity of microcomputers.

Microcomputer shows always draw huge crowds of all ages. The concept, current since the Industrial Revolution, that high technology is difficult and boring to learn seems to be under revision. By supplying microcomputers to society, high technology may finally attract the interest of a great many hobbyists.

The potential for women in the work force also deserves attention. As it seems quite probable that automation in production will displace a considerable number of unskilled workers, their retraining is of prime importance. At the same time, women with higher education should be encouraged to take part to alleviate the shortage of software workers. Because software can be developed and produced away from an office and on a part-time basis, homemakers should be encouraged to freelance through the use of mail service and home terminals.

Production of the enormous amount of software that is envisaged will be possible only through an international division of labor. In particular, application programs should be produced locally to meet end users' needs. Developing countries, especially those that have a well-developed higher-education system, should be encouraged to participate in software development and production.

It should be noted that software workers are skilled specialists (known as white-collar workers) and that the present society has never had any experience in accomodating a very large number of skilled specialists. Can a software worker in an on-line banking center perform well as a branch manager of that bank if he is promoted? Probably not. A university graduate employed by a bank may not want to work on software even if he or she is interested in it. Computer users should reconsider their organizational structures so as to assure the status of their software workers.

It should also be noted that automation may transfer a worker from manipulating simple machines to merely monitoring complex machines. The worker may be bored, if everything is normal, or frustrated and confused if something goes wrong, because the malfunctioning machines may prove too complex to control properly. He or she may lose the feeling of accomplishment and become unhappy in dealing with these new, not-too-friendly machines. It seems that there should be a conservation law for the feeling of accomplishment so that there would be other new things for the worker to do that would be at least as rewarding as the old activities. Computer-aided crafts manufacture, in which each individual can communicate interactively with a computer in realizing his or her creativity, may be a future solution.

Minerva was born from the head of Jupiter, fully armed and with a

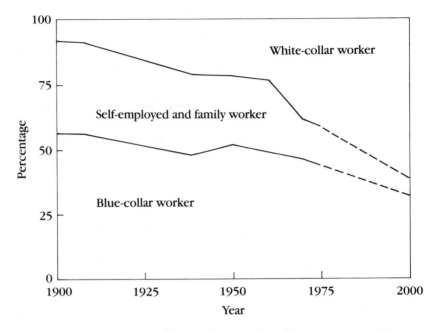

Figure 7-8   The trend toward the white-collar worker in Germany in the twentieth century, actual and anticipated. (SOURCE: *Microelectronics, Productivity and Employment*, OECD, ICCP Series No. 5, Paris, 1981)

tremendous battle cry. However, she turned out to be a goddess of wisdom and the patroness of the arts and trades. Werewolf, a medieval aristocrat, could turn himself into a man-eating wolf with a bulletproof skin. Is a micropocessor a Minerva or a Werewolf? It is up to us whether we make it a guardian of the arts and trades or turn it into a devourer of civilization.

7-7   Home Life

During the past quarter of a century, the time and effort required for such housekeeping chores as cooking, cleaning, washing, heating, and bookkeeping have been greatly reduced by the use of such appliances as refrigerators, cooking ranges, vacuum cleaners, washing machines, air conditioners, and electronic calculators. Each home in the developed part of the world is now served by a Shakespearean Mistress Quickly who says, "I wash, wring, brew, bake, scour, dress meat and drink, make the beds, and do all myself." Basic needs for efficient housekeeping seem to have been nearly filled, although manufacturers try to promote sales by introducing microprocessors into these appliances.

In view of the rising cost of energy and an increasing concern for security, however, information technology still has an important role to play in the home. In fact, microcomputerized security systems are rapidly appearing on the market, and private guard firms are now providing on-line security services. Centralized and adaptive surveillance and control of lighting, air conditioning, and other utilities may contribute considerably to energy saving. If an adaptive-pricing mechanism is introduced for peak and off-peak hours of utility consumption, computerized control of utilities will bring significant benefits to both suppliers and consumers.

Security information relating to smoke, fire, unlocked doors, intruders, appliance failures, gas or water leaks, and the like, can be gathered and processed quickly by sensors and microprocessors. The system can then be used to sound alarms or send messages to a center for emergency assistance. In view of the fact that more and more houses are left unattended during work hours, a remote surveillance and control capability can contribute significantly to security. Such systems will also be helpful in the case of an earthquake or other natural disaster by providing early warnings and guidance as well as shutting off utilities to minimize further hazard.

To reduce the fatigue in commuting to and from offices and plants, and to reduce the expense of transportation systems, a new work pattern, known as "work away from the office," is being tried out. It has been a common practice for scientists to work at home by using time-sharing system terminals. Some people also now have their own personalized computers so that they can work at home.

A high-technology home plant is also emerging in which an engineer working at home can program and run highly sophisticated, numerically controlled machine tools for producing small components with high values added. Homemakers who have programming skills are now producing software on a part-time basis, and some of them are using on-line terminals in their homes for this work.

Work away from the office is more easily arranged in situations where the work can be performed individually and relatively independently of the work of others, where physical transportation of bulk material and products is not required, and where the investment at home is not too high. In this context, and in view of the fact that information-oriented service industries are gaining significant shares in the developed countries' economy, software development and production is one of the most exciting prospects for work away from the office. We see on-line terminals playing the major role, supported by stand-alone systems in a mixture to be determined by costs, capabilities, and needs. The dispersal of work is encouraged by information technology, whether it is to individual homes, branch offices, or plants in neighborhood communities. The amount of dispersal must be determined case by case to share capital costs and maximize efficiency.

Videotex and other services will soon introduce electronic shopping into the home. The pattern of shopping may be divided into two types, in accordance with the characteristics of merchandise. Routine shopping for standard items such as some foods, utensils, and other daily necessities as well as certain appliances, is done mainly at nearby supermarkets and convenience stores or by mail- or telephone-order services. Shopping for these items is generally a task. Shopping for commodities such as fashionable apparel, jewelry, furniture, and other quality goods is done at department stores or specialty stores. Shopping for these items is generally a pleasure. Consumers want to do the former type of shopping as efficiently as possible, avoiding time and effort to the greatest possible extent. This is the area in which electronic shopping can be introduced with greatest benefit.

Inventory-control computers with a large number of point-of-sales (POS) terminals have been extensively used by large-scale retailers and are now being more widely linked directly to wholesale dealers and warehouses as well as to credit centers and banks. These on-line connections will be further extended to homes and delivery centers. The consumers at home will be able to select merchandise by watching television screens that display sales catalogs and advertisements. The consumers then use keyboards to send orders for the merchandise to an electronic shopping center. The shopping center asks credit centers and banks to verify credit and transfer funds and at the same time sends instructions to the appropriate warehouses or delivery centers concerning shipment and delivery of the merchandise to the customers. In some cases, an electronic shopping center may ask customers to pick up merchandise at a community pickup center. The success of electronic shopping will depend largely on the variety and quality of merchandise, the time and effort required for physical delivery, and the cost of home terminals.

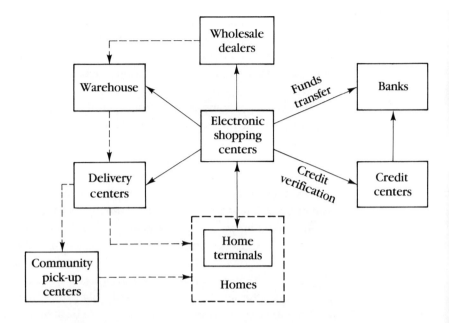

Key: Information flow ─ ─ ─ ─
      merchandise flow ─────

Figure 7-9 Flow chart for electronic shopping

As a result of the extensive use of some appliances and reduced work hours, people at home now have more time for learning, health care, and entertainment. In the future, computerized learning systems will be used by students to complement school education and by citizens of all ages to refresh and extend their knowledge. Hardware for home learning may either be stand-alone systems or on-line terminals. In the case of stand-alone systems, videotapes or video disks that contain teaching programs, dictionaries, and other teaching materials can be purchased or leased from distributors. In the case of on-line terminals, sophisticated interactive learning programs will be implemented in central computers that permit simultaneous access from a number of terminals.

Health care systems for home use will also be stand-alone systems or on-line terminals. Stand-alone systems will monitor temperature, blood pressure, pulse rate, and other vital signs and enhance mechanical aids for the aged and physically disabled. On-line terminals will be able to send cardiograms and other information for centralized monitoring, provide instruction from doctors, and allow access to emergency medical centers.

Hardware for home entertainment will be very diverse. Videotapes and video disks, which are already used for viewing movies and television programs, will also provide sophisticated programs for video games. Interactive use of video disks will follow, and highly sophisticated stand-alone systems that include audio and visual synthesizers will appear on the market. The capability of on-line terminals that already provide videotex-type information will be enhanced by linking them to broad-band cables and by including microprocessors and video disks. Videotex and cable television services will strengthen local communities of interest by providing information for daily life. Some of these communities are of a civic nature and others are of a commercial nature.

To meet the needs of terminals with high resolution and powerful local capabilities, central systems will have to be able to switch between a large number of broad-band cables and to input, store, retrieve, and update very large amounts of information in various forms. In addition to this, software development will be a crucial factor for learning, health care, and entertainment at home.

7-8 Concluding Remarks

In this chapter, we have described some of the significant benefits and problems that have been and will be accompanied by progress in information technology.

Perhaps the most significant of the benefits is the rapid growth of many diverse communities of interest. These range from very small ones that serve very narrow scientific or cultural interests to the very large ones such as today's nongovernmental organizations. Members of these communities of interest understand the problems within their specific range of interest better than anyone else and therefore can find solutions better than anyone else. Communities of interest form an enormous number of invisible nets that span the world, and each individual belongs to several of these nets.

Through overlapping memberships in a variety of communities of interest, a valuable, indeed, an essential network of interconnection has come into being. These invisible nets are networks of mutual interest, understanding, and problem-solving ability. They have solved and will be able to solve a host of problems so numerous and diverse that governments and intergovernmental organizations could not begin to address them all.

Sometimes, communities of interest of a propagandist nature grow up, interested, not in gathering data and learning from it, but in fabricating data to support their programs. This is an old phenomenon in human society. We can only hope that a growing familiarity with the importance of integrity of data (see Section 7-4) will expose or mitigate against the acceptance of fabrication or misinterpretation of data for propagandist purposes. It is our belief that sound and honest communities of interest will outweigh purely propagandist groups.

To solve problems of the sorts we have discussed, information technologies should be fostered as much as possible to promote the growth of communities of interest. Among other things, data bases that provide selective dissemination of information as well as retrospective search will be a powerful tool for strengthening communities of interest. The communities of interest should be encouraged and supported to participate in the formation of a great variety of data bases that require their specific knowledge.

Governments should not interfere in any way with the growth of communities of interest across national boundaries, for the strengthening of communities of interest not only helps citizens of all countries by aiding in the solution of particular problems but, more importantly, works toward greater world stability by allowing people to identify and solve common problems across national boundaries. Thus, the strengthening of these linking communities of interest allows for a gradual and constructive reorganization of world communities based on cooperation and mutual help. These positive and integrative forces engender world stability based at a deeper level than diplomatic bargaining or a mere balance of military forces. Given the perilous situation of the world today, we feel that world stability should be a foremost concern of every government, and for this reason, all governments should join in promoting communities of interest.

Data bases can provide, for the first time in human history, a way of quickly and accurately selecting specific information that people need. This technology will allow people in information-rich regions to select the information they need from the flood of facts loosed on them by today's information explosion. People in information-poor regions will have access to the information they need through communication networks. To establish a data base to serve many needs for everyone, a great deal of information in various forms has to be collected, entered in machine-readable form, collated, coded for retrieval, and updated. Information providers, information vendors, and common carriers should be organized and encouraged to promote the formation and operation of data base services. When information is collected and processed, due attention should be given to its authenticity and validity. Governments should not prevent people from having access to data bases across national boundaries. Rather, they should support the growth of data bases in their own countries and free access to all public data bases.

As the service industries grow and become increasingly information oriented, proper emphasis needs to be placed on the implications of information technologies for service industries and, particularly, for the quality of service. Better tools are needed in this area to aid our understanding and our ability to evaluate quality. The computerized-information industry itself is turning from a capital-intensive manufacturing industry to a labor-intensive service industry because of the drastic reduction of hardware cost and the rapid increase both in the need for software and, in software cost. The future of the information industry is almost solely dependent on the progress of software technology and, in particular, the improvement of productivity in software production, and the reasonable evaluation of software products.

For the information industry to flourish and to support various industrial, economic, and cultural activities, the enormous job opportunities that are being created in the area of software development and production must be filled by competent engineers and technicians. During a transition period, while information technologies allow and encourage automation in industry and business, a considerable number of workers may be displaced. Continuing education and retraining should be provided during this period in order to shift displaced workers to the newly created jobs. There should also be a strengthening of education and training for younger generations in order to fill needs. Women at home should be encouraged to participate in software production. An international division of labor for software production should be promoted to fill needs, to share new jobs among the peoples of the world, and to produce application programs better fitted to end users' needs.

Work that can be done without much interaction with others, such as software development and production, may be done at home in order to avoid time and fatigue of commuting to and from offices and to enable housewives or househusbands to work on a part-time basis. Home information systems for security and energy conservation can bring considerable benefits to households. A large variety of sophisticated programs must be developed and an enormous amount of information must be collected to provide such conveniences as shopping, learning, and entertainment at home.

References

Directory of Online Databases, Vol. 4, No. 3, Cuadra Associates, Inc., Santa Monica CA, 1983.

Information Activities, Electronic and Telecommunications Technologies: Impact on Employment, Growth and Trade, Vol. I. OECD, ICCP Series No. 6, Paris, 1981.

H. Inose. "Information and the Household." *Microprocessing and Microprogramming* 7 (1981):211–219.

Microelectronics, Productivity and Employment. OECD, ICCP Series No. 5, Paris, 1981.

J. R. Pierce. "Communication." *Scientific American* 227, 3 (September 1972):31–41.

Georges Rosch. *Economique Médicale, un Système de Services Collectifs.* Flammarion Médecine-Sciences, Paris, 1978.

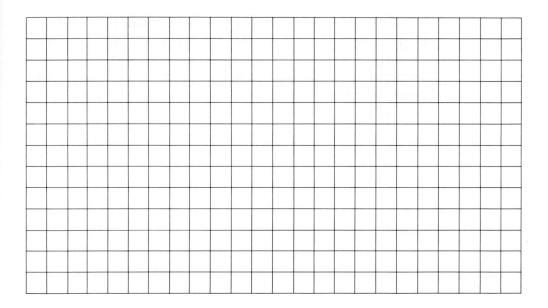

8-1 Introduction
8-2 The State of the Art
8-3 Toward an Evaluation
8-4 Responsibility
8-5 The Role of the Government
8-6 Concluding Remarks

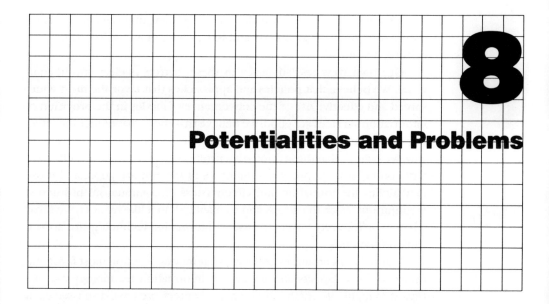

Potentialities and Problems

8-1 Introduction

This book is concerned with information technology and civilization, particularly with three interwoven aspects of information technology and civilization, which we will restate here.

Through the convergence of modes, parts of information technology that were once diverse in nature and use are coming together in one common digital technology for the processing, transmission, storage, and retrieval of information. Pictures and graphs, sounds, and data can be intermingled and used together in communication, in transactions, and in all aspects of our culture.

In our increasingly complex and diverse society, knowledge and its advancement reside in communities of interest made up of those who are active and informed in various fields of endeavor. Increasingly, the speed, the reduction in cost, and the increase in power of information technology, brought about through the convergence of modes, encourage the formation of communities of interest that span many countries. Fast and economical air travel works together with the convergence of modes in fostering widespread communities of interest. Such communities of interest can advance knowledge and reveal—and perhaps overcome—cultural biases.

We have also emphasized the impact of new, powerful, and unified information technology on arts and letters, old, new, and yet to be—on culture, if you will.

Our own view and advocacy in these matters is clear and unequivocal. We believe that policies and approaches that favor the most widespread and effective use of the convergence of modes in the provision of information services are good; we believe that those that hinder the effective exploitation of the convergence of modes are undesirable. In a similar way, we believe that those things that promote the formation and effective functioning of widespread communities of interest are good, and those that hinder the formation and effectiveness of communities of interest are injurious, both to nations and to mankind. In a like manner, we favor whatever effectively fosters the use of information technology for artistic and cultural ends.

Our only uncertainties concern what modes of action most favor and promote those aspects and impacts of information technology that we regard as highly desirable. In previous chapters, we have discussed such matters in detail. In this chapter, we will summarize much of what we have already said.

Before turning to such a summary, we wish to point out once again that there is far more to our lives than information technology and what it can directly provide. A society cannot live by words alone. People demand goods that make our easy, diverse, and mobile way of life possible. They demand good food, good clothing, good shelter, and good medical attention. They demand that police protect them from criminals and that armies protect them from hostile states. Whether or not these and other things that people demand are either good in themselves or good for the people is beside the point. A nation that does not meet the reasonable demands of its people will be judged as backward; it will lose in status and influence, and it may well disappear. Though information technology has become essential in providing the goods of life, it is not enough in itself. Goods can be produced effectively only through high intelligence and hard work.

However, not all nations need to produce all goods. Through both information technology and advanced means of transportation, our world has become a world of interdependence and trade. Nations with great mineral or agricultural resources will continue to produce and export minerals or foods. Nations with fewer resources will do well if they can produce some high-technology products that have high values added. This has an additional merit in that high-technology production has few adverse effects on the environment. Many high-technology products are associated with information technology. Integrated-circuit design and the production of software are ideal for nations and people who have few resources beyond their intelligence and enterprise. Software production, especially application programs, has proved to be an ideal (though still small-scale) industry in a number of countries which are not ordinarily counted among leaders in technology. Moreover, the fostering of these important technologies will help a growing nation to manage its own affairs.

8-2   The State of the Art

It is not difficult to recognize the importance of information and information technology in our lives. We are all familiar with the personal communication of writing letters and with the postal system. The telephone call, like the letter, puts us in touch with anyone in the world whom we want to reach, instantly and surprisingly cheaply. We are all familiar with books, which are quite different, and with newspapers, which are different still, and which were once all of mass media. Most of us are familiar with the mass medium of radio and that newer mass medium, television, and many of us are avid watchers. How much we retain of what we see and hear on television is difficult to determine, but we can certainly estimate the amount of time we spend staring at the screen.

While computers can store and transmit information, we usually think of them as operating on data to get some sort of answer or result. Most of us have used hand calculators, and a surprising number are acquiring recreational computers or at least digital games of some sort. Today, computers are merging with other areas of information and application. Computerized robots are drastically improving productivity and relieving workers from adverse working environments. Word processors are creeping into offices and even into homes, which are increasingly being protected by electronic burglar alarms, many of which can call the police. Microprocessors now control television sets, microwave ovens, and a host of gadgets. Information technology is before the eyes of all, and much more serves us but is hidden from our eyes.

In thinking about the use and impact of information technology, we should try to be well informed. We should neither underestimate nor overestimate the state of the art. Large computers cost fantastic amounts, operate at fantastic speeds, and solve fantastic problems, but they do not solve all problems. Computers can be used to teach well, but the cost has been too high for most instruction. Yet, recreational computers and computer games teach a great deal under the guise of play. While computers can recognize and respond to a limited set of words or phrases, the voice typewriter seems very far away. Computers can translate deliberately simple text with less than 100 percent accuracy. While the dictionary look-up and word-processing aspects of translation are highly effective, full and unedited machine translation of text seems very far away. Computers can act as "experts," but only in narrow and special fields, such as mathematical manipulation or knowing the items and proper interconnection of a computer company's catalog. An on-board computer saw the Viking orbiter through an extended mission with only occasional help from the ground. It was a real robot, and perhaps the first, but its sterling qualities were accuracy and reliability, not intelligence. It was inconceivably stupid and limited compared with a five-year-old, but its attention span was far greater. Computers have been made to write queer poems and undistinguished music, but their chief contribution to music, and to other arts, appears to be as tools in the hands of artists.

Indeed, perhaps the best way to avoid either underestimating or overestimating the power of computers is to think of them always as tools and to ask who has used them effectively and what useful things have really been accomplished. We should ask the same question concerning all of electronic communication and information services: What useful things have been accomplished?

We have noted that while we may think of this as the age of information, more than information alone is necessary for civilized life. The food we eat, the cars we drive, the airplanes we travel in, the showers, heating systems, and air conditioners in our homes, are clearly a part of our civilization. Information technologies are important in their production and use, but in their purpose and function, they are not a part of information technology.

8-3   Toward an Evaluation

The part of our civilization in which our growing information technology is inextricably entwined is growing, and it is to this part that our consideration has been addressed. In a short space, we have tried to describe the potentialities and problems of these areas of life in an orderly way. In a book, such order must have a linear form; one goes from one chapter to the next. But the interrelations of information technology and civilization are more complex than any linear stringing together. Similar considerations occur many times in somewhat different contexts. This has made the writing of this book difficult. It makes any attempt at summary or recommendation more difficult still.

Yet the reader has a right to ask what the authors think after considering the various matters touched on, and what, if anything, they recommend. Further, among all of the things the authors mentioned or treated, are some seen as matters of greater urgency or concern than others? To help answer this question, we have provided a sort of checklist of observations and questions, a list of some things (surely not all, in this world of imperfect knowledge and judgment) that we recommend to the reader's further study and consideration. This list has a certain amount of necessary duplication.

Beyond any such list, and beyond any deferring to the judgments of others, the observations we have made concerning the importance of the convergence of modes, the importance of communities of interest, and the impact of information technology on culture seem to us to be crucial in understanding the present and working toward the future.

Through the ages, our technological world has grown increasingly complicated and diverse. This has been true of information technology. Printing served or created a need for books and periodicals. The telegraph served the written word. So did the postal system. Radio, the phonograph, and other recording means served the spoken word and music. Television serves chiefly the eye and the ear, although some text and charts do appear on television screens. In our age, digital technology and the computer are bringing the whole world of information together once again. Information technology may grow more and more complicated, but, through the convergence of modes, it is no longer divided into separable technological areas. The same means of transmission, processing, and storage that serve text also serve the ear and the eye. We see this graphically in television games in which the player uses a keyboard or another device to interact with a color display on a screen. We see it in speak-and-spell toys, which unite spoken words with the spelling of words.

Because of the capability of today's digital technology in handling all modes of information, information technology no longer presses civilization in a particular direction, as printing and writing, the postal service,

CHECKLIST

Computers and Control

Large-scale integration

Supercomputers

Data bases

The ubiquitous microprocessor (automated production, distributed processing, office automation, home computers, games, learning)

Software engineering and copyright protection

Communication Technology

The unique and very different capabilities of satellites and optical fibers

Integration through digital transmission, switching, and storage

Mobile communication in an era of computers and satellites

Line switching versus packet switching

Communication protocols

Facsimile and teletext

New media for mass communications

Information Authentication and Security

Citation of source

Control and tracing of data entries and changes

Checking through communities of interest

Reliability and security technology

Information Processing

Data base management

Distributed processing

Array processing

Text editing

Composition and reproduction

Information Distribution

Mass media (press, radio, television, books)

Communities of interest (books, journals, data bases)

Person to person (mail, telephone, facsimile, electronic mail)

Convergence of service modes (sight, sound, data transmission, switching, storage, processing)

Information Retrieval

Books and libraries

Catalogs, Yellow Pages

Data banks (commercial systems, professional systems, technical and scientific systems)

Videotex and teletext

Design

Graphics

Analysis

Computer-aided design (CAD) and computer-aided manufacturing (CAM)

Information-Oriented Infrastructure

Communication

Medical care

Transportation

Energy

Education

Administration

Finance

Industry

Information-oriented products

Productivity improvement of agriculture and conventional industries

Computerized robots

Software production

Language and Letters

Preservation of languages and dialects

(continued)

Checklist *continued*

Language translation (computer aids, full translations from restricted sources)

Computers and instruction (teaching programs, the computer as a toy for experimental learning)

Recognition of written and spoken language (character recognition, speech recognition, keyboards and nonalphabetic languages)

Information and the Arts

Recording and conservation

Analysis and critical study

Synthesis of text, music, form

The computer as a tool in producing musical sounds, designs, pictures, and sculpture

Interactive, integrated art

Standardization

Through adoption of good practices

Through consensus of producers and users

Through national and international associations

Through governmental action

Through intergovernmental bodies

and the telegraph pressed it toward the written word or as the telephone, the phonograph, and the radio pressed it toward the spoken word. An improved and universal technology gives us a great deal of freedom to go where we will. We can call by telephone, write a letter, or use a word processor together with various means of reproduction to publish a pamphlet that rivals letterpress in quality. A new sort of freedom goes with the unity of digital information processing.

The unity of information technology goes far deeper than surface manifestations. Those who work in information technology understand this is a fact of life, but government regulators have difficulty coping with it. In questions of regulated services versus competition, regulators do not always propose, like Solomon, to give half of the child to each contending party. Rather, they may propose to divide the child into many

Governmental Functions

Standardization

Regulation and antitrust

Promotion of cooperative effort

Freedom of information

Protection of privacy

Supplying of infrastructure

Supporting research

Supporting scientific and cultural data bases

Promoting societal acceptance of change

Smoothing international cooperation

Services to People

Problems of reliance on mass media—the information explosion

Accessibility and authenticity of information

Evaluation of information services and software

Communities of interest as sources of information and judgment

Labor issues (Obstacles to change, retraining)

Home life (work at home, security devices, electronic shopping, home computers)

parts, with the idea that its identity and overall function will be best served by competition among limbs. That a divided child may not live or function is a consideration foreign to this philosophy.

It seems reasonable that a single entity can in principle provide a national service at lower cost than competing services. Postal service is an example. If competition were allowed, those in small and remote communities would pay very high rates or get no service, and the total cost of service would be higher, though charges would be "fairer." Further, both analyses and evidence indicate that the overall cost of a single service can be less than that of a divided service.

But will a single entity provide, and continue to provide, good, up-to-date communication service cheaply? Not if it is hampered in using its background and resources—and, perhaps, not without competition. But competition is no stimulus unless all those who provide a service can afford to compete.

Perhaps cooperation is better than either competition or monopoly and regulation. It seems most reasonable that news-gathering organizations, such as newspapers, should contribute the materials that are distributed through such services as videotex and teletext. It seems reasonable that those who gather information should band together with those who process it and with those who have the facilities to distribute it to offer a service that none alone could provide as well. Indeed, should not enterprises with joint interests but diverse capabilities band together to conduct the research and development necessary for a successful joint venture? Such activity would be more than frowned on in most advanced societies; in some instances, it would be illegal, contravening laws designed to prevent cartels in restraint of trade.

It is hard to say anything definitive about regulation, competition, and cooperation in our real world. One thing is certain: If there is competition, users will be ill served if standardization is inadequate. Having incompatible television tape recorders is awkward. Recreational computers that won't talk to one another's peripherals are awkward. Data bases that can be interrogated by some terminals but not by others lead to frustration, unnecessary expense, lack of use, or all three.

At present, there is a lack of standards in the digital world. More standardization is needed. But what should be standardized, and by whom? Only what is necessary and profitable to standardize, whatever that is, and only with the full participation of people who have actually built and operated things that are effective and good.

It is worth noting that in the history of information technology, a necessary and desirable degree of standardization has often emerged through a sort of common consent, as in language, type fonts, morse code, and the keyboard of the typewriter (which is almost standard). Some other standardizations, such as that which gave us the metric system, have occurred only by governmental and intergovernmental action.

We have noted that the digital art has given humanity great freedom. It serves well whether the medium of communication be text, speech, or diagrams and pictures. And it provides a freedom comparable to that provided by the letter or the telephone, but potentially far more popular. The mass media—the newspapers, radio, television—carry messages from them to us. They also carry the same message by the same means to each of us. Because everything depends on a few publishers or a few broadcast stations and networks, standardization can be worked out among a relatively small number of people and organizations.

The mass media of an earlier era were the newspapers and the mass-circulation magazines. The latter have been largely replaced by television. The remaining magazines are largely addressed to particular communities of interest, such as sports, boating, and commercial, technological, and scientific communities. In such periodicals, there is a diversity of interest but also a common, inherent mode of production and set of standards.

The growing use of hand calculators, computer games, and personal computers is putting very diverse equipment into the hands of very diverse people. So far, most of the electronic equipment is stand-alone equipment—it does not have to interconnect with anything else. But some of it would be much more powerful if it did. We already see problems in connecting peripherals to recreational computers. There will be a greater problem in interconnecting various computers through existing and new communication paths. Because the diversity is great at the start, standardization may be very difficult. Yet, in the long run we must have enough standardization to allow different pieces of equipment to operate together. And we must have international standardization if there is to be free and effective commerce in equipment across national boundaries. Some countries with a large and essential export trade are aware of this; some large lands with huge internal markets seem to have been less aware.

8-4 **Responsibility**

In this chapter, we have noted two important matters. One is that television has largely displaced general-circulation magazines; it has become the successful medium that appeals to everyone, or tries to. The other is that our world has become a world of interdependence, and not all nations need to produce all goods. Indeed, not all nations will be sources of all sorts of information. Further, scientific information and much technical and other information is neither the product nor the property of nations or even of formal international organizations. Rather, it is the product of transnational communities of interest whose members push investigations forward, gather or interpret data, and critically examine their common fields of interest. Governments can gain national advantage by supporting education and research and development wisely, but this can be as much through the advancement of the skills and expertise of the citizenry as through temporary proprietary information. Nations stay ahead by working hard and effectively in advancing, not by guarding jealously what they already have. Knowledge gained should be shared within one worldwide community of interest.

Worldwide communities of interest have a positive value to nations. Self-deceit is common in this world, especially among those who feel that new knowledge should bolster their cultural or social or political dogmas. The most effective safeguard against such self deceit is the examination of one's beliefs by other expert and critical minds.

Thus, we have maintained that it is to the advantage of nations to foster a free flow of information. Indeed, information can be regarded as a curious good that, like the loaves and fishes, can be divided endlessly among the multitude so that all are fed. And, like the loaves and fishes, it can be had free—or almost so. If a country lacks information, it should be assured of obtaining it cheaply from abroad. And if it doubts the validity of the information it has, it can obtain some sort of free consultative evaluation through discussions within various worldwide communities of interest.

Here we encounter age-old matters of great current interest and importance. One of these is freedom of information. Another is privacy. Perhaps these two aspects of information are too narrow, and we should really be concerned with the *integrity* of information.

Suppose that we do encounter data or information in the course of our affairs, and that it seems important to us. What are we to make of it? What is it beyond marks on paper or on a computer screen?

Information is so diverse in sources and so great in quantity that it cannot possibly be collected, verified, or distributed by one agency. Useful information must come to us from very diverse sources, even when it is supplied through one information service, public or private. Certainly, we should distrust anything if we do not know its source. Sometimes newspapers quote "informed sources" without saying what or who these are. And sometimes people generally regarded as informed are dead wrong.

Thus, the integrity of information requires that users know the source of information. Beyond this, it is important that competent people in various communities of interest be able to learn exactly how data were gathered and how they were processed in producing summaries. Numbers such as percentage of unemployment or gross national product are almost meaningless unless we know how they were arrived at and how carefully the work was done. Freedom of information must mean—as it often does—getting at sources and methods as well as at quotable measures.

When information concerns the background, knowledge, or activities of individuals or corporations, integrity implies something else. It implies in part that the information is correct and can be verified by going to identified sources. It also implies confidentiality and privacy. Sometimes the information gathered is of a private, proprietary, or confidential nature, information whose disclosure might damage an individual or might be financially injurious to an organization and its many employees and owners. Insofar as possible, such information should be gathered only for very compelling reasons, should be kept only as long as necessary, and should be guarded diligently against ill use.

The integrity of information requires great care in the gathering and handling of data. Full documentation of sources and methods is essential. Only authorized persons should be allowed to enter important data into data banks, to change data, or to process data for use by others, and there must be a record of these persons and their activities. An audit trail must be provided through which entries into and changes in data banks and all steps in processing can be traced. This is already understood in the case of financial transactions, but it may not be well-enough appreciated in the handling of other sorts of information.

Lack of integrity of information is as old as embezzlement and blackmail; it is useless to blame it on new information technologies. Carelessly handled, information technology affords an opportunity for abuse, and, indeed, for computer crime. Carefully handled, it allows better supervision than hand-kept records, for it can be easier to guard and document.

8-5 The Role of the Government

We see in the foregoing discussions several important roles for government in connection with information technology and civilization. One role is to be a constructive force in standardization; another is to encourage the dissemination of information and to guard its integrity. A third role is to encourage the production and use of information in advancing the economic life of the nation.

A part of the role of the government lies in gathering data concerning national life that are important both to the operation of the government and to industry and commerce. Census, economic, and employment data are examples. Another role is to encourage and support research and development when these are beyond the capabilities of the private sector. While large industries can support advanced research and development, small businesses and some older industries do not have adequate capabilities to advance through their own resources. Some are doomed and will eventually fail because they are inherently obsolete. Others may be revivified through information technology and research. A government must act wisely if it is to build for the future rather than try to preserve an outmoded past.

Still another area of important government action is to provide, or help to provide, the infrastructure necessary for an effective functioning of the society and its economy. We live in a time of rapid changes and great dislocations. Industry declines in some sectors and in some geographic areas and grows in others. In the new areas, educational facilities and public service are needed for the growing population. In the old areas, retraining is needed, and information about opportunities elsewhere is essential. Some large companies can and do provide retraining, and they work constructively with employees. Some even help to create the required infrastructure in the communities to which they move. Small companies cannot do this.

In a world as complex as ours, no group of people, in government or out, can comprehend and plan the life of a nation. Particular aspects of national life are understood only by particular groups of people in particular communities of interest. If government is to be effective, it must be a partner with other elements in promoting the well-being of citizens. It has an important role in informing and helping them, but it must work in concert with the private sector, not at cross-purposes with it. Neither competition nor regulation can accomplish all necessary ends. Cooperation is essential.

8-6 Concluding Remarks

Whatever organizations we may deal with, we are all individuals, and we look on information technology from our own points of view. One thing that we see and suffer from is the information explosion. Its most common manifestation is that the mass media—specifically, television and newspapers—try to cover more and more, and they necessarily cover it thinly.

There are several possible remedies. One is a national party line that tells all people just what few things they should know and pay attention to. This would seem fantastic except that it has been tried in various countries.

Short of a collapse of civilization, information will grow rather than contract. Of course, it is important to avoid gathering useless and suspect data for frivolous purposes. But the bulk of data that is either essential or useful is bound to increase. No individual, no organization, can understand and make use of it all. Ultimately, important data comes from, and is used within, various communities of interest. The mass media can provide a person with some general information that is important in day-to-day life. If one is to be better informed, it will be through membership in various communities of interest. A person who is deeply interested in some sport will subscribe to specialized publications and join specialized organizations. A scientist or engineer will read technical journals, attend meetings in several countries and correspond with and talk with people from many lands.

In our world, each of us is a member of many communities of interest—as parent, local taxpayer, employee, citizen, expert, or amateur. In general, communities of interest are open to anyone who is interested and competent. Sometimes, however, the cost of journals and meetings is high.

It is communities of interest that the new convergence of modes in information technology promises to serve best. Libraries are an old and valued resource. Centralized computer cataloging, book loans, and book purchases already play an important part in some countries. One can get a good deal of information by telephone. In some parts of the world, there is now a host of computer-accessible data bases, some private, some institutional. At present, subscription to such services is expensive, but individual inquiries are within the reach of the individual worker. We may hope that the rapid fall in the cost of terminals coupled with new communication services will bring down the cost of addressing queries to various data bases, that the compatibility of data bases will increase, and that the number and variety will increase also.

It is not only through information that information technology can be of use to individuals. We have noted that communication, computerization, and remote terminals make it possible to work at home and, even on a part-time basis, to conduct what used to be called the paper work associated with such activities as banking and insurance. To these we may add the production of software. It appears that advances in information technology may well change the work patterns of a substantial number of individuals.

We have noted that information technology can benefit people in other ways. In a day in which both adults and children may be away from home, security of the home is of increasing concern. Here, burglar alarms, smoke detectors, and other safeguards can be very important, especially if an alarm alerts some agency, public or private, that can take prompt action. Also, it is highly desirable that a person absent from his or her home be able to check on it from a distance and perhaps turn household appliances and services on or off.

We have already discussed data bases, but it seems appropriate to mention the potential value of data services in making reservations, in shopping, and even in buying, and especially in searching for unusual products, services, or skills. And information technology promises to make medical, educational, and other services both better and more responsive to the particular needs of the individual.

It could be kept secret from only the most obtuse that through the increasing power and flexibility associated with the convergence of modes, information technology is transforming all aspects of life. It is changing how and where we live and what we do. It is transforming our culture, old, present, and to come. It is transforming what we call civilization.

In the present complex world, no one can know everything, but it is necessary to have accurate and deep knowledge if we are to make the most of our opportunities. Our world has become a world of communities of interest, each held together by shared information. In this world, individuals and institutions, public and private, can achieve the most by working together cooperatively. No one can lead a satisfactory life unaided by others; no organization can survive without the cooperation of others. Those people and organizations that are best able to cooperate to mutual advantage will prosper the most.

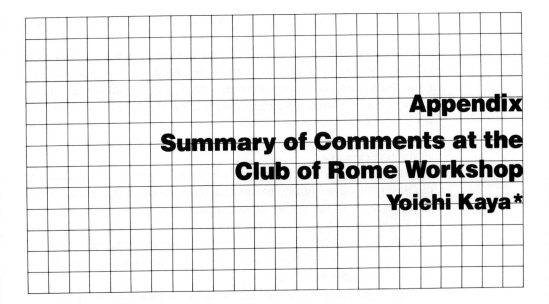

Appendix
Summary of Comments at the
Club of Rome Workshop
Yoichi Kaya*

The first draft of this report was read by numerous distinguished scholars, many associated with the Club of Rome. A workshop on this report was held under the sponsorship of the Japan Committee of the Club of Rome in Tokyo on October 25, the day before the 1982 Tokyo Conference of the Club. The authors were present along with some twenty members of the Japan Committee of the Club of Rome and distinguished scholars from outside, including Edward W. Ploman, Vice Rector of United Nations University, Sogo Okamura, Director General of the Japan Society for Promotion of Science, Alexander King, Chairman of IFIAS, and Hugo Thiemann, Counselor of Nestle S.A.

The authors were most grateful for all of the comments made by participants, many of which they were able to fully incorporate in revising the report. As the organizer of the workshop, I felt it would help readers understand the issues dealt with in the report if I summarized those comments. This has not been an easy task. Eventually, I found that the best approach was to classify the comments into a few broad categories so that the essence of the comments could be given briefly. Readers should remember that this description is my own interpretation and was not reviewed by the participants.

*Chairman of the Program Committee of the 1982 Tokyo Conference of the Club of Rome; member of the Club of Rome; Professor of Electrical Engineering, University of Tokyo

(1) Some participants expressed their dissatisfaction with the nature of the report as a "report to the Club of Rome." Nearly ten reports have been published under the name of "the report to the Club of Rome." In general, these reports expressed concerns about the world problematique. Participants also pointed out that this report should not duplicate a report entitled *Microelectronics and Society: For Better or For Worse,* which also dealt with these technologies.* Responding to the latter point, the authors put forth the following views, which I believe satisfied almost all the participants.

This report was written in a different context and by authors trained in a discipline—specifically, information technology—different from that of the authors of the earlier report. Readers of this report will find a number of issues that are scarcely touched upon in the other report and a number of views on related problems that are different from those in the other report. In this sense, each report is complementary to the other one, and both should be read.

Although the authors did not explicitly respond to the questions about problematique, I think I have the right to defend them in this regard, as I am a member of the Club of Rome, which asked the authors to conduct the research and write this report.

Japanese members of the Club of Rome have been concerned with recent rapid progress in information technology, because this has had, and will continue to have, revolutionary impact on modern society. We feel that a clear, authoritative overview of the historical trends of information technology is indispensable in discussing the world problematique and that such an overview is the only proper basis for an orderly investigation of related social, economic, political, and legal issues.

This report was written along this line, and the authors have done an excellent job, at least for the first part of the objective. Taking into account that the authors are both scientists working outside of the Club of Rome and that the report is not "by" but "to" the Club of Rome, I think the authors correctly put less emphasis on conveying a message of problematique to the public and greater emphasis on describing phenomena and issues. Stressing the problematique is a task, not for the authors, but for our members.

(2) Some participants expressed a dissatisfaction with the technol-

---

*Friedrichs, G. and Schaff, A. eds. *Microelectronics and Society; For Better or For Worse,* Pergamon Press, Oxford, 1982.

ogy-oriented nature of the report, specifically, with the relatively light emphasis on social, political, and economic impacts of new information and communication technologies. An example of an area that is almost completely neglected is military applications, an area of potentially very serious impact on the future of the world. One of the workshop participants stressed the necessity of touching upon this aspect, noting that special light might be shed here because one of the authors is from Japan, a nation that is a rare example of successful progress in information and communication technology not driven by military applications.

Another point made was the importance of more research on the possibility that these technologies would create more labor opportunities, especially in third world countries. The report touched on the possibility, but only rather briefly.

(3) The most controversial issue may be the impact of information and communication technology on third world countries. This impact could be positive, because information technologies may produce more employment in software development, as described in the report, but the impact might also be negative because of a widening of the technology gap between developed and developing countries. This might lead to reduction of employment in third world countries. A workshop participant from the third world stressed the necessity of research on this issue by the people in the third world instead of by those in the developed world; he believes the real problem is understood only by the people seriously involved in it. According to him, illiteracy is a basic barrier to development and should be tackled first; emphasis on recent technology should follow. This view fits with the authors' view in that they see information technology as continuously evolving, with reading and writing one of its most significant aspects.

There were many other comments, some favorable and some critical of the report. The purpose of the workshop was, not to generate a consensus of the participants on the content of the report, but to give advice to the authors for revising their report. This purpose was realized; the report will help people use information and communication technology "for better" rather than "for worse."

Reviewers of the First Draft of *Information Technology and Civilization*

Dr. David Z. Beckler
The Director for Science, Technology and Industry
Organization for Economic Co-operation and Development

Dr. Shumpei Kumonon
Professor of International Relations
College of General Education
University of Tokyo

Prof. Ithiel de Sola Pool
Center for International Studies
Massachusetts Institute of Technology

Prof. Soji Yamamoto
Faculty of Law
Tohoku University

Participants in the Workshop Held at the California Institute of Technology on June 1 and 2, 1982

Dr. Philip Abelson
Editor, *Science*

Prof. Yoichi Kaya
Department of Electrical Engineering
University of Tokyo

Dr. Roger Levien
Director, Strategic Systems Analysis
Xerox

Dr. George E. Mueller
Chairman and Chief Executive Officer
System Development Corporation

Dr. Peter Renz
Editor
W. H. Freeman and Company

Prof. Hiroshi Inose

Prof. John R. Pierce

Participants in the Inose—Pierce Project Workshop Held in Tokyo on October 25, 1982

Members of the Club of Rome

Name	Affiliation
Dr. James W. Botkin	Partner Technology & Strategy Group Cambridge, Mass.
Mr. Andre Danzin	President AFDAS Paris, France
Sr. D. R. Diez-Hochleitner	Chairman The Club of Rome of Spain Madrid, Spain
Dr. John E. Fobes	Chairman U.S. Association for the Club of Rome Washington, D.C.
Dr. Orio Giarini	Secretary General "Genève Association (Intl. Assoc. for Risk and Insurance Economics Research) Geneva, Switzerland
Dr. T. Ranald Ide	Chairman, Canadian Communication Research Advisory Board Ontario, Canada
Prof. Mohamed Kassas	Department of Botany Faculty of Science University of Cairo Cairo, Egypt
Dr. Yoichi Kaya	Professor, Department of Electrical Engineering University of Tokyo Tokyo, Japan
Dr. Alexander King	Chairman, IFIAS Paris, France
Mr. Koji Kobayashi	Chairman of the Board Nippon Electric Co., Ltd. Tokyo, Japan

Prof. Pentti Malaska	Turku School of Economics Turku, Finland
Prof. Donald N. Michael	Professor Emeritus of Planning and Public Policy University of Michigan
Dr. Paulo Moura	President Institute of Political and Social Studies São Paulo, Brazil
Dr. Saburo Okita	Chairman, Institute for Domestic and International Policy Studies Tokyo, Japan
Dr. Aurelio Peccei	President, Club of Rome c/o Intergovernmental Bureau for Informatics (IBI) Rome, Italy
Prof. Ing. Eduard Pestel	c/o Universitat Hannover Institut für Mechanik A Hannover, Federal Republic of Germany
Dr. Jørgon Randers	Dean Norwegian School of Management Bekkestua, Norway
Mr. Jean Saint-Geours	President Credit National Paris, France
Prof. Adam Schaff	President European Coordination Center for Research & Documentation in Social Science Vienna, Austria
Mr. John G. Stokes	Vice President International Development Gang-Nail Systems, Inc. West Perth, Western Australia
Dr. Hugo Thiemann	Counselor, Nestle S.A. Switzerland

Mr. Dan Tolkowsky	Vice Chairman and Managing Director, Discount Investment Corporation Ltd. Tel Aviv, Israel

Guests

Prof. Mahdi Elmandjra	University Mohamed V Rabat, Morocco
Mr. Fernando Elzaburu	Madrid, Spain
Prof. Hiroshi Inose	Professor of Electronic Engineering University of Tokyo Tokyo, Japan
Dr. Hiroshi Kida	Director General National Institute for Educational Research Tokyo, Japan
Dr. Boris J. Milner	Doctor of Economics, Professor Deputy Director Institute for Systems Studies Moscow, USSR
Dr. Shigeichi Moriguchi	Professor Emeritus of Mathematical Engineering University of Tokyo Tokyo, Japan
Mr. Peter North	Australian Club of Rome c/o Streeton Consulting Pty. Point Piper, Australia
Dr. Sogo Okamura	Director General Japan Society for the Promotion of Science Tokyo, Japan
Dr. Howard Perlmutter	Professor of Social Architecture Worldwide Institutions Research Center The Wharton School of the University of Pennsylvania Philadelphia, Pa.

Prof. John R. Pierce

Professor Emeritus of Engineering
California Institute of Technology
Pasadena, California

Mr. Edward W. Ploman

Vice Rector
United Nations University
Tokyo, Japan

Dr. Claudio Stern

Professor
El Colegio de Mexico, A.C.
Mexico, D.F.

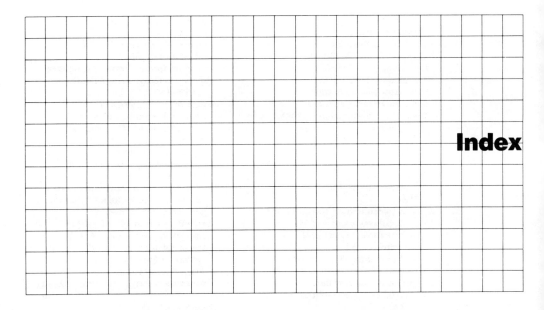

Index